T0093553

Praise for *Trust in Computer Systems and the Cloud*

"The problem is that when you use the word trust, people think they know what you mean. It turns out that they almost never do." With this singular statement, Bursell has defined both the premise and the value he expounds in this insightful treatise spanning the fundamentals and complexities of digital trust. Operationalizing trust is foundational to effective human and machine digital relationships, with Bursell leading the reader on a purposeful journey expressing and consuming elements of digital trust across current and future-relevant data lifecycles.

—Kurt Roemer,
Chief Security Strategist and Office of the CTO, Citrix

Trust is a matter of context. Specifically, "context" is one of the words most repeated in this book, and I must say that its use is justified in all cases. Not only is the meaning of trust analysed in all possible contexts, including some essential philosophical and psychological foundations, but the concept is also applied to all possible ICT contexts, from basic processor instructions to cloud and edge infrastructures; and different trust frameworks are explored, from hierarchical (CAs) to distributed (DLTs) approaches. A must-read book to understand how one of the bases of human civilization can and must be applied in the digital world.

—Dr. Diego R. Lopez,
Head of Technology Exploration, Telefónica and
Chair of ETSI blockchain initiative

As we have moved to the digital society, appreciating what and what not to trust is paramount if you use computer systems and/or the cloud. You will be well prepared when you have read this book.

—Professor Peter Landrock, D.Sc. (hon),
Founder of Cryptomathic

Trust is a complex and important concept in network security. Bursell neatly unpacks it in this detailed and readable book.

—Bruce Schneier, author of
Liars and Outliers: Enabling the Trust that Society Needs to Thrive

This book needs to be on every technologist's and engineer's bookshelf. Combining storytelling and technology, Bursell has shared with all of us the knowledge we need to build trust and security in cloud computing environments.

—Steve Kolombaris
- CISO & Cyber Security Leader with 20+ years experience.
Formerly Apple, JP Morgan Chase, Bank of America.

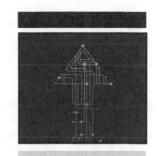

Trust in Computer Systems and the Cloud

Mike Bursell

WILEY

Published by John Wiley & Sons, Inc., Hoboken, New Jersey.
Published simultaneously in Canada.

978-1-119-69232-4
978-1-119-69301-7 (ebk.)
978-1-119-69231-7 (ebk.)

For general information on our other products and services or for technical support, please contact our Customer Care Department within the United States at (800) 762-2974, outside the United States at (317) 572-3993 or fax (317) 572-4002.

Wiley also publishes its books in a variety of electronic formats. Some content that appears in print may not be available in electronic formats. For more information about Wiley products, visit our web site at www.wiley.com.

Library of Congress Control Number: 2021944020

Cover Image: © amtitus/istock.com
Cover Design: Wiley

SKY10030658_102221

To Catherine, Josephine, and Miriam.

#YNWA

About the Author

Mike Bursell is a UK-based security, distributed systems, and open source architect and enthusiast who has recently found himself coding again.

He studied English Literature and Theology at King's College Cambridge, where he also sang in the choir, met his wife, spent too much time playing computer games, got into online communities, played some rugby badly, read lots of books, and spent as much time as feasible punting on the River Cam. After graduating in 1994, he joined Cambridge University Press to work on electronic publishing with CD-ROMs but quickly moved to creating and running their nascent website, learning Perl and Java to provide automation.

His subsequent jobs for a variety of global companies fostered his interests in distributed systems and security. An MBA from the Open University in 2001 expanded his horizons into the interface between engineering, systems, and the business world—a milieu he has inhabited ever since in roles spanning software engineering, systems architecture, patent creation, and product management.

Mike is a passionate open source advocate and a contributor and Correspondent at Opensource.com. He is co-founder with Nathaniel McCallum of the open source security project Enarx (`https://enarx.dev`) and has even written code for it in Rust. He speaks globally at conferences (when not in pandemic lockdown) and maintains the security-leaning blog *Alice, Eve and Bob* at `https://aliceevebob.com`. Since mid-2021, he has been CEO and co-founder of Profian, a start-up in the Confidential Computing space.

About the Technical Editor

Aeva Black is a dot-com veteran, an open source hacker, and a queer and non-binary geek. They work in the Azure Office of the CTO to improve the state of open source software supply chain security, and to support teams working on cloud security and digital privacy. Back in 2012, they launched OpenStack's Bare Metal Cloud program, enabling performance-sensitive cloud native workloads to run without a hypervisor.

Aeva currently serves on the Board of the Open Source Initiative, the non-profit which stewards the definition of "open source", and works within several other foundations including the Confidential Computing Consortium and the Cloud Native Computing Foundation.

Aeva is a lifelong student of the buddha dharma and an advocate for LGBTQIA+ rights. They served for several years on the Board of the Consent Academy, a Seattle-area educational non-profit, and were recently published in Transcending, an anthology of trans buddhist authors.

Acknowledgements

First, family: to Catherine, Josephine, and Miriam for being supportive and long-suffering; to my parents, without whom I wouldn't be writing this; to my parents-in-law, without whom I wouldn't have a wife and kids; and to my brother and sister, who feature at the beginning of this book—I *would* trust you with my life.

Second, work and education: Steve Watt of Red Hat, who encouraged me; and Jen Huger (also of Red Hat), who provided great advice and opportunities to trial some of the material on Opensource.com. Richard D'Silva, who ran the computers at Bryanston; and the redoubtable Mrs Macquarrie (Jenny), who encouraged me from an even earlier age. Andrew Herbert and Chris Phoenix deserve a mention for hiring me when I didn't really know how to program and giving me space to learn. Peter Landrock, Ross Anderson, and Stephe Walli have also provided formative guidance at times, even if they never knew it.

Friends and colleagues on projects I care about, and who have been important to this book's creation, include Nathaniel McCallum and the entire Enarx team, Michael Bilca (whose advice I should have taken with relation to cryptocurrency around a decade ago), and Aeva Black, who has contributed invaluable technical editing input and beyond (remaining errors are mine).

People who have had an immense formative on my leisure life, but whom I've never met, include (in alphabetical order by surname) David Braben, William Gibson, Anne McCaffrey, Sid Meier, Melissa Scott, and Neal Stephenson. I salute your accomplishments, all. I have met Nick Harkaway and knew him before his hair was short and his eyebrows grew out. He gets a salutation, too.

Hats off to Adnams, Bishop Nick, Laphroaig, Lagavulin, Talisker, and the Scotch Malt Whisky Society. And to the barflies at EMRC (you know who you are).

The year in which I wrote most of this book, 2020, has been weird, to say the least, but there has been one positive throughout, which leads me to Jürgen

Klopp, the Liverpool team, coaching staff and wider network at Anfield in Liverpool, my second birthplace (by marriage). After a season like that, it's a toss-up between Jonny Wilkinson and Jürgen. I should be so lucky.

Last, and far from least, thanks to the editorial team at Wiley for making this happen: special thanks to Jim Minatel, Candace Cunningham, and Pete Gaughan, but not forgetting everyone behind the scenes.

There are others too numerous to mention, and I apologise if I've missed you. Please contact me to remedy the situation if there's a second edition. I don't believe there are any rules about accepting bribes in this situation, so you know what to do.

Mike Bursell

August 2021

I'm not going to pretend that listening to the songs on this playlist will help make sense of the book, but they all (with many others) featured in its writing, so I've included them here. Note that some of them may contain words or sentiments that you may find disturbing: *caveat auditor*.

"Secret Messages"—ELO

"Bleed to Love Her"—Fleetwood Mac

"Alone in Kyoto"—Air

"She's So Lovely"—Scouting for Girls

"Prime"—Shearwater

"Stay"—Gabrielle Aplin

"The Way I Feel"—Keane

"Come On, Dreamer"—Tom Adams

"Congregation"—Low

"Go!"—Public Service Broadcasting

"The Son of Flynn"—Daft Punk

"Lilo"—The Japanese House

"Scooby Snacks"—Fun Lovin' Criminals

"My Own Worst Enemy"—Stereophonics

"All Night"—Parov Stelar

"Long Tall Sally (The Thing)"—Little Richard

"Sharp Dressed Man"—ZZ Top

"Dueling Banjos"—Eric Weissberg, Steve Mandell

"The Starship Avalon (Main Title)"—Thomas Newman

"A Change Is Gonna Come"—Sam Cooke

"This Place"—Jamie Webster

Contents at a Glance

Introduction   xv

Chapter 1   Why Trust?   1

Chapter 2   Humans and Trust   19

Chapter 3   Trust Operations and Alternatives   53

Chapter 4   Defining Trust in Computing   79

Chapter 5   The Importance of Systems   93

Chapter 6   Blockchain and Trust   151

Chapter 7   The Importance of Time   161

Chapter 8   Systems and Trust   185

Chapter 9   Open Source and Trust   211

Chapter 10   Trust, the Cloud, and the Edge   233

Chapter 11   Hardware, Trust, and Confidential Computing   247

Chapter 12   Trust Domains   281

Chapter 13   A World of Explicit Trust   301

References   309

Index   321

Contents

Introduction		xv
Chapter 1	**Why Trust?**	**1**
	Analysing Our Trust Statements	4
	What Is Trust?	5
	What Is Agency?	8
	Trust and Security	10
	Trust as a Way for Humans to Manage Risk	13
	Risk, Trust, and Computing	15
	Defining Trust in Systems	15
	Defining Correctness in System Behaviour	17
Chapter 2	**Humans and Trust**	**19**
	The Role of Monitoring and Reporting in Creating Trust	21
	Game Theory	24
	The Prisoner's Dilemma	24
	Reputation and Generalised Trust	27
	Institutional Trust	28
	Theories of Institutional Trust	29
	Who Is Actually Being Trusted?	31
	Trust Based on Authority	33
	Trusting Individuals	37
	Trusting Ourselves	37
	Trusting Others	41
	Trust, But Verify	43
	Attacks from Within	43
	The Dangers of Anthropomorphism	45
	Identifying the Real Trustee	47

Chapter 3	**Trust Operations and Alternatives**	**53**
	Trust Actors, Operations, and Components	53
	Reputation, Transitive Trust, and Distributed Trust	59
	Agency and Intentionality	62
	Alternatives to Trust	65
	Legal Contracts	65
	Enforcement	66
	Verification	67
	Assurance and Accountability	67
	Trust of Non-Human or Non-Adult Actors	68
	Expressions of Trust	69
	Relating Trust and Security	75
	Misplaced Trust	75
Chapter 4	**Defining Trust in Computing**	**79**
	A Survey of Trust Definitions in Computer Systems	79
	Other Definitions of Trust within Computing	84
	Applying Socio-Philosophical Definitions of Trust to Systems	86
	Mathematics and Trust	87
	Mathematics and Cryptography	87
	Mathematics and Formal Verification	89
Chapter 5	**The Importance of Systems**	**93**
	System Design	93
	The Network Stack	94
	Linux Layers	96
	Virtualisation and Containers: Cloud Stacks	97
	Other Axes of System Design	99
	"Trusted" Systems	99
	Trust Within the Network Stack	101
	Trust in Linux Layers	102
	Trust in Cloud Stacks	103
	Hardware Root of Trust	106
	Cryptographic Hash Functions	110
	Measured Boot and Trusted Boot	112
	Certificate Authorities	114
	Internet Certificate Authorities	115
	Local Certificate Authorities	116
	Root Certificates as Trust Pivots	119
	The Temptations of "Zero Trust"	122
	The Importance of Systems	125
	Isolation	125
	Contexts	127
	Worked Example: Purchasing Whisky	128
	Actors, Organisations, and Systems	129
	Stepping Through the Transaction	130
	Attacks and Vulnerabilities	134

Trust Relationships and Agency   136
  Agency   136
  Trust Relationships   137
The Importance of Being Explicit   145
  Explicit Actions   145
  Explicit Actors   149

Chapter 6   Blockchain and Trust   151
Bitcoin and Other Blockchains   151
Permissioned Blockchains   152
  Trust without Blockchains   153
  Blockchain Promoting Trust   154
Permissionless Blockchains and Cryptocurrencies   156

Chapter 7   The Importance of Time   161
Decay of Trust   161
  Decay of Trust and Lifecycle   163
  Software Lifecycle   168
    Trust Anchors, Trust Pivots, and the Supply Chain   169
    Types of Trust Anchors   170
  Monitoring and Time   171
  Attestation   173
    The Problem of Measurement   174
    The Problem of Run Time   176
Trusted Computing Base   177
  Component Choice and Trust   178
  Reputation Systems and Trust   181

Chapter 8   Systems and Trust   185
System Components   185
Explicit Behaviour   188
  Defining Explicit Trust   189
  Dangers of Automated Trust Relationships   192
Time and Systems   194
Defining System Boundaries   198
  Trust and a Complex System   199
  Isolation and Virtualisation   202
  The Stack and Time   205
  Beyond Virtual Machines   205
  Hardware-Based Type 3 Isolation   207

Chapter 9   Open Source and Trust   211
Distributed Trust   211
How Open Source Relates to Trust   214
  Community and Projects   215
    Projects and the Personal   217
  Open Source Process   219
    Trusting the Project   220
    Trusting the Software   222

		Supply Chain and Products	226
		Open Source and Security	229
Chapter 10	**Trust, the Cloud, and the Edge**		**233**
	Deployment Model Differences		235
		What Host Systems Offer	237
		What Tenants Need	237
	Mutually Adversarial Computing		240
	Mitigations and Their Efficacy		243
		Commercial Mitigations	243
		Architectural Mitigations	244
		Technical Mitigations	246
Chapter 11	**Hardware, Trust, and Confidential Computing**		**247**
	Properties of Hardware and Trust		248
		Isolation	248
		Roots of Trust	249
	Physical Compromise		253
	Confidential Computing		256
		TEE TCBs in detail	261
		Trust Relationships and TEEs	266
		How Execution Can Go Wrong—and Mitigations	269
		Minimum Numbers of Trustees	276
		Explicit Trust Models for TEE Deployments	278
Chapter 12	**Trust Domains**		**281**
	The Composition of Trust Domains		284
		Trust Domains in a Bank	284
		Trust Domains in a Distributed Architecture	288
	Trust Domain Primitives and Boundaries		292
		Trust Domain Primitives	292
		Trust Domains and Policy	293
		Other Trust Domain Primitives	296
		Boundaries	297
		Centralisation of Control and Policies	298
Chapter 13	**A World of Explicit Trust**		**301**
	Tools for Trust		301
	The Role of the Architect		303
		Architecting the System	304
		The Architect and the Trustee	305
	Coda		307
References			**309**
Index			**321**

Introduction

I am the sort of person who reads EULAs,[1] checks the expiry dates on fire extinguishers, examines the licensing notices in lifts (or elevators), and looks at the certificates on websites before I purchase goods from retailers or give away my personal details to sites purporting to be using my information for good in the world. Like many IT security professionals, I have a (hopefully healthy) disrespect for authority—or, maybe more accurately, for the claims made by authorities or those claiming to be authorities in the various fields of interest in which I've found myself involved over the years.

Around 2001, I found myself without a job as my employer restructured, and I was looking for something to do. I had been getting interested in peer-to-peer interactions in computing, based on a project I'd been involved with at a previous company and the question of how trust relationships could be brokered in this sphere. I did a lot of reading in the area and nearly started a doctorate before getting a new job where finding time to do the requisite amount of study was going to be difficult. Not long after, my wife and I started trying for a family, and the advent of children in the household further reduced the amount of time—and concentration—available to study at the level of depth that I felt the subject merited.

Years went by, and I kept an eye on the field as my professional interests moved in a variety of different directions. Around 2013, I joined a group within ETSI (the European Telecommunications Standards Institute) working on network function virtualisation (NFV). I quickly gravitated to the Security Working Group (Sec-WG), where I found several people with similar professional interests. One of those interests was trust, how to express it, how to define it, and how

---

[1] End user licenses or license agreements.

to operate systems that depended on it. We did some interesting work in the group, producing a number of documents that looked at particular aspects of telecommunications and trust, including the place of law enforcement agencies and regulators in the sector. As the telecommunications industry struggled to get its collective head around virtualisation and virtual machines (VMs), it became clear to the members of the security group that the challenges presented by a move to VMs were far bigger—and more complex—than might originally have been expected.

Operators, as telecommunications providers are known in the industry—think Orange, Sprint, or NTT Docomo—have long known that they need to be careful about the hardware they buy and the software they run on it. There were a handful of powerful network equipment providers (NEPs) whose business model was building a monolithic software stack on top of well-defined hardware platforms and then selling it to the operators, sometimes running and monitoring it for them as well. The introduction of VMs offered the promise (to the operators) and the threat (to the NEPs) of a new model, where entrants into the market could provide more modular software components, some of which could run on less-specialised hardware. From the operators' point of view, this was an opportunity to break the NEPs' stranglehold on the industry, so they (the operators) were all for the new NFV world, while the NEPs were engaged in the ETSI process to try to show that they were still relevant.

From the security point of view, we quickly realised that there was a major shift taking place from a starting point where operators were able to manage risk by trusting the one or two NEPs that provided their existing infrastructure. This was beginning to develop into a world where they needed to consider all of the different NFV vendors, the components they supplied, the interactions the components had with each other, and, crucially, the interactions the components had with the underlying infrastructure, which was now not going to be specialised hardware dedicated to particular functions, but generic computing hardware bought pretty much off the shelf. I think the Sec-WG thoroughly exasperated much of the rest of the ETSI NFV consortium with our continuous banging on about the problem, but we were equally exasperated by their inability to understand what a major change was taking place and the impact it could have on their businesses. The trust relationships between the various components was key to that, but *trust* was a word that was hardly even in the vocabulary of most people outside the Sec-WG.

At about the same time, I noticed a new trend in the IT security vendor market: people were beginning to talk about a new model for building networks, which they called *zero trust*. I was confused by this: my colleagues and I were spending huge amounts of time and effort trying to convince people that trust was important, and here was a new movement asserting that the best way to improve the security of your networking was to trust nothing. I realised after some research that the underlying message was more sophisticated and nuanced than that, but I also had a concern that the approach ignored a number of important abstractions and trust relationships. That concern has not abated as zero trust has been adopted as a rallying cry in situations where significantly less attention has been paid by those involved.

As virtualisation allowed the growth of cloud computing, and as Linux containers[2] and serverless computing have led to public cloud offerings that businesses can deploy simply and quickly, security is becoming more of a concern as organisations move from using cloud computing for the odd application here and there to considering it a key part of their computing infrastructure. The issue of trust, however, has not been addressed. From the (seemingly) simple question, "Do I trust my cloud service provider to run my applications for me?" to more complex considerations around dynamic architectures to protect data in transit, at rest, and in use, trust needs to be central to discussions about risk and security in private and public clouds, telecommunications, finance, government, healthcare, the Edge, IoT, automotive computing, blockchain, and AI.

The subject of trust seems, at first blush, to be simple. As you start delving deeper and examining how to apply the concept—or multiple concepts—to computing, it becomes clear that it is actually a very complex field. As we consider how business A deploys software from software provider B, using libraries from open source community C and proprietary software provider D, for consumption by organisation E and its user group F on hardware supplied by manufacturer G running a BIOS from H, an operating system from I, and a virtualisation stack from J, using storage from K, over a network from L, owned by cloud service provider M, we realise that we are already halfway through the alphabet and have yet to consider any of the humans in the mix. We need, as a security and IT community, to be able to talk about trust—but there is little literature or discussion of the subject aimed at our requirements and the day-to-day decisions we make about how to architect, design, write, deploy, run, monitor, patch, and decommission the systems we manage. This book provides a starting point for those decisions, building on work across multiple disciplines and applying them to the world of computing and the cloud.

---

[2]Popularised by Docker, Inc.

Why Trust?

I trust my brother and my sister with my life. My brother is a doctor, and my sister trained as a diving instructor, so I wouldn't necessarily trust my sister to provide emergency medical aid or my brother to service my scuba gear. I should actually be even more explicit because there are times when I *would* trust my sister in the context of emergency medical aid: I'm sure she'd be more than capable of performing CPR, for example. On the other hand, my brother is a paediatrician, not a surgeon, so I'd not be very confident about allowing him to perform an appendectomy on me. To go further, my sister has not worked as a diving instructor for several years now, so I might consider whether my trust in her abilities should be impacted by that.

This is not a book about human relationships or trust between humans, but about trust in computer systems. In order to understand what that means—or even *can* mean—however, we need to understand what we mean by trust. *Trust* is a word that arises out of human interactions and human relationships. Words are tricky. Words can mean different things to different people in different contexts.

The classic example of words meaning different things depending on context is the names of colours—the light frequencies included in the colours I identify as mauve, beige, and ultramarine are very likely different to yours—but there are other examples that are equally or more extreme. If I discuss "scheduling" with an events coordinator, a DevOps expert, and a kernel developer, each person will almost certainly have a different view of what I mean.

Trust is central to the enterprise of this book, and to discuss it, we must come to some shared understanding of what is meant by the word itself.[1] The meaning that we carry forward into our discussion of computer systems must be, as far as is possible, shared. We must, to the extent we can, come to agree on a common referent, impossible as this exercise may seem in a post-modern world.[2] Our final destination is firmly within the domain of computing, where domain-specific vocabulary is well-established. But since day-to-day usage of the word *trust* is rooted in a discussion about relationships between humans, this is where we will start.

The sort of decisions that I have described around trusting my sister and brother are ones that humans make all the time, often without thinking about them. Without giving it undue thought, we understand that multiple contexts are being considered here, including:

- My relationship to the other person
- Their relationship to me
- The different contexts of their expertise
- The impact that time can have on trust

This list, simple as it is, already exposes several important points about trust relationships to which we will return time and time again in this book: they are asymmetric (trust may be different in one direction to another), they are contextual (medical expertise and diving equipment expertise are not the same), and they are affected by time. As noted earlier, this book is not about human relationships and trust—though how we consider our relationships will be important to our discussions—but about trust in computing systems. Too often, we do not think much about trust relationships between computing systems (hardware, software, and firmware), and when we do, the sort of statements that tend to emerge are "This component trusts the server" or "We connect to this trusted system". Of course, in the absence of significantly greater levels of artificial intelligence than are currently in evidence at the time of writing, computing systems cannot make the sort of complex and nuanced decisions about trust relationships that humans make; but it turns out that trust is vitally important in computing systems, unstated and implicit though it usually is.

There is little discussion about trust—that is, computer-to-computer or machine-to-machine trust—within the discipline or professional practice of computing, and very little literature about it except in small, specialised fields. The discussions that exist tend to be academic, and there is little to find in the popular professional literature—again, with the exception of particular specialised fields.

---

[1] I sympathise with anyone tasked with translating this book: "trust" is a concept that is very culturally and linguistically situated.

[2] This book is not a work of literary criticism, and we will generally be steering clear of Derrida, Foucault, deconstructionism, post-structuralism, and other post-modernist agendas.

When the subject of trust comes up in a professional IT or computing setting, however, people are often very interested in discussing it. The problem is that when you use the word *trust*, people think they know what you mean. It turns out that they almost never do. What one person's view of trust entails is almost always different—sometimes radically different—from that of those to whom they are speaking. Within computing, we are used to talking about things and having a shared knowledge, at least to some degree of approximation. Some terms are fairly well defined in the industry, at least in general conversation: for example, *cryptography*, *virtualisation*, and *kernel*. Even a discussion on more nebulous concepts such as *software* or *networking* or *authentication* generally starts from a relatively well-defined shared understanding. The same is not true of trust, but trust is a concept that we definitely need to get our heads around to establish a core underpinning and begin to frame an understanding of what shared meaning we hope to convey.

Why is there such a range of views around trust? We have already looked at some of the complexity of trust between humans. Let us try to tease out some of the reasons for people's confusion by starting with four fairly innocuously simple-looking statements:

- I trust my brother and my sister.
- I trust my bank.
- My bank trusts its IT systems.
- My bank's IT systems trust each other.

When you make four statements like this, it quickly becomes clear that something different is going on in each case. Specifically, the word *trust* signifies something very different in each of the four statements. Our first step is to make the decision to avoid using the word *trust* as a transitive verb—a word with a simple object, as in these examples—and instead talk about trust relationships *to* another entity. This is because there is a danger, when using the word *trust* transitively, that we may confuse a unidirectional relationship with a bidirectional relationship. In the second case, for example, the bank may well have a relationship with me, but it is how I think of the bank, and therefore how I interact with it, which is the relationship that we want to examine. This is not to say that the relationship the bank has with *me* is irrelevant to the one I have with *it*—it may well inform my relationship—but that the bank's relationship with me is not the focus. For the same reason, we will generally talk about the "trust relationship *to*" another entity, rather than the "trust relationship *with*" another, to avoid implying a bidirectional relationship. The standard word used to describe the entity doing the trusting is *trustor*, and the entity being trusted is the *trustee*—though we should not confuse this word with other uses (such as the word *trustee* as used in the context of prisons or charity boards).

Analysing Our Trust Statements

The four cases of trust relationships that we have noted may look similar, but there are important differences that will shed light on some important concepts to which we will return throughout the book and that will help us define exactly what our subject matter is.

Case 1: My Trusting My Brother and Sister   As we have already discussed, this statement is about trust between individual humans—specifically, my trust relationship to my brother, and my trust relationship to my sister. There are two humans involved in each case (both me and whichever sibling we are considering), with all of the complexity that this entails. But we share a set of assumptions about how we react, and we each have tens of thousands of years of genetics plus societal and community expectations to work out how these relationships should work.

Case 2: My Trusting My Bank   Our second statement is about trust between an individual and an organisation: specifically, my trust relationship to a legal entity with particular services and structure. The basis of the expression of this relationship has changed over the years in many places: the relationship I would have had in the UK with my bank 50 years ago, say, would often have been modelled mainly on the relationship I had with one or more individuals employed by the bank, typically a manager or deputy manager of a particular branch. My trust relationship to the bank now is more likely to be swayed by my views on its perceived security practices and its exercising of fiscal and ethical responsibilities than my views of the manager of my local branch—if I have even met them. There is, however, still a human element associated with my relationship, at least in my experience: I know that I can walk into a branch, or make a call on the phone, and speak to a human.[3]

Case 3: The Bank Trusting Its IT Systems   Our third statement is about an organisation trusting its IT systems. When we follow our new resolution to rephrase this as "The bank having a trust relationship to its IT systems", it suddenly feels like we have moved into a very different type of consideration from the initial two cases. Arguably, for some of the reasons mentioned earlier about interacting with humans in a bank, we realise that there is a large conceptual difference between the first and second cases as well. But we are often lulled into a false sense of equivalence because when we interact with a bank, it is staffed by people, and it also enjoys many of the legal protections afforded to an individual. There are still humans in this case, though, in that we can generally assume that it is the intention of certain humans who represent the bank to have a trust relationship

---

[3]Or at least what appears to be a human—a topic to which we will return in a later chapter.

to certain IT systems. The question of what we mean by "represent the bank" is an interesting one when we consider when we might use this phrase in practice. Might it be in a press conference, with a senior executive saying that the bank "trusts its IT systems"? What might that mean? Or it could be in a conversation between a regulator or auditor with the chief information security officer (CISO) of the bank. Who *is* "the bank" that is being referred to in this situation, and what does this trust mean?

Case 4: The IT Systems Trusting Each Other   As we move to our fourth case, it is clear that we have transitioned to yet another very different space. There are no humans involved in this set of trust relationships unless we attribute agency to specific systems; and if so, which? What, then, is doing the trusting, and what does the word *trust* even mean in this context? The question of agency raised earlier—about an entity *representing* someone else, as a literary agent represents an author or a federal agent represents a branch of government—may allow us to consider what is going on. We will return to this question later in this chapter.

The four cases we have discussed show that we cannot just apply the same word, *trust*, to all of these different contexts and assume that it means the same thing in each case. We need to differentiate between them: what is going on, who is trusting whom to do what, and what *trust* in that instance truly means.

What Is Trust?

What, then, is trust? What do we mean, or hope to convey, when we use this word? This question gets a whole chapter to itself; but to start to examine it, its effects, and the impact of thinking about trust within computing systems, we need a definition. Here is the one we will use as the basis for the rest of the book. It is in part derived from a definition by Gambetta[4] and refined after looking at multiple uses and contexts.

> **Trust is the assurance that one entity holds that another will perform particular actions according to a specific expectation.**

This is a good start, but we can go a little further, so let us propose three corollaries to sit alongside this definition. We will go into more detail for each later.

First Corollary   "Trust is always contextual".

Second Corollary   "One of the contexts for trust is always time".

Third Corollary   "Trust relationships are not symmetrical".

---

[4]Gambetta, 1988.

This set of statements should come as no surprise: it forms the basis for the initial examination of the trust relationships that I have to my brother and sister, described at the beginning of this chapter. Let us re-examine those relationships and try to define them in terms of our definition of trust and its corollaries. First, we deal with the definition:

- The entities identified are a) me and b) my siblings.
- The actions ranged from performing an emergency appendectomy to servicing my scuba gear.
- The expectation was fairly complex, even in this simple example: it turns out that trusting someone "with my life" can mean a variety of things, from performing specific actions to remedy an emergency medical condition, to performing actions that, if neglected or incorrectly carried out, could cause my death.

We find that we have addressed the first corollary—that trust is always contextual:

- The contexts included my having a cardiac arrest, requiring an appendectomy, and planning to go scuba diving.

Time, the second corollary, is also covered:

- My sister has not recently renewed her diving instructor training, so I might have less trust in her to service my diving gear than I might have done 10 years ago.

The third corollary about the asymmetry of trust is so obvious in human relationships that we often ignore it, but is very clear in our examples:

- I am neither a doctor nor a trained scuba diving instructor, so my brother and sister trust me neither to provide emergency medical care nor to service their scuba gear.

Let us restate one of these relationships in the form of our definition and corollaries about trust:

I hold an assurance that my brother will provide me with emergency medical aid in the event that I require immediate treatment.

This is a good statement of how I view the relationship from me to my brother, but what can we gain with more detail? Let us use the corollaries to move us to a better description of the relationship.

First Corollary   "The medical aid is within an area of practice in which he has trained or with which he is familiar".

Second Corollary "My brother will only undertake procedures for which his training is still sufficiently recent that he feels confident that he can perform them without further detriment to my health".

Third Corollary "My brother does not expect me to provide him with emergency medical aid".

This may seem like an immense amount of unpacking to do on what was originally presented as a simple statement. But when we move over to the world of computing systems, we need to consider exactly this level of detail, if not an even greater level.

Let us begin moving into the world of computing and see what happens when we start to apply some of these concepts there. We will begin with the concept of a *trusted platform*: something that is often a requirement for any computation that involves sensitive data or algorithms. Immediately, questions present themselves. When we talk about a *trusted platform*, what does that mean? It must surely mean that the platform is trusted by an entity (the workload?) to perform particular actions (provide processing time and memory?) whilst meeting particular expectations (not inspecting program memory? maintaining the integrity of data?). But the context of what we mean for a *trusted platform* is likely to be very different between a mobile phone, a military installation, and an Internet of Things (IoT) gateway. That trust may erode over time (are patches applied? Is there also a higher likelihood that an attacker may have compromised the platform a day, a month, or a year after the workload was provisioned to it?). We should also never simply say, following the third corollary (on the lack of trust symmetry), that "these entities trust each other" without further qualification, even if we are referring to the relationships between one trusted system and another trusted system.

One concrete example that we can use to examine some of these questions is when we connect to a web server using a browser to purchase a product or service. Once they connect, the web server and the browser may establish trust relationships, but these are *definitely not* symmetrical. The browser has probably established that the web server represents the provider of particular products and services with sufficient assurance for the person operating it to give up credit card details. The web server has probably established that the browser currently has permission to access the account of the user operating it. However, we already see some possible confusion arising about what the entities are: what is *the web server*, exactly? The unique instance of the server's software, the virtual machine in which it runs (if, in fact, it is running in a virtual machine), a broader and more complex computer system, or something entirely different? And what ability can the browser have to establish that the person operating it can perform particular actions?

These questions—about how trust is represented and to do what—are related to agency and will also help us consider some of the questions that arose around the examples we considered earlier about banks and their IT systems.

What Is Agency?

When you write a computer program that prints out "Hello, world!", who is "saying" those words: you or the computer? This may sound like an idle philosophical question, but it is more than that: we need to be able to talk about entities as part of our definition of trust, and in order to do that, we need to know what entity we are discussing.

What exactly, then, does *agency* mean? It means acting for someone: being their agent—think of what actors' agents do, for example. When we engage a lawyer or a builder or an accountant to do something for us, we set very clear boundaries about what they will be doing on our behalf. This is to protect both us and the agent from unintended consequences. There exists a huge legal corpus around defining, in different fields, exactly the scope of work to be carried out by a person or a company who is acting as an agent for another person or organisation. There are contracts and agreed restitutions—basically, punishments—for when things go wrong. Say that my accountant buys 500 shares in a bank with my money, and then I turn around and say that they never had the authority to do so: if we have set up the relationship correctly, it should be entirely clear whether or not the accountant had that authority and whose responsibility it is to deal with any fallout from that purchase.

The situation is not so clear when we start talking about computer systems and agents. To think a little more about this question, here are two scenarios:

- In the classic film *WarGames*, David Lightman (Matthew Broderick's character) has a computer that goes through a list of telephone numbers, dialling them and then recording the number for later investigation if they are answered by another machine that attempts to perform a handshake. Do we consider that the automatic dialling Lightman's computer performs is carried out as an act with agency? Or is it when the computer connects to another machine? Or when it records the details of that machine? I suspect that most people would not argue that the computer is acting with agency once Lightman gets it to complete a connection and interact with the other machine—that seems very intentional on his part, and he has taken control—but what about before?

- Google used to run automated programs against messages received as part of the Gmail service.[5] The programs were looking for information

---

[5]Hern, 2017.

and phrases that Google could use to serve ads. The company were absolutely adamant that *they*, Google, were not doing the reading: it was just the computer programs.[6] Quite apart from the ethical concerns that might be raised, many people would (and did) argue that Google, or at least the company's employees, had imbued these automated programs with agency so that philosophically—and probably legally—the programs were performing actions on behalf of Google. The fact that there was no real-time involvement by any employee is arguably unimportant, at least in some contexts.

This all matters because in order to understand trust, we need to identify an entity to trust. One current example of this is self-driving cars: whose fault is it when one goes wrong and injures or kills someone? Equally, when the software in certain Boeing 737 MAX 8 aircraft malfunctioned,[7] pilots—who can be said to have trusted the software—and passengers—who equally can be said to have trusted the pilots and their ability to fly the aircraft correctly—lost their lives. What exactly was the entity to which they had a trust relationship, and how was that trust managed?

Another example may help us to consider the question of context. Consider a hypothetical automated defence system for a military base in a war zone. Let us say that, upon identifying intruders via its cameras, the system is programmed to play a recording over loudspeakers, warning them to move away; and, in the case that they do not leave within 30 seconds of a warning, to use physical means up to and including lethal force to stop them proceeding any further. The base commander trusts the system to perform its job and stop intruders: a trust relationship exists between the base commander and the automated defence system. Thus, in the language of our definition of trust:

"The base commander holds an assurance that the automated defence system will identify, warn, and then stop intruders who enter the area within its camera and weapon range".

We have a fair amount of context already embedded within this example. We stated up front that the base is in a war zone, and we have mentioned the

---

[6]There is an interesting point about grammar here. In British English, collective nouns or nouns representing an organisation, such as Google, can often take either a singular or a plural verb form. In the US, they almost always take the singular. So, saying "The company were adamant that *they*. . .", an easy way to show that there are multiple actors possibly being represented here, works in British English but not in US English. Thus British English speakers may be more likely than US readers to consider an organisation as a group of individuals than as a monolithic corporate whole.

[7]Wikipedia, "Boeing 737 MAX groundings", 2021.

range of the cameras and weapons. A problem arises, however, when the context changes. What if, for instance:

- The base is no longer in a war zone, and rules of engagement change
- Children enter the coverage area who do not understand the warnings or are unable to leave the area
- A surge of refugees enters the area—so many that those at the front are unable to move, despite hearing and understanding the warning

These may seem to be somewhat contrived examples, but they serve to show how brittle trust relationships can be when contexts change. If the entity being trusted with defence of the base were a soldier, we would hope the soldier could be much more flexible in reacting to these sorts of changes, or at least know that the context had changed and protocol dictated contacting a superior or other expert for new orders. The same is not true for computer systems. They operate in specific contexts; and unless they are architected, designed, and programmed to understand not only that other contexts exist but also how to recognise changes in contexts and how their behaviour should change when they find themselves in a new context, then the trust relationships that other entities have with them are at risk. This can be thought of as an example of programmatically encoded bias: only certain contexts were considered in the design of the system, which means inflexibility is inherent in the system when other contexts are introduced or come into play.

In our example of the automated defence system, at least the base commander or empowered subordinate has the opportunity to realise that a change in context is possible and to reprogram or switch off the system: the entity who has the relationship *to* the system can revise the trust relationship. A much bigger problem arises when *both* entities are actually computing systems and the context in which they are operating changes or, just as likely, they are used in contexts for which they were not designed—or, put another way, in contexts their designers neglected to imagine. How to define such contexts, and the importance of identifying when contexts change, will feature prominently in later chapters.

Trust and Security

Another important topic in our discussion of trust is security. Our core interest, of course, is security in the realm of computing systems, sometimes referred to as *cyber-security* or *IT security*. But although security within the electronic and online worlds has its own peculiarities and specialities, it is generally derived from equivalent or similar concepts in "real life": the non-electronic, human-managed world that still makes up most of our existence and our interactions, even when the interactions we have are "digitally mediated" via computer screens and mobile phones. When we think about humans and security, there is a set of things that we tend to identify as security-related, of which the most obvious and common are probably stopping humans going into places they are not supposed to visit, looking at things they are not supposed to see, changing things they are not supposed to alter, moving things that they are not supposed to shift, and stopping processes that they are not supposed to interrupt. These concepts are mirrored fairly closely in the world of computer systems:

Authorisation: Stopping entities from going into places

Confidentiality: Stopping entities from looking at things

Integrity: Stopping entities from moving and altering things

Availability: Stopping entities from interrupting processes

Exactly what constitutes a core set of security concepts is debatable, but this is a reasonably representative list. Related topics, such as identification and authentication, allow us to decide whether a particular person should be stopped or allowed to perform certain tasks; and categorisation allows us to decide which things which humans are allowed to alter, or which places they may enter. All of these will be useful as we begin to pick apart in more detail how we define trust.

Let us look at one of these topics in a little more detail, then, to allow us to consider its relationship to trust. Specifically, we will examine it within the context of computing systems.

Confidentiality is a property that is often required for certain components of a computer system. One oft-used example is when I want to pay for some goods over the Web. When I visit a merchant, the data I send over the Internet should be encrypted; the sign that it is encrypted is typically the little green shield or padlock that I see on the browser bar by the address of the merchant. We will look in great detail at this example later on in the book, but the key point here is that the data—typically my order, my address, and my credit card information—is encrypted before it leaves my browser and decrypted only when it reaches the merchant. The merchant, of course, needs the information to complete the order, so I am happy for the encryption to last until it reaches their server.

What exactly is happening, though? Well, a number of steps are involved to get the data encrypted and then decrypted. This is not the place for a detailed description,[8] but what happens at a basic level is that my browser and the merchant's server use a well-understood protocol—most likely HTTP + SSL/TLS—to establish enough mutual trust for an encrypted exchange of information to take place. This protocol uses algorithms, which in turn employ cryptography to do

---

[8]See Rescorla 2000 for a definition of the HTTP protocol, the core component of the communication.

the actual work of encryption. What is important to our discussion, however, is that each cryptographic protocol used across the Internet, in data centres, and by governments, banks, hospitals, and the rest, though different, uses the same cryptographic "pieces" as its building blocks. These building blocks are referred to as *cryptographic primitives* and range from asymmetric and symmetric algorithms through one-way hash functions and beyond. They facilitate the construction of some of the higher-level concepts—in this case, confidentiality—which means that correct usage of these primitives allows for systems to be designed that make assurances about certain properties.

One lesson we can learn from the world of cryptography is that while using it should be easy, designing cryptographic algorithms is often very hard. While it may seem simple to create an algorithm or protocol that obfuscates data—think of a simple shift cipher that moves all characters in a given string "up" one letter in the alphabet—it is extremely difficult to do it well enough that it meets the requirements of real-world systems. An oft-quoted dictum of cryptographers is, "Any fool can create a cryptographic protocol that they can't defeat"; and part of learning to understand and use cryptography well is, in fact, the experience of designing such protocols and seeing how other people more expert than oneself go about taking them apart and compromising them.

Let us return to the topics we noted earlier: authorisation, integrity, etc. None of them defines trust, but we will think of them as acting as building blocks when we start considering trust relationships in more detail. Like the primitives used in encryption, these concepts can be combined in different ways to allow us to talk about trust of various kinds and build systems to model the various trust relationships we need to manage. Also like cryptographic primitives, it is very easy to use these primitives in ways that do not achieve what we wish to achieve and can cause confusion and error for those using them.

Why is all of this important? Because trust is important to security. We typically use security to try to enforce trust relationships because humans are not, sadly, fundamentally trustworthy. This book argues that computing systems are not fundamentally trustworthy either, but for somewhat different reasons. It would be easy to think that computing systems are *neutral* with regard to trust, that they just sit there and do what they do; but as we saw when we looked briefly at agency, computers act *for* somebody or something, even when the actions they take are unintended[9] or not as intended. Equally, they may be maliciously or incompetently directed (programmed or operated). But worst, and most common of all, they are often—usually—*unconsciously* and *implicitly* placed into trust relationships with other systems, and ultimately humans and organisations, often outside the contexts for which they were designed. The main goal of this book is to encourage people designing, creating, and operating computer systems to be conscious and explicit in their actions around trust.

---

[9]Wikipedia, "Morris Worm", 2020.

Trust as a Way for Humans to Manage Risk

Risk is a key concept to be able to consider when we are talking about security. There is a common definition of risk within the computing community, which is also shared within the business community:

$$risk = probability \times loss$$

In other words, the risk associated with an event is the likelihood that it will occur multiplied by the impact to be considered if it were to occur. Probability is expressed as a number between 0 and 1 (0 being no possibility of occurrence, 1 being certainty), and the loss can be explicitly stated either as an amount of money or as another type of impact. The point of the formula is to allow risks to be compared; and as long as the different calculations use the same measure of loss, it is generally unimportant what measure is employed. To give an example, let us say that I am interested in the risk of my new desktop computer failing in the first three years of its life. I do some research and discover that the likelihood of the keyboard failing is 4%, or 0.04, whereas the likelihood of the monitor failing is only 1%, or 0.01. If I were to consider this information on its own, it would seem that I should worry more about the keyboard than the monitor, until I take into account the cost of replacement: the keyboard would cost me \$15 to replace, whereas the monitor would cost me \$400 to replace. We have the following risk calculations then:

$$risk = probability \times loss$$

$$risk\,(keyboard) = 0.04 \times 15 = 0.6$$

$$risk\,(monitor) = 0.01 \times 400 = 4$$

It turns out that if I care about risk, I should be more concerned about the monitor than the keyboard. Once we have calculated the risk, we can then consider mitigations: what to do to manage the risk. In the case of my desktop computer, I might decide to take out an extended manufacturer's warranty to cover the monitor but just choose to buy a new keyboard if that breaks.

Risk is all around us and has been since before humans became truly human, living in groups and inhabiting a social structure. We can think of risk as arising in four categories:

ASSESSMENT	MITIGATION
Easy	**Easy**
If there are predators nearby, they might kill us . . .	. . . so we should run away or hide.
Easy	**Difficult**
If our leader gets an infection, she may die . . .	. . . but we don't know how to avoid or effectively treat infection.
Difficult	**Easy**
If the river floods, our possessions may be washed away . . .	. . . but if we camp farther away from the river, we are safer.
Difficult	**Difficult**
If I eat this fruit, it may poison me . . .	. . . but I have no other foodstuffs nearby and may go hungry or even starve if I do not eat it.

For the easy-to-assess categories, both the probability and the loss are simple to calculate. For the difficult-to-assess categories, either the probability or the loss is hard to calculate. What is not clear from the simple formula we used earlier to calculate risk is that you are usually calculating a risk against something that is generally a benefit. In the case of the risk associated with the river, there are advantages to camping close to it—easy access to water and ability to fish, for example—and in the case of the fruit, the benefit of eating it will be that it may nourish me, and I do not need to trek further afield to find something else to eat, thereby using up valuable energy.

Many of the risks associated with interacting with other humans fit within the last category: difficult to assess and difficult to mitigate. In terms of assessment, humans often act in their own interests rather than those of others, or even of a larger group; and the impact of an individual not cooperating may be small—hurt feelings, for example—or large—inability to catch game—or even retribution towards a member of the group. In terms of mitigation, it is often very difficult to guess what actions to take to encourage an individual, particularly one you do not already know, to ensure that they interact with you in a positive manner. You can, of course, avoid any interactions at all, but that means you lose access to any benefits from such interactions, and those benefits can be very significant: new knowledge, teamwork for hunting, more strength to move objects, safety in numbers, even having access to a larger gene pool, to name just a few.

Humans developed trust to help them mitigate the risks of interacting with each other. Think of how you have grown to know and trust new acquaintances: there is typically a gradual process as you learn more about them and trust them to act in particular ways. As David Clark points out when discussing how we develop trust relationships, this "is not a technical problem, but a social one".[10] We see here both time and various other contexts in which trust relationships can operate. Once you trust an individual to act as a babysitter, for instance, you are managing the risks associated with leaving your children with that person. An alternative might be that you trust somebody to make you a cup of tea in the way that you like it: you are mitigating the chance that they will add sugar to it or, in a more extreme case, poison you and steal all of the loyalty points you have accrued with your local cafe.

Trust is not, of course, the only mitigation technique possible when considering and managing risk. We have already seen that you can avoid interactions altogether,[11] but two alternatives that are different sides of the same coin are punishment and reward. I can punish an individual if they do not interact with me as I wish, or I can reward them if they do. Many trust relationships between individuals are arguably built up over time with a combination of these mitigations, even if the punishment is as little as a frown and the reward as little as a smile. What is even more interesting is that the building of the trust relationship is two-way in this case, as the individual being rewarded or punished needs to trust the other individual to be consistent with rewards or punishments based on the behaviour and interactions presented.

Risk, Trust, and Computing

Risk is important in the world of IT and computing. Organisations need to know whether their systems will work as expected or if they will fail for any one of many reasons: for example, hardware failure, loss of power, malicious compromise, poor software. Given that trust is a way of mitigating risk, are there opportunities to use trust—to transfer what humans have learned from creating and maintaining trust relationships—and transfer it to this world? We could say that humans need to "trust" their systems. If we think back to the cases presented earlier in the chapter, this fits our third example, where we discussed the bank trusting its IT systems.

Defining Trust in Systems

The first problem with trusting systems is that the world of trust is not simple when we start talking about computers. We might expect that computers and computer systems, being less complex than humans, would be easier to consider with respect to trust, but we cannot simply apply the concept of trust the same

---

[10]Clark, 2014, p. 22.
[11]Or attempt to do so: humans are quite good at seeking out those who do not want to interact with them, and bothering them anyway, as any tired parent of young children will tell you.

way to interactions with computers as we do to interactions with humans. The second problem is that humans are good at inventing and using metaphors and applying a concept to different contexts to make some sense of them, even when the concept does not map perfectly to the new contexts. Trust is one of these contexts: we think we know what we mean when we talk about trust, but when we apply it to interactions with computer systems, it turns out that the concepts we think we understand do not map perfectly.

There is a growing corpus of research and writing around how humans build trust relationships to each other and to organisations, and this is beginning to be applied to how humans and organisations trust computer systems. What is missing is often a realisation that interactions between computer systems themselves—case four in our earlier examples—are frequently modelled in terms of trust relationships. But as these models lack the rigour and theoretical underpinnings to allow strong statements to be made about what is really going on, we are left without the ability to allow detailed discussion of risk and risk mitigation.

Why does this matter, though? The first answer is that when you are running a business, you need to know that all the pieces are correct and doing the correct thing in relationship to each other. This set of behaviours and relationships makes up a system, and the pieces its components, a subject to which we will return in Chapter 5: The Importance of Systems. We can think of this as similar to ensuring that your car is made up of the correct parts, placed in the correct locations. If you have the wrong brake cable, then you may find that when you press the relevant pedal, your brakes don't engage. In the same way, if you have multiple computer systems trying to talk to each other, and your database is not correctly integrated with the other components, you may find that when somebody places an order with your company, the order is not processed. When discussing these relationships and integrations in computing and IT, we sometimes talk about one component having a *contract* that it offers to other components. This contract will describe the expected behaviour of the component in terms of the inputs it receives and output that it provides. Providers of such components generally try to keep these contracts as firm and unchanging across versions as possible because any changes can significantly impact the behaviour of the rest of the system.

Think, for instance, of a component that is calculating the risk associated with an event. It takes as input a probability in a range from 0 to 1 and a dollar amount and then outputs the product of the two according to our formula. What would happen if a new version was released that, instead of taking the probability as a range from 0 to 1, expected a percentage (in the range from 0 to 100)? This would be a change to the contract, and any components integrated with this one—either for input or output—would need to be informed of the change and possibly updated in order for the system to work as expected.

To return to our definition:

"Trust is the assurance that one entity holds that another will perform particular actions according to a specific expectation".

The contract is the "specific expectation" in this case. The contract is usually defined with an application programming interface (API), either expressed using one of a common set of descriptive languages or specific to the particular language in which the component is written. The first reason that being able to discuss risk management and mitigation is important, then, is to allow us to construct a business by integrating various systems along the lines of the contracts they provide. The second reason for its importance is security.

Defining Correctness in System Behaviour

Earlier, we skirted slightly around the idea of *correctness* in terms of components and their behaviours, but one way of thinking about security is that it is concerned with maintaining the correctness of the behaviour of your systems in the face of attempts by malicious actors to make them act differently. Whether these malicious actors wish to use your systems to further their own ends—to mine crypto-currency, exfiltrate user data, attack other targets, or host their own content—or to disrupt your business, the outcome is the same: they want to use your systems in ways you did not intend.

To guard against this, you need to know:

- How the systems *should* act
- How to recognise when they do *not* act as expected
- How to fix any problem that arises

The first goal is an expression of our trust definition, and the second is about monitoring to ensure that the trust is correctly held. The third—fixing the problem—is about remediation. All three of these goals may seem very obvious, but it is easy to miss that many security breakdowns arise precisely because trust is not explicitly stated and monitored. The key thesis of this book is that without a good understanding of the trust relationships between systems in contexts in which they operate *or might operate*, it is impossible to understand the possibilities available for malicious compromise (and, indeed, unintentional malfunction). Many attacks involve taking systems and using them in ways—in contexts—not considered by those who designed and/or operate them. A full understanding of trust relationships allows better threat modelling, stronger defences, closer monitoring, and easier remediation when things go wrong, partly because defining contexts where behaviours are defined allows for better consideration of where and how systems should be deployed.

We can state our three aims differently. To keep our systems working the way we expect, we need to know:

- What trust relationships exist
- How to recognise when a trust relationship has broken
- How to re-establish trust

There is, of course, another thing we need to know: how to defend our systems in the first place and design them so that they can be defended. These are topics we will address later in the book.

CHAPTER 2

Humans and Trust

As Richard Harper points out in his preamble to a collection of essays on trust, computing, and society,[1] much of the literature around trust is not really about trust at all, but about *mistrust*. It is the setting up—and maybe the demolishing—of a trust relationship that could be labelled as mistrust; and given the consequences of its failing, getting this part right is important. If you take a simple view of trust as something which is binary—it is either there or it is not—rather than considering it as a more complex relationship or set of relationships, then the area which is not black and white, but tinged with complications, is what is relevant.

That is what could fairly be labelled, within the literature, as mistrust.

It would be nice to believe that we can take a reductionist view of trust, which allows us to follow this lead, moving all the complicated parts into a box labelled *mistrust* and having a well-defined set of parts we need to consider that are all just about *trust*; but we saw in the previous chapter that trust is itself complex. We certainly do want to get to a clearer, more refined definition, but we first need to delve deeper into what trust looks like and how it is defined in the various spheres of relevant academic study. Although our interest is less in the human-to-human realm than in trust relationships that involve computer systems (whether human-to-computer or computer-to-computer), it is important to understand the theoretical and academic underpinnings of trust

---

[1]Harper, 2014, p. 10.

in the human-to-human realm. This is not just because there is utility in being able to relate some of this thinking to our realm by being able to compare what we mean with what we do not mean, but also because any application of trust between realms must necessarily be metaphorical and deserves a thorough examination. As discussed in Chapter 1, "Why Trust?", metaphors are useful but can be misleading and need to be employed with care. The other reason is that if we cannot unpick what *can* be intended when the word *trust* is used, then it is difficult to define what we *wish* to communicate as we try to restrict some of the various associated concepts and choose those that we want to use.

First, we need to admit that the field of study regarding trust is both active and wide: there are a lot of definitions of human-to-human trust, many of which are not easily reconcilable. Most of the definitions, understandably, focus on social elements, and, as noted by Harper, there is a strong overtone of mistrust. Here are some examples supplied by other noted authors ruminating on the notion of trust:

- Trust in social interactions is "the willingness to be vulnerable based on positive expectation about the behaviour of others".[2]
- Cheshire notes that Baier's definition[3] "depends on the possibility of betrayal by another person".
- For Hardin, when considering interpersonal trust, "my trust in you is encapsulated in your interest in fulfilling the trust".[4]
- Cheshire distinguishes *trustworthiness* from *trust* and discusses how risk-taking can act as a signal that one party considers another trustworthy.[5]
- Dasgupta[6] has seven starting points for establishing trust, of which three are related directly to punishment, one to choice, one to perspective, one to context, and one to monitoring.

All of these examples may be helpful when considering human-to-human trust relationships—though even there, they generally seem a little vague in terms of definition—but if we are to consider trust relationships involving computers and system-based entities, they are all insufficient, basically because all of them relate to human emotions, intentions, or objectives. Applying questions around emotions to, say, a mobile phone's connection to a social media site is clearly not a sensible endeavour, though we will examine later how intention and objectives may have some relevance in discussions about trust within the computer-to-computer realm.

One further definition that deserves examination is offered by Diego Gambetta, the source of our original *trust* definition. We will spend a little time on this as

---

[2]Mayers et al., 1995, cited in Harper p. 230.
[3]Baier, 1986, referenced in Cheshire, p. 55.
[4]Hardin, 2001.
[5]Cheshire, 2001, p. 52.
[6]Dasgupta, 1988.

it will set up some interesting issues to which we will return at some length later in the book. Gambetta proposes the following definition:

> **trust (or, symmetrically, distrust) is a particular level of the subjective probability with which an agent assesses that another agent or group of agents will perform a particular action, both before he [sic] can monitor such action (or independently of his capacity ever to be able to monitor it) and in a context in which it affects his own action.**[7]

There are some interesting points here. First, Gambetta discusses agents, though the usage is somewhat different to that which we employed in Chapter 1. We used *agents* to describe an entity acting for another entity, whereas he is using a different definition, where an agent is an actor that takes an active role in an interaction. Confusingly, the usage within computing sometimes falls between these two definitions. A software agent is considered to have the ability to act autonomously in a particular situation—the term *autonomous agent* is sometimes used equivalently—but that is not necessarily the same as acting as a person or an organisation. However, in the absence of artificial general intelligence (AGI), it would seem that software agents must be acting on behalf of humans or human organisations even if the intention is to "set them free" to act autonomously or even learn behaviour on their own.

The second important point that Gambetta makes is that a trust relationship—he is specifically discussing human trust relationships—is partly defined by expectations before any actions are performed. This resonates closely with the points we made earlier about the importance of collecting information to allow us to form assurances. His third point is related to the second, in that he discusses the possible inability of the trustor to monitor the actions in which they are interested. Given such a lack of assuring information, the ability to evaluate the likelihood of trust is based on the same data: that presented beforehand.

For his fourth point, however, Gambetta also identifies that there are contexts in which actions can be monitored, though he seems to tie such actions to actions the trustor will take. This seems too restrictive on the trustor, as there may be actions taken by the trustee that do not lead to corresponding actions by the trustor—unless the very lack of such actions is considered action in itself. More important, however, is the implicit assumption (from the negative explicit in the previous statement) that monitoring should take place.

The Role of Monitoring and Reporting in Creating Trust

This assumption about monitoring should not be glossed over. Monitoring is important because without it, there is no way for us to check or update a trust relationship. Without some sort of feedback mechanism to allow us to monitor

---

[7]Gambetta, 1988.

the actions being taken by the trustee, any trust relationship that we have created to the trustee can only be based on our original expectations. It is difficult to feel that we have modelled a trust relationship well if there is no way to verify or validate the assurances we have, so monitoring definitely has a role to play.

One difference that we will encounter when we start examining trust relationships to computer systems, however, is that the opportunities for direct sensory monitoring of actions are likely to be more limited than in human-to-human trust relationships. When monitoring human actions, they are often readily apparent, but the same is not true for many computer-performed actions. If I request via a web browser that a banking application transfer funds between one account and another, the only visible effect I am likely to see is an acknowledgement on the screen. Until I get to the point of trying to spend or withdraw that money,[8] I realistically have no way to be assured that the transaction has taken place. It is as if I have a trust relationship with somebody around the corner of a street, out of view, that they will raise a red flag at the stroke of noon; and I have a friend standing on the corner who will watch the person and tell me when and if they raise the flag. I may be happy with this arrangement, but only because I have a trust relationship to the friend: that friend is acting as a trusted channel for information.

The word *friend* was chosen carefully because a trust relationship is already implicit in the set of interactions that we usually associate with someone described as a friend. The same is not true for the word *somebody*, which I used to denote the person who was to raise the flag. The situation as described is likely to make our minds presume that there is a fairly high probability that the trust relationship I have to the friend is sufficient to assure me that they will pass the information correctly. But what if my friend standing on the corner is actually a business partner of the flag-waver? Given our human understanding of the trust relationships typically involved with business partnerships, we may immediately begin to assume that my friend's motivations in respect to correct reporting are not neutral.

The example of the flag was chosen as a simple one: it is binary (either performed or not performed), and the activity was not imbued with any further significance. If, however, we give or associate our example with some value—say, a signal that money should be transferred into my bank account from the flag-waver and their business partner's bank account—it is clear that a lot more is at stake. If, for example, my friend chooses to favour the business relationship over our friendship, my friend might collude with the flag-waver and tell me that they raised the red flag even when they did not. Or, my friend might

---

[8]There is a wider question about whether money is *real* and whether bank accounts truly *transfer* anything when balances are updated, but such discussions are beyond the scope of this book.

tell me the flag-waver has not raised the flag when they have, colluding with a third party with the intention of defrauding both me and the third party by somehow accessing the funds in my bank account that I do not believe to have been transferred.

The channels for reporting on actions—i.e., monitoring them—are vitally important within trust relationships. It is both easy and dangerous to fall into the trap of assuming they are neutral, with the only important one being between me and the acting party. In reality, the trust relationship that I have to a set of channels is key to maintaining the trust relationships that I have to the main actor that is the monitor—who or what we could call the *primary trustee*. In trust relationships involving computer systems, there are often multiple entities or components involved in actions, and these form a chain of trust where each link depends on the other: the chain is typically only as strong as the weakest of its links.

There is a further complication to be considered, which is how rarely we have control over—and can therefore have significant trust towards—the reporting or monitoring of channels in a relationship to a computer system. Channels are often under the control of the acting party or can be compromised in ways over which I have very little control. Let us look back again at the example of the bank transfer via a web browser. The reporting of the transfer is via the application, which is presumably written by the bank or at least is under the control of the bank: I have no control of this channel. Even if I am using a downloaded application and it is running on my computer or mobile phone—and even if it is open source,[9] meaning I have the chance to check that what it is displaying is "correct"—I cannot be sure that it is "valid" as the information it has comes from the bank, in the final analysis. In terms of compromise, I can at least take some steps to decrease vulnerabilities and, therefore, the chance of compromise, for the pieces over which I have control: I can keep my computer or phone as secure as possible, check that the versions of any downloaded applications—web browser or banking application, for instance—are verified as being from the expected suppliers, and check that the connection they have to the bank is as secure as I can make it.

In the end, however, it is up to my bank to provide valid information and ensure its correctness, though I will be the one who pays for these measures and am likely to bear any cost of invalid data: security economics raises its head again. This discussion about trust chains and monitoring will reappear later in the book as an important issue when designing and managing trust.

One final point to bear in mind about Gambetta's definition of trust is his description of the *subjective probability* with which an assessment is made about whether actions will be performed. We dropped this phrase in our definition,

---

[9]*Open source* software "is software with source code that anyone can inspect, modify, and enhance"— Opensource.com (2021).

replacing it with *assurance*, as subjective probability frankly seems difficult to quantify or apply. The use of the word *assurance* should not be taken to imply 100% certainty, but words like *subjective* are problematic. The first reason is that the *subject* in this case may not be human. The second is because if we are to tie trust relationships back to discussions of risk, then objectivity and external qualifiability are insufficient: we also require external quantifiability.

We have examined, then, a variety of different trust definitions in the human realm, though none of them seems a perfect fit for our needs. Before we throw all of these out with no further consideration, however, there is an interesting question about the overlap between human-to-human relationships and human-to-computer relationships when the computer has a closely coupled relationship with an organisation. This is different to case 3 that we discussed in Chapter 1, when we discussed the relationship between a bank and its systems, and more like case 2, where my trust relationship to the bank, and the bank's relationship to me, are characterised by interactions largely with their computer systems. In this case, punishment or other social impacts (positive or negative) may be more relevant, as we may be able to relate them to people rather than to the computers with which the actual interaction takes place. We will return to this question later, once we have addressed questions around trust to institutions—which is related but distinct—later in this chapter.

Game Theory

Much of the recent discussion around trust in the human-to-human realm has revolved around game theory and cooperation, either separately or in conjunction. *Game theory* is the study of social interactions from a theoretical point of view, typically looking at strategies for interaction that yield particular outcomes (usually the "best" for an actor or set of actors). Different styles of interaction, competition, and cooperation are studied, and mathematical approaches are applied, usually with the proviso that the actors are "rational"[10] though not necessarily in possession of perfect information about their situation.

The Prisoner's Dilemma

The best-known example of game theory is the Prisoner's Dilemma. The classic scenario of the Prisoner's Dilemma is where two members of a criminal gang are arrested and held separately from each other so that they cannot communicate. Each of them is presented with a choice: they may either stay silent or betray the other. Each is told the consequence of whichever action they may decide to

---

[10]The definition of what exactly counts as "rational" behaviour may be in itself an issue of debate.

take, combined with that of the fellow gang member. There are four outcomes, of which two are the same for both criminals, reducing the total number of distinct outcomes to three:

- Both prisoners stay silent, in which case they are both sentenced to one year in prison.
- One prisoner stays silent, but their colleague betrays them, in which case the betrayer goes free but the silent prisoner receives a sentence of three years in prison.
- Both prisoners betray the other, in which case they both end up in prison for two years.

The rational position for each prisoner to take is to betray the other because betrayal provides a better reward than staying silent. Three interesting facts fall out of this game and the mountains of theoretical and experimental data associated with it:

- If the prisoners play repeatedly but know the number of repeated games, then the most rational strategy is to punish the other for bad behaviour and keep betraying.
- If they do *not* know the number of repetitions, then the most rational strategy is to stay silent.
- In reality, humans tend to a more cooperative strategy when playing variants of this game, working together rather than betraying each other.

I have attended events where groups of people—unaware of the theory—have participated in multiple rounds of this game or a modified version of the Prisoner's Dilemma (sometimes, for instance, the payoffs are adjusted and counts kept of notional money won and lost). It is fascinating to watch people trying out strategies whilst reacting to past rounds and also being locked into a history of their own behaviour that they cannot change. Much of the foundational modern work around the Prisoner's Dilemma—and broader game theory—was done by Robert Axelrod.[11] He noted the same points and posited that cooperation—in such games or more broadly—is a positive evolutionary trait. It encourages behaviours that are likely to benefit the survival of the species adopting them. He also suggested ways to encourage cooperation, based on computer models contributed by various academic institutions:

- Enlarge the shadow of the future (make players more aware of future games and less bound into their—and their fellow player's—histories).
- Ensure that the payoffs are immediate, clear, and motivating.

---

[11] Axelrod, 1990.

- Teach players to care about each other.

- Teach reciprocity (rewarding positive actions—typically cooperation—and punishing negative actions—typically betrayal).

- Improve recognition abilities (being able to recognise what the other party's strategy is).

Although proposed as a thought experiment, it turns out that the Prisoner's Dilemma can be used to model rather closely a number of different situations. Game theory arguably suffered, in the last years of the twentieth century and the early years of the twenty-first, from being the blockchain of its day: it was seen by some as the future foundation for all rules and types of societal interaction. As Heap and Varoufakis[12] noted, people's motivations are typically more complex than the somewhat simplistic models provided by game theory and are affected by what they called people's *social location*: the cultures and societies in which they live and their relative positions in terms of wealth, power, etc.

This does not mean, however, that game theory has nothing to offer us. What Axelrod's tactics to encourage cooperation seem to be promoting are ways to build some sort of trust between the two parties. Let us revisit our definition of *trust* and apply it to game theory:

"Trust is the assurance that one entity holds that another will perform particular actions according to a specific expectation".

We need, of course, to consider our corollaries as well: how do they apply in this case?

First Corollary   "Trust is always contextual".

Second Corollary   "One of the contexts for trust is always time".

Third Corollary   "Trust relationships are not symmetrical".

The two entities are easily identified in this case: the two participants in the game. The context here is the game—one way of understanding the concerns of Heap and Varoufakis is that trying to extend the context beyond the game means we are extending the context too far. It is clear that time is a vital component of this relationship, given the impact of multiple games. And the final corollary is that although the trust relationships from each player to the other in this example are not necessarily symmetrical, the best outcome is achieved when they are. Most important, as the games proceed, each party is building an assurance that the other will perform certain actions—staying silent or betraying—when asked. It is interesting to note that in our definition of *trust*, there is no value associated

---

[12]Heap and Varoufakis, 1995.

with whether the outcome is positive or negative: each party can have an assurance that the other party will perform particular actions (always staying silent; alternatively betraying and then staying silent; staying silent in response to the first party's previous silence) without the outcome necessarily being positive.

Reputation and Generalised Trust

The Prisoner's Dilemma is not the only type of game covered in the field of game theory. There are many, of which most are two-player games, and most can also have multiple participants (with no theoretical limit). The two-player games serve to give an example of how assurances about future behaviour—what we are referring to as *trust relationships*—can be formed between two participants.

What about the case for multiple participants? When I set about forming a trust relationship "from scratch"—with no prior interactions—to someone (let us call her Alice), then I do so based on my expectations, biases, and interactions over time. If, on the other hand, somebody (we will call her Carol) asks me for information on Alice in order for her to form an initial opinion, and then asks multiple other people who have also formed a trust relationship to Alice for the same or similar information, then something else is happening: Carol is finding out information not first-hand, but based on information from others.

The standard term for this is *reputation*, and it does not map directly from a trust relationship that Carol has to Alice but is a second-order construct. Carol cannot directly map my views on my trust relationship to Alice, alongside the views of others on their trust relationships to Alice, directly to her trust relationship to Alice: rather, she derives enough information to describe a reputation that she can relate to Alice and use to decide how best to form a trust relationship.

In the Prisoner's Dilemma example, we discussed the best strategic approach but also noted that many humans often end up taking a much more positive approach than would be expected by theoretical analysis. One reason for this may be that humans do not always act rationally—that is, in ways that suggest informed self-interest. One alternative to a self-interested approach is known as *generalised trust*. Rather than assuming that all trust relationships need to be formed from an initial position of distrust, generalised trust suggests that the default should be to trust, in the absence of any evidence to suggest it would be wise to do the contrary.[13] Given our interest in trust for security within computing, this approach may not be a very sensible one: it is much easier to assess risk from the point of view of starting from a position of no trust and build up a trust relationship built on known precepts than to reduce trust. Further, as Brian Rathburn points out,[14] such trust relationships typically rely greatly on

---

[13]Rathburn, 2011, p. 24.
[14]Rathburn, 2011, p. 28.

reciprocity; and given our focus on the asymmetry of trust relationships, we should be wary of relying overly on this approach.

The reputation approach is interesting because rather than having to start her trust relationship to Alice from scratch or with only the tools that she has (her experience, biases, and some expectations), Carol starts with some specific information about Alice that she can use. We can think of this type of information as inputs to the idea of "trustworthiness" proposed by some of the writers we have mentioned when considering human-to-human trust.

What other types of information might we have up front? Another way of looking at this is asking what pressures can be brought to bear on the trustee that allow me, the trustor, to have a high assurance that this will affect the trustee's behaviour in ways that are likely to influence them to act in ways consistent with my expectations. Bruce Schneier writes in detail about this in *Liars & Outliers: Enabling the Trust That Society Needs to Thrive*.[15] He discusses societal pressures, moral pressures, reputational pressures, institutional pressures, and security systems, all in the context of society. Sanctions, punishments, and incentives all fit into this model of trust establishment and management, and reputation is one of the key concepts required to evaluate relationships.

We know in our day-to-day human interactions that reputations can be ill-formed or unfairly earned and also that they can change significantly over time. We will look at indirect trust relationships in Chapter 3, "Trust Operations and Alternatives", and at the importance of time in Chapter 7, "The Importance of Time", but another point arises from reputations: over the many years that humans have grown into larger and larger groups, creating societies and forming organisations, reputations are important for another type of trust relationship. This is the area on which Schneier spends much attention, as evidenced by his chapter headings on organisations, corporations, and institutions, and which we can broadly label *institutional trust*.

Institutional Trust

A great deal of the literature on trust revolves around our trust—and mistrust—in institutions: or, as we would clarify with our new understanding about these concepts, the trust relationships we have to institutions. This type of trust is related directly to our second case in Chapter 1: my trust relationship to my bank. Banks are, in fact, a key example of institutions where their customers' or users' trust is self-evidently vital. Banks and other financial institutions are so important to the smooth running of (capitalist) society that governments will not infrequently move in to prop up a bank when trust in it begins to falter.

---

[15]Schneier, 2012.

The assurance associated with trust here is generally around whether a bank has sufficient assets to be able to provide its customers with their money when requested. But there is a greater and more dangerous concern against which financial institutions—or maybe, more broadly, frameworks—must guard: trust in a currency itself. By this, we really mean there is a generally accepted assurance that the currency will hold its value over time, or at least not deviate (particularly downwards) too sharply over time in terms of its purchasing power.

It has become clear, with the rise of blockchain-backed crypto-currencies as an alternative (for some) to traditional *fiat* currencies, that the types of assurance, and how they are managed, are more complex than had generally been assumed. This topic is so important for our understanding of how trust is embodied in a particular set of systems that we will return to crypto-currencies in more detail in Chapter 6, "Blockchain and Trust".

For now, we will concentrate on more traditional institutions and some of the discussions on how trust is relevant to them. It should come as no surprise that this is a topic that has garnered a great deal of attention over the years. The idea that institutions are required because individual humans cannot "scale" to provide all of the services required is clearly not new. Monarchs and generals have appeared to manage large groups of people, trustworthy individuals have been appointed to dispense justice (at, for instance, Jethro's urging to Moses in Exodus 18), and the people who they serve—or are supposed to serve—need to have a trust relationship to them.

Theories of Institutional Trust

One of the most famous and influential early modern writers on the topic of institutional trust in the West, at least, was Thomas Hobbes,[16] in his *Leviathan*, originally published in 1651. In fact, the full title of his book was *Leviathan: Or the Matter, Forme and Power of a Commonwealth, Ecclesiasticall and Civil*, and it is considered an important early work in *social contract theory*. This theory—the name is taken from another giant in the field, Jean-Jacques Rousseau's *The Social Contract*[17]—suggests that we—members of societies—give up some rights that we might otherwise exercise and give them, instead, to institutions.

Hobbes's central thesis is that people (he would say "men") are, by default, in "a state of nature" in which they are "brutish and at warre" with one another. In other words, without some sort of authority structures, there can be no society beyond simple interpersonal relationships. To overcome this restriction, humans create agreements to give up some of their rights to take from each other—though never to defend themselves—by imbuing rights into a sovereign body. This

---

[16]Hobbes 1651; 1996.
[17]Rousseau, 1762.

sovereign body is preferably, in Hobbes's view, a monarch and has the power to create laws and exact punishment. Though the work is a masterpiece and still worth reading, certain issues stand out to a more modern reader, including, crucially, how such sovereign bodies are ordained[18] and sustained if there is no continual re-establishment of the sovereignty by its body politic.

If we ignore Hobbes's preference for a monarch as the structural centre and over-look for now the question of how exactly a central authority is established (a topic to which we will return in Chapter 3, "Trust Operations and Alternatives") we may consider the possibility that trust in this central authority could be continually re-established, but we must remember that such trust is really made up of many separate trust relationships to the authority. There is a distinction here between the set of trust relationships held and the reputation of the authority: the latter, while theoretically a reflection of all the former, is not a true view of it in the context of two important measures:

- The conglomeration of information about trust relationships will always be imperfect in practice, in the same way that a map is never a true representation of a tract of land (a perfect representation becomes more than a representation and becomes part of what it is representing[19]).

- Reputation is information allowing an entity to consider the formation—or tuning—of a trust relationship rather than the relationship itself.

This is a distinction that often seems to be lost in discussions of institutional trust—or, more specifically, trust relationships to institutions. Either little difference is evinced between reputation and trust, or the fact that different parties hold different relationships is overlooked. One notable exception to this is Francis Fukuyama, whose 1995 book *Trust: The Social Virtues and the Creation of Prosperity*[20] is one of the canonical works in the modern discussion of institutional trust. In it, he examines the role of social capital, familism, individualism, and sociability in economic growth, in particular their effects on how corporations and companies form. He argues strongly that mutual trust, a commodity linked to the concept of social capital,[21] is very important to how people in different cultures form groups and corporations.

Another approach is that taken by Onora O'Neill,[22] who takes as one of her starting points that "trust is social", and then goes on to discuss the "crisis of trust" in public institutions, another example of mistrust being taken as a

---

[18]Chomsky's criticisms of the British Empire, for example, are particularly trenchant in this regard (Chomsky, 2015, p. 109).
[19]Carroll, 1889.
[20]Fukuyama, 1995.
[21]Coleman, 1986.
[22]O'Neill, 2002.

core aspect to be studied. O'Neill then goes on to consider how this can be managed, suggesting that transparency (a removal of secrecy) is not enough if we cannot remove deception and that true accountability involves the ability to make informed, deliberate (and individually autonomous) choices. Although the language here may seem somewhat different to what we have been using, the accent on choices that are both informed and individual is very consonant with our approach.

A final example in this area is a work by Diego Gambetta, whose 1988 essay "Mafia: the Price of Mistrust"[23] both explicitly deals with mistrust and also discusses very different alternatives to institutions as instantiations of Hobbes's structural authorities as the centre for trust networks. He suggests that the Mafia in Sicily and southern Italy is successful for a variety of reasons: through fear of sanctions; because cooperation with the Mafia enhances people's mutual economic interests; because people have general reasons (cultural, moral, or religious) for believing that cooperation is good irrespective of sanctions and rewards; and because people are related by bonds of kin or friendship. It is worth considering, as in the case of the Prisoner's Dilemma, whether the sort of trust relationship that an individual might have to the Mafia might actually meet our definition of trust, remembering that the assurance of bad behaviour meets it equally as well as assurance of good behaviour.

We might also consider the differences between informal institutions like the Mafia and formal institutions like a monarchy. Author Henry Farrell[24] makes an interesting distinction between trust/distrust in informal institutions as opposed to formal institutions such as those we have been examining so far. To state it in the terms we have been using, the distinction is that the context(s) of the trust relationship that a person holds to the Mafia are very far being well-defined: in this case, they are very ill-defined. This means a "certain fuzziness" in how to behave in certain situations dominates the relationship, as the institution itself is informal.

Who Is Actually Being Trusted?

The main problem with discussions around institutional trust is that although they use similar terms to those we use around individual human-to-human trust, they are all about conglomerations of trust relationships or about second-order derivations such as reputation. Economists are well aware that it is difficult to extrapolate from the theoretically rational individual actors modelled in game theory to multiple actors, particularly when neither the institution being

---

[23]Gambetta, 1988, pp. 158–175.
[24]Farrell, 2009.

trusted nor the context(s) for that trust relationship tend to be well-defined. Consider, for example, the phrase *I don't trust the government* and what different overtones that may hold when uttered by a single parent in their twenties and a multi-millionaire venture capitalist in their sixties. What do they trust the government to do or not to do, and what do they mean by the government? We are even further hampered by the geographical and jurisdictional differences. What I might mean by the government, writing this in the United Kingdom, is likely to be different to what is meant by a person of similar background in the US, Singapore, or Kazakhstan: even granted that we are talking about different bodies, the functions of those governments, their responsibilities to us, and our expectations of them are likely to be radically different.

Although it can cause confusion around the definition of party and of context, this territoriality—the connection to a particular territory or locality—as Axelrod[25] calls it, provides some help when trying to define trust relationships and derive reputation, as it forces repeated interactions with known and easily recognised individuals. What is interesting about this is that Axelrod is pointing out the fact that institutions are represented by actual people who act as agents for the institution, as we noted in our discussion of our second case in Chapter 1.

Not all institutions are central authorities—although central or state banks exist, many institutions do not fit into either category—but one development that has been particularly significant is the rise in what Coleman[26] identifies as explicitly social contracts with multiple corporate actors, over and beyond those with, and sometimes to the detriment of, the structural authorities that Hobbes described. Given that Coleman was writing in the mid-1980s, much of his forecast seems extremely prescient. From the move (in much of the world) from the support of party political manifestos to a much more issue-led political activism (the example *du jour* being Extinction Rebellion), to the astonishing power of search engines and social media sites, most of us maintain many more trust relationships to institutions in many more contexts than we would have done even 10 or 20 years ago. Nor does this disallow the possibility of some of those being state actors even outside our territory: the government of Estonia, for instance, has started offering e-residency[27] for those who are not existing citizens, with a variety of mainly digital services attached. Of course, such non-territorial or extra-territorial authorities have existed for centuries—examples being the Roman Catholic Church, CND (the Campaign for Nuclear Disarmament), and Communist International (Comintern or the Third International)—though often, association with them has carried significant political risk for those involved.

---

[25] Axelrod, 1990.
[26] Coleman, 1986.
[27] e-Residency, 2019.

Trust Based on Authority

The word *authority* has its etymology in the Latin word *auctor*: creator or originator. The English word *author* still carries this meaning, usually describing the person who wrote a particular novel, paper, poem, or other work of text. In most contexts, however, when we think of the word *authority*, we tend to think about being told to do something, as in phrases such as "Does she have the authority to tell me to do this?" There is another meaning as well, related to an entity—typically a person or an organisation—with expertise in a particular area, who may act as a trustee. Sometimes these authorities will endorse ideas, people, organisations, or systems, creating a second level of authority.

How are these secondary authorities endorsed and established? Historically, authority was vested in figures or texts that had become established through either consensus or endorsement by another type of authority, such as the Roman Catholic Church. Notable examples include:

- The Bible—or, specifically, particular interpretations of the Bible that led to astronomical theories of geocentricism (with the Earth and planets revolving around the Sun) and that were defended by the Roman Catholic Church against the Copernican theories for which Galileo argued

- Galen, a Roman doctor and writer on medicine in the Greek tradition, whose incorrect theories around the circulation of the blood, for instance, were accepted for centuries

- Trofim Lysenko, a scientist (or arguably, pseudo-scientist) whose theories espousing inherited characteristics between generations led to a campaign against Darwinism and genetic theory pursued by the Soviet Union

The establishment of the endorsing authorities for these three examples are notably different. The first example is the theocratic rule of the Roman Catholic Church, whose control of much of Mediæval Europe was almost total, with spiritual power being backed up by economic and political (and concomitant military) power. The second example is the mediæval academe, whose practices and understandings of authority were established mainly through historical precedent and lack of philosophical means or impetus to challenge them, though they were also shored up by the Roman Catholic Church. The third was the autocratic regime of the Soviet Union, whose ability to influence research and teaching through political control—backed up by propaganda and force of arms—allowed them to endorse a particular viewpoint as authoritative.

The established endorsing authorities of the Middle Ages, including Biblical authority, the divine right of kings, and simplistic assumptions that force was sufficient to establish authority, came under question and then attack with the Renaissance and the Age of Reason (or Age of Enlightenment). Personal experience and the scientific method came to the fore, and the basis for authority was questioned. We have already looked at Thomas Hobbes's views on institutional authority: the assumptions that underlined these were exactly what Thomas Paine criticised as he attempted to find a new basis for social institutions and government in his late-eighteenth-century treatise *The Rights of Man,*[28] which defended the French Revolution. It had a significant impact on political and societal theory and reflected the broader move to a more individualistic view of human rights and experience, at least within European and American society.

This move to a more individual-centric world view led both to a debasing of the Roman Catholic Church as the sole endorsing authority for matters spiritual within the West and to a new approach to science, where experimentation challenged and developed scientific theory. This move has arguably never been fully complete, as the study of the philosophy of science shows us; neither is the search for "objective scientific truth" a simple acceptance of new ideas as they come along—a point addressed by Thomas Kuhn in his work on paradigm shifts.[29] The general march of society over the past few hundred years has, however, been towards an acceptance of science as an authority, with the scientific method its endorser, and experts in particular fields—we might say *contexts* for our purposes—as its practitioners.

We have more recently also seen a new set of ways in which endorsing authorities have become established and maintained their power. In a capital-based economy, money can be equally as powerful as force. In the modern era, wielding the two together is typically the reserve of nation-states, but in the past, organisations such as the East India Company were able to combine the two with great effectiveness. The multinational nature of much business in the modern era generally allows the effective exercise of economic power without employing military force: the overwhelming success of the x86 instruction set, pushed by the silicon chip vendor Intel, is a case in point. Other types of endorsing power in the modern era include:

Standards Bodies   Organisations come together to create an industry standard that will benefit multiple parties.

De Facto **Standards**   Enough groups start following the same specification that it becomes more valuable to keep to it than to diverge from it.

Fiscal Power   The power of central banks, even when not fully controlled by a government, allows them significant control over fiscal matters domestically and sometimes internationally.

---

[28]Paine, 1791, 1792; 2000.
[29]Kuhn, 1962.

Cultural Power   Latterly, the position of the BBC (British Broadcasting Company) within Great Britain, the British Empire, and later the British Commonwealth was such that it wielded considerable cultural power, allowing, even in the 1980s, the rise of the Acorn BBC microcomputer as a significant computing platform in the UK.

Utility Power   A particular organisation has sufficient effective control over a utility, tool, or device that they gain significant power, such as Google's power to promote companies in search results or Facebook's ability to influence what news we see.

Perhaps the most important example of an endorsing authority in our context is that of certificate authorities. As the Internet grew and the World Wide Web exploded in popularity in the mid-1990s, it became clear that there was a need to be able to identify the computer system—typically the web server—to which you were connecting. More accurately, there was a need to tie the identity of the entity—person or organisation—owning or operating that computer to that computer and the information it was providing. The invention of public-key cryptography and associated public-key infrastructure (PKI) based on asymmetric cryptography offered a way to do this, and a number of companies started offering a service by which they cryptographically signed certificates that could be requested by companies and then hosted on computers to prove their ownership: these companies became known as certificate authorities (CAs). They checked the identity of the requesting party and their ownership of the computer system (or associated DNS record), issued a certificate, and made legal representations around the service they were providing.

The complexity and importance of the trust relationships to CAs and public-key cryptography within our day-to-day interactions with computing systems should not be underestimated, and we will be undertaking a deep analysis of the issue later in the book. The relevant point here is that CAs became endorsing authorities through the identification of a need, the development of clearly defined processes, and the application of legal frameworks to support the services offered, which led to a new type of endorsing authority. The particular authority that they were endorsing was a series of cryptographic root certificates to which other certificates could be linked, leading to a chain of trust. These root certificates have come to be known as *trust anchors*, creating a concept that we will adopt and expand as we look beyond just PKI and into trust more generally.

While this shift to an expert-led, rationality-based, authority-endorsed approach to trust has been largely successful, particularly in the fields of science and technology, it is not without its detractors. Whether it is the doubt cast on the radical logical positivism that was proposed in the 1920s to the more recent populist antiscience movement, there has been a growing reaction against the authority of science and expert knowledge to what is becoming, in certain circles, a more post-expert world. The results of this move are concerning to many and have led to such extremes as:

- The anti-vaccination (anti-vaxxers) movement
- The leading British politician Michael Gove refusing to name any economists who supported his "pro-Brexit" stance and saying that "people in this country have had enough of experts"[30]
- Holocaust deniers
- A move by some to deny the validity of the scientific consensus on climate change[31] Exactly what has brought this antiscience movement about—and how to try to reverse it—is the subject of much debate, but this is not a new concern. In the 1990s, for instance, Steven Nock suggested that the change in who and what people trust could be traced to young people moving away from larger family units, arguing that an increase in privacy leads to a reduction in sufficient social relationships to allow trust to build up.[32] This change away from trusting established authorities has not all been bad nor all based on the rejection of qualified experts, however. Some of the foundations on which Western civilisation has long been considered to be based have come under prolonged and justified fire. The most obvious example of such an attack would be that of feminism on the patriarchal Establishment, with multiple waves of action and theoretical underpinnings (such as those put forward by Julia Kristeva and Luce Irigaray), but colonialism, racism, and many other long-held assumptions around authority have also come under scrutiny. Philosophical and literary critical theories such as post-structuralism and the deconstructionism espoused by Jacques Derrida have provided approaches that allow for the criticism of established authorities without a free-for-all rejection of their values and underpinnings (an example being the hermeneutics of suspicion).

Some of these approaches have led to developments that are important and relevant to our field of study, the most obvious being interest in using blockchains as the basis of crypto-currencies, providing an alternative to *fiat* currencies and research into self-sovereign identity (SSI). This approach rejects state, national, regional, or commercial organisations as the appropriate repositories for, and owners of, personal information held about individuals, such as their health or financial data, and seeks to provide means to allow the individuals to control this data and how it is collected, used, and changed. The mechanics of handling different types of data and its various usages are still under debate, and the trust issues also are still being studied. Other movements that we could associate with

---

[30]Katz, 2020.
[31]Chomsky, 2015, p. 135.
[32]Nock, 1993, pp. 147-148.

these approaches include the copyleft movement, which attempts to undermine the controls put in place to support copyright, and the open source movement,[33] a subject of discussion later in the book.

To return to the more general anti-authority, pro-individualist movement, the problem with trusting only in oneself is that it makes it almost impossible to build systems and processes involving other people in ways that allow for any useful cooperation or economies of scale or scope. Authorities of some type do end up being important to our larger set of requirements, and even movements that aim to reduce the number of trust relationships to as few as possible generally recognise the need for authorities in some guise or another. A good example of this is *oracles*, a concept within the field of blockchain that accepts the need to trust information from certain sources. Equally, standards—whether formal or *de facto*—are typically vital in allowing individual entities to work together, two classic historical examples being the regularisation of time across the United Kingdom with the rise of the railway and the standardisation of the systems of measurement that allowed government, commerce, and science to collaborate with less friction and confusion (the canonical example of this within the science community is the loss of a Mars Rover in 1999, due to a lack of standardisation on a particular measurement—metric or imperial units[34]—but the problem has been around for much longer than this[35]). We can expect that as we delve deeper into considerations of trust, we will need to consider what authorities we need to establish a trust relationship with, and the question of endorsement: one of the most troubling concerns around existing discussions of trust is how often such relationships are created with little or no consideration, and sometimes just assumed, leaving implicit relationships that, as they are not stated, cannot be critically examined.

Trusting Individuals

Having spent some time considering the questions associated with trusting institutions of various types, we need to look at issues around trusting individuals. In what may seem like a strange move, we are going to start by asking whether we can even trust ourselves.

Trusting Ourselves

William Gibson's novel *Virtual Light*[36] includes a bar that goes by the name of Cognitive Dissidents. I noticed this a few months ago when I was reading the

---

[33]Related movements include "open management" and "open data".
[34]Lloyd, 1999.
[35]Horrible Histories, 2017.
[36]Gibson, 1993.

book in bed, and it seemed apposite because I wanted to write a blog article about cognitive bias and cognitive dissonance (on which the bar's name is a play on words) as a form of cognitive bias. What is more, the fact that the bar's name had struck me so forcibly was, in fact, exactly that: a form of cognitive bias. In this case, it is an example of the *frequency illusion*, or the *Baader-Meinhof effect*, where a name or word that has recently come to your attention suddenly seems to be everywhere you turn. Like such words, cognitive biases are everywhere: there are more of them than we might expect, and they are more dangerous than we might initially realise.

The problem is that we think of ourselves as rational beings, but it is clear from decades, and in some cases centuries, of research that we are anything but. Humans are very likely to tell themselves that they are rational, and it is such a common fallacy that there is even a specific cognitive bias that describes how we believe it: the *illusion of validity*. One definition of cognitive biases found in Wikipedia[37] is "systematic patterns of deviation from norm or rationality in judgment". We could offer a simpler one: "our brains managing to think things that seem sensible but are not".

Wikipedia provides many examples of cognitive bias, and they may seem irrelevant to our quest. However, as we consider risk—which, as discussed in Chapter 1, is what we are trying to manage when we build trust relationships to other entities—there needs to be a better understanding of our own cognitive biases and those of the people around us. We like to believe that we and they make decisions and recommendations rationally, but the study of cognitive bias provides ample evidence that:

- We generally do not.
- Even if we do, we should not expect those to whom we present them to consider them entirely rationally.

There are opportunities for abuse here. There are techniques beloved of advertisers and the media to manipulate our thinking to their ends, which we could use to our advantage and to try to manipulate others. One example is the *framing effect*. If you do not want your management to fund a new anti-virus product because you have other ideas for the currently ear-marked funding, you might say:

"Our current product is 80% effective!"

Whereas if you do want them to fund it, you might say:

"Our current product is 20% ineffective!"

---

[37]Wikipedia, "List of Cognitive Biases", 2020.

People generally react in different ways depending on how the same information is presented, and the way each of these two statements is framed aims to manipulate your listeners to the outcome you have in mind. We should be aware of—and avoid—such tricks, as such framing techniques can subvert conversations and decision-making around risk.

Three further examples of cognitive bias serve to show how risk calculations may be manipulated, either by presentation or just by changing the thought processes of those making calculations:

Irrational Escalation, or the Fallacy of Sunk Costs   This is the tendency for people to keep throwing money or resources at a project, vendor, or product when it is clear that it is no longer worth it, with the rationale that to stop spending money (or resources) now would waste what has already been spent—despite the fact that those resources have already been consumed. This often comes over as misplaced pride or people not wishing to let go of a pet project because they have become attached to it, but it is really dangerous for security. If something clearly is not effective, it should be thrown out, rather than good money being sent after bad.

Normalcy Bias   This is the refusal to address a risk because the event associated with it has never happened before. It is an interesting one when considering security and risk, for the simple reason that so many products and vendors are predicated on exactly that: protecting organisations from events that have so far not occurred. The appropriate response is to perform a thorough risk analysis and then put measures in place to deal with those risks that are truly high priority, not those that may not happen or that do not seem likely at first glance.

Observer-Expectancy Effect   This is when people who are looking for a particular result find it because they have (consciously or unconsciously) misused the data. It is common in situations such as those where there is a belief that a particular attack or threat is likely, and the data available (log files, for instance) are used in a way that confirms this expectation rather than analysed and presented in ways that are more neutral. Clearly, such manipulation of data will alter risk calculations, as it will alter the probability assigned to particular events, skewing the results.

Given the pervasiveness of cognitive biases—further study of the field is definitely worthwhile for anyone involved with security, risk, or trust—it should come as no surprise that there are examples particularly relevant to trust. Amos Tversky and Daniel Kahnemann[38] identify a multitude of different biases to

---

[38]Tversky and Kahneman, 1982.

which humans are prone when looking at statistical data, of which two are particularly relevant:

Misconceptions of Regression   Regression suggests that if a particular sample is above a mean, the next sample is likely to be below the mean. This can lead to misconceptions such that punishing a bad event is more effective—as it leads to a (supposedly causal) improvement—than rewarding a good event—as this leads to a (supposedly causal) deterioration. The failure to understand this effect tends to lead people to "overestimate the effectiveness of punishment and to underestimate the effectiveness of reward". This feels like a particularly relevant piece of knowledge to take into a series of games like the Prisoner's Dilemma, as one is most likely to be rewarded for punishing others, yet most likely to be punished for rewarding them.[39] More generally, in a system where trust is important, and needs to be encouraged, trying to avoid this bias may be a core goal in the design of the system.

Biases on the Evaluation of Conjunctive and Disjunctive Events   People are bad at realising that a number of improbable but conjunctive events are likely to yield a bad outcome. This is important to us when we consider chains of trust, which we will examine in Chapter 3, "Trust Operations and Alternatives", as the chance of having a single broken chain of trust where all the links in the chain enjoy a high probability of trustworthiness may still in reality be fairly high.

How relevant is this to us? For any trust relationships where humans are involved as the trustors, it is immediately clear that we need to be careful. There are multiple ways in which the trustor may misunderstand what is really going on or just be fooled by their cognitive biases. We have talked several times in this chapter about humans' continued problems with making rational choices in, for instance, game theoretical situations. The same goes for economic or purchasing decisions and a wide variety of other spheres. An understanding—or at least awareness of—cognitive biases can go a long way in trying to help humans to make more rational decisions. Sadly, while many of us involved with computing, IT security, and related fields would like to think of ourselves as fully rational and immune to cognitive biases, the truth is that we are as prone to them as all other humans, as noted in our examples of normalcy bias and observer-expectancy effect. We need to remember that when we consider the systems we are designing to be trustors and trustees, our unconscious biases are bound to come into play—a typical example being that we tend to assume that a system that *we* design will be more secure than a system that *someone else* designs.

---

[39]Tversky and Kahneman, 1982.

Another point is that when we are evaluating trust relationships, we need to realise that we will always have incomplete information. This should encourage us to look for further information where possible but also to be aware that our brains may not even be allowing us to make correct—that is, rational—use of the information we have, or may be creating or falsifying information that we think we do have.

Trying to apply our definition of trust to ourselves is probably a step too far, as we are likely to find ourselves delving into questions of the conscious, subconscious, and unconscious, which are not only hotly contested after well over a century of study in the West, and over several millennia in the East, but are also outside the scope of this book. However, all of the preceding points are excellent reasons for being as explicit as possible about the definition and management of trust relationships and using our definition to specify all of the entities, assurances, contexts, etc. Even if we cannot be sure exactly how our brain is acting, the very act of definition may help us to consider what cognitive biases at play; and the act of having others review the definition may uncover further biases, allowing for a stronger—more rational—definition. In other words, the act of observing our own thoughts with as much impartiality as possible allows us, over time, to lessen the power of our cognitive biases, though particularly strong biases may require more direct approaches to remedy or even recognise.

Trusting Others

Having considered the vexing question of whether we can trust ourselves, we should now turn our attention to trusting others. In this context, we are still talking about humans rather than institutions or computers, and we will be applying these lessons to computers and systems. What is more, as we noted when discussing cognitive bias, our assumptions about others—and the systems they build—will have an impact on how we design and operate systems involved with trust. Given the huge corpus of literature in this area, we will not attempt to go over much of it, but it is worth considering if there are any points we have come across already that may be useful to us or any related work that might cause us to sit back and look at our specific set of interests in a different light.

The first point to bear in mind when thinking about trusting others, of course, is all that we have learned from the discussions of cognitive bias in the previous section. In other words, other human entities are just as prone to cognitive bias as we are, and also just as unaware of it. Whenever we consider a trust relationship to another human, or consider a trust relationship that someone else has defined or designed—a relationship, for instance, that we are reviewing for them or another entity—then we have to realise not only that they may be acting irrationally but also that they are likely to believe that they *are* acting rationally, even given evidence to the contrary.[40] Stepping away from the complexity of cognitive bias, what other issues should we examine when we consider whether we can trust other humans? We looked briefly, at the beginning of this chapter, at some of the definitions preferred in the literature around trust between humans, and it is clear both that there is too much to review here and also that much of it will not be relevant. Nevertheless, it is worth considering—as we have with regards to cognitive bias—if any particular concerns may be worthy of examination. We noted, when looking at the Prisoner's Dilemma, that some strategies are more likely to yield positive results than others. Axelrod's work noted that increasing opportunities for cooperation can improve outcomes, but given that the Prisoner's Dilemma sets out as one of its conditions that communication is not allowed, such cooperation must be tacit. Given that we are considering a wider set of interactions, there is no need for us to adopt this condition (and some of the literature that we have already reviewed seems to follow this direction), and it is worth being aware of work that specifically considers the impact when various parties are allowed to communicate.

One such study by Morton Deutsch and Robert M. Krauss[41] looked at differences in bargaining when partners can communicate with each other or not (or unilaterally) and when they can threaten each other or not (or unilaterally). Their conclusions, brutally relevant during the Cold War period in which they were writing, were that bilateral positions of threat—where both partners could threaten the other—were "most dangerous" and that the ability to communicate made less difference than expected. This may lead to an extrapolation to non-human systems that is extremely important: that it is possible to build—hopefully unwittingly—positive feedback loops into automated systems that can lead to very negative consequences. Probably the most famous fictional example of this is the game Global Thermonuclear War played in the film *WarGames*,[42] where an artificial intelligence connected to the US nuclear arsenal nearly starts World War III.

Schneier talks about the impact that moral systems may have on cooperation between humans and the possibly surprising positive impact that external events—such as terrorist attacks or natural disasters—tend to have on the tendency for humans to cooperate with each other.[43] Moral systems are well beyond the scope of our interest, but there are some interesting issues associated with how to deal with rare and/or major events in terms of both design and attacks on trust relationships. We will return to these in Chapter 8, "Systems and Trust".

---

[40]We are not helped in this task by the fact that our view of the evidence of their behaviour is equally prone to cognitive bias: we may be convinced that they are acting irrationally even when they are acting rationally. This endless cycle of second-guessing is one of the reasons human-to-human trust relationships are so complex and have generated so much study in the literature.

[41]Deutsch and Krauss, 1960.

[42]WarGames, 1983.

[43]Schneier, 2012, pp. 79–80.

Trust, But Verify

Without wanting to focus too much on mistrust, we should not, however, assume good intent when interacting with other humans. Humans do not always do what they say they will do, as we all well know from personal experience. In other words, they are not always trustworthy, which means our trust relationships to them will not always yield positive outcomes. Not only that, but even if we take our broader view of trust relationships, where we say that the action need not be positive as long as it is what we expect, we can also note that humans are not always *consistent*, so we should not always expect our assurances to be met in that case, either.

There is a well-known Russian proverb popularised in English by President Ronald Reagan in the 1980s as "trust, but verify". He was using it in the context of nuclear disarmament talks with the Soviet Union, but it has been widely adopted by the IT security community. The idea is that while trust is useful—and important—verification is equally so. Of course, one can only verify the actions—or, equally, inactions—associated with a trust relationship over time: it makes no sense to talk about verifying something that has not happened. We will consider in later chapters how this aspect of time is relevant to our discussions of trust; but Nan Russell, writing for *Psychology Today* about trust for those in positions of leadership within organisations,[44] suggests that "trust, but verify" is only the best strategy when the outcome—in our definition, the actions about which the trustor has assurances of being performed by the trustee—is more important than the relationship itself. Russell's view is that continuous verification is likely to signal to the trustee that the trustor distrusts them, leading to a negative feedback loop where the trustee fails to perform as expected, confirming the distrust by the trustor. What this exposes is the fact that the trust relationship (from the leader to the person being verified) to which Russell is referring actually exists alongside another relationship (from the person being verified to the leader) and that actions related to one may impact on the other. This is another example of how important it is to define trust relationships carefully, particularly in situations between humans.

Attacks from Within

To return to the point about not necessarily trusting other humans, there is often an assumption that all members of an organisation or institution will have intentions broadly aligned with each other, the institution, or the institution's aims. This leads to trust relationships between members of the same organisation based solely on their membership of that organisation, and not on any other set of information. This, we might expect, would be acceptable and,

---

[44]Russell, 2015.

indeed, sensible, as long as the context for expected actions is solely activities associated with the organisation. If, say, I join a netball club, another member of the club might well form a trust relationship to me that expects me to lobby our local government officers for funding for a new netball court, particularly if one of the club's stated aims is that it wishes to expand by getting one or more new courts.

But what if I have daughters who play rugby and who train at an adjacent rugby club that also wishes to expand? I may have joined the netball club with no intention of lobbying for increased resources for netball, but with the plan of lobbying the local government with an alternative proposal for resources, directed instead towards my daughters' rugby club. This might seem like an underhanded trick, but it is a real one and can go even further than external actions, with plans to change the stated aims or rules of the organisation. If I can get enough other members of the rugby club to join the netball club, it may well be that the constitution of the club, if not robust enough, might be vulnerable to a general vote to change the club's goals to stay with existing resources or even reduce the number of courts, ceding them to the adjacent rugby club.

Something a little like this began to happen in the UK around 2015, when animal rights campaigners demanded that the National Trust, a charity that owns large tracts of land, ban all hunting with dogs on its land. Hunting wild animals with dogs was banned in England and Wales (where the National Trust holds much of its land) in 2004, but some animal rights campaigners complain that trail hunting—an alternative where a previously laid scent is followed instead—can be used as a cover for illegal hunting or lead to accidental fox chases. The policy of the National Trust—at the time of writing—is that trail hunting is permitted on its land, given the appropriate licences, "where it is consistent with our conservation aims and is legally pursued".[45] Two years later, in 2017, the League Against Cruel Sports supported[46] a campaign by those opposed to any type of hunting to join the National Trust as members, with the aim of forcing a vote that would change the policy of the organisation and lead to a ban on any hunting on its land. This takes the concept of "revolt from within" in a different direction because the idea is to try to recruit enough members who are at odds with at least one of the organisation's policies to effect a change.

This is different to a single person working from within an organisation to try to subvert its aims or policies. Assuming that the employee has been hired in good faith, then their actions should be expected to be aligned with the organisation's policies. If that is the case, then the person is performing actions that are at odds with the trust relationship the organisation has with them: this assumes that we are modelling the contract between an organisation and an employee as a trust relationship from the former to the latter, an issue to which

---

[45]National Trust, no date.
[46]League Against Cruel Sports, no date.

we will return in Chapter 8, "Systems and Trust". In the case of "packing" the membership with those opposed to a particular policy or set of policies, those joining are doing so with the express and stated aim of subverting it, so there is no break in any expectations on the individual level.

It may seem that we have moved a long way from our core interest in security and computer systems, but attacks similar to those outlined above are very relevant, even if the trust models may be slightly different. Consider the single attacker who is subverting an organisation from within. This is how we might model the case where a component that is part of a larger system is compromised by a malicious actor—whether part of the organisation or not—and serves as a "pivot point" to attack other components or systems. Designing systems to be resilient to these types of attacks is a core part of the practice of IT or cybersecurity, and one of our tasks later in this book will be to consider how we can use models of trust to help that practice. In the case of the packing of members to subvert an organisation, this is extremely close, in terms of the mechanism used, to an attack on certain blockchains and crypto-currencies known as a *51% attack*. At a simplistic level, a blockchain operates one or more of a variety of consensus mechanisms to decide what should count as a valid transaction and be recorded as part of its true history. Some of these consensus mechanisms are vulnerable to an attack where enough active contributors (miners) to the blockchain can overrule the true history and force an alternative that suits their ends, in a similar way to that in which enough members of an organisation can decide to vote in a policy that is at odds with the organisation's stated aims. The percentage required for at least some of these consensus mechanisms is a simple majority: hence the figure of 51%. We will be returning to blockchains later in this book, as the trust models are interesting, and many of the widely held assumptions around their operation turn out to be much more complex than are generally considered.

The Dangers of Anthropomorphism

There is one last form of trust relationships from humans that we need to consider before we move on. It is not from humans to computer systems exactly, but from humans to computer systems that the humans *believe* to be other humans. The task of convincing humans that a computer system is human was suggested by Alan Turing,[47] who was interested in whether machines can be said to think, in what has become known as the *Turing Test* (though he called it the Imitation Game). His focus arguably was more on the question of what the machine—we would say *computer*—was doing in terms of computation and less on the question of whether particular humans believed they were talking to another human.

---

[47]Turing, 1950.

The question of whether computers can—or may one day be able to—think was one of the questions that exercised early practitioners of the field of artificial intelligence (AI): specifically, hard AI. Coming at the issue from a different point of view, Rossi[48] writes about concerns that humans have about AI. She notes issues such as explainability (how humans can know why AI systems make particular decisions), responsibility, and accountability in humans trusting AI. Her interests seem to be mainly about humans failing to trust—she does not define the term specifically—AI systems, whereas there is a concomitant, but opposite concern: that sometimes humans may have too much trust in (that is, have an unjustified trust relationship to) AI systems.

Over the past few years, AI/ML systems[49] have become increasingly good at mimicking humans for specific interactions. These are not general-purpose systems but in most cases are aimed at participating in specific fields of interaction, such as telephone answering services. Targeted systems like this have been around since the 1960s: a famous program—what we would call a *bot* now—known as ELIZA mimicked a therapist. Interacting with the program—there are many online implementations still available, based on the original version—quickly becomes unconvincing, and it would be difficult for any human to consider that it is truly "thinking". The same can be said for many systems aimed at specific interactions, but humans can be quite trusting of such systems even if they do not seem to be completely human. In fact, there is a strange but well-documented effect called the *uncanny valley*. This is the effect that humans feel an increasing affinity for—and presumably, an increased propensity to trust—entities, the more human they look, but only to a certain point. Past that point, the uncanny valley kicks in, and humans become *less* happy with the entity with which they are interacting. There is evidence that this effect is not restricted to visual cues but also exists for other senses, such as hearing and audio-based interactions.[50] The uncanny valley seems to be an example of a cognitive bias that may provide us with real protection in the digital world, restricting the trust we might extend towards non-human trustees that are attempting to appear human. Our ability to realise that they are non-human, however, may not always be sufficient to allow it to kick in. *Deep fakes*, a common term for the output of specialised ML tools that generate convincing, but ultimately falsified, images, audio, or even full video footage of people, is a growing concern for many: not least social media sites, which have identified the trend as a form of potentially damaging misinformation, or those who believed that what they saw was real. Even without these techniques, it appears that media such as Twitter have been

---

[48]Rossi, 2019.
[49]The fields of artificial intelligence (AI) and machine learning (ML) are intertwined and often listed together as *AI/ML*.
[50]Grimshaw, 2009.

used to put messages out—typically around elections—that are not from real people, but that, without skilled analysis and correlation with other messages from other accounts, are almost impossible to discredit.

Anthropomorphism is a term to describe how humans often attribute human attributes to non-human entities. In our case, this would be computer systems. We may do this for a number of reasons:

- Maybe because humans have a propensity towards anthropomorphism in order to allow them better to understand the systems with which they interact, though they are not consciously aware that the system is non-human

- Because humans are interacting with a system that they are clear is non-human, but they find it easier to interact with it as if it had at least some human characteristics

- Because humans have been deceived by intentionally applied techniques into believing that the system is human

By this stage, we have maybe stretched the standard use of the term *anthropomorphism* beyond its normal boundaries: normal usage would apply to humans ascribing human characteristics to obviously non-human entities. The danger we are addressing here goes beyond that, as we are also concerned with the possibility that humans may form trust relationships to non-human entities exactly *because* they believe them to be human: they just do not have the ability (easily) to discriminate between the *real* and the generated.

Identifying the Real Trustee

When security measures are put in place, who puts them there, and for what reason? This might seems like a simple question, but often it is not. In fact, more important than asking "for what" are security measures put in place is the question "for whom are they put in place?" Ross Anderson and Tyler Moore are strong proponents of the study of *security economics*,[51] arguing that microeconomics and game theory are vital studies for those involved in IT security.[52] They are interested in questions such as the one we have just examined: where security measures—which will lead to what we termed *behaviours*—are put in place to benefit not the user interacting with the system but somebody else.

One example is Digital Rights Management (DRM). Much downloadable music or video media is "protected" from unauthorised use through the application of security technologies. The outcome of this is that people who download media

---

[51]Anderson and Moore (2009).
[52]Anderson and Moore (2006).

that are DRM protected cannot copy them or play them on unapproved platforms or systems. This means, for example, that even if I have paid for access to a music track, I am unable to play it on a new laptop unless that laptop has approved software on it. What is more, the supplier from which I obtained the track can stop my previously authorised access to that track at any time (as long as I am online). How does this help me, the person interacting with the music via the application? The answer is that it does not help me at all but rather inconveniences me: the "protection" is for the provider of the music and/or the application. As Richard Harper points out, "trusting" a DRM system means trusting behaviour that enforces properties of the entity that commissioned it.[53] Is this extra protection, which is basically against me, in that it stops my ease of use? Of course not: I, and other users of the service, will end up absorbing this cost through my subscription, a one-off purchase price, or my watching of advertisements as part of the service. This is *security economics*, where the entity benefiting from the security is not the one paying for it.

When considering a DRM system, it may be fairly clear what actions it is performing. In this case, this may include:

- Decrypting media ready for playing
- Playing the media
- Logging your usage
- Reporting your usage

According to our definition, we might still say that we have a trust relationship to the DRM software, and some of the actions it is performing *are* in my best interests—I do, after all, want to watch or listen to the media. If we think about assurances, then the trust relationship I have *can* still meet our definition. I have assurances of particular behaviours, and whether they are in my best interests or not, I know (let us say) what they are.

The issue gets murkier when I cannot necessarily discover what behaviour is happening, because if I cannot, then I have no way to know if it is in my best interests or not. One might even expect that if behaviours *are* in my best interests, they would be disclosed to me as part of the description of the actions about which I am deciding to accept assurances. When I have significant concerns that there are behaviours that are explicitly *against* my interests, things become concerning. A large-scale example of this is the trust relationship that governments need to have to critical national infrastructure. The exact definition of *critical national infrastructure*—often capitalised or abbreviated to CNI—varies between experts and countries but is the collection of core hardware, software,

---

[53]Harper, 2014, p. 78.

and services that are key to keeping citizens safe and key elements of society functioning. A list might include the following:

- Power generation
- Water and sewerage
- Basic transport networks
- Emergency services
- Healthcare
- Location services (e.g., GPS)
- Telecommunications
- Internet access

For the purposes of many governments, the final two have become so intertwined that they can hardly be separated. What is noteworthy about telecommunications and core Internet capabilities is the small number of suppliers across the world. One of those is Huawei, which is based in the People's Republic of China. The government of the United States, whose relationship with the Chinese state and government can be characterised as a rivalry, if not out-and-out enemies, takes the view that given the nature of the ownership of Huawei, and its base in China, the telecommunications equipment that it manufactures and provides cannot be trusted.

This is a strong stance to take, and the concerns that are expressed are well-defined. The US government asserts that there is a real risk that a telecommunications equipment—and associated software—provider who is based within China may be under enough pressure from the Chinese government to include hidden features that could affect the confidentiality, integrity, or availability of services that are part of the United States' critical national infrastructure. If this were the case, it would allow communications that could be critical to the United States to be eavesdropped on or even tampered with by the Chinese government or those acting for it. The suggestion that the Chinese government would ever exert pressure to insert such capabilities—typically known as *back doors*—is strongly disputed by the Chinese and Huawei itself. However, to frame these concerns within our definition of trust relationships as well as from the point of view of the US government, there is insufficient assurance that the actions to be taken by such pieces of equipment are as expected and, therefore, the US government has taken the view that there should be no trust relationship formed with equipment that might be supplied by Huawei.

This is an extreme example, but when we see relationships of this type, where there are or may be actions that are hidden from us, it must be appropriate to say that we cannot have assurance and, therefore, should not label this as a proper trust relationship. In order to be adequately informed about entities and whether to form relationships to them, we need to have as much information about actions as possible before a trust relationship is formed, along with assurances about those actions. The problem with this is that one of the key sources of information about an entity is the entity itself, but we cannot trust any information that an entity provides about itself because, of course, we have no trust relationship to it to allow us to do so. This issue and how to mitigate it will be key as we move to deeper examinations about trust between computer systems and discussions around the topics of application programming interfaces (APIs) and open source software.

Anderson and Tyler[54] align this sort of effect with what economists call *externalities*. An externality is when there is a cost or benefit to a party who did not choose to incur that cost or benefit.[55] Certainly, in the case of the US government's concerns about Huawei telecommunications equipment, any back-door type of behaviour would count as a cost, even if that cost were not directly economic. Let us consider computer systems more generally. Sometimes actions might be performed by an entity (the trustee) without any intention of harm—that is, cost—to the party trusting it (the trustor); but if the trustor does not know about these actions, they have no way to evaluate any possible impact. In this case, the trustor needs to make explicit requirements either to exclude specific actions or even to require that no other actions will be performed beyond the expected ones. This second course of action may seem like the obvious one to take but is actually very difficult.

Many applications, when running, will perform actions that are not core to the functioning of the program itself, which we might call *side effects*. At the API level, there is a more formal use of this phrase, where actions are performed on data or variables that are not "local" to the function or operator being called. The general case where non-core actions are performed provides us with enough real concern. Two typical examples, which are recurring problems for IT security, will serve to illustrate the problem.

It is a truism that computer programs do not always function as they are designed. For that reason, log files are often collected to allow those who are tasked with managing the programs to understand any problems and maybe to feed back to those who designed and wrote the programs any bugs that are identified. Such logging is generally associated with the actions of the application; but, equally, logging may be performed on the data that is being entered, manipulated, and generated or on user logins and interactions, to allow someone auditing the application and its usage to track how it is being used.[56] The danger

---

[54] Anderson and Tyler, 2006, p. 611.
[55] Wikipedia, "Externality", 2020.
[56] There are, of course, problems associated with somebody who is not authorised to look at particular sets of logs accessing them and being able to view—or maybe manipulate—information to which they should not have access. This, however, is a failure of the broader system and not directly relevant to our point.

with which we are concerned is that information is being recorded in logs that should not be. This situation may mean that those who have legitimate access to a particular set of logs also get access to information that is not appropriate. A well-known example of this would be application logs designed to help a developer debug a payment application that logs credit card details, exposing them to the developer. The user of the site has a trust relationship to the application where they should expect that such information is not exposed but has no knowledge of the fact that this logging is taking place nor the ability to control or stop it.

Similar problems can occur with backup files. These differ from log files in that they are not intended for consumption by anything other than the application that may need to recover in the event of a problem, but the files need to contain enough data and information for the application to recover all of the state that it needs to continue operation. There is definitely a possible cost here to the user of an application if these files are accessed by unauthorised parties, but at least in this case, there is a possible benefit, too: the application can continue to be used. The question is whether this benefit outweighs the possible cost and, more specifically, whether the trustor even has the ability to make a choice as to whether backup files are stored or has enough information to make an informed choice as to whether they should be. While backup files on a local system are typically accessible to a user—though not always, nor always advertised—the likelihood of this being the case for remote or multi-user systems is significantly reduced. It would be good—that is, in my interests—if I, as trustor, were given the option to back up my own data in this case and insist that any backups generated by the trustee be anonymised or have any critical data removed. But even if I can insist on this, the chances that I can realistically enforce it are very low.

This is, in fact, another example of security economics: the backups are put in place not for my benefit but for the benefit of the entity operating the application or service I am using. Even if I have visibility into the actions they are performing, I have little or no chance or opportunity to influence them in my favour. Sometimes, despite the inability of individuals to have an impact on the practices of those whose services they are using, governments or other regulatory bodies put in place measures that force service providers to adopt practices that do benefit individuals. Good examples of this in the area we have been describing are the European Union's General Data Protection Regulation (GDPR) and the State of California's California Consumer Privacy Act (CCPA), both of which force service providers to protect consumers' data and put in place measures to prevent it from being misused. A slightly weaker type of protection, but one that can help, is the establishment of industry standards aimed at promoting good practice. Historically, however, standards have ended up benefiting industry players—service providers—rather than consumers or customers, who rarely have much—if any—representation on standards bodies.

In our definition of trust, we started with the following statement:

> **"Trust is the assurance that one entity holds that another will perform particular actions according to a specific expectation.**

It turns out that establishing that assurance can be more difficult than might be expected and that the performance of actions may also need to specify the non-performance of other actions to ensure that we can fully understand what behaviours we, the trustor, are trusting the other entity, the trustee, to perform. In the next chapter, we will examine trust in even more detail, the impact of different forms of trust, how trust is expressed, and some of the alternatives that may be appropriate in certain contexts.

CHAPTER 3

Trust Operations and Alternatives

We now have a comprehensive enough understanding of trust as a concept to look more critically at some of the ways that trust can be used. This chapter introduces a number of ways of using trust that we can think of as *operations* and associated trust components. These can be used alongside some of the foundational primitives that we considered in Chapter 1 to examine—and hopefully design—trust systems. We are also going to consider some alternatives to trust, what entities it may make sense to trust, and some ways of expressing trust.

Trust Actors, Operations, and Components

Before we dive further into trust relationships, we will take a moment to clarify who and what we are talking about when we discuss trust in systems.

Trustor The entity with the expectation of actions.

Trustee The entity expected to carry out actions.

System A set of components—for example, hardware, software, firmware, data, or human users—that can be considered as a single entity for the purposes of one or more specific architectural views of abstractions. A laptop might be considered a system, but so might a distributed blockchain, a nuclear power station, the Bolivian electrical power grid, or a cryptographic accelerator block within a network interface card. One important point is that interfaces with the system should be well-defined and that, from the point of view of an entity (itself possibly a system), communicating with it, the individual components of the system should be, if not indistinguishable, then governed by the same rules and behaviour and considered accountable to the system when abstracted as a whole. A system is non-decomposable within the frame of reference of the particular abstraction.

Implicit Trust   The property where a trust relationship is not explicitly defined and cannot therefore be assessed. Some trust relationships are known but still involve implicit trust. A key tenet of this book is that implicit trust relationships are dangerous and should always be transformed into explicit trust relationships, destroyed, or documented to allow mitigating actions.

Explicit Trust   The property where a trust relationship is known and defined and can therefore be assessed.

Endorsing Authority   An *endorsing authority* is a human or organisational entity to whom a trust relationship has been established. An endorsing authority can provide one or more trust anchors, endorsing them—that is, making a public or private claim—as representing properties of another human or organisation (such as their identity, physical location, or ability to access credit). Endorsing authorities are sometimes referred to as *trust anchors*—but for our purposes, we consider the endorsing authority an entity that endorses the trust anchor.

Trust Anchor   A *trust anchor* is a static component in a system whereby an endorsing authority allows trustors to assume trust in the system in which the anchor is contained. Trust anchors are static in terms of their interaction with a system, and the trust relationship to a trust anchor is assumed—based on the endorsing authority—rather than derived. We came across the concept of a trust anchor in Chapter 2 when discussing certificate authorities as endorsing authorities, and the root certificate endorsed by certificate authorities is the canonical example of a trust anchor. Note that a trust anchor is different from a root of trust, a concept to which we will return later in the book.

Trust Pivot   A *trust pivot* is a component (or set of components) and associated process (that is, an algorithm, rather than necessarily a process) that allows a trust relationship from one entity to a different entity to be transferred or added to another entity. An example from human-to-human relationships might be a person's will. A will is a legal document transferring to an executor the administration of a person's estate in the event of their death[1]. The validity of the pivot assumes the existence of one or more trust anchors—the legal authority of the will, for instance, and a counter-signature on the will of a party who is not a beneficiary of the estate.

Transitive Trust   *Transitive trust* describes the situation where one entity has a trust relationship to another entity via a third entity. The example in Chapter 2, "Humans and Trust", of my having a trust relationship to my friend with the expectation that they will tell me whether a flag has been raised, is an example of transitive trust, as are all trust relationships around monitoring. Another example from human-to-human relationships might be the creation of a contract that gives an accountant the authority to file tax records for an individual: the tax office now has a trust relationship to the individual through the accountant.

One or more trust pivots may be required to establish—or maybe maintain—a transitive trust relationship, such as the tax accountant's professional certification or the validity of the contract under local law. There is another case where trustor A trusts trustee C because B recommends C. Shown in Figure 3.1a, this situation is maybe the most common type of transitive trust.[2] We can model this as A having a trust relationship to B that B can be assured to provide good recommendations about trusting other parties (in this case, C) in a particular context. As trust should always be contextual, my trusting C in context X should not be based on B's trusting C in context X unless I also trust B in context Y, say—of making recommendations about context X (see Figure 3.1b).

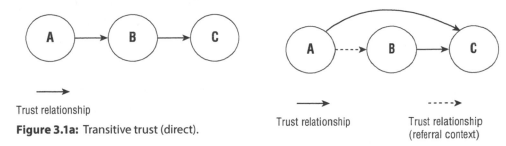

Trust relationship

Figure 3.1a: Transitive trust (direct).

Trust relationship

Trust relationship
(referral context)

Figure 3.1b: Transitive trust (by referral).

Chain of Trust   A *chain of trust* (or sometimes *trust chain*) is a linked set of transitive trust relationships (Figure 3.2). The simplest chain of trust would be a single trust relationship, but chains of trust can involve multiple

---

[1]Another example is the use of the general meaning of a *trust*, an agreement to allow an individual or organisation to administer the affairs of another person. But the potential to cause confusion by using this as an example, given its name, was too great to choose this as our example in the main text.
[2]See, for example, Abdul-Rahman and Hailes, 1997, pp. 49–50, on "Transivity".

entities and multiple relationships. Remarkably few trust relationships in computing systems consist of a single relationship, and chains of trust are very common. A chain of trust is only as strong as its weakest link, and a typical attack on a security system is to look for vulnerabilities on various parts of the chain of trust, which the system embodies until one is found that can be compromised.

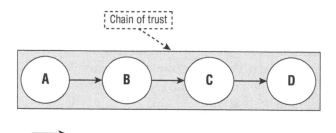

Trust relationship

Figure 3.2: Chain of trust.

Distributed Trust   Distributed trust involves multiple trust relationships spread across different entities, some or all of which may consist of chains of trust. While these multiple trust relationships can be considered separately, it is ultimately the way in which they are combined that allows expectations about assurances of actions to be made, rather than a reliance on any particular relationship. An example of distributed trust would be the trust relationship that a supporter of a sport has to their favourite team to win a game: there are trust relationships to each player, not to mention coaching and support staff; and even if one player fails to perform the actions for which the supporter has an assurance, other players may be able to make up for any failures and perform in such a way that the team still performs. Indeed, part of the trust relationship that the supporter has to each player is the expectation that a player will act as a part of the team and perform actions that are in the best interests of the team rather than the individual (Figure 3.3).

An alternative, and somewhat different, example is the trust that a patient has in the team in an operating theatre. In this case, it may be that there is little opportunity for an individual member to compensate for the failure of another, as a surgeon, even if sufficiently motivated, may not have the skills to catch or remedy a mistake by an anaesthetist. A final example of distributed trust, which we will examine in more detail later, is that of open source software, where my trust in the correct operation of the software is, at least in part, based on my trust relationship to the members of the open source community who were or are responsible for its creation, maintenance, and maybe even support (Figure 3.4).

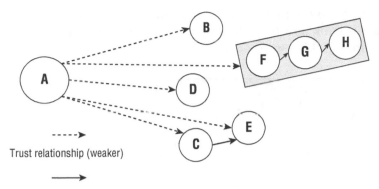

Trust relationship (weaker)

Trust relationship (stronger)

Figure 3.3: Distributed trust to multiple entities with weak relationships.

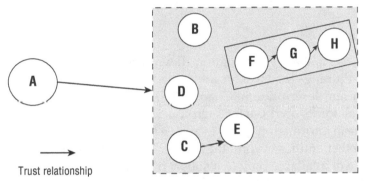

Trust relationship

Figure 3.4: Distributed trust with a single, stronger relationship. A set of weak trust relationships to multiple entities may be equivalent to a single, stronger distributed trust relationship.

Trust Domain   *Trust domains* are sets of entities or components that can be considered to form a single unit from the point of view of a trust relationship.[3] Such a trust relationship must—like all trust relationships—be bounded by context(s). Trust domains are actually all around us in human-to-human interactions: when I visit my bank to withdraw money from it, I typically do not care whether I have a particular trust relationship to the bank employee with whom I interact or the ATM from which I withdraw money. The trust relationship I have to the bank incorporates these entities into a trust domain, such as that shown in Figure 3.5, where three different contexts for trust are shown: α, β, and γ. This is simpler for the bank, of course, and simpler for me, as I do not need to maintain sets of distributed trust relationships or manage long chains of trust in order to perform standard tasks. In terms of context, though, I should not expect

---

[3]Trust domains are a key concept in this book and merit a dedicated chapter (Chapter 12) where we will describe them in more detail.

a bank employee to counter-sign a will: the context for the trust relationship I have to the bank as a trust domain does not include expectations or assurances around this type of action.[4]

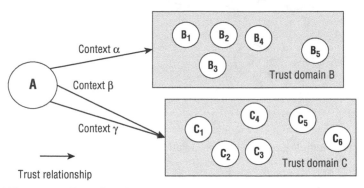

Context α

A

Context β

Context γ

→
Trust relationship

B_1 B_2 B_4 B_5 B_3
Trust domain B

C_4 C_5 C_1 C_6 C_2 C_3
Trust domain C

Figure 3.5: Trust domains.

Reputation   *Reputation* is shared information allowing an entity to consider the formation—or tuning—of a trust relationship rather than the relationship itself (as per our description in Chapter 2). Although an entity may collect information for its own use for such considerations, by *reputation*, we specifically mean information that is available to—and may be affected or changed by—other entities beyond the trustor. The information may be publicly available or available only to a subset of other entities. Equally, reputation need not be used solely at the formation of a trust relationship but also for its maintenance and subsequent destruction. Equally important is that reputation should be a function of whether a trustee meets the expectations within a trust relationship, and reputation should also be contextual. My relationship to an author may be based on my perception of their novels, and the author's reputation as a novelist may be formed by whether their books meet the expectations of their many readers; but that does not mean I should consider the author's reputation as a neurosurgeon when deciding to buy their next book.[5]

Intentionality   *Intentionality* is what a trustee (or designer of a component to be trusted) intends to be the actions to be performed on behalf of the party being represented. Much of our discussion around trust relationships thus far has looked at whether assurances about expectations of actions to

---

[4]This does not preclude my bank from offering such services to me, of course, but I should be clear that I am extending my trust relationship to them into an additional context when I do this. It may be very convenient for me to accept the bank's endorsing authority of a trust anchor of a trained department of will counter-signers, and very profitable for them if they can encourage me to spend money on legal advice as part of the relationship.
[5]Unless, of course, the author's latest novel is about neurosurgery.

be performed are met, but we have spent little time on how these can be expressed. To allow us to discuss how to talk about our expectations, we will use the word *intentionality*.[6] In order for a trustor to form an informed trust relationship to a trustee, the trustor needs to have some knowledge of the trustee's intentionality, which is provided by a trust action description.

Trust Action Description   The *trust action description* defines what actions are expected to be performed. In order for the trustor to know what expectations to have of a trustee, there must be a description of the actions to be performed. In the realm of computer systems, this has similarities to the application programming interface (API) description or software contract and may in fact be provided by one of these artefacts. We need a broader description, however, which refers not only to software or even hardware, and which also concentrates not solely on the inputs and outputs associated with the trustee but on broader actions as well. In order for the trustor to make a decision as to whether to form a trust relationship with the trustee, the trust action description must either be provided directly by the trustee or advertised or relayed by another party (which may involve a transitive trust relationship).

Reputation, Transitive Trust, and Distributed Trust

In the previous section, we spent some time defining *reputation* and introduced the concepts of transitive and distributed trust, all of which deserve a little more discussion before we move on.

As with so many of the concepts that we are seeking to define, the word *reputation* is employed in a number of different contexts, from narrowly defined definitions to more popular uses in day-to-day speech. In the same way that it would be possible to define specific formats for trust action descriptions, we could attempt to define exactly how reputation is calculated, measured, and employed. We will look at some of the ways in which this has been attempted later in the book when we consider the impact of time on trust—an area where reputation can provide some interesting insights. Even if we cannot provide a generalised description of how to define and utilise reputation across all different types and contexts of trust relationships, reputation is nevertheless important. To return to Prisoner's Dilemma–type games, Magnus Enquist and Olof Leimar[7] posit that cooperation—and therefore, in our terms, trust—will be difficult to encourage in systems where mobility is high, as free-riders have more chance of defecting and getting away with it. They show that

---

[6] A term used in philosophy with particular meanings, not all of which are relevant to our needs.

[7] Engquist and Leimar, 1993.

suspiciousness (waiting before committing to a new partner) and gossiping (members of the population discussing other members) are good ways of encouraging cooperation. *Suspiciousness* can be thought of as having a low appetite for risk in forming new trust relationships. One way of reducing this risk, of course, is to consider the reputation of the party to whom you are considering forming a trust relationship; and in this context, *gossiping* is how reputations are formed and communicated across the group.

Reputation can also be important to transitive and distributed trust relationships. In both cases, the ability of the root trustor to assess directly whether to trust their various trustees may well be constrained beyond the difficulties that might present themselves in a normal case. For example, if I have a direct trust relationship to my local mechanic, I may well be able to assess whether they are competent based on seeing the maintenance and repairs they have performed on other people's cars. If, however, my trust relationship is to an online mechanic service, which comes to my door, picks up my car, and returns it once the work is done, my ability to make assessments is restricted. For transitive trust relationships, the trustor may have to rely on the intermediate trustee (or, in the case of a chain of trust, intermediate trustees) to provide sufficient information or attempt to find an endorsing authority to allow a proper assessment, as depicted in Figure 3.6. There may be more than one endorsing authority, as depicted in Figure 3.7, in which case the trustor has to decide how best to combine the information it receives from each and then form a trust relationship to the trustee, as shown in Figure 3.8. It should be noted that although the root trustee needs to have a trust relationship to the endorsing authority in this case, this does not mean the root trustee is forming a direct trust relationship to the endorsed entity.

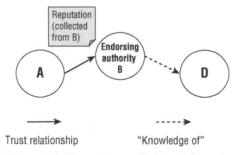

Trust relationship   "Knowledge of"

Figure 3.6: Reputation: collecting information.

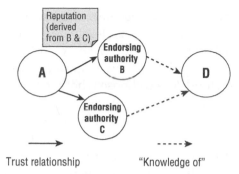

Trust relationship   "Knowledge of"

Figure 3.7: Reputation: gathering information from multiple endorsing authorities.

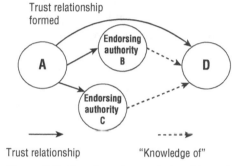

Trust relationship   "Knowledge of"

Figure 3.8: Forming a trust relationship to the trustee, having gathered information from multiple endorsing authorities.

Such an endorsing authority may not always be available, and reputation can act as an alternative. In this case, the community that forms and maintains the reputation is acting as a type of endorsing authority, and reputation can be considered a type of weak trust anchor, but it should be acknowledged any trust relationship based on this type of trust anchor must be very aware of these weaknesses.

Another concern to be borne in mind when considering transitive trust relationships—particularly long chains of trust, where visibility of the relationships along the chain is low—is implicit trust relationships. A real-world example of this is organisations deploying applications on public cloud services. If I deploy my application on public cloud A instead of on public cloud B, I may have chosen to do so because I trust the provider of public cloud A to maintain an acceptable level of service more than I trust the provider of public cloud B to do the same. There may, however, be a trust relationship from public cloud A to public cloud B, in that all support staff for public cloud A use a bug database hosted on public cloud B, which means if public cloud B becomes unavailable, then the continued running of my application is at risk. I was clearly not aware of the relationship held from public cloud A to public cloud B, so I could not use such information—about what was, from my point of view, an implicit trust relationship, even if it was known to public cloud A—to choose whether or not to form a trust relationship with public cloud A in the first place.

Although similar dangers exist for distributed trust relationships, their impact is likely to be less than the issue of the ability to gather sufficient information about various trustees. We could consider the trust relationship held to each trustee separately, but in the case of a distributed trust relationship, it is the conglomeration of these separate trust relationships that is the defining feature of the distributed relationship, rather than each individual relationship. Distributed trust relationships can be useful in cases where I do not have expertise in the area of the actions to be performed or other occasions where my ability to collect sufficient information to make an informed decision about the formation of a trust relationship is constrained. In these cases, the availability of endorsing authorities and trust anchors is likely to be low, and I may choose to use reputation as an alternative. For example, if I were a keen gambler, I might make decisions on which horses or teams to bet on based on statistics published by media outlets or third party compilers.

Agency and Intentionality

In the section on trust operations and components, we described intentionality as expressing what the trustee—or the designer of the component to be trusted—intends to be the actions to be advertised to be performed and by what or whom. This may seem a somewhat clumsy definition, but the various constituent pieces are important. First, there is an acknowledgement that in non-human systems, there may be a need to note the existence of a system's designer as an entity of interest. There may not be a specific trust relationship associated with the designer—though they may act as an endorsing authority—but their intent may be important. Second, rather than describing intentionality simply as an advertisement of the actions to be performed, we turned this phrase around. This is because the advertised set of actions—the trust action description—may be different to the actions that the trustee (or designer or the component to be trusted) intend to be performed. For example, I may design a system that I say will perform in a particular way (e.g., performing a virus scan of your computer) but that actually is intended to perform completely different actions (e.g., encrypting your hard drive and allowing me to extort money from you—also known as *ransomware*).

There are positive aspects to intentionality, however, which we will consider from the point of view of trust relationships to computer systems. The first, and most obvious, is that intentionality, as part of the design process, allows for statements to be made about what trustors of the component being designed can expect: *without intentionality, there can be no well-defined trust action description*. The second flows from the first: the stating of intentionality allows the person designing the component to be explicit about what should be implemented and to consider appropriate documentation, testing, operational concerns, and functional and non-functional properties of the component alongside the implementation process. In other words, *intentionality can be part of the component lifecycle*—and must be, if we are to create components and systems to and between which trust relationships can be created, maintained, and ultimately destroyed.

Another aspect is less obvious but equally important: *intentionality allows agency to be designed into a system* and flow, as it were, through the system during its lifecycle. As we move to thinking more about trust relationships to computer systems rather than to humans, the issue of agency will become more important in our discussions. In our initial four use cases, in Chapter 1, we introduced agency and looked at how complex it can be to understand exactly what person, organisation, or other entity a component was representing. This is described in the final part of our definition of intentionality: by what or whom actions can be designed to be carried out on behalf of an entity. Imagine that you are designing a component of a program or application[8] and that you want the component[9] to perform actions on behalf of you, your business, or another entity. In the simplest of cases, this could be a single, stand-alone component that forms the entire application, and the entity runs it directly on their own hardware; but many use cases are much more complex than this. Even in the simple case, how are entities that interact with this component to know that they can trust it? The danger is that implicit assumptions will be made, and we will end up with a component in which implicit trust is placed. As noted earlier, such implicit trust is considered harmful to system design, as it cannot be assessed. We should note, therefore, that not all components will need to consider trust relationships; but in the case we are examining here, where agency is being placed in a component, trust does need to be assessed.

To form a trust relationship to something—a component—that is not the direct human trustee, we need to consider how that component is endowed with *agency*: the ability or authority to act on that trustee's behalf. There are several ways the placing of agency into a component can be managed, including:

Inserting a Trust Anchor   In this case, a trust anchor such as a root certificate is inserted into the component, and access is provided to it by other entities that are considering establishing a trust relationship to it.

---

[8]The same goes for more complex systems, including those with hardware components, as we will explore in later chapters.
[9]The question of the extent to which different components in an application can have different agency is discussed in Chapter 12 on trust domains.

This means when the component is executed, it is the core trust component for the application, and the trust anchor inserted at design time represents the final entity to be used by the application and cannot be changed.

Preparing a Trust Anchor   This is similar to the case of inserting a trust anchor but leaves the selection of the trust anchor to a different stage in the deployment process. It may be that a component is written to be run by a different person or entity or that the precise trust anchor to be used is not known at design time. The precise mechanism by which this is managed may or may not be provided by this component, but care must be taken, as a compromise of the establishment of this trust anchor is a key vulnerability point in such a system.

Acting as a Transitive Actor in a Chain of Trust   This is actually by far the most common way in which agency is managed, though it is usually implicit. Of course, we only need to be concerned when (as noted earlier) the component will be trusted by another entity, which suggests that there will be some communication channel. If the other entity is to assess whether or not to form a trust relationship to the one we are designing, then sufficient information about the other entities in the chain of trust needs to be explicitly provided and the chain itself exposed for assessment.

Preparing a Trust Pivot   Although many components will act under the same agency for their entire execution lifecycle, there are times when an application or component needs to change the entity that it represents. A typical example is when I use my web browser to access my personal email and then my work email. In this case, the move between accounts is probably easily accomplished: I open a new browser tab and log in to my work account, at which point the emails I am sending are endorsed by a different trust anchor. What is actually happening, however, is that the browser has pivoted the trust that is being represented. This may be clearer if we think of reusing the same browser window: as I enter my work email account details and authenticate myself, the previous trust relationship that the browser was enabling to my personal email is discarded and a new one created. A more complex example might be when I give my old phone to a family member, who wipes my current details—associated with a Google or an iOS account, say—and replaces them with their own. In this case, the component of the phone that allows this to happen must be able to allow this pivot to take place.

There is a risk in these examples that we might assume that all we are worrying about is allowing an identity to be associated with this component (the identity of the trustee for whom the component provides agency). Although it is true that identity is often a key property that is being assessed when a trust relationship is being formed, it is not the only one. There are many cases—such as crypto-currency, voting, or auction applications—where identity is explicitly not one of the properties we should be considering, and anonymity or pseudo-nymity is a key property of the trust relationship.

Alternatives to Trust

Before we move on, we should remember that trust relationships are not the only ways humans have created to deal with risk. Let us look at some of the others.

Legal Contracts

Aside from trust, the first mechanism to consider is that of legal contracts. Legal contracts are older than you might expect: the development of legal contract law in England and the United States, for example, can be directly traced to ancient Roman law, and there are records of contracts at least as far back as the Sumerian Empire around 2600 BCE. To have contracts, there need to be author-ities to which the parties involved in the contract can appeal and mechanisms for enforcement to encourage compliance and punish wrongdoing. The authorities also build bodies of jurisprudence, but we should not overlook the place of social contracts in this milieu. The acceptance of authorities and the legitimacy of the rules—such as laws—that authorities create are, for J.S. Coleman,[10] one of the pioneers of applying mathematical modelling to sociology, at least a reflection of the social contracts that individuals—natural persons—establish implicitly or explicitly with multiple corporate actors—our authorities—one of whom may be the state. Fukuyama,[11] an American political scientist, argues that such social contracts are insufficient to explain aspects of community such as charity and public-spiritedness. But Coleman's analysis does seem consistent with how societies and communities coalesce around norms of acceptable behaviour and how civil disobedience can break out when norms change—such as around the US Civil Rights movement—or when corruption and self-interest cause ele-ments of the populace or citizenry to question the status quo being seen to be preserved by the Establishment—such as around the environmental protests organised by groups like Extinction Rebellion.

On the whole, legal contracts can act as a mechanism to mitigate risk when trust relationships from one party to another are insufficient—for instance, when the temptation to default is too high for one party—or the ability to form them is constrained—due, for instance, to imperfect or incomplete information being available about the trustee. Though there are risks to legal contracts, they

---

[10]Coleman, 1986.
[11]Fukuyama, 1995.

are generally a good fit for situations where trust relationships are not appropriate; and though we could model legal contracts as complex trust relationships around transitive trust, this seems to be a stretch: the language and definitions we have formed do not seem to be a particularly good fit. Contracts also represent an agreement between at least two parties, whereas we have modelled trust relationships as being in a single direction.

This does not mean legal contracts are always simply an alternative to trust relationships. In many cases, contracts form an adjunct to a trust relationship and are put in place to try to address possible future breakdowns that might occur or to cover situations with which the context of the trust relationship—which is, in the human sphere at least, typically implicit—is not necessarily well-equipped to deal. One example might be a contract between an employer and employee, which, in the best of cases, should embody two trust relationships: one from the employer to the employee, and vice versa. Specifying a notice period—common in some jurisdictions and required in others—means that the case where an employee is offered a job by another employer or needs to leave to care for a sick relative, is managed, possibly with similar provisions for the case when the employer may wish to remove or replace the employee from their position.

Overall, given the types of relationship in which we are most interested—those between computer systems—legal contracts are not our main interest. Although there may be contracts associated with the entities for which the trustor and trustee are agents, the fact that these operate in a different milieu—that of jurisprudence—means they are not directly relevant to our core interest.

Enforcement

Another alternative to trust relationships is one that ignores social contracts as positive building blocks for jurisprudence and uses force as the mechanism by which assurance is provided: this is the situation that Gambetta describes in his paper "The Price of Mistrust" about the Mafia. At this level of discussion, where we are considering individual trust relationships, we are not concerned with the societal impact of such an approach, but we should consider what such an approach means for our discussions. The first point to note is that the trustor, rather than relying on assurances from the trustee, is now creating a new context where the trustee must have a trust relationship (albeit dysfunctional) back to the trustor, with the assurance that there will be payback or sanctions imposed if the assurances are not met. This is easy to model in human-to-human trust relationships but more complex in the case of computer systems. It is also likely to be the case—for humans or computers—that the party performing the sanctions is not the initial trustor, meaning the modelling becomes yet more complex. Given these complexities and the difficulty in applying this approach to computer systems, we will not spend any more time addressing this approach.

Verification

What about verification on its own: can this be a sufficient alternative to a trust relationship? Rather than "trust, but verify", can we manage simply by verifying? Let us consider what is being verified in a trust relationship: the performance of actions by a particular actor. If we are verifying them, then we must have some assurance that they are to be performed, in which case, we have, by definition, a trust relationship in place. It is much better to be explicit about this and know that it is occurring, rather than just to "perform verification". This does not mean, however, that the trustee needs to be aware of the verification process, or even that specific actions are part of verifications rather than normal requests to which the trustee should respond. The standard examples of this in security contexts are penetration testers or red teams, who are typically employed by a trustor to verify correct behaviour from a trustee by performing actions that should provoke specific reactions from the trustee in line with expectations.

Assurance and Accountability

Throughout our discussion on trust relationships, we have used the word *assurance* to describe the expectation that an action will be performed and the probability associated with that. There are a couple of other properties around assurance that we should consider. The first is related to the discussion we had of side effects and the fact that we cannot be sure that even when an action is being performed, it is fully correct. Gambetta suggests that there is what we could call an *imbalance of proof*: once untrustworthy behaviour happens, the evidence is never difficult to find; but it is virtually impossible to prove its mirror image: trustworthy—that is, expected—behaviour.[12] This is similar, of course, to the problem of proving scientific theories: we develop and accept theories that fit the facts unless or until new facts arise, disproving them, but we do not generally consider them provable in the way that mathematical theorems may be. Schneier makes a similar point in his essay "Why Cryptography Is Harder Than It Looks" when he notes that there is no test possible that can prove the absence of flaws.[13]

The other point about which we wish to be as certain as possible is the identity of the party that has performed the action about which we have assurances. It may be that a trustor observes an action that is in keeping with the trust relationship's expectations and therefore believes the assurances

---

[12]Gambetta quotes Iago's "proof" of Desdemona's infidelity in Shakespeare's *Othello*.
[13]Schneier, 1997.

associated with that trust relationship are met, when actually the actions—or the observations that led to a positive report of the actions—were performed by another actor rather than the expected trustee. The problem is compounded if the observing/monitoring party is not trustworthy—a point we have already discussed. But even when it is, such occurrences may be less far-fetched and more common than we expect. To give an example, consider a set of automated tests designed to provide assurance that a particular component of a computer system is functioning as expected. A test might observe disk activity and, if it falls within a particular range, give a result indicating a pass, even though the disk activity was due to another application entirely. This is arguably a failure of the monitoring party—the test program, in this case—but it may not always be possible to ascertain with certainty—a high enough level of assurance—exactly which party performed an action and which is ascribed to the trustee.

We may assume that in most use cases, the core point of a trust relationship is to ensure that actions are performed as expected: it is the actions themselves that are central to the relationship. This is not always the case. There may be occasions when it is the performance of the actions *by the specific trustee* that matters most, rather than the actions themselves. This can be difficult, given the constraints that we have noted around ascribing specific actions to a particular trustee. Nancy Buchan[14] talks about the "diagnosticity of information" and "accounting" in ways that mirror some of our monitoring discussions but in a context of trust relationship-building that relies too heavily on human aspects such as vulnerability to be exactly applicable to our focus on computer systems.

Trust of Non-Human or Non-Adult Actors

The remaining chapters of this book will focus almost exclusively on computer systems, but it is worth considering what sorts of trust relationships might be formed with other types of actors. The first type of actor we might consider would be children. Generally, however, when we are discussing human actors, we will be considering the case of (assumedly) rational adults. The question of whether (even adult) humans can be expected to act rationally is one we have touched on previously, but we can certainly expect children to act in ways that we do not consider rational or that require us to understand that their perceptions of context may differ significantly from ours, given their differences in thought processes and relative lack of world experience. If we do not share context or are concerned that context may be considered to vary, then we are missing one of the key requirements for trust relationships, and we should be careful about forming significant trust relationships to children.[15]

---

[14]Buchan, 2009, pp. 386–389.

[15]This will come as no surprise to parents or those who have spent much time with children. It does not mean, of course, that we cannot ever form trust relationships to children, but we must be particularly wary of the expectations we place on them: this is an area of study well outside the scope of this book.

While such care should be echoed when we consider how we form trust relationships to those from different cultural backgrounds—the expectations around trust establishment in Chinese societies may differ significantly from expectations in a Western business context, for example[16]—there is an assumption that the relationship being formed is to rational adults.

Another possible target for trust relationships might be animals. It does not sound too bizarre to hear people say, "I trust my dog to do so and so . . .", for a number of reasons. The first is that many animals have fairly predictable responses to particular situations and stimuli, so our assurances around actions could be considered fairly clear. The second is that, as noted in the previous sentence, the situations in which we interact with animals are usually fairly restricted, so we have a small number of identifiable contexts. The third is less positive; we tend to anthropomorphise animals with which we come in contact, meaning we ascribe to them motivations and reactions that we associate with humans, even when doing so is not justified. Considering a different context, Patrick Bateson[17] makes a case for considering cooperation between animals and among animal groups as consonant with the theory of evolution, but his description of trust is not close enough to ours to be useful for our needs. We might consider animals a halfway house between humans and computers: on the one hand, they seem not to be very intelligent and to react in expected ways (treating them like computers); but on the other hand, we know that their behaviour is not always as we expect, and we also tend to anthropomorphise them (treating them as we might treat humans).

People—including children—animals, and computers are not the only things that we might say we trust. We may say the same about mechanical systems like cars or boats, or even processes. Although these might have similarities to computer systems—and processes may, of course, be implemented by computer systems—they are outside the scope of our interest.

Finally, there is the question of what it means to trust an organisation. We have discussed this in previous chapters, and from this point on, our assumption will be that when we talk about trust in the context of an organisation, we will be considering a party that is acting as the agent of that organisation. If we need to be more specific about the agency or consider different aspects of an organisation, we will state this explicitly.

Expressions of Trust

As humans, the most obvious way of expressing trust is to say "I trust you" or "I trust person X". We have seen how such expressions are insufficient for explicit trust relationships, and we looked at how context and time affect how

---

[16]De Cremer, 2015.
[17]Bateson, 1988.

we express those relationships. Clearly, however, there are many other ways of expressing trust, some of which we have already addressed in our studies of different forms of trust. Contracts of various types are typically backed by the endorsing authority of a body such as a state, though other bodies such as sporting associations, guilds, religious institutions, and schools may all have sufficiently expressive bodies of rules to allow contracts to be created. We can express trust in processes, as well: the process for issuing a driving licence; the process for getting my luggage transferred with me from San Francisco airport to Austin, Texas; the process for avoiding a penalty fare or additional charge when boarding a train. Some of these processes are associated with one or more obligations enshrined in contracts I have entered into with the various parties executing the processes, but other processes may be more based in societal norms than contractual relationships: think of the process that embodies the societal norm of letting a person with just a few items move in front of you in a checkout queue. You may or may not have trust to let someone go ahead of you, depending on where you are, what is being queued for, the relative ages of the various parties, how many items you have, and many other factors.

These examples are things *in which* we trust, but there is a different kind of expression of trust: the embodiment of trust relationships, which we began to examine when we considered the placing of agency. The contractual relationships just noted can be examples of such embodiments, and we might say that trust in processes is a way of embodying the sorts of social capital and social contracts in which Fukuyama and Coleman are interested. As we move further into the realm of computer systems, however, we can see that there trust embodiment types that are more definable and also more complex in the way that they realise trust relationships than the design or placement of agency into a particular component of a system. The embodiment of trust relationships, their ramifications, and the opportunities they present will be our topics for the rest of this book.

Let us start with a case from cloud computing. In this type of service, one party, the cloud service provider (CSP), owns and operates[18] a number of computer systems (hosts) on which a customer (the tenant) may run applications or processes (workloads). The precise mechanisms for how this works vary from CSP to CSP, the service provided, and the workload being executed, but the basic idea is that a tenant's workload executes on the CSP's host. This arrangement is sometimes expressed by the adage "the cloud is just somebody else's computer". While this may sound like a truism, it has important security and

---

[18]There are situations when a cloud service provider does not necessarily own the systems, but for our purposes, they are considered to have full control over each machine: other cases may present a more complex set of trust relationships. For this example, the key parties at this level of complexity are the CSP and the tenant.

trust implications. When I operate a computer system, I have close to full control over what happens on that machine.[19] This includes control not only over the core operating system and applications that I am running on the machine but also over any workloads that I am executing for a tenant.

Within the security field, a triad of properties are often considered when evaluating the security of a process or system: *confidentiality, integrity*, and *availability* (CIA). In fact, we touched on these properties in the section "Trust and Security" in Chapter 1. To evaluate security more fully, other properties may be required, but these three are a good starting point for our discussions. As the operator of a machine with full administrator access (sometimes referred to as *root*, which is the standard UNIX and Linux user name for the administrator) or the same privileges as the kernel (the core part of the operating system), I have control over all these properties:

Confidentiality Processes such as workloads store their executable code and data in memory, segmented into pages. With sufficient privileged access, such as root, the operator of the machine can inspect all the memory pages for a workload and see all the code and data associated with it, removing the property of confidentiality.

Integrity With the ability to inspect memory pages comes another ability: that of changing the data in the memory pages. With sufficient privileged access, the operator of the machine can change the data in all the memory pages of the workload, altering any or all of the code and data associated with it, removing the property of integrity.

Availability Another ability associated with sufficient privilege on a host machine is the ability to deny a workload sufficient resources to run. This is typically associated with not allowing the workload sufficient time on a shared processor (typically one of the CPUs or CPU cores) to execute, though such restraints may also involve other resources such as network access, storage, or interrupt handling. With sufficient privileged access, the operator of the machine may remove the property of availability.

All this sounds very damaging to the tenant and the tenant's relationship to the CSP, and it can be; but in most cases, there is no incentive for the CSP to do any of these things, and many incentives (including legal and contractual ones) not to do so. This explains why many millions of workloads are executed on cloud hosts every hour.

There may be occasions, however, when you have workloads whose data and/or code are too sensitive to risk being run on the CSP's host: i.e., on somebody else's computer. In this case, what I need to do is be aware that the trust

---

[19]Some of the exceptions to this state are interesting and very important to topics discussed later in this book, but we will concentrate on this case for now.

relationship that I have to the CSP does not extend to the context of allowing my more sensitive workloads on their hosts. One way to express this is to design an architecture for deploying my workloads that expresses this trust relationship. We will examine this use case next (also see in Figure 3.9) and continue to work on and extend it throughout the rest of the book. We will see issues of trust, security, and risk all coming into play and will begin to use some of the concepts that have been introduced in earlier chapters.

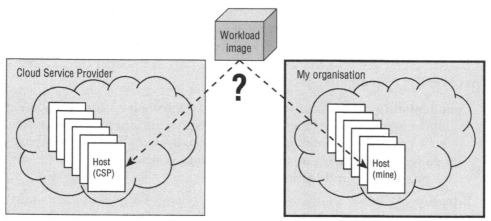

Figure 3.9: Deploying a workload to a public or private cloud.

For example, let us say that as the architect of a workload management system, or *orchestrator*,[20] I have two options for deploying workloads: I can deploy them on the CSP's hosts, or I can deploy them on hosts that are owned and operated by my organisation. Running workloads on my own hosts may be a more expensive option operationally, but we will assume that a risk evaluation has been taken that indicates the impact of the CSP on one or more of the confidentiality / integrity / availability triad of properties is too high, based on the sensitivity of some of these workloads.

What might such workloads look like, and why might they be sensitive? Some might be specific to organisations or sectors, such as:

- Medical data
- Credit card or other financial data
- Details of energy or mineral explorations
- Troop deployment information
- Automobile designs
- Next season's fashion designs

---

[20]Open source examples of orchestrators include Kubernetes and OpenStack, which are focussed on Linux containers and virtual machines, respectively.

Other workloads are more generic and could apply to many different organisations, such as:

- Customer addresses
- Employee payroll data
- Sales contracts
- Firewall configuration data
- Private keys associated with web server certificates

All of these types of workloads may be sensitive, and depending on the risk assessment performed, may be classified as suitable for deployment only to my organisation's systems, whereas other, less sensitive workloads may be deployed to the CSP's host machines.

As a software or systems architect, I may design a system that can deploy workloads either to the CSP or to my own organisation's systems, but that has rules about whether a particular workload can be deployed to either based on the classification of the workload's sensitivity. In doing so, I am creating an architecture that *expresses trust*, as I have embodied in at least two relationships:

- The trust relationship that my organisation has to the CSP in terms of sensitive workloads
- The trust relationship that my organisation has to the CSP in terms of non-sensitive workloads

In creating such an architecture, I have the opportunity to be explicit about these trust relationships, which is in keeping with one of the key precepts of this book: that trust relationships should be explicit.

In fact, while the two trust relationships just noted are probably the most obvious in the (so far rather simple) architecture we have described, there are several—possibly many—more types of trust and associated relationships that are being expressed. The first is in technology: I am trusting the orchestrator to deploy the workloads according to the rules I have designed. In fact, saying *technology* hides many different components and entities. Let us list some of them and the type or context of trust involved:

- The orchestrator: to follow the rules I have created
- The implementation of the language in which I have created the rules: to provide the orchestrator with the information it requires
- The compiler used to build the orchestrator: not to have introduced logic flaws

- The operating system of the orchestrator: to give correct details of network route hosts to the CSP's and my organisation's hosts

- The domain naming system (DNS): to identify correctly which hosts are in the CSP's network and which are in my organisation's

Then there are other factors that need to be considered, from humans—who may have intentionally or unintentionally introduced flaws into the system—to processes such as those that are supposed to test the architecture I have designed to ensure that it fits what I created, not to mention the documentation (itself most likely created by humans as the result of a set of processes) that I followed in order to understand what was being asked of me in the first place.

When we delve down to this level of complexity and granularity, it may seem that there is no end to the depths we need to go in order fully to understand and validate an architecture—and we have not even considered the issue of monitoring and verifying its operation. Luckily, the principles of computer system design can give us some help here, in the form of *abstraction*. Abstracting different components of a system allows us to concentrate only on those layers about which we need to care—in this case, probably the orchestrator and one or so layers below. With appropriate levels of description of the layers on which we rely—on which we have dependencies—we can be fairly sure that we are building on firm foundations.

Unluckily, abstractions are dangerous, too. One of the recurring issues with computer security is that even though dependencies may be well-defined, vulnerabilities and the attacks associated with them arise from two problems with abstractions:

- Attacks often occur at several points in a computer system, whose operation and design may be abstracted from each other, and where there is no way, at runtime or even design-time, to monitor the impact that a vulnerability in one may have on the operation of another.

- Security is typically a non-functional property of a system in that it is not core to its operation and, therefore, its design. Complex systems often display emergent behaviour, which is when components interact in ways that have unplanned or unexpected outcomes. Such behaviours are all the more likely with non-functional properties since the descriptions of expected component behaviours may well be more poorly described than the functional properties of the system.

There is another, deeper, problem for anyone interested in trust relationships in these systems: descriptions of components and systems rarely deal with trust at all. This means anyone trying to understand the trust properties of a system is likely to have to consider all the components that form the system, which may include having to go into at least as much detail as described in our examples. This is partly because trust is not well-defined in the literature and partly because people do not know that they should be considering it in detail and/or how to do so. Starting to remedy these problems is the goal of this book, and the following chapters aim to provide a technical introduction to trust in computer systems based on the underpinnings that we have established. They also aim to open our eyes to some of the pitfalls that may befall us.

Relating Trust and Security

One final point in this section is to underline the relationship between trust and security. In almost every context where security is important in computing and the cloud, trust relationships come into play. Once you start looking at security systems from the perspective of trust relationships, the connection between the two becomes obvious, and you will start to wonder what trust relationships are being expressed, whether they are implicit or explicit, and whether assumptions have been made about time, symmetry, or who the parties involved are. It will not always be easy to work out what the designers, implementers, and deployers of security in systems had in mind—where security measures are in place at all, of course—and this will most typically be because the people involved in these systems did not think about trust explicitly and therefore did not express any of these relationships explicitly.

This does not mean to say that all systems are lacking in trust thinking: there are some very sophisticated trust models within computing and the cloud, and we will look at some of these in detail in the forthcoming chapters. Nor does it imply that security without explicit expression of the relevant trust relationships is *ipso facto* poor; but the ability to talk about, describe, and design trust relationships into systems can make them more resilient, more usable, and, fundamentally, more secure.

Misplaced Trust

Having examined the types of entities we might consider appropriate to trust and some of the issues associated with expressing trust, we should take a moment to be aware of a problem that we addressed at some length in Chapter 2 and how it applies to where we form trust relationships. Security economics warns us to be careful to watch out for situations where the security in a system is benefitting not us but other parties. The same issue can apply to trust, and there are also occasions where trust may be unintentionally misplaced—that is, there is no intention to deceive any parties, yet a trust relationship should still not be established.

Consider the situation where you are contemplating buying a new financial product from your bank. You book an appointment with an adviser to discuss your needs. Typically, you are less informed about the products on offer than the adviser is, and so you need to form a trust relationship to them whereby you expect them to provide advice that is suited to your financial situation and goals. A good adviser—and by "good" we might say "talented" or "expert", rather than "motivated by goodwill"—will work hard to foster a relationship with you whereby you are happy to establish a trust relationship to them. The adviser is indeed likely to be worthy of trust, but that trust is typically a trust less appropriate for *you* to have to the adviser than it is for the bank by which they are employed and which will have given them and their colleagues incentives to sell you products that the bank is particularly interested in selling. In some jurisdictions, governments and consumer organisations have put measures in place to try to guard consumers against exactly this sort of abuse of trust. But can you be sure that the same abuse of trust is not a risk whenever you buy a high-value good or service such as a car, laptop, or Internet service plan?

Sometimes, as noted earlier, the misplacing of trust is unintentional, but this does not make it any less concerning. Let us take the example of a self-driving car designed in one country but being driven in another. We might say that we have a trust relationship to the car we are driving—more specifically, to the software which controls it—to make decisions around safety that we feel are appropriate or that mirror the decision we would make if we were in control ourselves. What we mean by *appropriate*, however, will depend on our cultural background. The canonical example is the relative value of human life that different cultures hold towards children and older people. In some cultures, if presented with the choice of hitting a child or an older person while driving, the vast majority of drivers would choose the older person with little hesitation, reasoning (possibly subconsciously) that the life of the child has more value than that of the older person. However, the same does not hold for all cultures because some would consider the older person's life more valuable. What should the car do when faced with such a dilemma?[21] The answer is that the designer will have to make a decision as to which action the driver might feel more appropriate—assuming that the hardware and software in the car are able to distinguish and make such a choice—and the designer is likely to choose along the lines that they find most culturally appropriate or, with sufficient awareness of the problem, will make a decision based on the expressed cultural values of the buyers of the car in a particular market. We might conceive of a situation where different software configurations are provided for cars to be sold in different geographical—and therefore cultural—markets; but what if the driver is renting a car away from home or takes their car with them to a country or region where the cultural expectations

---

[21]This is a reworking of a premise presented in the film *I, Robot* (2004), based on the series of short stories and novels by Isaac Asimov around the "The Three Laws of Robotics", which in turn built on a challenge in philosophy and ethics known as The Trolley Problem and its variants.

are different? In this case, the trust that the driver—or maybe the society—has that the self-driving car will do the right thing is misplaced.

In a similar but more concrete and less dramatic example, there are numerous examples of software or hardware systems that were designed for one situation failing or needing to be redesigned when applied to another. This is not always due to issues around trust, but one example is related to the sort of cloud services orchestrator described earlier. When it was originally designed, the OpenStack orchestrator—used to deploy virtual machines to host machines—had little concept of trust, as it had originally been designed for a different use case. The initial design assumption was made (whether explicitly or implicitly) that all hosts should be equally trusted, which, as we have noted, may be not appropriate when you are considering deploying sensitive workloads. Once this set of use cases was considered, the concept of trusted hosts and untrusted hosts was added to OpenStack,[22,23] but an assumption was made that could cause problems for actual deployments. The key rule for deploying workloads could be described thus:

Sensitive workloads can *only* be deployed to trusted hosts.

This expressed and dealt with the key requirement that sensitive workloads should be protected by being put onto trusted hosts, but unfortunately, it failed to deal with a significant and overlooked design requirement. The problem derived from the fact that there was no assumption that non-sensitive workloads should be trusted to behave well, and one of the behaviours they might exhibit would be that they might compromise a host or at least have a negative impact on the operation of the other workloads on that host (such as over-consuming shared resources: the *noisy neighbour problem*). This impact was acceptable if they were placed on an untrusted host, since even if the workloads on that host were themselves compromised, they were not sensitive. However, a problem could arise if a non-sensitive workload was placed on a trusted host. In this case, a non-sensitive workload could have a negative impact on the workloads on that host or even conceivably compromise the host itself, causing it now to be considered *untrusted*.

Surely this would not be a problem, though, because only sensitive workloads would be deployed to trusted hosts, and no untrusted workloads could therefore wreak such havoc. Unluckily, when the rules were written, there was no equivalent rule to *stop* the placement of non-sensitive workloads on trusted hosts. The rules should, in fact, have looked like this:

- Sensitive workloads can *only* be deployed to trusted hosts.

- Non-sensitive workloads can *never* be deployed to trusted hosts.

---

[22]Whether this level of granularity and description—trusted vs. untrusted—is sufficient is not an issue that we will address here.
[23]The functionality was never fully implemented and was removed from OpenStack. The description here is something of a simplification and is intended only to expose an example of unintended consequences of a design.

We might even consider an alternative set to give more flexibility in deploying non-sensitive workloads where resources are scarce:

- Sensitive workloads can *only* be deployed to trusted hosts.

- Non-sensitive workloads can *only* be deployed to trusted hosts where no sensitive workloads are already executing.

- Deploying a non-sensitive workload to a trusted host changes that host's classification to *untrusted*.

There are all sorts of ways in which we could address the particular problems associated with this system—which was fixed—but we can see that even for what seem to be fairly simple trust relationships, it is easy to make mistakes or put in place rules and trust relationships that have unintended consequences. In many of the cases we will be considering in the rest of the book, such complexities are part and parcel of the systems involved. Picking them apart is one of the key skills we hope to expose.

Defining Trust in Computing

As we move away from trust and human relationships and focus more on computer systems, we should re-examine our definition of trust and compare it with some of the definitions we find that are more relevant to a non-human context.

A Survey of Trust Definitions in Computer Systems

In their work on distributed trust, Adbul-Rahman and Hailes extend some of the simpler models in the literature into the world of distributed trust, Abdul-Rahman and Hailes[1] use Gambetta's definition of trust, which we analysed in Chapter 1, "Why Trust?"; they note the importance of these three points in any conversation around trust. Though they state them slightly differently, using the language we have adopted, they note the importance of:

1. The subjective nature of trust

2. The inability of the trustor to monitor all actions that might affect trust

3. That levels of trust depend on how the trustor's actions are affected by the actions of the trustee

---

[1] Abdul-Rahman and Hailes, 1997.

We can probably accept point 1, whilst being aware that subjectivity is not necessarily a problem if the scope of the trust is known and managed; and we have already noted the difficulties presented by point 2. The third point is either a truism because we accept that the trust relationship to the trustee is affected by the trustor's perception of the trustee's actions, or it is irrelevant because we believe that the trustor's actions are not directly related to the trust relationship in consideration. Despite these points and our rejection of Gambetta's original definition as insufficient for our needs, Abdul-Rahman and Hailes present some interesting and useful insights we can apply.

Their most important point is that, within the computing domain, systems are commonly labelled as *trusted* once they have been tested and shown to meet particular criteria, despite there being no concrete definition of trust that has been applied by the systems designers. This is something we have already noted, but Abdul-Rahman and Hailes go further, with the observation that the application of the label *trusted* can be taken to imply that nothing can go wrong and that all eventualities have been tested, rather than that the specific criteria previously specified—and only those criteria—have been applied. They note, somewhat laconically, that the suggestion that all eventualities have been tested is "not always true, and is difficult to guarantee",[2] an understatement if ever there were one.

Other useful definitions around trust include those gathered by the US National Institute of Standards and Technology (NIST). NIST publishes many sets of documents, and, sadly, the definitions between their own documents are not standardised. Nonetheless, it is worth our time to compare their various definitions for *trust*[3] and *trust relationship*[4] with each other:

1. Trust: a characteristic of an entity that indicates its ability to perform certain functions or services correctly, fairly and impartially, along with assurance that the entity and its identifier are genuine. (NIST SP 800-152[5])

2. Trust: The confidence one element has in another, that the second element will behave as expected. (NIST SP 800-161[6])

3. Trust: The willingness to take actions expecting beneficial outcomes, based on assertions by other parties. (NIST SP 800-95[7])

---

[2]Abuld-Rahman and Hailes, 1997, p. 49.
[3]https://csrc.nist.gov/glossary/term/trust.
[4]https://csrc.nist.gov/glossary/term/trust_relationship.
[5]Barker et al., 2015.
[6]Boyens et al., 2015.
[7]Singhal et al., 2007.

4. Trust relationship: An agreed upon relationship between two or more system elements that is governed by criteria for secure interaction, behavior, and outcomes relative to the protection of assets. Note: This refers to trust relationships between system elements implemented by hardware, firmware, and software. (NIST SP 800-160[8])

5. Trust relationships: Policies that govern how entities in differing domains honor each others' authorizations. An authority may be completely trusted—for example, any statement from the authority will be accepted as a basis for action—or there may be limited trust, in which case only statements in a specific range are accepted. (NIST 800-95[9])

6. Trust relationship: The access relationship that is granted by an authorized key in an account on one system (server) and a corresponding identity key in an account on another system (client). Once deployed, these two keys establish a persistent trust relationship between the two accounts/systems that enables ongoing access. (NISTIR 7966[10])

There are a number of interesting points to make here. First, definition 6 is referring to a very specific technical context[11]—SSH keys—where there are existing definitions that can be used. This may not coexist perfectly with our definition, but we should be pleased to note that there are some areas of computing where trust and trust relationships have been considered in some detail (and SSH is definitely one of those).

We can now look at the other definitions. The first point we should note is in definition 1:

"Trust: a characteristic of an entity that indicates its ability to perform certain functions or services correctly, fairly and impartially, along with assurance that the entity and its identifier are genuine".

The point to consider is that trust is defined here as a *characteristic* of an entity rather than as a relational property. In many ways, the rest of the definition aligns quite closely with ours, but the definition of trust as a characteristic should make us pause. From the beginning of our discussion, our definition has been derived from an understanding of trust that was based on, or at least strongly informed by, human-to-human relationships. In human-to-human contexts, it is quite clear that trust is relational, though we have seen some

---

[8]Ross et al., 2016. This report has been superseded by Ross et al., 2016a, which no longer includes a definitions section.
[9]Singhal et al., 2007.
[10]Ylonen et al., 2015.
[11]A technical context of this type is different from a trust context: the former refers to a field of technology, the latter to a context that may exist within a trust relationship.

attempts to define *trustworthiness* as a more objective consideration. But as we have explicitly chosen non-human contexts as our main context, is there an opportunity to take a different view and follow this definition in understanding trust as an objective characteristic? A brief example serves to show that this approach, tempting as it is, will not serve our needs and that the definition actually contains a self-contradiction, as depicted in Figures 4.1a and 4.1b.

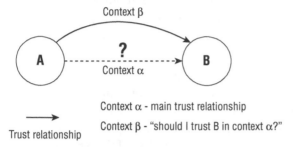

Context α - main trust relationship

Context β - "should I trust B in context α?"

Trust relationship

Figure 4.1a: Trying to establish a new trust context with the same trustee.

Circular trust context

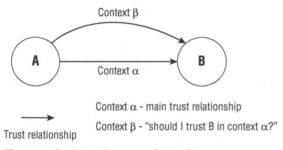

Context α - main trust relationship

Context β - "should I trust B in context α?"

Trust relationship

Figure 4.1b: A circular trust relationship.

To examine the issue of insufficiency, there is no way, according to the definition as provided, for different entities (trustors) to hold differing views of the entity with whom the trust characteristic is associated (the trustee). This might be understandable if what was being discussed was actually reputation in a particular context, but the addition of "assurances" to the definition makes it clear that there is actually a trust relationship being discussed. If all trustors have the same relationship with the trustee, then either they are all in the same trust domain—a concept we will define and discuss in detail in Chapter 12—or we have a problem with time as a context. The reason for this problem is that if the trustee defaults in its performance of any functions or services, there is no mechanism for the trustors to be updated with the new status of the trust. Worse, there is no trusted entity that can provide such an update, as the trust is associated with the trustee, in whom we have lesser trust than before. And our definition assumes that one of the services the trustee provides is giving details of the state of its own trust characteristic, which is clearly circular and nonsensical.

This implicit circularity of this assurance about the trustee providing its own trustworthy updates is no less important than the explicit circularity of assurances associated with the trustee. To take an example from the human-to-human realm, if I make assurances to you about my trustworthiness, then what reason do you have to accept my assurances if you do not know if you can trust me in the first place? The same goes for this definition: without an existing trust relationship with the putative trustee, a putative trustor entity has no way to bootstrap a relationship with the trustee.

Moving down the list, definition 2 is not that far from our own definition, though less detailed; and while the third definition explicitly addresses the issue of circularity we noted in the first, it does focus specifically on actions leading to "beneficial outcomes", which, as we have noted elsewhere, are not necessary to our definition. The question of to whom the benefit accrues would also be a concern we would wish to address if we were to adopt this particular definition.

The fourth definition, from NIST 800-160, is particularly interesting:

"Trust relationship: An agreed upon relationship between two or more system elements that is governed by criteria for secure interaction, behavior, and outcomes relative to the protection of assets. Note: This refers to trust relationships between system elements implemented by hardware, firmware, and software".

NIST 800-160 has been superseded, and the new version—which replaces only part of the original—does not include this definition. The first thing to note is that the scope defined actually seems very close to our area of interest as the relationships described are between system elements. The description of relationships as being "between two or more . . . elements" does not fit perfectly with our uni-directional approach; and its inclusion of "the protection of assets" makes definition 4 more specific than ours, though it does relate to the area covered by the NIST 800-160.

Definition 5 is also about trust relationships:

"Trust relationships: Policies that govern how entities in differing domains honor each others' authorizations. An authority may be completely trusted for example, any statement from the authority will be accepted as a basis for action or there may be limited trust, in which case only statements in a specific range are accepted".

This definition is less relevant to our interest in machine-to-machine trust relationships, but it does accord with concerns raised about the circularity that we discussed in definition 1. Also interesting is the point around authorities, where the definition takes a similar view to us around trusting authorities, particularly if we map the idea of *ranges* to our *contexts*.

Other Definitions of Trust within Computing

In addition to organisations such as the NIST, several computing groups have addressed the topic of trust, with results on which we can draw. There is another organisation within the IT industry that is very relevant to our deliberations and that we have not yet mentioned: the Trusted Computing Group[12] (TCG). The TCG describes itself thus:

> **"The Trusted Computing Group (TCG) is a not-for-profit organization formed to develop, define and promote open, vendor-neutral, global industry specifications and standards, supportive of a hardware-based root of trust, for interoperable trusted computing platforms"[13].**

The TCG is an industry consortium[14] associated principally with Trusted Platform Modules (TPMs), a set of hardware components technologies that we will examine later in the book. The TCG has also published a protocol definition called Trusted Network Connect (TNC) and is active across various sectors and technologies, including storage, the Internet of Things, the cloud, and automotive computing. TPMs are common components in consumer and enterprise hardware, and their standardisation has been an important security achievement within the industry. They are commonly used as a hardware root of trust in systems, a concept we will examine later in this chapter. In its document "TCG Glossary",[15] the TCG provides this definition for trust:

> **"Trust is the expectation that a device will behave in a particular manner for a specific purpose".**

As might be expected, given the TCG's focus on hardware, the specificity of "device" is unsurprising. We might hope for specificity around the "particular manner" in which the device is expected to behave, though the mention of a "purpose" suggests the expectation of something similar to what we have termed a *context*.

One important set of definitions of computing terms in the security realm is the IETF Security Glossary,[16] which both provides its own definitions and also

---

[12]See https://trustedcomputinggroup.org.
[13]Trusted Computing Group, 2020.
[14]Aaron Weiss gives an interesting negative critique of the TCG in an article from a 2006 issue of *netWorker*, which may best be contextualised within the debate at that time around digital rights management (DRM).
[15]Trusted Computing Group, 2017.
[16]Shirey, 2007.

cites those from other authorities. The Security Glossary provides two definitions of trust. The context for the first, provided without external reference or citation, is information systems:

> **"A feeling of certainty (sometimes based on inconclusive evidence) either (a) that the system will not fail or (b) that the system meets its specifications (i.e., the system does what it claims to do and does not perform unwanted functions)".**

The language—particularly the use of the word "feeling"—is clearly unsatisfactory in the context of computer systems, and the two requirements—that the "system will not fail" or that it "meets its specification" are very broad, even with the parenthetical clarification.

The context for the second is much less broad and is related to the context of public key infrastructure (PKI):

> **"A relationship between a certificate user and a CA [certificate authority] in which the user acts according to the assumption that the CA creates only valid digital certificates".**

This is generally what we would expect for this context. What is interesting is the "tutorial" (example) that the Security Glossary provides,[17] citing the ITU Recommendation on X.509[18] (parentheses provided by the Security Glossary):

> **"Generally, an entity is said to 'trust' a second entity when the first entity makes the assumption that the second entity will behave exactly as the first entity expects. This trust may apply only for some specific function. The key role of trust in [X.509] is to describe the relationship between an entity [i.e., a certificate user] and a [CA]; an entity shall be certain that it can trust the CA to create only valid and reliable certificates".**

This is interestingly consistent with our definition. If we substitute the phrase "makes the assumption" with "has assurance", then the statements are similar. Again, their use of *function* can be considered equivalent to our use of *context*, and the final sentence serves as a concrete example in the context of PKI. This is unsurprising: PKI is an area where the issue of trust has been considered and defined with care since its inception, as it is a key set of infrastructure technologies within the modern IT world.

---

[17]Shirey, 2007.
[18]International Telecommunication Union, 2001.

Applying Socio-Philosophical Definitions of Trust to Systems

As we have discussed in previous chapters, we have many definitions of trust when we talk about human relationships. Some of these definitions provide insight that can further our understanding of what we mean by trust in computing systems.

One author whose interest in trust extends into the online world, albeit with a continued focus on what he labels "human to system" trust, is Coye Cheshire. He talks about various concepts of interest to our discussion, including trust, trustworthiness, cooperation, and assurance, two of which we have already identified as important. He also notes the difficulty in talking about trust when referring to systems, pointing out that:

> "...the potential difference in meaning for terms such as intention, agency, cooperation, and choice is difficult to ignore when considering programmed systems versus human actors. For example, philosopher Annette Baier argues that relational, interpersonal trust depends on the possibility of betrayal by another person. Information systems and computer programs appear to lack the agency and consciousness to choose freely to betray the trust that users place in them".[19]

In a similar vein, there are some authors who, though approaching the topic of trust from a sociological point of view, still provide concepts that we are able to borrow. Barry Wellman, for example, presents six "analytic principles"[20] in his work on network analysis (an area where trust is relevant and that is related to the concept of trust domains). Of these, the first four are directly relatable to our concerns:

- Ties are usually asymmetrically reciprocal, differing in content and intensity.

- Ties link network members indirectly as well as directly. Hence, they must be defined within the context of larger network structures.

- The structuring of social ties creates nonrandom networks, hence clusters, boundaries, and cross-linkages.

- Cross-linkages connect clusters as well as individuals.

It is clear from our brief review that although there is literature around trust in computing, much of it is still related to human interactions, albeit with computer systems, and the material that does relate specifically to computer-to-computer

---

[19]Cheshire, 2011, p. 55.
[20]Wellman, 1988, p. 55.

interactions seems to be very domain-specific. There is nothing wrong with this, and we will be mining the domain-specific material in our later considerations; but what we are looking for is something more generally applicable to computing and trust that also allows us to make useful decisions about how trust may be created, maintained, and managed between different systems. Sometimes, borrowing concepts from outside the pure domain of computing will serve us well, but first we should consider what insights have already been brought to the field of computing from other areas of research.

Mathematics and Trust

Mathematics offers certainty. That, at least, is the promise to computing since the field's inception, and arguably one of the reasons that "computer science" is taught at universities, rather than "computer arts": computers, operating on ones and zeros, pure numbers, are governed, at the basic level, by mathematics. Mathematics, when applied to computing, should give us a black and white, binary determinism of the type that scientists profess to love.[21] Game theory, as we noted in Chapter 2, provides insights into trust relationships, just as Bayesian theory does to economics. In both these domains, however, it is the long game, with multiple actors or rounds of interaction, where mathematics brings the most value. Are there mathematical concepts and fields that can provide value in more focussed domains of trust?

Mathematics and Cryptography

The first and most obvious answer to the question is cryptography. We have touched briefly on cryptography earlier in the book, partly to note how difficult it is to do correctly. Cryptography, however, is one of the tools—or sets of tools—that is going to be important to our study of trust, and therefore it deserves some attention. Before we proceed, however, we should be aware that despite being firmly rooted in the "clean" world of mathematics, cryptography can be messy, too. In the introduction to their (rightly celebrated) book *Practical Cryptography*, Neils Ferguson and Bruce Schneier note:

"We [the community] have developed, implemented, and fielded cryptographic systems over the past decade. What we've been less effective at is converting the mathematical promise of cryptographic security into a reality of security. As it turns out, this is the hard part".[22]

---

[21]The black and white nature of science is, as students of the history of science will tell you, something of an illusion. It may be useful as a basis for teaching less-experienced pupils, but when science is applied to the real world, things typically get messy very quickly, one reflection of this being the separation of both mathematics and physics into "theoretical" and "applied" in many academic contexts.

[22]Ferguson and Schneier, 2003, pp. xvii.

Cryptography on its own is not a solution: it is part of the solution and provides some of the primitives that we need to define and build trust relationships. Cryptography, when correctly implemented, allows us to make and accept assurances about particular aspects of the world and within particular confines.

One of the most important assurances that we care about is that of identity. Cryptography allows us to be assured that an entity presenting a cryptographic key is the same entity that presents it to us in the future and was the same entity that presented it to us in the past. This is true only, however, if the key cannot be copied. But in the realm of computing, the presentation of a key is sufficient for it to be copied; therefore, a specific cryptographic capability is required: public-private key pairs, a branch of asymmetric cryptography. Without delving into the details of how asymmetric cryptography works, an entity that creates a pair of keys—a public key and a private key—and maintains the confidentiality of the private key can present the public key in such a way that it can convince other entities that it (the holding entity) and *only it* holds the private key that is the other half of the pair. This is enormously helpful, as we can now accept the assurance of identity, assuming that the following pre-requisites are met:

- That the key has not been copied either

  - Intentionally, by the holding entity to another entity (this would generally be against the interests of the holding entity, as identity is an important property to be guarded)

  - Or unintentionally, through some failure of the holding entity to maintain the confidentiality of the private key

- That the mathematics underlying the creation of the public-private key pair has not been sufficiently undermined to allow the private key to be derived or inferred from the public key or otherwise generated by another entity

Assuming, therefore, that the confidentiality of the key has not been compromised, we are left with the issue of mathematical protection of the key. The likelihood of compromise at the mathematical level is dependent on a variety of issues, including the algorithm used; the underlying mathematical problem employed; the "state of the art" of mathematics[23]; the time available to attack the keys; and the availability of technologies for attack, including quantum computers.[24]

There is one final prerequisite that we missed, and it is definitely the most important in terms of likelihood of vulnerability: implementation. The vast

---

[23]It is maybe ironic that mathematicians are generally happy to refer to their field as "an art", given our earlier note about "computer science".

[24]There are algorithms intended for public key cryptography that are designed to be "quantum-resistant", but none of these, at the time of writing, are considered proven in terms of the resistance they are likely to provide once sufficiently powerful quantum computing devices become available.

majority—by an overwhelming margin—of vulnerabilities in cryptographic primitives, algorithms, and protocols come not from underlying weaknesses in the mathematics or design of the cryptography[25] but from errors in implementation. Humans—who still write most of the code that is deployed in production—are notoriously bad at writing bug-free code, and cryptographic code is not only tricky to write due to the complexities that often underpin the primitives, algorithms, and protocols but also very fragile. By *fragile*, in this context, we mean minor errors—bugs—in implementation can lead to catastrophic failure in operation. Specifically, in this context, if cryptographic code is incorrectly implemented, then a vulnerability, once found and exploited, may lead to all the assurances provided by the underlying cryptography being completely removed.

Mathematics and Formal Verification

Luckily, mathematics provides a way to help us with the problem of bug-ridden code, though unluckily, as we shall see, it turns out that the help it can give us is limited. The field of study associated with this help is referred to as *formal verification*. Formal verification aims to start with proofs—at best, with an equivalent level of assurance to that of formal mathematical proofs—of the correctness of the algorithms to be implemented in code to ensure that they perform the operations expected and as set forth in a set of requirements. Though implementation of code can often fall down in the actual instructions created by a developer or set of developers, i.e., in the programming, mistakes are equally possible at the level of the design of the code to be implemented in the first place, and so proper design must be a minimum step before looking at any actual implementations. What is more, these types of mistakes can be all the more hard to spot, as even if the developer has introduced no bugs in the work they have done, the implementation will be flawed by virtue of it being incorrectly defined in the first place.

It is with an acknowledgement of this type of error, and an intention of reducing or eliminating it, that formal verification starts.[26] But some approaches within formal verification go much further, with methods to examine concrete implementations and make statements about *their* correctness with regard to the algorithms they are implementing.

Where we can make our verifications work, they are extremely valuable, and the sorts of places they are applied are exactly where we would expect: in systems where security is paramount and to prove the correctness of cryptographic designs and implementations. Another major focus of formal verification is

---

[25]All these points are specific to peer-reviewed cryptography, which has been subject to research and investigation before adoption by the wider cryptographic world.
[26]MacKenzie, 2001, provides a starting point for the sorts of correctness that formal verification aims—or may be able—to provide.

software for safety systems, where the "correct" operation of the system—by which we mean "as designed and expected"—is vital. Examples might include oil refineries, fire suppression systems, nuclear power station management, aircraft flight systems,[27] and electrical grid management. Although most of the focus of this book is on software, formal verification of hardware is also an important field of study. The practical application of formal verification methods to software is, however, more limited than we would like. As Alessandro Abate notes in his paper on formal verification of software:

> **"Two known shortcomings of standard techniques in formal verification are the limited capability to provide system-level assertions, and the scalability of large, complex models".[28]**

To these shortcomings, we can add another extremely significant one, and it is an issue that will haunt us throughout the rest of the book: how sure can you be that what you are running is what you think you are running?

Surely knowing what you are running is exactly why we write software, look at the source, and then compile it under our control. That, certainly, is the basic starting point for software that we care about.

The problem is arguably one of layers and dependencies and was outlined by Ken Thompson, one of the founders of modern computing, in the lecture he gave when he accepted the Turing Award in 1983.[29] It stands as one of the establishing artefacts of computing security and has weathered the test of time: if there is one work cited in this book that I would recommend all readers follow, it is Thompson's. In his talk (which he subsequently published), he describes how careful placing of malicious code in the C standard compiler could lead to vulnerabilities (his specific example is in account login code) that are not only undetectable by those without access to the source code but also not removable. The final section of the paper is entitled "Moral", and Thompson starts with these words:

> **"The moral is obvious. You can't trust code that you did not totally create yourself. (Especially code from companies that employ people like me.) No amount of source-level verification or scrutiny will protect you from using untrusted code".**

---

[27]Failures in the flight software for Boeing's 737 MAX 8 aircraft are believed to have caused two crashes, leading to the deaths of 346 people.
[28]Abate, 2017.
[29]Thompson, 1984.

However, as he goes on to point out, there is nothing special about this compiler:

> **"I could have picked on any program-handling program such as an assembler, a loader, or even hardware microcode. As the level of program gets lower, these bugs will be harder and harder to detect. A well-installed microcode bug will be almost impossible to detect".**

These are the problems that we need to consider whenever we think about computer systems. Thompson uses the word *trust*, though he does not define it. But it is clear from his description of the problem that we could choose almost any definition of the word, and his statements would still hold true.

It is for the reasons noted by Thompson that open source software, firmware, and hardware are so vital to the field of computer security and to our task of defining and understanding what *trust* means in the context of computing. We will examine issues around open source—and how distributed trust in the open source community can work—in a later chapter. However, without the ability to look at the source code of all the layers of software and hardware on which you are running code, you can have only reduced trust that what you are running is what you think you should be running, whether you have performed formal verification on it or not.

The Importance of Systems

Throughout this book, we have talked about computer systems. In Chapter 3, we offered a definition, of which the initial statement was:

> **A system is a set of components—for example, hardware, software, firmware, data, human users—which can be considered as a single entity for the purposes of one or more specific architectural views of abstractions.**

This, and the broader issue of non-decomposability, will be useful when we consider the importance of trust relationships. However, in order to understand some of the problems around trust within systems made up of computers, or within the components of computers that are considered, when composed, as *systems*, we need to consider in more detail what computer systems look like.

System Design

While we have neither the space nor the need to perform a full examination of computer systems design—a whole field of research and endeavour of its own—there are nevertheless some core concepts and considerations that we need to consider and understand as they have—or can have—a direct bearing on the trust relationships between components and systems.

Those designing computer systems—typically known as *architects* of one type or another (systems architects, software architects, cloud architects, security architects, et al.)—tend to talk about *layers* when they discuss or describe the various components in which they are interested. Layers are important because it is well-nigh impossible for any one person to hold the details in their head of all the various components that form a modern computer system. Nor is it likely that any single person will be expert in enough of the various fields required to build all of the components to break each one down in detail. This is generally fine, however, as one of the key characteristics of modern computer systems is the extent to which the various interfaces are carefully defined and standardised precisely to allow the abstraction of what makes a particular system to be safely applied, and the expectations of the behaviours at each level of the system to be understood and managed. Often, a set of component layers are applied in standard or at least similar ways to create what is known as a *stack*—the best known of these probably being a *network stack*. To give us an idea of some of the types of abstractions employed when designing and then interfacing with systems, we will briefly examine three different sets of components, each made up (more or less) of separate layers. These examples will also provide us with use cases to employ when we want to look more deeply at the trust relationships within them and that can be created *to* them.

The Network Stack

Our first example is the network stack. When a process running on a computer wishes to send some data to a process on another computer, it employs a network stack. The network stack takes the data to be sent, packages it up, and sends it through a well-defined set of layers—basically abstractions of sets of behaviours—all the way to an actual physical component that translates the data into electronic pulses on a wire or light pulses on a fibre optic cable.[1] There are two standard models to represent the network stacks used in most modern computer systems: the Internet Protocol[2] and OSI[3] models (Figure 5.1 and Figure 5.2, respectively).

That there are two different models does not mean that different instances of a network stack are produced to one specification or the other: it is more that one of the two models will typically be chosen when describing the operations

---

[1]Other media of transmission are possible. The descriptions and definitions of the various steps are so well-known and well-developed that a specification for sending packets using pigeons has been proposed as an April Fool's joke: IP over Avian Carriers (IPoAC). See Waitzman, 1990 for details (though two further versions, superseding the initial version, have also been proposed at the time of writing).

[2]Postel (ed.), 1981.

[3]International Organization for Standardization, 1994.

of a system or specific stack. The abstraction(s) appropriate for any particular discussion or architectural view will be selected, though sometimes it may be helpful to use both at different points in the same conversation. The actual components employed do not change—and given the differences in the models (not least the different numbers of layers), it should come as no surprise that there continues to be discussion as to exactly what components fit into which layer(s) for each model.

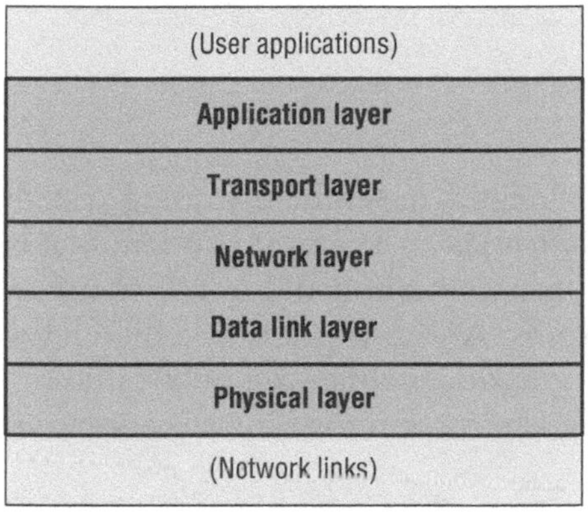

| (User applications) |
| Application layer |
| Transport layer |
| Network layer |
| Data link layer |
| Physical layer |
| (Notwork links) |

Figure 5.1: Internet Protocol suite layers.

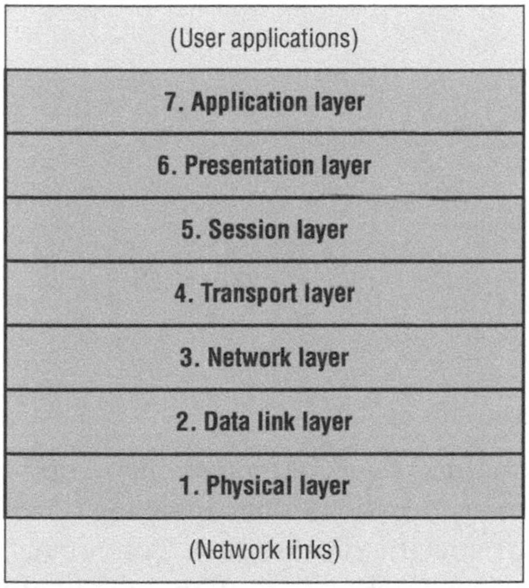

| (User applications) |
| 7. Application layer |
| 6. Presentation layer |
| 5. Session layer |
| 4. Transport layer |
| 3. Network layer |
| 2. Data link layer |
| 1. Physical layer |
| (Network links) |

Figure 5.2: OSI layers.

In each model, the different layers are conceptually responsible for different tasks, and it is generally possible, when sending data, for a layer (for instance, the Session layer in the OSI model) to pass the data to the layer directly below it (the Transport layer in the same model) according to a known set of specifications. In the case of receiving data, the lower layer can pass the data up to the layer immediately above it in the same way. In both sending and receiving cases, the passing layer should "know" that the other layer will "do the right thing" with the data: e.g., process it, drop it (where appropriate), or raise an error. The words "know" and "do the right thing" are in quotation marks for good reason here: although the expected actions may be well-defined in the general literature, there is (as elsewhere) less emphasis on what we define as *trust* than we need in order to start making any statements about relationships. This lack of clarity is a recurring problem—with a few notable exceptions—to which we will return.

Linux Layers

Linux (specifically GNU/Linux,[4] but we will refer to the entire operating system by the more common *Linux* or as a *Linux system*) is an operating system that is based on the Linux kernel and can run on many common and not so common hardware platforms and silicon architectures. Android phones, which have approximately 70% market share[5] of the worldwide mobile/cell phone market, run versions of Linux. A common layering abstraction for Linux is shown in Figure 5.3.

	user applications
User mode	low-level system components
	C standard library
Kernel mode	Linux kernel
Hardware	

Figure 5.3: Linux layering.

Any modern operating system—including Linux—is, of course, made up of myriad different components, and there are many occasions when breaking down these layers into more detail is required for specific discussions. Conversely, there are occasions when even the high-level abstractions are all that are likely required. An example would be a conversation about the architectural impact of siting a component in *user space* or *userland* (where it runs in User Mode) or *kernel space* (where it runs in Kernel Mode). Typically, there is a lot of computational overhead associated with context switches, where the system needs to transition between user space and kernel space, so a more detailed

---

[4]Stallman, 2019.
[5]StatCounter Global Stats, 2020.

definition may not be required: this level of abstraction is entirely appropriate in this context. Equally, Linux systems will (almost always) include a network stack, as described in the previous section. There is rarely a need to decompose the various layers of the network stack (regardless of model) when discussing the general operation of the system unless network-specific concepts are being discussed.[6]

Virtualisation and Containers: Cloud Stacks

Our final examples are also based on Linux and relate specifically to cloud computing. There's a joke that goes,

---

There is no cloud: it's just somebody else's computer.

Running applications *in the cloud* means running them on a computer system (host) that is either in a public cloud—owned and operated by a cloud service provider such as Microsoft (Azure), Amazon (AWS), or Alibaba (Alibaba Cloud)—or in a private cloud—typically run by a department of a large organisation, and dedicated to applications from that organisation. The application you run is often called a *workload* and can be of several types. You might, for instance, run an entire operating system within a virtual machine (VM), run an application within a container, or run a *serverless* application—all on the host.

In each case, the host needs to provide not just the resources for your workload to execute—CPU cycles, networking, storage, backup, administration, etc.—but also isolation for your workload so that other workloads cannot interfere with yours, or vice versa. We can refer to this as *workload-from-workload isolation*. The host also wants to ensure that the workloads executing on it cannot interfere with its operation—*host-from-workload isolation*. There is another type of isolation that is more difficult to achieve: *workload-from-host isolation*, where the workload has assurances that the host cannot interfere with its operations. We will return to all of these, how they may be achieved, and how they can be expressed in terms of trust relationships later on, but in order to do so, we need to have a basic understanding of layers in at least two of the standard cloud deployment scenarios: the Linux virtualisation stack (Figure 5.4) and the Linux container stack (Figure 5.5). It is worth noting that these are representative diagrams only: for instance, Middleware and Userspace components may be provided by different vendors, as may the Management Engine and CPU.

---

[6]Although there are times, such as when describing resource management of side-channel attacks, when such discussion may be required, even when the core components under examination are not directly related to networking.

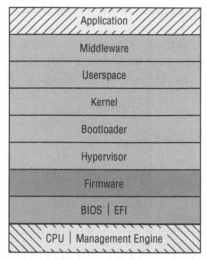

Figure 5.4: Linux virtualisation stack.

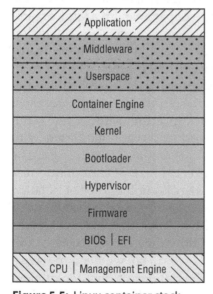

Figure 5.5: Linux container stack.

It is worth noting that these two stacks share the same layers at the bottom and top but that the actual implementations—at least for the top two or three layers—are generally different for instances of the different layers and even for different workloads. Also important to note is a point to which we will return once we start examining the different trust models associated with these stacks: the shadings in each stack represent the fact that different layers are likely to be supplied by different vendors. For example, in the virtualisation stack, the Middleware, Userspace, Kernel, Bootloader, and Hypervisor layers will often be provided by a single vendor (such as an operating system vendor), whereas the Firmware, BIOS/EFI, and CPU/Management Engine layers will all usually come from different vendors.

Other Axes of System Design

Layering models are not the only abstractions employed by those involved in system design. There is a whole discipline around the depiction and modelling of systems, of which the best-known set of "views" is the Unified Modeling Language[7] (UML), originally closely tied to object-oriented programming models. Many of these approaches are useful for understanding exactly how systems behave and interact. For our purposes, some of the most important issues to consider will be where components are deployed, which components have administrative control over others, and which are owned by which entities. In order to understand the trust relationships between systems and entities, we need to look in detail at some of the options for each of these and how they impact trust.

"Trusted" Systems

The idea that trust is important for systems design and implementation is not new. By 1985, the famous "Orange Book" (so named for its orange cover) had been published by the United States Department of Defense: it was officially titled *Trusted Computer System Evaluation Criteria*[8] and officially abbreviated to TCSEC. The TCSEC was a guide to the evaluation of computer systems to be used for sensitive or classified information. By 1993, Dorothy Denning issued a now almost equally famous critique of the Orange Book, entitled "A New Paradigm for Trusted Systems".[9] She starts her paper thus:

> The current paradigm for trusted computer systems holds that trust is a property of a system. It is a property that can be formally modeled, specified, and verified. It can be designed into a system using a rigorous design methodology. For high levels of assurance, the design methodology uses formal models and methods in order to prove that trust is present.[10]

These formal methods are exactly those we discussed in the previous chapter when looking at formal verification. In fact, Denning goes on to list eight shortcomings of the TCSEC, the fourth of which corresponds to a problem we identified:

---

[7]Object Management Group, 2017.
[8]Department of Defense, 1985.
[9]Denning, 1993.
[10]Denning, 1993, p. 36.

---
4. Real systems are vastly more complex than their security models.[11]

While this idea is important in terms of addressing one of the sets of problems with the TCSEC, her proposal of a new paradigm for trusted systems is even more so:

The current paradigm of treating trust as a property is inconsistent, with the way trust is actually established in the world. It is not a property, but rather an assessment that is based on experience and shared through networks of people in the world-wide market. It is a declaration made by an observer, rather than a property of the observed.[12]

Demolishing the idea that trust is an inherent property of a system and making it *relational* changed the way that systems designed for security would be thought of and would eventually bring about a new approach to evaluation by the US Government and associated organisations, known as the Common Criteria,[13] originally published in 2005. The approach of the Common Criteria is that users of a system can specify functional and assurance requirements, against which the system is then tested. A system is not considered "trusted" in this context: rather, it has been tested to particular requirements about how it is expected to behave.

This does not stop systems being referred to as "trusted". In Denning's description, it was people who decided what systems should be trusted, but we are interested in how systems interact with each other. This brings us to one of the central questions of this book: how can we define what we mean when we say that one (computer) system *trusts* another? As we have discussed throughout the earlier chapters, and as highlighted by Denning, we do not accept the premise that trust is a *property*, so any description needs to be relational. More than that, we need to consider what assurances we are expecting to be fulfilled. This is our first opportunity to explore our definition of trust.

Let us remind ourselves of that definition.

Trust is the assurance that one entity holds that another will perform particular actions according to a specific expectation.

First corollary: "Trust is always contextual".

Second corollary: "One of the contexts for trust is always time".

Third corollary: "Trust relationships are not symmetrical".

---

[11]Denning, 1993, p. 36.
[12]Denning, 1993, p. 38.
[13]Commoncriteriaportal.org, 2020.

We will be dealing later on with how assurances can be made and what mitigations may be possible: for now, we will concentrate on the expectation of what actions might be required. We will specify a context and note the asymmetry of trust relationships, but we will leave the context of time for examination later in the book. For our examples, we will use the stacks we examined earlier in the chapter and look at trust relationships between specific layers in those stacks. In all of the examples we will consider, there are already well-defined interfaces (usually APIs) to describe the functional behaviour of the different layers (or, as we might think of it, across the layer boundary): we are generally not interested in this type of behaviour. We care about behaviour (a set of actions) that is typically security-related and, though less likely to be defined, is important to achieve the correct and expected ("according to specific expectation") operation of the various parts of the system.

Trust Within the Network Stack

Our first example is from the network stack. We will use the Internet Protocol model (Figure 5.1) and, specifically, the trust relationship from the Internet layer to the Link layer in the case of transmission. When an instance of an Internet layer wishes to transmit packets directed to a specific IP address, it will use an instance of the Link layer—implementing Wi-Fi (one of the 802.11 family), for instance—to do so. There may be all sorts of routing required, and the basic functional requirement is that the packets received by the Link layer from the Internet layer are transmitted as received (subject to protocol requirements), but one of the expectations required to meet certain security contexts might be that the packets are not copied to another entity. It may be that such an action—copying to another entity—might be considered entirely appropriate by the designer of the Link layer (maybe for data backup or reliability checking), but from the point of the trustor, *in this particular context*, it is important that this possibility be explicitly excluded. The Internet layer's *trust relationship* to the Link layer includes this expectation of particular actions.

It is clear that, in this context, there is no concomitant trust relationship from the Link layer to the Internet layer. Though there might be occasions (though unlikely) for the reverse situation, when the Link layer does hold expectations that the Internet layer will not copy data, this would be data being received by the Link layer and sent "up" to the Internet layer, which is a different context to the one defined here.

Here we fill out a table that we will use when describing trust relationships. It includes both the trustor and the trustee, any contexts, a section for time-specific context concerns, actions, expectations, assurances, and mitigations. As noted previously, we will leave some of these sections for consideration later.

We can start filling in our table (Table 5.1) by noting that there are several contexts in which interactions occur between the layers. We are, of course, interested only in contexts that are relevant from the trustor (Internet layer) to the trustee (Link layer), but others might include integrity of data (transmitted or received), timeliness of data (transmitted or received), ordering of data (transmitted or received), and availability of error messages. Some of these may be considered functional (in particular, integrity and ordering) and others non-functional (for instance, availability of error messages); which contexts fall into which category will depend on the exact definition of the interface.

Table 5.1: Trust from Internet layer to Link layer in the IP suite

FROM (TRUSTOR)	INTERNET LAYER	TO (TRUSTEE)	LINK LAYER
Context(s)		Confidentiality of data transmitted.	
Time-specific		*Considered in later chapters.*	
Action(s)		Transmit packets as received from Internet layer.	
Expectation(s)		Transmit only to receiving party of routing rules.	
Assurance(s)		*Considered in later chapters.*	
Mitigation(s)		*Considered in later chapters.*	

Trust in Linux Layers

For our second example, we look at trust between layers in the Linux stack. We will examine the trust relationship between a user application and a low-level system component. In this case, we will be specific about the instances of each: we are interested in the bash shell (other shells exist, but we choose a specific one for this example) and the login program that the shell calls in order to log in users. We choose this example because it is exactly the one which Ken Thompson called out in his paper:

> **The actual bug I planted in the compiler would match code in the UNIX "login" command. The replacement code would miscompile the login command so that it would accept either the intended encrypted password or a particular known password.[14]**

The bash shell wants, in this context, to ensure that all authentications are valid and that only valid authentication attempts (a username and password that exist in the appropriate user database(s)) lead to a login. This is an example

---

[14]Thompson, Ken, 1984.

of a requirement that might actually be listed as functional in this context, given that the "login" application exists within a security context.

When considering context in this case, we may note that the action and the expectation we examine here represent only a subset of those likely to be considered within the "valid authentication" context. Another expectation might include "error logged on incorrect authentication attempt" and "user account locked after X number of failed password attempts". Equally, if different authentication methods are supported, one expectation might be "all users in group X required to provide a One-Time Password" – see Table 5.2.

Table 5.2: Trust from the bash shell to the login program

FROM (TRUSTOR)	BASH SHELL	TO (TRUSTEE)	LOGIN PROGRAM
Context(s)		Valid authentication.	
Time-specific		*Considered in later chapters.*	
Action(s)		Processing of login data.	
Expectation(s)		Only valid user + password sets lead to login.	
Assurance(s)		*Considered in later chapters.*	
Mitigation(s)		*Considered in later chapters.*	

Trust in Cloud Stacks

The two examples we have looked at so far have both involved trust relationships from components in "higher" layers calling "down" into "lower" layers, but trust contexts can exist in the other direction as well. Here, we will consider the trust relationships in two directions around the same actions. The entities we will consider are the kernel and the hypervisor from the Linux virtualisation case (Figure 5.6). At first glance, these two layers are separated by another layer—the bootloader—but this is an example where time plays a role. Unsurprisingly, given its name, the bootloader's role is to manage the booting of the kernel. The picture we are looking at is, in fact, a simplified one; and what we see here, above the hypervisor, are the layers that make up the *guest*—the workload instance owned by the tenant. Although there seem to be many layers shown, the reality is, in fact, *more* complex, and the exact makeup of each layer depends on the implementation. A more accurate version (for one implementation) might replace "Hypervisor" with "host bootloader + host kernel + host VMM".[15] The example shown assumes that the Hypervisor layer is provided by the same vendor as the guest layers upon which the tenant runs their application.

---

[15]Virtual Memory Manager.

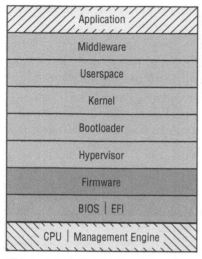

Figure 5.6: A Simple Cloud Virtualisation Stack.

The Hypervisor layer provides resources to the Kernel layer, allowing it to execute the layers above. The hypervisor also manages both workload-from-workload isolation and host-from-workload isolation. At a simplified level, the Kernel layer relies on the Hypervisor layer to service requests (*system calls*, or *syscalls*) for resources, whether they be storage, networking, GPU, or just the CPU cycles the guest needs in order to execute.

Now let us start filling in our table (Table 5.3) dealing with one context of the trust relationship that the Kernel layer has to the Hypervisor layer—syscalls processing—and, specifically, their processing in a timely manner. Although this is not a security-specific requirement, there are definitely occasions where a lack of such timely processing might be considered a security issue.

We should, by now, recognise that other contexts of trust from the Kernel layer to the Hypervisor layer may be available, as may other actions and expectations within the context we have chosen to examine. For instance, the Kernel layer may have actions and expectations around the provision of sufficient CPU clock cycles to perform the processing required, or that the Hypervisor layer will provide integrity protection for the memory of the guest kernel from tampering by other workloads on the host. Similar contexts may exist in the other direction, and we will not necessarily call them out for every trust relationship that we examine from now on.

Table 5.3: Trust from kernel to hypervisor

FROM (TRUSTOR)	KERNEL (GUEST KERNEL)	TO (TRUSTEE)	HYPERVISOR
Context(s)		Syscalls processing.	
Time-specific		*Considered in later chapters.*	
Action(s)		Syscalls processed.	
Expectation(s)		Syscalls processed in a timely manner.	
Assurance(s)		*Considered in later chapters.*	
Mitigation(s)		*Considered in later chapters.*	

Table 5.4, and our second trust relationship, is that from the hypervisor to the kernel. It may seem that the only important trust relationship is in the other direction, but there are definitely aspects of trust in the relationship from the Hypervisor layer to the Kernel layer. One such—and an important one from the point of view of security—could be labelled "lack of malicious intent toward other workloads". Given that the hypervisor has the job of protecting the rest of the host and any other workloads from interference (host-from-workload isolation and workload-from-workload isolation), then any attempt by the Kernel layer to request resources that might impact other workloads should lead the hypervisor to reconsider its trust relationship to the Kernel layer.

Table 5.4: Trust from hypervisor to kernel

FROM (TRUSTOR)	HYPERVISOR	TO (TRUSTEE)	KERNEL (GUEST KERNEL)
Context(s)		Workload-from-workload isolation.	
Time-specific		*Considered in later chapters.*	
Action(s)		Resources requested by Kernel layer.	
Expectation(s)		Kernel layer does not attempt to break workload-from-workload isolation.	
Assurance(s)		*Considered in later chapters.*	
Mitigation(s)		*Considered in later chapters.*	

Before we go on, let us reflect on these trust relationships briefly in terms of the human (or organisational) entities for which these two layers have agency, lest the description seems too abstract. Let us consider a cloud service provider

(CSP), that owns and operates host machines on which multiple tenants pay to run workloads. Tenant A wishes to ensure that its workload will be able to execute as expected on the CSP's host. This wish is expressed in the relationship from the Kernel layer—which is at the bottom of the stack of layers representing the tenant's workload (the guest)—to the hypervisor—which is at the top of the stack of layers representing the CSP's host. Equally, tenant B wishes the CSP to ensure that its workload is not negatively impacted by the behaviour of tenant A's workload (or any other tenant's workload). This wish is expressed in the relationship from the Hypervisor layer to the Kernel layer, as the CSP tries to ensure isolation. There are other levels at which we could abstract these relationships (we could just abstract at the host and guest layers, for instance). One of the aims of this chapter is understanding how these wishes, themselves trust relationships that may well be embodied in contracts or service-level agreements (SLAs), relate to more specific technical requirements.

Without these kinds of abstractions, modern computing would be next to impossible. Given the number of layers that are involved in deployments of software and hardware systems—from transistors to CPU instructions, all the way up to databases and web servers—the chances of anybody being able to hold in their head all the necessary information seems unlikely. Abstractions, then, are necessary. But as we have noted, most abstractions generally do not specify anything to do with trust or what trust might look like. This is unsurprising, and this lack of a trust definition can probably be traced back, at least in part, to the evolution of the Internet from the original set of mutually trusting systems. There are some areas of computing, however, where trust has been considered in some detail. The most obvious of these is the hardware root of trust—an issue that deserves, and will get, its own chapter, but that we will introduce here.

Hardware Root of Trust

There is a story oft-told within the IT security community: this story is so well-known, in fact, that uttering a single word, when casting judgement on a system or a design, can lead to instant understanding, and nodding—or shaking—of heads among the Enlightened, who will know that the speaker is noting a particular design or implementation failure. That word is *turtles*. The story goes like this.

Back in the days of popular public lectures, some time around the end of the nineteenth century or the beginning of the twentieth, a famous luminary (some say George Bernard Shaw, others William James, maybe it was someone else) was presenting to an audience of the general public. He (the lecturer is always a "he") spoke with great erudition about evolution, astronomy, physics, cosmology, and all manner of interesting topics. At the end of the lecture, as was his wont, he accepted questions from individual members of the public. He noticed a little old lady (the questioner is always a little old lady) who was waiting patiently to ask him a question. Once all of the other people had left, she approached him.

"That was a very interesting lecture", she told him.

"I'm glad you enjoyed it", he replied.

"Of course, it was all wrong", she continued.

Somewhat taken aback, the lecturer asked her for an example of something in his lecture that she felt was incorrect.

"Well, that bit about the Earth circling the sun, for a start", she retorted.

"What theory do you espouse, madam?"

"The Earth sits on the back of a giant turtle".

Sensing a possible fallacy in her argument, he responded, "But what supports the turtle?"

The little old lady regarded him with a withering look of disdain, "Well, everybody knows that it's turtles *all the way down*".

The point of the story as told within the context of security is not, of course, about cosmology but about the problems of infinite regression. When building a system that we need to secure as much as possible, each layer needs to trust—have a trust relationship to—the layer below it. But in the end—at the bottom—there must be a layer in which trust can reside. When we were describing the various operations and components associated with trust earlier in the book, we named this the *root of trust* because it needs to be at the root of the system we build—the basis or foundation on which all other layers are built. Typically, the root of trust is considered to reside in hardware. This is for a variety of reasons:

- Software is prone to the sorts of problems we considered earlier around provability.

- Hardware underpins software: it is what software runs on. Therefore, the lowest layer of a system, considered in reductive detail, is likely to be hardware.

- Hardware is what ultimately executes the instructions of the layers above it, so if there can be no trust in this layer (or set of layers), then there can be no trust in the system at all.

Life, of course, is not this simple: not only is considering hardware as a single layer overly simplistic, but we also need to remember that all hardware components above a very basic level of simplicity are, in fact, designed using software. We should also remember the issues around trust that were raised when we discussed the US government's attitude to Huawei and the hardware (and software) produced by the Chinese company and other vendors that might be considered subject to the influence of possibly unfriendly governments or state actors. On the whole, however, the considerations around trust in a running system in which we are most interested are such that denoting a single hardware component as a root of trust is either sufficient for the purposes of system design and implementation or at least the best we can achieve in the circumstances. When they are the latter, it is important to record that as a part of the documentation and description of the system.

Acceptance of this trusted root will almost always be based on its endorsement by one or more endorsing authorities. Examples might be the vendor and/or manufacturer of the component, a certification and testing body, and a standards body that came up with the specification to which certification and testing is performed. The Trusted Computing Group (TCG) is one such standards body, and a TPM (Trusted Platform Module) is an example of one such component.

In fact, TPMs are one of the most common roots of trust in modern computing. Their architecture, manufacture, and operating limits are well-defined, the technologies they use and the designs they embody are mature, and their cost is such that their presence in most general computing devices (such as laptops, desktops, and server systems) incorporate them by default on their motherboard. We will look in more detail at the specific capabilities that TPMs provide in a later chapter, but they allow for two very useful properties with regard to systems and trust: *measured boot* and *trusted boot* (sometimes known as *secure boot*). We will be careful with these terms and not capitalise them, as the TCG provides specifications for well-defined steps and standardisations, and our aim here is not to pick apart specific implementations but to understand the basic intentions of the processes and consider possible issues.

TPMs are not the only hardware roots of trust available to us: one other class of component, in particular, is worth our attention: hardware security modules (HSMs). HSMs were originally designed for military and government use and can generally offer a broader and deeper set of security assurances than TPMs. Of particular note are features around tampering: tamper-evidence, tamper-resistance, and tamper-responsiveness.

Tampering is a term that has slightly different usage from the standard meaning, in that it tends to imply that the damage done to a system or component was done with the intention that it not necessarily stop normal operation but alter it in such a way that the attacker could gain some advantage (often, but not always, snooping on activities being performed). This may have been the intention, but it may be that the damage did actually stop or at least affect normal operation, whether or not the attacker gained the advantage they were attempting. Tampering attacks are typically difficult to manage. From time to time, products will appear that are marketed as "tamper-proof". The problem with saying that any system is tamper-proof is that it clearly is not, particularly if you accept the second part of the definition that the system or component was altered to give the attacker some sort of advantage. This is one of those phrases, then, that should immediately raise concerns within a security context: there are no absolutes (or, at least, positive absolutes) in security, and it is impossible to be sure that something *can* be constructed to be tamper-proof, for the same reason that the adage that "any fool can create a cryptographic protocol that he/she can't break" is true: you cannot fully assess or forecast the skills and abilities of all future attackers of your system, and new technologies (such as quantum computing) may provide new opportunities for attackers.

The best options available to protect against tampering are those that HSMs may offer:

- *Tamper-evidence*: A property whereby attempts to tamper with the HSM are made clear through software or hardware controls (e.g., logging to a file, or an LED being illuminated)

- *Tamper-resistance*: A property whereby the designers of the HSM increase the protections against tampering (e.g., by providing a second casing inside the main external one)

- *Tamper-responsiveness*: A property whereby specific actions are performed if tampering is detected (e.g., deletion of cryptographic keys or disabling of particular functions)

Unlike TPMs, HSMs are separate physical components, rather than a single chip on a motherboard (the standard implementation of a TPM) and may be either local to the system using them (mounted, for example, inside the chassis, attached to a PCI slot) or remote (providing functionality via a network connection). Like TPMs, HSMs typically provide a range of cryptographic functions to be used by external parties. At their simplest, HSMs may provide little more than basic cryptographic functions—hashing, encryption, decryption, and key generation—and key storage. There are a number of standards and certifications that can be applied to HSMs and address specific capabilities, including dealing with tampering.

Although the range of functionality offered by TPMs has increased significantly with the TPM v1.2 specification, HSMs have long offered broader sets of capabilities than TPMs. While the simplest uses of HSMs include basic key creation, management, and manipulation (including use within cryptographic algorithms), some HSMs are more generally programmable, and it is possible to implement protocols and more complex functionality such as cryptographic signature creation and verification following RFC 5485.[16]

---

[16]Housley, 2009, superseded by Housley, 2018.

Given the broader capabilities of HSMs compared to TPMs, it would seem obvious to ask why the former are not the default option for cryptographic operations. The answer is that HSMs are both much (typically, orders of magnitude) more expensive than TPMs and also much more difficult to provision, program, and operate correctly. While HSMs—particularly those with the highest ratings according to the relevant specifications—remain the gold standard for hardware roots of trust for cryptographic key management, in particular, TPMs are cheaper, simpler to use, and more available. TPMs have the added benefit of being embedded into the system motherboard of a machine and therefore, better placed to provide a hardware root of trust functionality around system integrity (see the section Measured Boot and Trusted Boot).

Cryptographic Hash Functions

Before we look at the different processes, there is a tool in the security practitioner's repertoire whose use we need to understand: cryptographic hash functions. This is one of the cryptographic primitives that we noted in passing in Chapter 1, and it turns out to be a vital one in understanding many of the issues we are about to discuss. A cryptographic hash function, such as SHA-256 or MD5 (now superseded and deprecated for cryptographic uses as it is considered "broken") takes as input a set of binary data (typically as bytes) and gives as output a *hash* that is hopefully unique for each set of possible inputs. The length of the output—the hash—is typically the same for any pattern of inputs (for SHA 256, it is 256 bits, or 32 bytes). It should be computationally implausible (cryptographers hate the word "impossible") to work backward from the output hash to the input: this is why they are sometimes referred to as *one-way hash functions*. The phrase "hopefully unique" when describing the output is extremely important: if two inputs are discovered that yield the same output, the hash is said to have *collisions*. The reason MD5 has become deprecated is that it is now trivial to find collisions with commercially available hardware and software systems. Another important property is that even a tiny change in the message (e.g., changing a single bit) should generate a large change to the output (the *avalanche effect*).

What are hash functions used for, and why is the property of being lacking in collisions so important? The simplest answer to the first question is that hash functions are typically used to ensure that when someone hands you a piece of binary data (and all data in the world of computing can be described in binary format, whether it is text, an executable, a video, an image, or a complete database of data), it is what you expect. Comparing binary data directly is slow and arduous computationally, but hash functions are designed to be very quick. Given two files of several megabytes or gigabytes of data, you can produce hashes of them ahead of time and defer the comparisons to when you need them.[17]

---

[17]It is also generally easier to sign hashes of data, rather than large sets of data themselves—this happens to be important as one of the most common uses of hashes is for cryptographic (*digital*) signatures.

Indeed, given the fact that it is easy to produce hashes of data, there is often no need to have both sets of data. Let us say that you want to run a file, but before you do, you want to check that it really is the file you think you have and that no malicious actor has tampered with it. You can hash that file very quickly and easily, and as long as you have a copy of what the hash should look like, you can be fairly certain that you have the file you wanted. This is where the "lack of collisions" (or at least "difficulty in computing collisions") property of hash functions is important. If the malicious actor can craft a replacement file that shares the same hash as the real file, then the process of hashing is essentially useless.

In fact, there are more technical names for the various properties, and what I have described here mashes three important properties together. More accurately, these properties are as follows:

Pre-Image Resistance   If you have a hash, it should be difficult to find the message from which it was created, even if you know the hash function used.

Second Pre-Image Resistance   If you have a message, it should be difficult to find another message that, when hashed, generates the same hash.

Collision Resistance   It should be difficult to find any two messages that generate the same hash.

Collision resistance and second pre-image resistance sound like the same property at first glance but are subtly (and importantly) different. Pre-image resistance says that if you already have a message, finding another with a matching hash should be hard; whereas collision resistance should make it hard for you to find any two messages that will generate the same hash, and is a much harder property to fulfil in a hash function.

Let us go back to our scenario of a malicious actor trying to exchange a file (with a hash that we can check) with another one. Now, to use cryptographic hashes "in the wild" (i.e., out there in the real world with actual implementations), there are some important and difficult provisos that need to be met. More paranoid readers may already have spotted some of them. In particular:

■ You need to have assurances that the copy of your hash has *also* not been subject to tampering.

■ You need to have assurances that the entity performing the hash performs and reports it correctly.

■ You need to have assurances that the entity comparing the two hashes reports the result of that comparison correctly.

These three reasons all sound like the bases for trust relationships, and they are: in order to build a process on top of hash function calculations, trust relationships encapsulating these three requirements must be in place to one or more entities. It should come as a relief to discover that one of the functions of a TPM is to provide exactly the functionality required to support all three of these trust relationships; as long as we accept the assurances of the endorsing authorities of the TPM(s) we wish to use, we are now in a position to start building the processes of measured boot and trusted boot that we wanted to consider.

Measured Boot and Trusted Boot

We will reuse our description of the layers in the Linux virtualisation stack depicted in Figure 5.6 to consider what measured boot and trusted boot aim to achieve. We will concentrate on the bottom four layers: CPU/Management Engine, BIOS/EFI, Firmware, and Hypervisor. Here, as before, we should note that the abstraction we have chosen is not a perfect match for this discussion, but it should provide sufficient detail for us to understand the process. Consider the addition of a layer *just* above the CPU/management engine, where we interpose a TPM and some instructions for how to perform one of our two processes. Once the system starts to boot, the TPM is triggered and then starts its work (alternative roots of trust such as HSMs might also be used, but we will use TPMs, the most common root of trust in this context, as our example).

In both cases, the basic flow starts with the TPM performing a measurement of the BIOS/EFI layer. This measurement involves checking the binary instructions to be carried out by this layer and then creating a cryptographic hash of the binary image. The resultant hash is then stored in one of several *PCR (platform configuration register)* slots in the TPM. These can be thought of as pieces of memory that can be read later on, either by the TPM for its purposes or by entities external to the TPM, but that cannot be changed once they have been written. This provides assurances that once a value is written to a PCR by the TPM, it can be considered constant for the lifetime of the system until power-off or reboot.

After measuring the BIOS/EFI layer, the next layer (Firmware) is measured. In this case, the resulting hash is combined with the previous hash (which was stored in the PCR slot), and then the combined hash is stored in a PCR slot. The process continues until all of the layers involved have been measured and the results of the hashes stored. There are (sometimes quite complex) processes to set up the original TPM values (we have omitted some of the more low-level steps in the process for simplicity) and allow (hopefully authorised) changes to the layers for upgrading or security patching, for example. What this process— *measured boot*—allows is for entities to query the TPM after the process has completed and check whether the values in the PCR slots correspond to the expected values precalculated with *known good* versions of the various layers—that is, prechecked versions whose provenance and integrity have already been established. Various protocols exist to allow parties *external* to the system to check the values (e.g., via a network connection) that the TPM attests to being correct: the process of receiving and checking such values from an external system is known as *remote attestation* and will feature prominently in later discussions, particularly with regard to cloud computing.

This process—measured boot—allows us to find out whether the underpinnings of our system—some of the lowest layers—are what we think they are. But what if they are not? Measured boot, unsurprisingly, given the name, only measures but does not perform any other actions. The alternative, *trusted boot*, goes a step further. When a trusted boot process is performed, the process not only measures each value but also performs a check against a known good value at the same time. If the check fails, then the process will halt, and the booting of the system will fail. This may sound like a rather extreme approach to take to a system, but sometimes it is absolutely the right approach. The failure of a trusted boot process is a likely indicator of a compromised system. Therefore, it is better that a compromised system not be available than for you to establish a trust relationship based on flawed expectations.

There is an interesting point here, which is that this is an example of a transitive trust relationship. Entity A (the trustor) is trusting Entity B (the TPM and associated process) to block the creation of a trust relationship to Entity C (a particular instantiation of the Linux virtualisation stack) if Entity B believes it to be flawed. This may often be exactly the correct behaviour, as it may well be that Entity B has better information about possible failure or compromises of Entity C than Entity A is able to have. It is probably unrealistic, for example, to expect Entity A to hold measurements for all the possible systems to which it may connect. This is another point to which we will return when we consider remote attestation servers within cloud computing.

There is a major problem that we must address before moving on, however, which is that trusting Entity B to say—*attest*—that Entity C should not be trusted should not automatically mean that we can also accept Entity B's assurances (based, for instance, on a lack of failure in a process) that Entity C *should* be trusted. This is the problem with the nomenclature *trusted boot* and, even worse, *secure boot*. Both imply that an absolute, objective property of a system has been established: it is "trusted" or "secure". Obviously, it would be unfair to expect the designers of such processes to name them after the failure states—"untrusted boot" or "insecure boot"—but unless the trustor can establish a very clear transitive trust relationship to the attesting entity *for all the contexts of all the trust relationships to be established*, then we can make no stronger assertions. We can take this issue of contexts further: there is an enormous temptation to take a system that has gone through a trusted boot process and to label it a "trusted system", where *the very best* assertion we can make is that the particular layers measured in the measured and/or trusted boot process have been asserted to be those that the process expected to be present. Such a process says nothing at all about the fitness of the layers to provide assurances of behaviour or about the correctness (or fitness to provide assurances of behaviour) of any subsequent layers on top of those.

We should note that designers of TPMs are quite clear about what is being asserted and that assertions about trust should be made carefully and sparingly. Unluckily, however, the complexities of systems, the generally low level of understanding of trust, and the complexities of context and transitive trust that we have just identified make it very easy for designers and implementers of systems to do the wrong thing and assume that any system that has successfully performed a trusted boot process can be considered "trusted".

It is also extremely important to remember that TPMs, as hardware roots of trust, offer us one of the best mechanisms we have for establishing a chain of trust in systems that we may be designing or implementing.

Certificate Authorities

We already spent some time considering certificate authorities (CAs) in Chapter 2 when discussing endorsing authorities and when considering different definitions of trust in Chapter 1. We promised to return to the subject later, as CAs are such a core part of how trust is considered in many situations. In order to understand how CAs work, we first need to divert our attention briefly to public-key cryptography, on which public key infrastructures (of which CAs are an important constituent part) are constructed.

The mathematical principles behind public-key cryptography are beyond the scope of this book, but public keys are based on asymmetric cryptography. One of the key principles of asymmetric cryptography is that it is possible to create a *key pair* with two parts: a *private key* and a *public key*. The private key is secret (kept private), while the public key can be shared (made public). *Cipher text* (encrypted data, whether actually text or not) encrypted using the private key can be decrypted using the public key, and vice versa. This means that if I encrypt a document with a private key, you can use the associated public key to check that I (the holder of the private key) was the entity who performed the encryption. Equally, if you send me a document encrypted using the same public key, only I (the holder of the private key) can decrypt it.[18] These basic operations allow an important set of associated operations to be achieved, including digital signatures, certificates, and cryptographic session key establishment for protocols such as TLS and HTTPS.

---

[18]In fact, in both cases, it is unusual to encrypt the actual document with the public or private key, as asymmetric cryptography is quite slow. Encryption of cryptographic hashes or *session keys* is the more normal usage of public-private key pairs.

The first point we should make about the phrase *certificate authority* (CA) is that it is often used in two very different ways, or, more specifically, to refer to two different types of entities. The key characteristic of a CA from the point of view of trust relationships is that it is an endorsing authority: "a human or organisational entity to whom a trust relationship has been established", by our definition. In both uses of the term, this characteristic is preserved, but the type of entity being considered differs. A CA issues certificates attesting to the identity of the entity to which the certificate was issued and from whence other trust relationships are typically derived, but the basis for the endorsement differs in the two usages of the term. We can give the two types of CAs the labels *Internet certificate authorities* and *local certificate authorities*.

Internet Certificate Authorities

When we refer to Internet CAs, the sort of entities we are describing are those whose creation was outlined in Chapter 2: organisations set up to issue certificates to other parties such as companies that wish to show web site visitors that the system to which their browser is connected is owned and operated by them, the company to whom the certificate was issued. The root of trust for such an Internet CA is the private key associated with the *root certificate* for the CA. Each certificate that the CA issues is associated with this root certificate through a chain of trust whereby a series of different CAs signs the next, starting with the root certificate and ending at the certificate issued to the party requesting it. Typically, the requesting party will create a *self-signed certificate*, which it then sends to the CA, and which, after (hopefully exhaustive) checking, the CA endorses through the certificate chain that it issues to the requester, whose final certificate is the self-signed one, now fully endorsed.

It should be fairly obvious that the private key and root certificate for a global CA are (as suggested by the name) at the root of the trust chain and therefore need to have both their integrity and their confidentiality protected. This is one of the most common uses for HSMs in the infrastructure of the Internet. The credibility (and associated authority) of an endorsing authority is good only as long as the confidentiality of the private key is maintained, because as soon as another party has access to it (or the ability to use it to sign other certificates, making valid, but ill-endorsed certificate chains), there is no way to be certain whether or not any certificate issued by that CA is valid (at least, from the date that the private key's confidentiality was compromised, if the date can be established, and sometimes not even then). Access to root keys—and other core artefacts in the CAs' infrastructure—must be extremely carefully controlled; the processes and mechanisms for generating, using, and revoking them are subject to elaborate *key ceremonies*, so named because of the complexity and number of steps that need to be performed by named and checked individuals or roles.

Given the role that Internet CAs hold in securing transactions and operations across the Internet, the benefits to a malicious attacker in managing to gain access to signing capabilities should not be underestimated. The root *public* certificates of many (some suggest too many) Internet CAs are embedded within most web browsers and are used to check the identity of and establish encrypted connections to banks, government agencies, merchants, suppliers, software vendors, video conferences services, and beyond. In September 2011, it was discovered that DigiNotar, a Dutch Internet CA, had been subject to a successful attack on its system and that fraudulent certificates were being issued in its name. Digi-Notar's operations were taken over by the Dutch government, and by the end of the month, the company was bankrupt. The compromise and subsequent failure of the company led to web browsers having to remove certificates issued by DigiNotar from their list of trusted certificates. Various theories were put forward as to the identity of the party compromising DigiNotar, but state actors were among the plausible candidates.

In the absence of specific proofs of fraudulent use—that is, negative proof of security—there is, as we noted when we cited Gambetta in Chapter 2, no way to be assured of security, as there can be no *positive* proof of security. This is particularly true for Internet CAs, where the trust placed in them as endorsing authorities is entirely based on human trust relationships, corporate and individual. Alongside the legal and standards-based assurances that underpin the functioning of Internet CAs, their reputation is an important asset because once it erodes, the extent to which customers will be willing to form trust relationships to them will significantly reduce.

Local Certificate Authorities

The other type of certificate authority to examine we will label *local*. By this, we do not necessarily mean local geographically, but rather with respect to the scope of use of the issued certificates. Our use of *local* here is more akin to the use of *local* when discussing variables in programming languages but more specific: the use of the certificates is scoped by the context within which they are employed. Rather than using an Internet CA, whose context is generally endorsing companies or organisations in the public sphere and in terms of web- or more broadly Internet-based certificates, there are many contexts where a different type of authority is more appropriate.

Let us examine a set of public key infrastructures (PKIs) that many of us use every day—debit and credit card associations—and, specifically, when we make a chip payment at a vendor. We will use a somewhat simplified description of the process, which should allow us to understand what is going on. When we wish to make a purchase, we present the card to the vendor, who (in the absence of contactless payment options) inserts our credit or debit card into a reader. The reader attempts to sign details of the purchase transaction using a certificate that is kept within the chip on the card. We are usually expected to enter a PIN as part of the transaction process, which is an authentication step to allow the *issuer bank*[19] to perform two-factor authentication, where we have to provide two pieces of information: something we have (the physical card) and something we know (the PIN). Once this has been accepted, the chip is able to sign the transaction, which is sent to the *acquirer bank*, typically the bank with whom the vendor does their banking. Given that we expect credit and debit cards to work globally these days, a little thought might lead us to expect that this process would require every acquirer bank to hold a public key for every issuer bank that issues cards, which would be an enormous undertaking. Luckily, this is where credit and debit card associations such as Visa and Mastercard come in. Issuer banks can become members of the association, and when they issue a credit or debit card, they use a certificate issued to them by the card association to sign that individual card's certificate.[20] This means that when the signed transaction is received by the acquirer bank, they can check the *certificate chain* (the chain of trust formed through the various certificates signing each other) and ensure that its root is a valid one from a card association of which they are a member, and should then be happy to accept the transaction.

This example shows not only the complexity of such systems—PKI is notoriously difficult to set up and manage—but also that such *local* arrangements make sense in the scope of particular contexts (even where the geographical context is obviously global). Internet CAs are generally not set up to perform the sort of financial due diligence required to set up and run a multi-billion payment reconciliation network, which is best managed by dedicated systems and networks. If nothing else, the trust relationships required by the various parties are very different in the two cases.

There can be other, much smaller examples of local CAs. Imagine that you are creating a multi-component, distributed system where the various components need to establish some sort of trust relationships to each other and will need to establish encrypted connections. The obvious way to do this is with certificates: but who should sign them? The answer is that if the scope of the system is the context within which the certificates are to be used, then a simple, local CA may be entirely appropriate. In this sort of context, there is likely to be little need for the huge process required for a larger CA such as an Internet CA. As long as you can protect the root private key and certificate from possible misuse by actors identified in your threat model, this may be all the process and infrastructure that you require, though consideration of questions such as how to manage revocation of certificates should always be undertaken.

---

[19]Some associations, such as American Express, issue cards directly rather than through issuer banks.

[20]This is also somewhat of a simplification of exactly how the various certificates fit together—there are more certificates and keys involved in the actual process.

It is in systems and contexts such as these where the use of the phrase *certificate authority* to denote the (fairly basic) process of managing what may be a single private key and certificate can lead to confusion. Most people, hearing the phrase, assume that an *Internet* CA is the subject under discussion. This confusion may be further fuelled if any of the components of your system need to talk to *external* systems, acting, for instance, as a web server on the Internet. In this case, some components may require two (or more) separate certificates derived from different and distinct certificate chains—one being your local CA and the other being an Internet CA.

While this may seem confusing, let us step back and look at why the need for separate certificates fits exactly with our view of trust. We have two trust contexts that are being managed:

The Internal Context   Here, each component needs to be assured that the other component with which it is communicating is part of the same system. For each communication of this type, the component needs to form a trust relationship to the other component, and this is where the local CA acts as an endorsing authority, allowing the basis of trust. This basis may not solely be identity: capabilities information may be included in the certificate, signalling, for example, that a particular component should be trusted to perform DNS lookups and another for database or file access.

The External Context   Here, one or more external systems wish to communicate with a component of your system. The external system does not need to know or form a trust relationship to any other components of your system: just the one that is presenting an external interface. And as the external system needs no knowledge of the internal trust relationships within the system, it needs no knowledge of the PKI managed by your system's local CA. It does, however, need to establish the identity (and, optionally, permitted capabilities) of your system, so it needs access to a certificate whose chain it can check. This is more likely to be a fit to the services provided by an Internet CA. If this is the case, you will need to acquire such a certificate and ensure that it is associated with your system.

This distinction between what we might think of as the "inner" and "outer" lives of systems will turn out to be important in our discussions later on, and we will cover it in much more depth in *Chapter 12, Trust Domains*.

It is worth noting the TPMs can be used as part of a system within either a local CA or an Internet CA. TPMs generally come with an endorsement key (EK) certificate, which is embedded in the TPM by the manufacturer. Once the TPM is added to a platform (such as a motherboard), a platform certificate may be added, typically by the original equipment manufacturer (OEM). These can be considered part of a local CA, but it is also possible to *provision* keys and certificates into a TPM as the *owner* of the system (processes and protocols are built into the TPM in an attempt to stop unauthorised provisioning at some later point in time). The addition of keys and certificates from a different local CA—such as a CSP—using these processes allows a trust pivot, allowing the TPM to act as a root of trust for a different trust domain (see Chapter 3 for definitions of *trust pivot* and *trust domain*).

Before we move from the question of local CAs, there is one more issue that we should address: "Are self-signed certificates always bad?" If you have ever deployed a system including a local CA of the type outlined here, you may have come across a problem with auditors or security experts. The problem tends to be with the root certificate that acts as the basis for the local CA. As you—whether an individual or organisation—are acting as the endorsing authority, that certificate is not, by definition, signed by an external authority (by which people usually mean an Internet CA). Even if those who will be using the system accept your or your organisation's assurances as to the provenance of the components (in other words, they have a trust relationship to you in the appropriate trust context), they may question the use of self-signed certificates.

This situation can be thought of as an example of what linguists refer to as *hyper-correction*, where we have a rule so firmly ingrained into our usage that we misuse it. A standard example from the English language is when we are taught that "correct grammar" requires us to say "You and I can go to the beach" rather than "You and me can go to the beach". This ingrains a tendency in us to eschew saying "you and me", even when it is correct; so rather than saying, "He came gaming with you and me" (which is correct), you will often hear people saying, "He came gaming with you and I" (which is incorrect).[21] To return to our context, security professionals have been drilled so frequently with the mantra that "you should never accept a self-signed certificate" that they forget, or do not understand, that what is really being asserted is that "you should never form a trust relationship to an entity on the web in the context of communications confidentiality and integrity where that entity presents a self-signed certificate as part of the TLS protocol handshake" (though, to be fair, this is a bit of a mouthful). Where there is a good trust relationship (in the appropriate context) to an endorsing authority for the certificates being used in a system, the use of self-signed certificates should be considered entirely acceptable.

Root Certificates as Trust Pivots

We have now spent enough time discussing root certificates issued by certificate authorities (whether Internet CAs or local CAs) and how they are used to allow signed certificates further down the certificate chain to consider how

---

[21]To check correct usage in this case, the easy rule is to take out the "you and" and see whether "me" or "I" sounds correct. "He came gaming with I" is clearly incorrect in this context, unless your local dialect allows this construction, which I heard not infrequently growing up in Somerset in the United Kingdom.

certificates can be used by components acting as trust pivots to transfer or add a trust relationship to another entity. In our earlier example, the combination of the credit or debit card, the certificate on the chip (and associated certificate chain), the card reader, and the protocol established by the card association allowed trust to be established in the ability of the card's issuer bank to cover the transaction being made to the acquirer bank. More specifically, in terms relevant to our discussion, the card association has an existing trust relationship to the issuer bank and their ability to cover the transaction, and a trust pivot allows that trust relationship to be transferred to the acquirer bank.

Another, more common example is Internet CAs' *raison d'être*: the use of certificates to allow you to form a trust relationship to a web server acting as an agent for an organisation on the web. When the web server's owner applies for a certificate, the Internet CA performs checks allowing it to ascertain that the applicant is who they assert themselves to be. If these checks pass, then the Internet CA establishes a trust relationship to the web server owner and issues a certificate that basically asserts this fact (further assertions may be made but are not necessarily required). When I point my web browser at the site operated by the organisation, my browser uses the issued certificate, its knowledge of a public root certificate from the Internet CA (which is generally bundled with the browser), and any other relevant protocols (such as checking for revocation and performing a TLS handshake) to allow me to form a trust relationship to the web server's owner (assuming, of course, that the web server has not been compromised).

What we should be careful of in these situations is exactly what that trust relationship means—what its context is. The checks that Internet CAs perform tend not to be exposed as part of the process, and there is a real risk that we make assumptions about the scope of the trust relationship we have formed based on the endorsement of the Internet CA. In other words, we assume contexts beyond what are actually being asserted and that are outside the scope of the trust pivot, which can only act in contexts associated with the trust anchor. The standard example is the assumption that if my browser accepts a certificate from a web server, I can trust the owner of that site to act as a vendor of goods to be shipped to my home. It *may* be that the web server's owner can be trusted in this way (it may be appropriate to form such a trust relationship to the owner of the web server), but I should not do this solely on the basis of the trust pivot. Unless I can verify that the Internet CA has taken the following steps, I have no basis to form such a trust relationship:

1. Established a trust relationship to the web server's owner in this context.

2. Made such an assertion as one of the contexts of the issued certificate.

Beyond these issues is the question of whether I have a trust relationship to the Internet CA in the context of it being an appropriate referrer of entities in this context. The claims that Internet CAs make are rarely considered explicitly, and even the ability to ascertain which certificate chain (to which Internet CA) a browser is using to check and "approve" a web server is generally opaque to users. These complexities are part and parcel of our human trust relationships to technology and tend to be transferred to our design and implementation of computer-to-computer trust relationships. Understanding the role that CAs play as one of the underpinnings for trust is an important step in having informed conversations about trust.

The following figures show an example of a trust pivot. In Figure 5.7, an entity, C5, exists within trust domain C. By means of a trust pivot process, C5 moves (Figure 5.8) into trust domain B, where it now resides at the completion of the process (Figure 5.9).

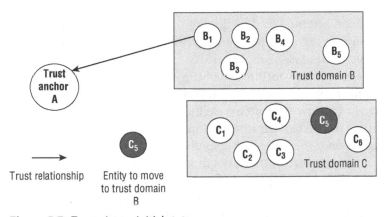

Figure 5.7: Trust pivot—initial state.

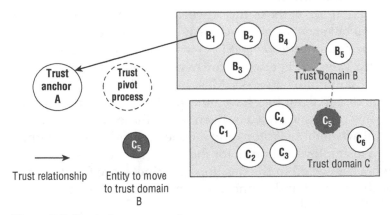

Figure 5.8: Trust pivot—processing.

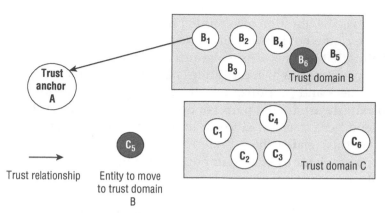

Figure 5.9: Trust pivot—complete.

The Temptations of "Zero Trust"

Zero-trust networks are an attempt to describe an architectural approach that addresses the disappearance of macro-perimeters within the network. The phrase seems to have appeared around 2010, as people realised that inserting a firewall or two between one network and another has little effect when network traffic flows across an organisation—or between different organisations. They are very complex and do not follow one or two easily defined or defended routes, taking, instead, multiple routes to their destination. This problem is exacerbated when the routes are not only multiple but also virtual. At one level, of course, *all* network traffic is virtual; but in the days of simpler network topologies, ingress and egress of traffic all took place (allegedly) through a single physical box, even if there were multiple routing rules, and, therefore, this was a good place to put controls. Those days of simple network topologies are long gone. Now, when multiple components may be hosted on the same physical host as VMs or Linux containers, much of the traffic between them may never reach the physical network at all but stay "local", never leaving the host on which they are executing. *Software-defined networking* (SDN) may route packets around in previously unexpected ways, and networks are overwhelmingly porous.

Consider "internal" corporate networks. Most have desktops, laptops, and mobile phones connected to them that have multiple links to other networks that do not traverse any corporate firewalls. Even where those links *do* traverse the corporate firewall, when those laptops and mobile phones leave the corporate network and go to employees' homes for the night, the devices—and the USB drives that were connected to the desktop machines—are free to roam the hinterlands of the Internet and connect to almost any global connected system with no effective controls.

However, this new reality addresses not only end-point devices but also components of the infrastructure that are much more likely to have—and need—multiple connections to different other components, which may or may not be on the corporate network. The rise of *cloud computing* further means that while some of the infrastructural components start on the "internal" network, they may well migrate during their lifetime to a completely different network. The rise of micro-services further exacerbates the problem, as placement of components seems to become irrelevant, leading to an ever-growing (and, quite possibly, exponentially growing) number of flows around the various components that form an application infrastructure.

What the concept of *zero-trust networks* says about this—and rightly—is that a classical, perimeter-based firewall approach becomes pretty much irrelevant in this context. There are so many flows, in so many directions, between so many components, which are so fluid, that there is no way firewalls can be placed between all of them. Instead, according to zero-trust networking, each component should be responsible for controlling the data that flows in and out of itself and should have no trust for any other component with which it may be communicating.

The first part of this statement is unproblematic from our point of view— that each component should have responsibility for data ingress and egress to and from itself. All users should always be authenticated to any system and authorised before they access any service provided by that system. In fact, we can even extend this principle to all components on the network and require that a component should control access to its services with API controls. Using this model, it is possible to build distributed systems made of micro-services or similar components that can be managed in ways that protect the data and services that they provide.

The problem becomes clear as soon as we extend this principle and are explicit about what is being implemented, and is encapsulated in two words: "be managed". In order to make, implement, and design systems espousing such a principle, there needs to be one or more policy-dictating components (a descriptive term is *policy engines*) from which other components can derive their policy for enforcing controls. The client components must have a level of trust in these policy engines so that they can decide what level of trust they should have in the other components with which they communicate. This in turn exposes a connected issue: these low-level components (making use of the policy engines) are not, in fact, in charge of making the decisions about who they trust—which is how "zero-trust networks" are often defined. The components may be in charge of enforcing these decisions, but not the policy with regard to the enforcement. It is like a military camp: sentries may control who enters and exits (enforcement), but those sentries apply orders that they were given (policies) in order to make those decisions: this is delegation by policy, or *transitive trust*. There is, of course, nothing wrong with this—transitive trust and agency are topics we have already addressed in this book—but it is not *zero trust*.

Since its original application to the world of networking, the term *zero-trust* is gaining a foothold and being used in different contexts, such as in p2p (peer-to-peer) and Web 3.0 discussions. The underlying principle seems to be that there are some components of the ecosystem that we do not need to trust: they are "just there", doing what they were designed to do. These components are basically *neutral* in terms of the rest of the actors in the network. The idea that there are neutral components in the ecosystem—not owned or operated by named actors in our system—is useful. If we consider the agency and intended actions of every possible component in a system, we lose opportunities for abstraction and will also likely never be able to define the core parts of the system over which we have control. The issue, however, is the suggestion that we should have zero trust in those components. On the contrary, these are often the components that we must trust the most of all the entities in the system. If they do not do what we expect them to do, everything falls apart pretty quickly—and the same argument can also be applied to zero-trust networking.

Let us consider this dilemma in terms of our definition of trust:

Trust is the assurance that one entity holds that another will perform particular actions according to a specific expectation.

In this context, the phrase "will perform particular actions according to a specific expectation" is most relevant. The description of these "zero-trusted" neutral components "doing what they're designed to do" should have brought exactly these words to mind because it is this trust in their correct functioning that is a key foundation in the systems being described.

It may be that the confusion arises because the focus of most trust design thinking around the sort of p2p systems being described is the building, maintaining, and decay of trust between the components in the system, rather than the neutral infrastructure components, which are easier to consider out of scope. This focus is both understandable and important because it's a visible and core property of many p2p systems. It is, however, very dangerous. In this equation, the "neutral" components have zero change in trust unless there is a failure in the system, which, being a non-standard state, is not a property that is top of mind. If the system design focus for a p2p application or system is the constant evaluation and re-evaluation of the level of trust held to other actors, then it is easy to consider the components in which you can hopefully have constant, unchanging trust relationships as islands in the stream, uninteresting and static. If they can truly be considered neutral in terms of the trust relationships other components need to hold to them—in other words, they are considered neither friendly nor malevolent, as they are neither allied to nor suborned by any of the actors—then their static nature is uninteresting in terms of the standard operation of the system you are building.

This does not mean that they *should* be uninteresting or unimportant, however. Their correct creation and maintenance are vital to the system itself. It is for this reason that we should be very wary of the phrase *zero-trust*, as it seems to suggest that these components are not worthy of our attention. When considering the world from a security point of view, these components should count as among the most fascinating parts of any system, partly because they are likely to be the first point of attack for a malicious actor.

We can distil our preferred view of the world into a few points that can be contrasted with the zero-trust viewpoint of the world, which raises so many concerns:

- Although components may start from a position of having little trust in other components, they move to a position of known trust rather than maintaining a level of zero-trust.
- Components do not decide what other components to trust—they enforce policies that they have been given.
- Components absolutely do have to trust other components—the policy engines—or there can be no way to bootstrap the system or enforce policies.

Though it may not have the cachet of the phrase *zero-trust*, a much better term to describe networks and systems where we apply these principles is *explicit-trust*.

The Importance of Systems

At the beginning of this chapter, we considered what a *system* might be in the context of computing. The phrase *computer system* is often used to describe a single computer, with a CPU, RAM, firmware, an operating system, etc. But we should be careful, while accepting this as one instance of a *system* in computing, to recognise that other units can also be considered—as we did when we first proposed the definition. We have noted that layers of various stacks can provide useful ways of looking at components to which trust relationships may be created and how decomposability is a key measure for considering a system abstraction. If, from the point of an outside party (a putative trustor, for example), a set of components is presented as un-decomposable, then this is probably the correct set to consider a *system* from that party's point of view. The system, then, is a fundamental entity in a trust relationship.

Isolation

We need to add another characteristic to our definition of a system related to un-decomposability: isolation. We have already seen, when considering layers, how important isolation can be, but it is not just in the software stack that it has a role to play. Isolation between systems allows the definition of boundaries between them, which means that interfaces and actions on those interfaces can be defined. Isolation allows agency to be associated with a set of components, and with that agency comes the possibility of assurances associated with actions—one of the key building blocks for trust relationships. If isolation is not a characteristic of a particular set of components, knowing *what* you are trusting becomes impossible. Isolation is difficult; but if the owner of a system does not enforce isolation and provide assurances to possible trustors about that isolation, then any trust relationships that those trustors make to the system can only be considered flawed, as its agency has to be considered compromised.

Is a system the only unit to which a trust relationship can be created: in other words, is a system what we could call the *minimum trustable entity?* Probably not. There are occasions when we want to be able to talk about trusting small, conceptually stand-alone components, but to describe them as *systems* would be overkill. Our earlier definition of *system* noted that it is made up of "a set of components", which are, if not indistinguishable by an external party, then "governed by the same rules and behaviour". Though un-decomposable and isolated, a TPM, for most abstractions, would be too small a unit to be considered a system, whereas the host computer of which it is a part might be. The reason for placing so much importance on systems is to make it clear that if we are to consider them trustable entities, they must act at the level of abstraction required for the trust relationship, as if they were single components: un-decomposable and isolated.

The level of abstraction is in itself an important point. We noted in the previous paragraph that a host computer of which a TPM is part might be considered a system. It is made up of multiple components, but it may provide an abstraction where various interfaces are available for interaction with it, and no further level of decomposability is available to external parties. At a different level of abstraction, however, it may itself be part of a larger system: a bank may consider the host machine a single component in a larger transaction-management system. Systems, then, may be made up of other systems, each with concentric layers of isolation[22]; but in order to define system behaviours—the expected actions that will be part of the trust relationship—a description of the boundaries of the system is required, and isolation to those boundaries must then follow.

While accepting that a system presents an abstraction to which we can consider creating a trust relationship, we should not assume that there is no work to be done by a putative trustor in examining how that system operates and

---

[22]The issue of how we manage trust relationships when a component system may be considered part of more than one system—such as a host computer owned by a CSP and running workloads for multiple tenants—is complex and something we will examine in Chapter 12, "Trust Domains".

how the various components relate to each other. In order to have assurances about expected future actions of our trustee system—which is what our trust relationship enshrines—due diligence such as auditing and analysing the trustee system may be appropriate at the design stages. The extent to which this will be possible will depend on questions such as the relationship between the various parties, whether there are parts of the system that are considered confidential and proprietary—both possible reasons to downgrade assurances—and a multitude of other factors. These assurances may also need to be backed up with information at the time of the actual creation of the trust relationship, such as attestation information—bearing in mind, of course, the proviso we noted about agency being essential to any assurance of trust.

Contexts

One aspect of systems that we must remember is that they exist and operate within contexts and that the contexts need always to be taken into consideration when we are looking at how they interoperate. Furthermore, different actors interacting with a system will have different expectations about its operation and how they think about it. Creating a system description with stated boundaries and defined interfaces can be a difficult task. We should be aware that the requirements related to a trust relationship may be different to those required for system definitions in other contexts, such as power management, organisational responsibility, or auditing. These different contexts can often be muddied, and the role of a systems designer is to take into account the context—or contexts—of trust. There is little literature in this area, with the notable exception of Appendix E of *NIST Special Report 800-160: Systems Security Engineering—Volume 1*,[23] which includes an excellent description of "The Characteristics and Expectations of a Systems Security Engineer". Though aimed at security engineers specifically, this appendix—and indeed the rest of the document—is almost required reading for anyone considering systems from the point of trust and is as relevant to designers, testers, operators, and auditors of a system as it is to any engineers who may be implementing one.

Nor is systems security the sole concern when considering contexts. In Chapter 3, we looked at the issue of *misplaced trust* and how there are dangers when a system or component is reused in a context for which it was not originally designed. This is a common problem when considering various contexts including resilience and system hardening, for instance, and extends well beyond trust contexts. Nor is it restricted solely to the deployment of systems in new contexts: many systems are used for purposes for which they were never intended, an issue that historically haunted the use of US driver's licenses as

---

[23]Ross, McEvilley, and Oren, 2016a, p. 201ff.

proof of age in bars, for instance (rather than proof of permission to operate a vehicle on public roads).

When we are designing or implementing a system, it is tempting to implement all the possible capabilities we can think of to allow it to operate in as many contexts as possible, but this can be a mistake. Often, it is safer to restrict the capabilities of a system to make it more difficult for people to use it incorrectly. There is a dictum—somewhat unfair—within computing that "users are stupid". While this is overstating the case somewhat, it is fairer to note that Murphy's Law holds in computing as it does everywhere else: "Anything that can go wrong, will go wrong". This can be applied to the point at issue by noting that *some* user *somewhere* can be counted upon to use the system that you are designing, implementing, or operating in ways that are at odds with your intentions. IT security experts, in particular, know that they cannot stop people doing the wrong thing; but where there are opportunities to make it *difficult to do the wrong thing*, then we should embrace them.

Equally, there are many occasions when it makes sense to reduce the capabilities of a system in order to reduce the risk of it being turned against us, either through compromise or just by being used in ways we had not considered. If we do not need an all-powerful administrator account after initial installation, it makes sense to delete it after it has done its job. If the logging of all transactions might yield information of use to an attacker, then it should be disabled in production. If older versions of cryptographic functions might lead to protocol attacks, it is better to compile them out than just to turn them off in a configuration file. As Thomas Schelling writes in *The Strategy of Conflict*,[24] a book firmly rooted in its time (it was published during the Cold War), there are times when it's useful to reduce your capacity for action, as this will force your opponent to take a particular course of action: if I drop my wallet into a postbox, what's the point of a (rational!) mugger attacking me?

Worked Example: Purchasing Whisky

We now have a good understanding of how systems can be described and composed. Now it is time to look at a worked example, considering in some detail the various systems involved and the various trust relationships that exist. Imagine that I enjoy a single malt whisky from time to time (this *Gedanken-Experiment* is not designed to be too taxing on the reader) and that my favourite distillery has just announced that I can buy bottles from them online. I am excited and decide to buy something from their special bottling. For purposes of this book, we will consider the systems involved with the actual purchase and ignore the broader questions around delivery, not to mention consumption (which should

---

[24]Schelling, 1960.

hopefully be the most enjoyable part of the process). We will also make a few assumptions, including that the distillery has a sufficiently capable IT systems and operation group to run their own servers, that both they and I have an uninterrupted and uncensored connection to the Internet, and that both they and I have bought computing hardware from suppliers who have not tampered with it and are not going have any impact on our use of it.

Actors, Organisations, and Systems

We will start off by considering the actors and related organisations in the interaction. It might seem obvious that there are two main actors—the *distillery* and *me*—but there are others that we need to consider. As I plan to use a credit card to make the purchase, and the distillery needs to check it, we need to consider the *issuer* and *acquirer banks,* both of which are part of a *credit card association*. Given the age restrictions on buying alcohol where I live (which, for the sake of simplicity, we will say is in the same jurisdiction as the distillery), the *government* has an interest in ensuring that the purchaser (me) is old enough legally to buy alcohol (I am). We will be using an encrypted connection to communicate, and the distillery has a server certificate associated with their web server, which will need to be signed by an *Internet certificate authority*. I will be making the purchase on a laptop running a Linux distribution provided by an *open source community*, and the distillery will be running their systems on a different Linux distribution, which is backed by a *commercial software vendor*.

Before we have even started, we have collected a multitude of actors and related organisations:

- Me, the purchaser
- The distillery
- The bank that issues my credit card (the issuing bank)
- The bank the distillery will use to check the transaction (the acquirer)
- The credit card association
- The government in whose jurisdiction the distillery and I reside
- The Internet CA for the distillery's web server
- The open source community that creates my Linux distribution
- The open source community that creates my web browser
- The commercial vendor that creates the distillery's Linux operating system distribution
- The open source community that creates the web server software used by the distillery

Without trying particularly hard, we have already found eleven different actors or related organisations. One of the lessons we can draw immediately is that real-life interactions are complex and that the deeper and broader we look, the more actors we are likely to discover. We will stop looking for actors here and start addressing the various systems that are involved. We will delve deeper than is normal when people look at security issues, but one of the lessons to learn is the number of layers that are available to be considered. The decision about when to stop delving and trust other people to have made good choices is sometimes the hardest one we can make.

Stepping Through the Transaction

Now that we have a list of the main actors, let us walk through the various steps of the transaction at a high level. This will allow us to identify the systems involved in the purchase, and from there, we will be in a position to consider how they are associated with the various actors and organisations and to examine at least some of the trust relationships. We will also dig deeper into the steps to understand some of the complexities involved. At all points, we will assume that no errors occur (whether human or other) and all checks pass.

Our starting point is that the distillery web site is up and accepting orders, and I have started up and logged in to my laptop, which is connected to the Internet from my home wifi access point. These are the steps I now take in order to effect a purchase.

1. I start my web browser and enter the distillery's URL, which starts with `https://`, signalling that I wish to connect over the HTTPS protocol. I tell the web browser to connect.

2. My web browser looks up the address associated with the URL's domain name by asking my laptop to perform a DNS lookup.

3. The laptop contacts a DNS server, which provides the IP address of the distillery's web server and passes the address to the web browser.

4. The web browser starts a connection to the web server, requesting an HTTPS connection.

5. The web server provides a public certificate, signed by an Internet CA, as part of the initial protocol handshake.

6. The web browser checks the public certificate and validates that it is signed by a root certificate that it has in its preloaded store.

7. The web browser checks that the public certificate is associated with the web server to which it is attempting to connect.

8. The web browser and web server each check that the other supports a version of the TLS protocol that is accepted by local policy.

9. The web browser and web site perform a TLS handshake, establishing a session key that can be used for the rest of the HTTPS connection. All traffic between the two components is now encrypted for the duration of this session.

10. The web browser requests the page associated with the URL that I entered from the web site, and the site provides it. The web browser displays the page on my laptop screen.

11. I navigate to the page where I can make an order, select the bottle that I wish to buy, and head to the checkout page.

12. On the checkout page, I am asked to provide my name, billing address, and shipping address (which are the same in this case), and credit card details, including expiration date and CVV number. I am also asked for my date of birth. I enter these and submit my order.

13. The web site checks my date of birth and calculates my age, validating that I am old enough to purchase the bottle of whisky.

14. The web site checks that my billing address and shipping address are the same—if they were not, more information would be required.

15. The web site sends my credit card details, billing address, and transaction information to the acquiring bank using the online interface provided by them.

16. The acquiring bank approves the transaction. This provides an extra check of my age, as within my jurisdiction, credit cards are not provided to banking customers under the age of 18—the same as the legal age for buying alcohol in my area.

17. The web site sends the web browser a page confirming that the transaction was successful, and for the next few days, I stay close to the front door awaiting a delivery.

There are quite a lot of steps listed here, many of which are small and straightforward. But, as promised, we need to go a little deeper into some of them.

First, we should look at whether we have noted the involvement of the various actors and organisations we identified in the previous section. A quick check shows that there are four we have missed: the providers of the operating system distributions that are running on my laptop and the distillery's web server, and the providers of my web browser and the web server software. This is unsurprising, as most of us rarely spare much thought to the software that underpins the more visible applications we run, vital as they may be, particularly because our focus is typically on how we access more complex applications that exist on and via the World Wide Web. Their place is important, however, so let us consider where these organisations sit in our list of transactions.

The answer is that their existence is implicit in all of the steps and assumed based on our stated starting point and in the first step:

- The distillery web site is up and accepting orders, and I have started up and logged in to my laptop.
- "I start my web browser".

In terms of the operating system providers, it is quite possible that either the distillery or I am using software from companies such as Microsoft or Apple, and that the web browser and web server software are provided by the same companies, but this only reduces the number of organisations we need to consider and doesn't remove the need to consider any relevant implicit trust relationships.

Let us now think a little bit further about some of the steps. Despite the fairly large number of steps, the systems we are considering are quite high level because we are considering abstractions that exist equally at a high level: connecting to a web server, performing authentication, encrypting the session, providing credit card details, checking their validity for a particular transaction, and then completing the purchase. That does not mean we cannot dig deeper into them. As we do so, we will realise that, although the extent of decomposition is not infinite, even an initial investigation is likely to go well beyond what can generally be expected of a non-expert; and the further we decompose, the less likely it is that any single person will be able fully to consider all the salient points. In doing so, we will expose the importance—and dangers—of systems.

Let us start by considering steps 2 and 3 more closely:

2. My web browser looks up the address associated with the URL's domain name by asking my laptop to perform a DNS lookup.

3. The laptop contacts a DNS server, which provides the IP address of the distillery's web server and passes the address to the web browser.

These simple descriptions include a variety of steps and components, many of which are hidden at the level of abstraction stated here. The first question we can ask is what it means for the web browser to ask the laptop to "perform a DNS lookup". The word *ask* suggests that there is some communication going on, which is indeed the case. Some web browsers now have the ability to perform a DNS lookup on their own using the *DNS over HTTPS* protocol (DoH),[25] but DNS queries have typically been considered in the domain of the operating system and network stack. The web browser, then, will use one of a variety of tools available on Linux to retrieve an IP address from a DNS server—which we will discuss more shortly. There are, in fact, a bewildering number of ways in which this can happen, including commands such as host, nsswitch, and the file

---

[25]Hoffman and McManus, 2018.

/etc/resolv.conf. The exact mechanism used by the web browser is generally hidden from our view by abstractions—and anyone looking into the complexities of just this single system should be grateful that we only took on this one.

The request by the web browser for a DNS lookup requires not only that the laptop is connected to the Internet (which we have already established) but also that it has access to a *domain name system* (DNS) server. In fact, if I have visited this web site on a previous occasion, there is a good chance that the information will be cached locally and that a repeat lookup is not required, particularly if the visit was recent; but for this example, we will assume that no cached values are available. What is more, we are actually adding at least one other actor or organisation here: the entity operating the DNS server. There are, in fact, hundreds of *root servers* for DNS across the Internet, configured in 13 named authorities and operated by organisations as diverse as *Verisign* (a commercial Internet CA), the *University of Maryland* (a US academic institution), and *NASA* (the USA's National Aeronautics and Space Administration). They are coordinated by the *Internet Assigned Numbers Authority* (IANA) and all provide services according to the DNS protocol[26] and running over the Internet using the Internet Protocol.[27] This is one of the reasons we introduced the operating system providers: their function in this transaction is not just to shield us from all the code they collect together from multiple sources, but also to perform appropriate due diligence on the various organisations providing that code and the relevant configurations and other organisations on which the software relies to provide services.

Now let us skip down to step 13, which is simpler:

13. The web site checks my date of birth and calculates my age, validating that I am old enough to purchase the bottle of whisky.

In this case, the system in which we are interested is the web site and web server software, and it is the latter that has the responsibility to calculate my age. It is unlikely, however, that the web server itself includes software to perform this check. More likely, it will actually get the operating system to perform the check. This assumes the availability of at least the following components:

- The current date (at time of the transaction), which may be provided by a Network Time Protocol (NTP) server, introducing yet another organisation for us to consider

- A configuration setting to specify the legal age for purchasing alcohol

- A library function or binary to calculate my age based on the date of birth I provided

---

[26]And the DNS protocol is based on a set of standards originally laid out in RFC 882 and RFC 883. Mockapetris, 1983 and Mockapetris, 1983a.
[27]Postel (ed.), 1981.

- A comparison function to check that my age is greater than the configured minimum legal age setting

- Optionally, logic to check that I have filled in the data correctly: the calculation function should probably raise queries if I enter a date of birth suggesting that I'm over 150 years old, for instance

Exactly how each of these is implemented is beyond my scope of interest as the distillery's customer—unless the calculation somehow goes wrong, and I am denied the opportunity to make the purchase. And the details of some of them are likely to be beyond the interest of the distillery's IT function, though it should probably at least perform a few checks to ensure that these components work as expected.

It is clear, as suggested here, that we could dive almost *ad infinitum* into the various systems and components—we have not even begun to consider firmware and hardware, for instance!—but that we need, for practical purposes, to decide what levels of abstraction, and therefore what systems, we are willing to examine as we go through our description of the transaction. Key to our decision must be a direct communication of interaction as part of the transaction. Based on these considerations, let us propose the following set of systems as the core of our description:

- My web browser
- My laptop, including hardware, firmware, and software (but excluding the web browser)
- The distillery's web server
- The distillery's host machine, including hardware, firmware, and software (but excluding the web server)
- The acquirer's online systems (for checking the transaction)
- The DNS server queried by my laptop

What is notable about this list is how few of the actors and organisations noted earlier are directly represented. Their lack of appearance here does not mean that they are unimportant, however, and we will see how mapping trust relationships and agency finally allows us to bring all of these pieces together.

Attacks and Vulnerabilities

But before moving on, it is worth thinking about attacks and vulnerabilities. Trust relationships allow us to judge risk and make appropriate decisions about levels of security: they are the reason we are looking at this transaction in the first place. There is the possibility of vulnerabilities and attacks at any—or all—of the steps that we have identified, so we will choose just two to look at in some detail and ensure that we relate this to the trust relationships we will examine in the final section of this chapter.

The first attack we will look at concerns a step that we have already examined:

3.   The laptop contacts a DNS server, which provides the IP address of the distillery's web server and passes the address to the web browser.

There are two types of possible attacks here: local and remote. In a local attack, some compromise of the operating system may lead to an incorrect IP address being provided to the web browser. This might be somebody changing the application itself, which does the checking, so that if it returns the address of a malicious host when it notices my visits to my favourite distillery—quite a niche attack, but possible—or poisons the local cache with the fake information, the outcome is the same: my web browser will be directed to a web site that is not the one I planned to visit.

A remote attack may require more resources, but if access to my laptop is difficult, attackers may be able to compromise or subvert other pieces of infrastructure and fool my laptop into returning the wrong information. Although we have—for the sake of simplicity—ignored many of the various systems involved in this step, there are multiple opportunities for compromise, though the ease of compromising them would depend on the capabilities, location, and resources of the attacker. If, at any point in the DNS lookup, an attacker can intercept the packets sent by my laptop or the packets being returned to it, the information being returned may be spoofed. My Wi-Fi access point, my broadband router, my Internet service provider's systems, the DNS server being queried—all are attack points if the integrity of DNS queries is not protected. This is one of the core use cases for the *Domain Name System Security Extensions*, better known as DNSSEC,[28] which provide integrity protection and authentication for DNS lookups. Ultimately, the success of an attack of this type depends on a number of factors, including exactly what information the attacker is trying to obtain and how much effort they are willing to put into it. With the overwhelming majority of web sites now using HTTPS, and (hopefully!) my expectation that my credit card details, at least, should not be entered except via an HTTPS connection, the attackers may have to find a way to obtain a certificate that is accepted by my web browser as valid. We may hope that this should be a significant barrier to entry, but given what we already know about DigiNotar, it may be that this attack is still worthwhile—though maybe not if my maximum purchase is only for a bottle of single malt. There are other defences against this sort of attack, including the checks that the acquiring bank will hopefully perform, but these should serve as examples of some of the types of vulnerability—and hence attacks—that might be possible.

---

[28] Arends et al, 2005, 2005a, 2005b.

Our second example is an attack during one of the steps involving the distillery's systems: in this case, step 13 again. Let us say that someone below the age for purchasing alcohol wishes to buy some whisky online and has access to credit card details. They will be asked to provide their date of birth, but let us (for the sake of this example) assume that they are resistant to lying about this particular information and instead prefer to attack the age-verification function of the site, making it possible for anyone over the age of 16 to make a purchase. This may seem like a rather contrived example, but if we consider an online vendor shipping to a multitude of different jurisdictions with different ages for the legal purchase of alcohol, such an attack might be worthwhile for somebody who wished to get the vendor into trouble in several jurisdictions. They could also disrupt sales by making it impossible for anyone to make a purchase if they entered a date of birth indicating that they were over 30 . We have already looked at the various components involved with this validation and seen that there are a surprising number of them. This provides quite an attack surface for anyone wishing to compromise this particular step in the transaction.

Trust Relationships and Agency

We are now in a position to look at the various trust relationships and the agency expressed in the various systems at the level we have decided to focus on.

Agency

Given the various systems, which are expressing agency, and for which actors? The most obvious pairings are my web browser, which is acting as an agent for me as the purchaser, and the distillery's web server, which is acting as an agent for the distillery. Can we identify any others, however? Other obvious pairings are the systems that are clearly run by and for a particular actor—the DNS servers and the acquirer's servers—but there are a few more that we can also identify:

- The acquirer is acting as an agent for the credit card association, which is, in this context, acting as an agent for the issuing bank.
- The distillery's system is acting as an agent for the government when it checks my age—both directly by parsing my input and indirectly through the credit card validity check.

These are the obvious agency-agent pairings, and we should ask ourselves whether there is tension when a system is acting as the agent for multiple actors. The answer is that there is certainly a possibility of conflict of interest, but that in all of the cases we have noted, there are contractual or legislative arrangements in place that should allay our concerns. In each case, the agency is not directly through the system but indirectly through another actor or set of actors. The distillery can only (legally!) sell alcohol because it has a licence from the government, and it can also only take money from my credit card through a contractual arrangement that it has with its issuing bank, which in turn has an arrangement with the credit card association—an arrangement mirrored by a similar contractual arrangement with my bank, the issuer in this case.

Trust Relationships

We are now ready to consider the trust relationships between the systems that we have identified as being in scope for our considerations. Given that there are only six systems in our example, we might expect there to be only a few to define, but there are actually a number of different contexts that we need to examine, so we will go through the different steps in our example and lay out the relationships in table format. Note that we are only looking at trust relationships between systems, not other actors. Even though we will identify multiple different trust relationships, there are still many more that we could note; though this list is long, it is far from exhaustive.

1. I start my web browser and enter the distillery's URL, which starts with `https://`, signalling that I wish to connect over the HTTPS protocol. I tell the web browser to connect.

   Conclusion: No system trust relationships.

2. My web browser looks up the address associated with the URL's domain name by asking my laptop to perform a DNS lookup.

   Conclusion: Trust relationship from web browser to laptop system (Table 5.5).

Table 5.5: Trust relationship from web browser to laptop system

FROM (TRUSTOR)	WEB BROWSER	TO (TRUSTEE)	LAPTOP SYSTEM
Context(s)		DNS lookup	
Time-specific		For length of transaction	
Action(s)		Perform DNS lookup on URL's domain name	
Expectation(s)		Correct DNS information provided	
Assurance(s)		Web browser installed from same software repository as laptop system	
Mitigation(s)		Mismatch with certificate in future step: display warning to user	

3. The laptop contacts a DNS server, which provides the IP address of the distillery's web server and passes the address to the web browser.

Conclusion: Trust relationship from laptop to DNS server (Table 5.6).

Table 5.6: Trust relationship from laptop to DNS server

FROM (TRUSTOR)	LAPTOP SYSTEM	TO (TRUSTEE)	DNS SERVER
Context(s)		DNS lookup	
Time-specific		Duration of lookup	
Action(s)		Perform DNS lookup on domain name	
Expectation(s)		Correct DNS information provided	
Assurance(s)		Information added at system setup time by operating system community group	
Mitigation(s)		Choose a different DNS server; user can report errors to DNS providers	

4. The web browser starts a connection to the web server, requesting an HTTPS connection.

5. The web server provides a public certificate, signed by an Internet CA, as part of the initial protocol handshake.

Conclusion: Trust relationship from web browser to web server (Table 5.7).

Table 5.7: Trust relationship from web browser to web server

FROM (TRUSTOR)	WEB BROWSER	TO (TRUSTEE)	WEB SERVER
Context(s)		HTTPS protocol support	
Time-specific		HTTPS session	
Action(s)		Start HTTPS connection	
Expectation(s)		Accept connection on HTTPS port; follow HTTPS protocol; provide certificate	
Assurance(s)		Well-known port; web site well-known	
Mitigation(s)		Drop connection	

6. The web browser checks the public certificate and validates that it is signed by a root certificate that it has in its preloaded store.

Conclusion: Trust relationships from web browser to laptop system (Table 5.8).

7. The web browser checks that the public certificate is associated with the web server to which it is attempting to connect.

Table 5.8: Trust relationships from web browser to laptop system

FROM (TRUSTOR)	WEB BROWSER	TO (TRUSTEE)	LAPTOP SYSTEM
Context(s)		Certificate validation	
Time-specific		During validation	
Action(s)		Perform check on validity of certificate presented	
Expectation(s)		Positive result if valid, negative if invalid	
Assurance(s)		Web browser installed from same software repository as laptop system	
Mitigation(s)		Very few	
FROM (TRUSTOR)	**WEB BROWSER**	**TO (TRUSTEE)**	**LAPTOP SYSTEM**
Context(s)		Certificate retrieval from on-disk store	
Time-specific		Lifetime of certificate store—until update	
Action(s)		Laptop retrieves and provides root certificate	
Expectation(s)		Root certificates provided as originally stored	
Assurance(s)		Web browser installed from same software repository as laptop system	
Mitigation(s)		Very few	

8. The web browser and web server each check that the other supports a version of the TLS protocol that is accepted by local policy.

   Conclusion: Trust relationship from the web browser to the web server (Table 5.9). Trust relationship from the web server to the web browser (Table 5.10).

Table 5.9: Trust relationship from web browser to web server

FROM (TRUSTOR)	WEB BROWSER	TO (TRUSTEE)	WEB SERVER
Context(s)		HTTPS protocol establishment	
Time-specific		During the protocol handshake	
Action(s)		Cryptographic capabilities disclosure	
Expectation(s)		Cryptographic capabilities fully disclosed; best fit chosen	
Assurance(s)		Generally in best interests of browser to choose strongest cryptographic option	
Mitigation(s)		Refuse to complete connection if minimum capabilities policy not matched	

Table 5.10: Trust relationship from web browser to web server

FROM (TRUSTOR)	WEB BROWSER	TO (TRUSTEE)	WEB SERVER
Context(s)		HTTPS protocol establishment	
Time-specific		During the protocol handshake	
Action(s)		Cryptographic capabilities disclosure	
Expectation(s)		Cryptographic capabilities fully disclosed; best fit chosen	
Assurance(s)		Generally in best interests of server to choose strongest cryptographic option	
Mitigation(s)		Refuse to complete connection if minimum capabilities policy not matched	

9. The web browser and web site perform a TLS handshake, establishing a session key that can be used for the rest of the HTTPS connection. All traffic between the two components is now encrypted for the duration of this session.

Conclusion: Trust relationship established from web browser to web server based on validation of the certificate and successful protocol handshake in the previous steps (Table 5.11). Trust relationship established from web server to web browser based on successful protocol handshake in the previous steps (Table 5.12). Trust relationship from web browser to laptop system (Table 5.13).

Table 5.11: Trust relationship from web browser to web server

FROM (TRUSTOR)	WEB BROWSER	TO (TRUSTEE)	WEB SERVER
Context(s)		HTTPS session	
Time-specific		For duration of HTTPS session or expiration of certificate	
Action(s)		HTTPS protocol requests and responses	
Expectation(s)		HTTPS requests served in a timely fashion; HTTPS responses correctly formatted	
Assurance(s)		Certificate signed by Internet CA in preloaded store	
Mitigation(s)		Close connection; user can report to Internet CA	

Table 5.12: Trust relationship from web server to web browser

FROM (TRUSTOR)	WEB SERVER	TO (TRUSTEE)	WEB BROWSER
Context(s)		HTTPS session	
Time-specific		For duration of HTTPS session	
Action(s)		HTTPS protocol requests and responses	
Expectation(s)		HTTPS requests correctly formatted	
Assurance(s)		Web browser presents known USER AGENT string	
Mitigation(s)		Close connection; mark IP address as bad; report IP address to badlisting authority	

Table 5.13: Trust relationship from web browser to laptop system

FROM (TRUSTOR)	WEB BROWSER	TO (TRUSTEE)	LAPTOP SYSTEM
Context(s)		Date and time provision	
Time-specific		At time of request	
Action(s)		Provide date and time on request	
Expectation(s)		Correct end time provided	
Assurance(s)		Web browser installed from same software repository as laptop system	
Mitigation(s)		Very few	

10. The web browser requests the page associated with the URL that I entered from the web site, and the site provides it. The web browser displays the page on my laptop screen.

   Conclusion: Trust relationship from the web server to the web client (Table 5.14). Trust relationship from the web browser to the laptop system (Table 5.15).

Table 5.14: Trust relationship from web browser to web client

FROM (TRUSTOR)	WEB SERVER	TO (TRUSTEE)	HOST SYSTEM
Context(s)		Web page retrieval from storage	
Time-specific		As each page or component is requested	
Action(s)		Host system provides stored information on request from web server	
Expectation(s)		Information provided in a timely fashion; correct information provided	
Assurance(s)		Very few	
Mitigation(s)		Very few	

Table 5.15: Trust relationship from web browser to laptop system

FROM (TRUSTOR)	WEB BROWSER	TO (TRUSTEE)	LAPTOP SYSTEM
Context(s)		Rendering of pages to laptop display	
Time-specific		On request from web browser	
Action(s)		Information displayed when provided to laptop system	
Expectation(s)		No changes made by laptop to information before display	
Assurance(s)		Web browser installed from same software repository as laptop system	
Mitigation(s)		Very few	

11. I navigate to the page where I can make an order, select the bottle that I wish to buy, and head to the checkout page.

12. On the checkout page, I am asked to provide my name, billing address, and shipping address (which are the same in this case), and credit card details, including expiration date and CVV number. I am also asked for my date of birth. I enter these and submit my order.

Conclusion: Trust relationship from the web browser to the web server (Table 5.16).

Table 5.16: Trust relationship from web browser to web server

FROM (TRUSTOR)	WEB BROWSER	TO (TRUSTEE)	WEB SERVER
Context(s)		Confidentiality of sensitive data	
Time-specific		As long as the data is stored by the web server	
Action(s)		Web server protects sensitive data	
Expectation(s)		Sensitive data not shared with unauthorised parties	
Assurance(s)		Certificate signed by Internet CA in preloaded store	
Mitigation(s)		User can report to Internet CA if a breach is discovered	

13. The web site checks my date of birth and calculates my age, validating that I am old enough to purchase the bottle of whisky.

Conclusion: Trust relationship from the web server to the host system (Table 5.17).

Table 5.17: Trust relationship from web server to host system

FROM (TRUSTOR)	WEB SERVER	TO (TRUSTEE)	HOST SYSTEM
Context(s)		Age validation	
Time-specific		On request	
Action(s)		Host system validates age	
Expectation(s)		Approval if old enough according to jurisdiction; rejection if not old enough	
Assurance(s)		Very few	
Mitigation(s)		Very few	

14. The web site checks that my billing address and shipping address are the same—if they were not, more information would be required.

15. The web site sends my credit card details, billing address, and transaction information to the acquiring bank using the online interface provided by them.

16. The acquiring bank approves the transaction. This provides an extra check of my age, as within my jurisdiction, credit cards are not provided to banking customers under the age of 18—the same as the legal age for buying alcohol.

   Conclusion: Trust relationship from the web server to the host system (Table 5.18). Trust relationship from the web server to the acquiring bank (Table. 5.19).

Table 5.18: Trust relationship from web server to host system

FROM (TRUSTOR)	WEB SERVER	TO (TRUSTEE)	HOST SYSTEM
Context(s)		Confidentiality of sensitive customer data	
Time-specific		Jurisdiction-specific	
Action(s)		Transfer of sensitive customer data	
Expectation(s)		Data will only be transmitted to authorised parties; data will not be stored beyond time required for transmission; data will be encrypted at all times during transmission	
Assurance(s)		Very few	
Mitigation(s)		Very few	

Table 5.19: Trust relationship from web server to acquiring bank

FROM (TRUSTOR)	WEB SERVER	TO (TRUSTEE)	ACQUIRING BANK (TRANSITIVE RELATIONSHIP VIA HOST SYSTEM)
Context(s)		Approval of transaction	
Time-specific		During transaction	
Action(s)		Check customer details and transaction	
Expectation(s)		Check customer details; check validity of credit card; check card CVV; check card expiration date; check sufficient credit availability	
Assurance(s)		Acquirer bank's membership of credit card association	
Mitigation(s)		Reject transaction; report to credit card association	

17. The web site sends the web browser a page confirming that the transaction was successful, and for the next few days, I stay close to the front door awaiting a delivery.

Conclusion: Trust relationship from web server to web browser (Table 5.20).

Table 5.20: Trust relationship from web server to web browser

FROM (TRUSTOR)	WEB SERVER	TO (TRUSTEE)	WEB BROWSER
Context(s)		Display of completed transaction	
Time-specific		At time of transaction	
Action(s)		Display transaction details page	
Expectation(s)		Display in a timely manner; display correct details	
Assurance(s)		Very few	
Mitigation(s)		Very few	

Although this example has been lengthy, it has shown the complexity associated with everyday processes and transactions that we may generally never question. It has also exposed the number of trust relationships involved in such a transaction and the importance of each of them in the correct completion of the process. The next chapter looks in more detail at time and how important it is to consider whenever we are modelling, validating, or establishing trust relationships.

The Importance of Being Explicit

Being explicit when describing trust is important: not just being explicit about the expected actions associated with a trust relationship, but also about the entity to which the relationship is formed, the trustee. We will spend some time in this section examining how difficult such explicitness can be in the context of computing and the cloud and some of the problems that can arise when we fail to apply explicitness sufficiently. (And we'll see this again when considering blockchain systems in the next chapter.)

Explicit Actions

First, we will look at establishing what actions we are expecting to be performed. We noted, in Chapter 2, that "the performance of actions may also need to specify the non-performance of other actions as well, to ensure that we can fully understand what behaviours we, the trustor, are trusting the other entity, the trustee, to perform". This was in the context of our example with the network stack where we specified an action that network packets should only be transmitted to the intended entity. We could equally have expressed this as a negative: that network packets should not be transmitted to unintended entities. Sometimes, expressing a negative may in fact be a more powerful and explicit way of stating an action, but we should be wary of the temptation of a set of negatives in an *exclude list*[29] when an explicit "DENY ALL" is what is required. The writing of configuration of this type (often used for firewalls, remote access, or storage authorisation) is complex, and a guide to writing "safe" rules is outside the scope of this book.

Another example that we have already considered is that of logging, where a component automatically records information that it should not, such as credit card information. Even though there may be no negative or malicious intent associated with the action, the performance of this action represents a security risk. When writing requirements for a trust relationship, being explicit may be useful. For instance, we might include text in the action description such as "Only the following entities are considered authorised, and all others are considered unauthorised, including storage for logging and debugging. If logging is required for debugging, an explicit flag must be set, and the component should refuse to function if this flag is set and the execution mode of the system is 'production' or 'staging'". While this sort of language may seem excessive, there is a danger that without it, confusion may arise, or designers or implementers of the trustee component may overlook excluded actions that may be

---

[29]This book attempts to avoid language that is considered offensive to certain groups, such as *blacklist*. See Inclusive Naming Initiative, 2021.

important to the trustor but that might otherwise be considered unimportant to the trustee component.

This is also a good example of why contexts can be useful. In the action description above, we used the phrase *execution mode*. We could equally have expressed this as a context and listed several, such as *development, testing, staging,* and *production*. We can then write trust relationship descriptions for each context. Doing this allows us to specify the contexts in which certain actions are acceptable and those in which they are not. This should not stop us from making explicit exclusionary requirements where they are important, but noting that logging *is* acceptable in *development* and *staging* contexts should allow design and implementation choices that reflect the requirements more closely.

Such careful definition should address not only core functionality but also the issue of *side effects*, which we discussed in Chapter 2. Sometimes this can only be performed with an explicit "DENY ALL" type statement, requiring that actions that are not explicitly authorised are officially unauthorised. The problem with this approach is abstraction: the trustor may not have sufficient knowledge of the various contexts within which the trustee will be operating to be able to exclude actions that may occur. Most of our focus in the book thus far has been on the trustor's specifying the various parts of the trust relationship, but this discussion brings us to an important point: the responsibility of the trustee's designer to provide a full specification. In the context of computer hardware and software, the standard mechanism for specifying the behaviour of a component is the *application programming interface* (API), and it is to this API that programmers and integrators (and also most likely those specifying the trust relationship) will turn when they wish to understand the behaviour of a component. Typically, API descriptions only address the behaviour of the component *over the interface*—hence the name. For normal uses, this is appropriate, as it allows the abstractions of modular system design to be maintained, but it presents a problem when considering trust.

The practice of creating hardware or software components and specifying their behaviour over interfaces is well-established, and while the writing of good documentation is still often considered a secondary and unimportant function (though some languages and their associated toolchains now auto-generate some API-level documentation at compile time, e.g., Rust and Java™), correct and readable API and other documentation is an important and valuable artefact of any system. The discipline of documenting the actual behaviour of a component is less widespread, partly because it is more difficult and partly because there is often an assumption that component abstraction obviates the need for such information by "external" parties. Unfortunately, this may not be the case where trust relationships are concerned, and this is one of the shifts that component designers and implementers need to undertake if their components are to be utilised in explicitly trust-related contexts. Another, more complex shift is one that is yet more difficult and rarely considered except for components in security-related contexts: that of what behaviour is explicitly excluded by a design. Here again, we are beset by the problem that the abstractions we expect when we are considering a single component (not to forget that a complete system may act as a single component of a much larger system) do not hold when considering the trust relationships that may be formed to it. A knowledge of which components need to be considered as possible trustees is required, followed by not just the API definition but also a description of behaviour that may be relevant to the contexts in which that trust may be used, both allowed and prohibited. In order to do this, designers of possible trustee components need to consider contexts in which trust relationships may be appropriate and decide whether or not to support them. Documentation should explicitly exclude contexts where support is not provided.

Even with all these considerations of allowed and prohibited behaviour, there is a set of security concerns that are much more difficult to address: side-channel attacks. Side-channel attacks are based on information gained from how a system is implemented and are different from attacks on the design of an algorithm, for instance. Let us consider the example of cryptographic key generation. When a cryptographic key is generated for use in, for example, an RSA public-private key pair, a number of different components will typically be involved, from the CPU to various cache lines and memory buses. Even without direct access to the contents of these components, there are techniques that can often be used to infer information about the process of generation, which may lead to enough information to derive the private key. Some of these attacks may require the ability to run other processes at the same time; others may examine power, sound, or temperature fluctuations associated with the components. However, they do not rely on any *misimplementation* of the key generation if we consider only that a *correct* implementation is judged solely on whether, given a set of inputs, the output is a valid public-private key pair: that is, that the implementation is *functionally* accurate.

Mitigations are available to protect against certain side-channel attacks and are often implemented in security-critical systems such as TPMs. This requires the creation of requirements that are referred to as *non-functional*, in that they refer not to the characteristics of an implementation that relate to its correctly fulfilling its specified function but to other characteristics. One common mitigation for cryptographic operations is a *constant-time implementation*, which attempts to address a subset of side-channel attacks known as *timing attacks*. Here, non-functional requirements are applied such that data gained from recording how long specific methods or processes take to execute should not yield sufficient information to leak cryptographically sensitive material. Such non-functional requirements—which may be unrelated to security concerns, addressing, for instance, reliability or fail-over characteristics—often have a negative impact on other characteristics of the system and require a trade-off to be made. The trade-off typically made in constant-time implementations, for instance, is between resistance to timing attacks and speed of operation: the protection needed is likely to slow the normal functioning of the implementation.

Unluckily, the full range of side-channel attacks is inherently unknowable, and therefore perfect protection can be considered impossible. What can be done when specifying a component and its suitability as a trustee for trust relationships is to document that range of side attacks against which mitigations have been implemented. Also, note the known types of side effects to which the component might be considered vulnerable, but against which no implementation has been provided. It is important to note that such a document can only list attacks known at the time of implementation and also that the number of mitigations will depend on the contexts in which the component is expected to be deployed. A common mistake when building systems implementing sensitive operations is the use of a component in a context for which it is not suited. This sort of mistake is actually a trust failure: the trust relationship was insufficiently defined, or the trustee component was insufficiently documented to allow an informed decision to be made. By extension, a party deploying a system into an environment for which it is designed cannot assume that equivalent assurances of behaviours can be made in the new environment—in other words, do not try to create trust relationships to systems operating in environments for which there is no documented design expectation.

It will never be possible to foretell all of the possible uses for a component or all the possible side-channel attacks to which it could be subject, particularly as some of them may be *emergent properties*, meaning that they may not become apparent until the component is combined with others or included in a configuration in a different system. As designers of trustor and trustee parties in a trust relationship and specifiers of a trust relationship's constituent part, the best we can do is be as explicit as possible. Our focus should be to avoid *impedance mismatches* in terms of documentation. This occurs when the description level from one side of the relationship (particularly the trustee's) is defective or inadequate in terms of the other party's expectations.

Sometimes, the best tool in our armoury is societal, and this is one of those times. Training, professional bodies, compliance regimes, and regulation can help us in this context. The phrase *best practice* has fallen out of favour somewhat recently, particularly within the security field. It suggests that there may be an objective, provable "best"—an idea that security experts tend to reject, just as they reject the idea that something can be objectively, provably "secure". An alternative is *best-known practice*, a phase that leaves space not only for improvement in the field but also to acknowledge that there may be better practices available that are not yet known to the person or people communicating. Whatever phrase we use, establishing norms for the types of documentation that should be provided and the ways of thinking about what information needs to be considered at the various stages of the process must be part of understanding and managing trust.

Explicit Actors

Equally important to specifying the exact actions to be performed is the issue of specifying the actors to which trust relationships are made. When considering security economics, we noted that we cannot assume that actors necessarily have our best interests at heart. When we consider the actions that an actor takes, we need to know not only about those actions but also that any assurances we have can be linked to the actor. Otherwise, any assurances we have may not be associated with the actor and may be worthless.

One factor to consider is the possible disconnect between a chain of trust and the agency of a trustee. When we accept a chain of trust, we should be aware that it is typically a static description of a set of trust relationships at a particular time. A certificate chain may tell us that the web site to which our browser is connected was checked to belong to a particular company three months ago, but what if the domain has been transferred to another organisation, or the original company has been bought by another? Probably even more worrisome is the possibility of compromise: we may assume (or at least hope!) that a company will only apply for a certificate for a host that it believes to be secure. But, what if it is wrong, and there is an existing persistent compromise, or that site has been compromised since the granting of the certificate? This is a classic example of time being a vital context within trust relationships, and the reason that there is an increasing move within IT security to shorter-lived certificates. This would include so-called *ephemeral certificates*, which are designed to be issued only for the expected lifetime of a component. There are, of course, mechanisms to revoke certificates if they, or the component to which they relate, are found to be compromised. We saw an example when we looked at the case of DigiNotar. However, they are complex and not always well-implemented either by the trustee or by the trustor in such relationships.

In these cases, we have assumed that the chain of trust at least *started off* pointing to the entity associated with the component—the entity for which the component holds agency—but we must also beware of cases where this is not the case. We may take the chain of trust represented by *trusted boot* as an example. This chain asserts that all of the various hardware and software components in the stack have been measured and found to meet the expectations in the process. It is quite possible that a CSP may present me, a tenant wishing to run workloads on the host on which the trusted boot process was performed, with the measurements as an assurance that I can trust the host to perform as expected. The chain of trust in this example, however, does not relate to the likely actions of the host component, which expresses agency for the CSP, but only tells me that the components on the host are the ones that may be expected. The actions and operations of that host are under the control of the CSP, including the opportunity for the CSP to upgrade, downgrade, change, add components to, or remove components from the host between the time the measurement was made and when my workload *finishes* executing. Tempting as it may be to care only about the state of the system when I deploy my workload, any changes to the system during execution are equally important to the trust relationship I must hold to it. And, yet again, we must consider the possibility that the system has been compromised since the measurement by either software or a malicious actor such as a rogue administrator.

Blockchain and Trust

Another strong movement within computing is the use of blockchains. Originally associated solely with cryptocurrencies—of which Bitcoin is the oldest and best-known—blockchains are now being employed for uses from tracking chickens through the supermarket supply chain[1] to allowing individuals to control who gains access to their personal data.[2]

Bitcoin and Other Blockchains

Bitcoin, like all other blockchain-based systems, is based on work by Satoshi Nakamoto (believed to be a pseudonym) and first published in the whitepaper "Bitcoin: A Peer-to-Peer Electronic Cash System".[3] A full explanation of blockchains, the mathematics behind them, and their applicability is beyond the scope of this book. The original whitepaper, which provides a remarkably simple explanation, is recommended as an introduction to the subject. One of the basic concepts, however, is the linking of blocks of data to earlier blocks, to which they have a relationship, in a chain using cryptographic hash functions.

---

[1]Berman, 2018.
[2]Wang and De Filippi, 2020.
[3]Nakamoto, 2008.

The cryptographic hashes are embedded in the new blocks, and the provenance of the chain of blocks can be traced backward through these hash values.

Cryptocurrencies provide an ingenious alternative to relying on central banks to anchor monetary value and purchasing power, and many of the applications of blockchain are focussed on removing a central authority from a system: what we would refer to, in the context of trust, as an *endorsing authority*. The replacement of this centralised endorsing authority is an approach that we might identify as a problem with blockchains, but this approach is actually consonant with our views of trust, surprising though this may sound.

Let us return to the question of roots of trust. We looked in some detail at how root certificates can be roots of trust in public key infrastructure and how Trusted Platform Modules (TPMs) can provide a hardware root of trust for a system—in those cases, the root of trust was backed by a single endorsing authority. Clearly, this is not applicable in blockchains. We will consider two alternatives that are broadly espoused by two different types of blockchain systems.

Cryptocurrencies provide examples of the original type of blockchain, sometimes referred to as *public, permissionless,* or *unpermissioned blockchains*. The distinction—which can be a matter of some contention among blockchain aficionados—is with *private* or *permissioned blockchains*. In a cryptocurrency and other permissionless blockchains, there are no membership restrictions on anybody who wishes to join the system underpinned by the blockchain, whereas permissioned blockchains restrict those who can be members or at least restrict those who can write to the blockchain (with reading sometimes being allowed to non-members).

Permissioned Blockchains

An example of a permissioned blockchain might be a shipping cargo manifest and lading system: here, only authorised parties (such as shipping companies, logistics operators, or customs officers) are able to write valid data to the blockchain, though other parties (customers wishing to see the progress of their order, for instance) may be able to read the data. Another oft-cited example of a permissioned blockchain is a transaction reconciliation system that might be run between multiple banks: in this case, it may be that there is no visibility of the blockchain to any party beyond those who are able to write to it.

In the case of permissioned blockchains, there may be an endorsing authority to provide the root of trust. The organisations and individuals involved may come together to form a single organisation such as a joint venture—a commercial venture between a variety of parties that has legal standing in some jurisdictions. Alternatively, however, they could all decide to agree on the initial block. As long as this is well-established and agreed between the members, and the transitions to subsequent blocks are signed by authorised members of the system, all is well. Furthermore, new members can be added and members removed from the system as long as the rules for such changes are also well-established (in certain types of blockchain systems, such changes can in fact be recorded within the blockchain itself as *transactions* on blocks within the chain).

Trust without Blockchains

Let us consider what a trust relationship might look like in the case of such a blockchain, starting with the case where there is no blockchain system in place. We will use the example of the shipping cargo system where a set of members move goods around the world in cargo containers, from manufacturer to customer, through ports, docks, and customs authorities. This example moves us away from computer systems back to real-world systems, so we are not able to be as specific about the various components of the trust relationship. Nonetheless, Table 6.1 shows an example of one particular set of actions in such a system.

Table 6.1: Shipping company trust relationship without blockchain system

FROM (TRUSTOR)	CUSTOMER	TO (TRUSTEE)	SHIPPING COMPANY
Context(s)		Genuineness of goods	
Time-specific		Length of the contract	
Action(s)		Shipping company receives goods from manufacturer; shipping company delivers to docking company	
Expectation(s)		Goods are from expected supplier; goods are not substituted in transit	
Assurance(s)		Legal contract	
Mitigation(s)		Legal recourse; reputational damage to shipping company	

This seems relatively straightforward; and, indeed, systems to allow such trust relationships have been developed and formed the basis of international trade for hundreds—arguably, thousands—of years. What difference does a permissioned blockchain bring to the process? The answer is "not much" if you are considering solely this one trust relationship, but "a great deal" if you consider the many different trust relationships that need to be set up for the passage of just one shipping container through the various parties involved from its initial starting point to its final destination. Blockchains are sometimes seen as solving new technical problems, but where they generally bring value is actually in providing new technical approaches to solve societal or institutional problems. When considering multiple containers shipped by different companies through different ports, with many manufacturers and customers, the number of trust relationships that need to be considered starts to become enormous, and this is where blockchains have been purposed to help.

Blockchain Promoting Trust

What if, for example, we had a mechanism to allow transitions of a container between the various steps of the process, and the result of this mechanism was cryptographically signed by the parties involved visible to many parties but with a very low risk of their being forged or changed? This is what a blockchain can provide, and although each party *may* decide that they need to establish specific trust relationships for all the relevant contexts with all the various parties, all of which need to be tracked in separate transactions, there is an alternative: trust the blockchain as the record. If the transactions embedded in a block include information relating to trust contexts, and these blocks can be embedded into the blockchain, then the relationships can be tracked much more efficiently through the blockchain than via multiple different contracts—a radical change in how the system operates. The fact that the various transactions are also linked through the chain and have the quality of non-repudiability also provides efficiency improvements over a system that is based solely on multiple different contracts.

Non-repudiability is one of the key characteristics enshrined in most, if not all, blockchains. It describes the quality that once a transaction has been accepted into a block, and once that block has been accepted into the blockchain, it can be considered unchangeable both by the parties to which it relates and any other parties. If I have given you a sum of money and, in return, you have handed over a new car, it is in both of our interests (in general!) that neither of us can turn around and deny that the transaction took place. The ability to say that parties cannot deny that a transaction happened is non-repudiability.

There is a phrase in the preceding discussion that should raise some questions in our minds: the suggestion that parties "trust the blockchain as the record". This is not directly related to trust in computers, but it is related to trust in systems and has relevance to how we consider trust relationships in these contexts, so it is worth unpacking and trying to understand better what is going on here. How can we restate such a trust relationship in the terms that we have adopted? First, we can talk about a trust relationship to the *system* of which the blockchain is the artefact. The system we are considering, we should remember, is permissioned, so there is a mechanism for tracking and deciding whether to form a trust relationship to another party, *whether or not they are known to the trustor*. The various parts of the system, including the definition of the contexts it covers, the parties, the identification of the parties, and the mathematical and computational underpinnings of the blockchain, are all constituent parts of the blockchain system. Therefore, the trust relationship(s) that the trustor establishes to the system must consider all of these. There is, however, no trust relationship required to a single endorsing authority. Interestingly, there is no single endorsing authority in the pre-blockchain approach to managing these relationships in the example we considered of the shipping cargo system, which is part of the reason for the complexity of all the different contracts and relationships that need to be considered. The addition of the permissioned blockchain allows trustors to form transitive trust relationships to the trustees through the medium of the blockchain system, which is backed by distributed trust relationships from the multiple members of the system.

Let us consider what the trust relationship looks like in this case (detailed in Table 6.2). We will also assume that rather than set up a specific contract for this transaction, the members of the permissioned blockchain system have agreed that transactions entered in the blockchain should have the legal force of contracts and that the blockchain is imbued with evidentiary force.

Table 6.2: Shipping company trust relationship with blockchain system

FROM (TRUSTOR) CUSTOMER	TO (TRUSTEE) BLOCKCHAIN SYSTEM
Context(s)	Genuineness of goods
Time-specific	Length of the contract
Action(s)	Shipping company receives goods from manufacturer; shipping company delivers to docking company
Expectation(s)	Goods are from expected supplier; goods are not substituted in transit
Assurance(s)	Transactions entered on the blockchain
Mitigation(s)	Legal recourse with blockchain as evidence; shipping company's membership of blockchain system revoked or downgraded; reputational damage to shipping company

We can see that the blockchain is performing the same purposes as the contract in our non-blockchain use case but with different assurances and mitigations. In order for the blockchain to meet these requirements, however, there are some further important underpinnings to consider. We have already noted the evidentiary status that we are according the blockchain in our example. In order for this to be met, there are two interlocking characteristics that need to be supplied by the system. One we have already discussed: non-repudiation. If a party can tamper with the history of the blockchain, then previous transactions cannot be held to be unchangeable. There is a step required to get here, though, which is the question of how transactions get onto the blockchain in the first place: this is managed by a concept called *consensus*. For any blockchain system (permissioned or permissionless), there must be a mechanism whereby transactions are placed into blocks and those blocks are joined to the blockchain in such a way that the members of the system can agree on their repudiability. There are many consensus mechanisms and associated algorithms, and the choice of which mechanism (or mechanisms) is adopted for a particular blockchain system is one of the blockchain's key characteristics.

The reason that consensus mechanisms are important in our context is that they are one of the key components in which trust must be placed within a blockchain system, and their status as a core element to any blockchain system sometimes goes ignored or undervalued. A great deal of research has gone into consensus mechanisms with different characteristics. From our point of view—concentrating on the computing aspects of trust—it is typically mathematics and implementation of a particular consensus algorithm that we care about, in the broader context of blockchain systems, but this is generally not the overarching concern. We noted earlier that blockchain systems are less about solving technical problems than societal and institutional ones. Consensus mechanisms embody how different systems solve different societal, institutional, and even political and philosophical problems such as who should have access to your health data, how we can stop institutions from being coerced by local governments, and how we can allow journalists and workers in non-governmental organisations to report on corrupt regimes.

Permissionless Blockchains and Cryptocurrencies

Let us turn our attention to permissionless blockchains and cryptocurrencies. Cryptocurrencies tackle something that is not fundamentally a process problem (as in the case of the complexity of contracts and relationships involved in shipping and lading), but is a social, political, and philosophical problem. What if you do not trust (or do not wish to have to trust) the endorsing authority behind a fiat currency? A decision not to trust the endorsing authority may, in fact, be mirrored by or even informed by a suspicion that the endorsing authorities lack trust in the users or consumers of the fiat currency and the removal of agency from those users to control their access to or use of the currency. A *fiat currency* is one that is backed by a government agency such as a central bank rather than a commodity such as gold. Fiat currencies are subject to the whims—sometimes politically motivated—of the agency that endorses them, and, for some, this is reason enough to distrust them. When Nakamoto published his white paper, the revelation he provided was not that it was possible to provide an alternative to fiat currencies, but that it was possible to create an alternative that had characteristics such as immutability and anonymity (or at least pseudonymity), did not rely on a centralised endorsing authority, and was underpinned by (fairly) simple-to-understand protocols and mathematical and computational concepts.

In his white paper, however, Nakamoto made a bold claim: "We have pro-posed a system for electronic transactions without relying on trust".[4] According to our understanding of trust, this statement is, at best, a vastly misleading oversimplification and, at worst, simply false. It is false because, in order to use a cryptocurrency such as Bitcoin with any level of assurance, a user needs to establish multiple trust relationships. The most obvious is a trust relationship that we have already mentioned: a trust in the mathematical and computational concepts that underpin the system. One of these core concepts is one that we have already addressed: cryptographic hash functions. It is the output of these that ties the blocks together. Another important concept—which underpins the non-repudiability of bitcoin transactions—is that of digital signatures. These require a key pair of a public key and a private key, as described in Chapter 5. The continued non-repudiability of transactions within the bitcoin system is a core characteristic; any possible challenge to the mathematics of asymmetric cryptography, or attacks such as those potentially offered by quantum cryptog-raphy, would have a significant negative impact on the continued viability of Bitcoin, not to mention many other cryptocurrencies and blockchain systems. The difficulties of replacing or augmenting these underpinnings with others, should attacks or vulnerabilities emerge, is a continuing concern for the cre--ators of new blockchain systems since the fundamental assumptions of early blockchain currencies such as Bitcoin have become more obvious. While these concerns around the mathematical underpinnings of blockchains may seem esoteric, they are important and neglected by many of the more naive propo-nents of blockchain systems. This is possibly due to the influence of Nakamoto's statement, now something of a mantra, around the lack of need to rely on trust in blockchains. This is similar to the popular mis-description of "zero-trust" systems that we considered in Chapter 5.

The fact that trust is required actually turns out to be an *explicit* point in one aspect of most, if not all, permissionless blockchains: software implementations. We have already noted that the cryptography that underpins the blockchain needs to be trusted, but such trust is warranted only insofar as the software that implements it can also be trusted. The same goes for the protocols that allow the blockchain to function: how the various components agree on when a new block should be created, for instance—referred to as the *consensus* algorithm in blockchain systems.[5] In order for this agreement to be possible, system users need to be able to look at the elements of the blockchain system and judge whether they are a *proper* and *correct* implementation. It is for this reason that most per-missionless blockchain systems (and many permissioned blockchain systems as

---

[4]Nakamoto, 2008, p. 8.
[5]Bitcoin uses a particular type of consensus algorithm referred to as *proof of work*. While this algorithm has functioned well, it has a damaging environmental impact due to the computa-tional effort required as Bitcoin scales.

well) are released as open source software. We will address the interesting trust properties of open source software in Chapter 9, but the fundamental utility of open source software in this context is that users of the cryptocurrency can check for themselves that the software they are running correctly implements the system that they *think* they are running and have an assurance (if it is found to do so) that they can trust the blockchain to perform. While all such checks are, of course, subject to all the provisos introduced by Ken Thompson when considering trust in a software and hardware stack (discussed in Chapter 4), these checks allow the removal of another centralised authority: the vendor who creates software to run the system. They do not, of course, remove the need for any trust relationships at all; but along with the basic tenets of a cryptocurrency—that trust in the currency is distributed into the blockchain and all its users and that there is collective agreement to trust in the consensus algorithm that underpins it—there exists sufficient trust and a sufficient number of trust relationships to allow a form of monetary value to exist without a particularly troublesome trust relationship (at least for some people): that to a single endorsing authority embodied by at central bank.

Beyond the aspects of blockchain systems that we have already identified, there are other components where trust can be very important in permissioned and permissionless blockchains. Ethereum was one of the first blockchain systems to go beyond currency-based transactions within blocks and allow computational transactions to be recorded as well or instead.[6] We already hinted at some of the types of transactions that are possible when we talked about members of a permissioned blockchain being added to or removed from the system. It is possible to create a transaction that describes this type of action, like casting a vote, interacting with an application, and numerous other types of action. These types of transactions can include computational aspects, and it is possible to describe and encapsulate them in *smart contracts*. These contracts are arguably somewhat badly named: they are not smart in terms of requiring any artificial intelligence or machine learning, nor can they necessarily describe anything that would be considered a contract in a legal sense. However, they can describe computationally a set of actions that two or more parties can agree on, based on sets of inputs and leading to known outputs.

An example might be a smart contract to make a purchase of 5% of the stock of a named ice cream company if the average temperature in Norway exceeds a certain temperature for five consecutive days next June. This can be well-described computationally, and the possible inputs and outputs are well-defined. As the person making the funds available, the question to ask is, what

---

[6]Ethereum, 2021.

do I need to know before deciding if I should enter into such a contract? The obvious answer is that I need to *trust* the smart contract, but by this stage of our investigations, we know that such a statement is complex. What I actually need is a trust relationship to one or more entities, with one or more contexts, assurances, and actions. It is clear that there are multiple entities here, which include:

- The blockchain system
- The code of the smart contract
- The interpreter of the smart contract
- The mechanism for buying the stock
- The entity providing the input for the weather information

This last entity—the entity that is providing the temperature information about Norway—has a particular classification within blockchain systems: it is known as an *oracle*. An oracle *has* to be trusted if there is to be any trust to the smart contract, though one way to avoid it becoming a single point of failure (and therefore a single point of trust) is to use several different oracles as inputs. Even in this case, however, there must be a trust relationship to one or more entities, not to mention the channels they use to communicate the data on which the smart contract will act.

Here we also begin to see a more complex issue arising: one of the trusted entities is the interpreter of the smart contract. By this, we mean the program or application that is running the smart contract—which is just computer code like everything else in the system—which we need to hope is going to execute the instructions in the smart contract following the specification we expect. There is another level that we need to consider, however, which starts to be more visible when we talk about blockchain systems that not only have no centralised authority for data but also have no centralised authority for execution. In other words, the computational elements of a blockchain system are typically distributed across multiple computing platforms, such as private or public clouds.

Needless to say, anyone relying on blockchain systems with smart contracts needs to be certain that there are appropriate trust relationships to the systems that are actually executing these smart contracts. In the case of permissionless blockchain systems, one approach to reducing the need to trust any particular executing system is to run multiple instances and then run consensus algorithms to adjudicate cases where they provide different outputs, in the same way that the levels of trust in any particular oracle can be reduced by taking inputs from multiple instances. In the case of permissioned blockchains, there may be fewer options for multiple instances, and the protection of the smart contract may become vital, whether that is the *confidentiality* or the *integrity* of the data or algorithm, or the availability of computing resources for it to execute. If my "buy" decision on an ice cream company is held up so that other parties can purchase stock before me, my plans to gain a cheap foothold in a new market may be cruelly thwarted!

Whether we are considering permissioned or permissionless blockchain systems, however, the trust relationships to smart contracts, their constituent parts, and associated components are all important when considering the risk of participation. We must not be fooled into thinking that this is a "trust-less" system: it is just that trust is transferred into different entities. Sometimes, that transfer of trust actually makes it difficult to evaluate risk and reduces the opportunities available to designers and users of a system to understand the trust relationships involved.

The Importance of Time

As we have looked at our definition of trust and the corollaries associated with it, we have continually returned to the point that time is an important context to consider as part of a trust relationship. Sometimes the extent to which time is relevant is fairly obvious, such as in the case of the web transaction we examined at the end of the last chapter, where the length of the transaction, and the connection associated with it, determined the time context for most of the trust relationships. In this chapter, we will take a deeper look at trust and time in the context of computers and systems.

Decay of Trust

The very first examples of trust relationships that we examined in the book—my relationships to my brother and sister—made it clear that trust can decay. The example of my sister's not having worked as a dive instructor for a while was given as a reason for that trust relationship to decay: for my assurance in her to perform the correct actions to be reduced. To be clear, it is only in this context that the decay over time impacts in this particular way: I might (and would!) trust her to put me in the recovery position if I were rendered unconscious. While she might forget this skill over time, the rate of decay is different for this trust relationship, though they both relate to skills that could save my life—in the appropriate context.

How similar to these sorts of human trust relationship calculations (using the term *calculations* loosely) are computer trust relationships in terms of time? Can we apply similar approaches, or is time not actually applicable as a context in the realm of computer-computer trust? At first glance, the answer might seem to be that time should *not* necessarily be a context that we need to consider: after all, are computer systems not supposed to be deterministic in their operation? Sadly, as every person who has ever designed, implemented, operated, or monitored a computer-based system of any complexity knows, we can rarely rely fully on provably deterministic systems. Some of the reasons for this scepticism are also reasons for us to take time as an important context when considering trust relationships in this realm.

Another context that has a similar correlation to the realm of human-human relationships, and upon which we can touch briefly here, is along the chain of trust. This is an important point and worth a brief digression. When considering the security of a system, a certificate chain—the canonical example of a chain of trust in computing—is often considered a single unit: if all of the links in the chain are validated from the final certificate to the root of trust, then it is common to consider the final certificate trusted. Taking this approach leads to the possibility of having the same levels of assurance in a trust relationship to a component with a single link in the certificate chain that backs it as to a component with 10, 20, or 50 links in it.[1] This is a dangerous and erroneous assumption and confuses two separate contexts represented by the certificate chain, one cryptographic and one organisational. While we may be justified in having equal assurance in each of the cryptographic signatures in a certificate chain, having the same assurance about each of the organisations is a much more tricky—and unlikely—proposition. In fact, when we say that we have equal assurance in each cryptographic signature, there are arguably only two major trust relationships in play here:

- The relationship from the component that is performing the checking to the different components that created the signatures and certificate chain in the first place, embodied by the shared cryptographic algorithm (or set of algorithms and primitives, more accurately)

- The relationship from our system to the component that is performing the checking for us (and any other components involved in communicating to us the validity of the checks performed)

It should be clear, then, that assurance based on a chain of trust should decay—or, maybe better, should fall off or reduce—with the length of the chain,

---

[1] While there may be occasions where such a similar assurance *might* be justified, these are edge cases where we generally start off with a low level of trust in the root certificate that is signing the shorter certificate chain in the first place.

though the rate of that decay or reduction will vary. This actually accords with our experience of trust in human-human interactions: chains of trust—examples of transitive trust—are generally considered weaker as more people are added to the chain. Trusting my sister's friend's teacher's hairdresser to service my diving gear, or even to put me in the recovery position should I fall unconscious, is something I'm much less likely to consider, however strong each recommendation is, though I might be happy to consider my sister's friend, as long as my sister's recommendation is firm—a chain with a single link.

To return briefly to certificate chains, there is a link here to time as well. As we discussed in Chapter 5 when noting the rise in popularity of ephemeral certificates, we need to consider possible changes in the circumstances of the human institutions associated with the signatures and certificates in the chain over time. The longer the time since the initial signing, the greater the chance that one or more of the parties involved may have been compromised, turned malicious, been bought by a different party, or just gone out of business.

Decay of Trust and Lifecycle

Systems, when operating in the real world, are notorious for behaving in ways that do not follow the expectations of their designers or operators: in fact, they may display behaviour that can be described as *non-deterministic* in that the same set of inputs may not yield the same behaviour and outputs in repeated cases over time. When this happens, how can trustors to any such system hold assurances about the latter's expected behaviour? Computers—and therefore the systems that form them—should act as deterministic state machines, so what are the factors that lead to their diverging from their expected behaviour over time? We will look at some of the possible reasons that arise in running real-world systems and consider mitigations that may be available on the part of the trustor. Many of the examples that follow relate not only to security—which is a main focus of this book—but also to other system properties such as reliability, availability, and performance.

Vulnerability Discovery   Nobody (at least, no well-intentioned or honest actor) designs systems or components with vulnerabilities; but over time, most complex systems or components will be found to have vulnerabilities, and with these come exploits, and with these, attacks. The longer a trust relationship to a system or component is in place, the more likely that a vulnerability has been found—or, more accurately, the longer since an investigation into the security of the trustee has been carried out.

Mitigations   The standard mitigation to avoid exposure to vulnerabilities is to ensure that a system has the most recent patches from the vendor or provider. However, there is no obvious way for a trustor to be assured that the trustee has applied such patches. Even if interfaces report versions of software (and many do not, to avoid attackers from identifying old or unpatched instances), such information could be dishonestly spoofed. In cases where there may be concerns over vulnerability patching, it may be that the trustor needs to establish a trust relationship to the trustee around the context of the timeliness of applying patches.

Target of Attackers   While we might expect trust to decay linearly over time, there are definitely contexts where this is not the case, and we should not assume such a property. A good example is where a trustee system becomes a target for attackers when it had, in the past, not been considered at high risk. Whether for political or financial gain or ethical or personal dissatisfaction with an organisation, systems associated with these organisations may become targeted. This may lead to problems for systems that have a trust relationship to them, as it may be difficult for the trustee system to maintain the behaviour characteristics (such as performance and uptime) associated with the relationship.

Mitigation   It is difficult to plan for such occurrences as they are, almost by definition, unexpected. Where critical capabilities need to be maintained, the trustor may insist on extra capacity being available at all times to cover such changes or ensure that alternative trustee systems (possibly provided by a different provider) are available.

Upgrades and Changes   One of the most common causes of perturbation of system behaviour is upgrades and changes to the behaviour of systems that result from the introduction of new functionality. These changes—and whether a particular upgrade or change will have an impact—are difficult to predict, particularly in complex systems where multiple components have dependencies on the behaviour of others. A change in the behaviour of a component on which the trustee relies, even if it is not exposed directly to the trustor, may negatively impact the expected behaviour associated with the trust relationship. As with the previous example, where a system becomes a target for attackers, the decay pattern for this type of trust is unlikely to be linear or continuous, though it may be more possible to predict if upgrades and changes are planned or can be forecast.

Mitigations   There are two standard approaches to avoiding such negative impacts: (i) pre-deployment or "staging" testing, and (ii) definition of the application programming interface (API) and/or application binary interface (ABI) presented to external systems. Systems that are acting specifically as trustors should establish a context around the stability of any APIs and/or ABIs with which they integrate.

Breaking by Patching   The application of patches—outside the standard upgrade path—is always a source of concern for operational systems. In many ways, the issues involved in patching are similar to the issues associated with upgrades that we just discussed. Normally, patches are issued to fix urgent issues—often security-related, but sometimes for other reasons, such as performance or reliability. Because urgency generally means reduced testing time, patches have a higher likelihood of disruption than upgrades.

Mitigations   Though they can be disruptive and their impact difficult to predict, patches generally attempt to maintain the same API and ABI and to affect only small parts of a system.[2] These characteristics allow for decisions to be made about whether to apply patches depending on calculations made as to the likely business impact. From the point of view of the trustor, in order to allow such calculations to be made with the trustor's interests (and assurances) in mind, it is important that the trustor's business requirements are known and taken into consideration by the trustee.

Mean Time to Failure and Mean Time to Repair   Mean time to failure (MTTF) and mean time to repair (MTTR) are two measures that have typically been associated with hardware, where knowledge of the physical characteristics of components such as hard disks or power supply units (PSUs) can give good indications of when system-reliant components may fail. Similar measures can also be applied to software—software reliability is an important and growing field of study—and these may be combined, when considering a system, to allow predictions to be made about whether trust around security should be degraded. In the hardware case, at least, it is the security property of availability that is the most likely to be affected. But predictions about when exactly an effect will happen are difficult; and although the issue of *burn-in periods* (where hardware can take some time to "settle down" and is more likely to fail soon than after some prolonged use) is reduced with modern hardware, *planned obsolescence* is still definitely a factor.

Mitigations   The standard approach to MTTF and MTTR failures is to maintain redundant systems, either load-balanced in normal operation or in *hot*, *warm*, or *cold* backups (typically allowing immediate fail-over, fast fail-over, or guaranteed but slow fail-over, respectively). This area is one where standard practices in non-security-specific properties such as reliability and performance can provide immediate benefits in terms of trust relationship planning and maintenance.

User Error   User error may appear to be a strange area to address in a section on trust and lifecycle, but most—arguably all—systems rely on human users at some point, whether it is for entry of data, freeing up of disk

---

[2]This is not the case for all patch strategies, however. Some vendors, such as Microsoft, often provide multiple patches at a time ("Patch Tuesday" in Microsoft's case, which is once a month). This allows operational teams to plan their testing regimes but does tend to lead to "batching" of patches, where multiple unconnected patches are applied whether or not they directly impact operations.

space, replacing failing hardware, or just the correct operation of *fibre-seeking backhoes*[3]. Although, like *burn-in periods*, there may be some situations where errors reduce over time (as users gain more experience with the system), for others, the likelihood may rise, presumably following a Poisson distribution.

Mitigations   Mitigation for user entry error is a field of study within user-experience design (UXD); however, mitigating other types of user error is much more difficult, particularly when errors may not be catastrophic (unlike those induced by fibre-seeking backhoes) but compounded over time, or even combined with other errors. A classic example is a program that fails due to logging too many errors, filling up available disk space and triggering other errors, which cannot then be logged due to there being nowhere to record them.

Availability of Support   One last issue that we can consider is the lack of support for the trustee system: when there is no opportunity to manage or fix a system because appropriate resources are not available. This can occur for multiple reasons, including suppliers going out of business, experts retiring from an organisation, failure to upgrade versions that go "out of support", or just that specific hardware is no longer available (it has been reported that there are fewer than 10 specialist valves remaining in the world of a particular type required to allow a particular BBC service to continue broadcasting, for instance[4]).

Mitigations   This is arguably a *second-order* problem in that it comes into play only if another issue (such as one of those noted above) occurs, but it may significantly increase the impact on trustees being able to apply mitigations. The obvious mitigation, of course, is for the operator of the trustee system to ensure that the service they are offering *does* have support available; but when trustors have a long-established relationship to a system, and the trustor is a key part of their business, this can be difficult. If the software—and, to some extent, hardware—of the trustee system is open source, there may be an opportunity for an organisation, including the operator of the system, to take over support, but this can be very difficult for proprietary software and hardware.

What is clear from looking at the possible mitigations for many of these issues is that they may require one or more extra trust relationships with the trustee. An interesting point about these relationships is that many of them require deeper

---

[3]The category *fibre-seeking backhoe* has been defined as "any of a genus of large, disruptive machines which routinely cut critical backbone links, creating Internet outages and packet over air problems" in Raymond, 2001, though not in the third edition print version, Raymond, 1996.
[4]Sabbagh, 2011.

visibility into the trustee system than would normally be exposed, as they break to some degree the abstraction provided by the system in the first place. Usually, we think about interactions between systems as being well-defined by the API or ABI, but in order to have appropriate assurances for certain trust relationships, the trustor needs to go beyond this interface and have more visibility of other characteristics of the system (e.g., monitoring or operations) than is standard.

Providing more visibility gives the operators of trustee systems more than just an operational headache, however: there may be contractual and commercial issues at stake here as well. Service-level agreements (SLAs) are the standard mechanism within the industry to manage such matters, but the types of information provided in SLAs may well be insufficient to allow the sorts of assurances required for the types of trust relationship that we have been considering. The reasons for these insufficiencies are quite understandable: if a cloud service provider (CSP) publishes a list of software libraries they are using and their current versions, for instance, the CSP is giving malicious actors a great deal of information about what attack vectors may be available for exploitation. Major customers may be able to pressure CSPs into providing some of this information to them, but smaller customers have little or no chance. SLAs tend to concentrate on the availability of a service (which is still, of course, a significant concern for many of the issues we have identified), rather than allowing the amount of visibility into their systems that we might want to have not just to allow sufficient information to establish trust relationships, but to think about how to maintain them. The amount of visibility into other systems should be a major concern for those deciding where and how to deploy and manage systems in the Cloud. Rather than just adopt a *fire and forget* approach to deployment, where a contract is signed and applications are deployed with no further review, there should be regular, planned, and expert reappraisals of whether the services offered by CSPs and the SLAs associated with them are sufficient to provide the assurances required to allow a trust relationship to the CSP. The point about *expert* reappraisal is important here: SLAs are contractual documents, and although they may contain technical information, they need to be part not just of the operational design considerations for systems but also the trust considerations (though these may, of course, overlap).

In the end, SLAs are a mechanism for managing risk through contractual arrangements, something we considered briefly in Chapter 3, and are an entirely appropriate component of a risk mitigation strategy. Most SLAs are not written, however, with the express intention of allowing the customer of a CSP to make decisions about trust relations: this is not their main context, to use our terminology. Nor are those most likely to be reviewing them best equipped to consider them in this context. So unless SLAs *are* considered explicitly from a trust point of view, it is likely that the extent to which they can provide the assurances required as a backup to the direct relationship from the trustor to the trustee will be minimal, as they will be overloaded with expectations and assumptions that are actually out of the context of the (contractual) trust relationship that the SLA represents.

Software Lifecycle

There are various models of software lifecycle, sometimes referred to as the *software development lifecycle*, and the preferred model is typically dependent on the methodology used. Some restrict themselves to the actual creation of the software, whereas others, such as those focusing on *DevOps* (software development and IT operations) place an emphasis on the deployment and operation of the software, typically taking a cyclical view of operations. Such approaches often also consider the tools and processes involved in the lifecycle as important, creating tiers of concerns, all of which involve trust relationships! We will not dive down the rabbit hole of comparing software methodologies; but given that many of the trust relationships in which we are interested are in the operations phase, we can give a list of stages or phases of the software lifecycle, which is, if not necessarily exhaustive, at least fairly non-contentious:

- Application of governance and regulatory frameworks
- Policy creation
- Design
- Coding
- Testing
- Staging
- Operations
- Patching
- Upgrading
- Monitoring
- End of life

The point of providing such a list in this context is two-fold: (i) to note that the list of issues that we considered in the previous section applies to many of them; and (ii) to think about when in the lifecycle different trust relationships should be considered.

Exactly when such considerations take place will depend on a number of factors, but this is a situation in which the DevOps approach to the software lifecycle embraces an important fact: that if developers do not consider how their software will be deployed and operated, the operation of the software will be impeded. This is even more true for trust relationships, and we should extend this thinking through all the different phases of the lifecycle of a system. If, for example, a piece of software is designed without consideration for the trust relationships it will require to operate within a cloud and whether those relationships will meet any relevant regulatory requirements, the coding, testing, and operations phases will suffer.

Another good example is monitoring operational software, and the principle of "trust, but verify", which we examined in Chapter 2. This dictum is a good example of where time is clearly exposed as an important consideration within trust relationships because the two separate actions—trust and verify—must occur over time. In order to *continue* to hold an assurance, we need to check whether the assurance is still valid: we need to verify that the actions are in line with our expectations. This may require checks on inaction, continuous checks, or atomic checks at particular points in time; but if our assurance is not fulfilled, then the trust relationship should be stopped or at least modified.

Trust Anchors, Trust Pivots, and the Supply Chain

When considering the issues of establishing and maintaining trust relationships, two sets of trust operations require very specific thought: management of trust anchors and the use of trust pivots. A trust anchor is a static component to which the trust relationship is assumed rather than derived, whereas a trust pivot is both a component and an associated process that allows a trust relationship from one entity to another to be transferred or added to a third entity.

The establishment of a trust anchor in a system allows the development and establishment of new trust relationships to and from that system to take place and is therefore a major milestone in the deployment of the system. Trust anchors are not only about deployment, however. There has been a growing realisation that consumers of software need to become more aware of the *software supply chain*, the set of steps that occur before consumers are presented with a product. Similar concerns are also expressed about hardware in some cases—we have already looked at the US government's attitude to Huawei. These steps are most easily visible in open source software, where the process of software creation is, perforce, more open than that for proprietary software.

If we cast our minds back to Ken Thompson's declaration in Chapter 4 about the ease with which malicious alterations to code can be made, it should become clear to us that the more steps there are in producing code, the more opportunities there are for compromise. Not all of them will be as difficult to spot as Thompson's example, but knowing what dependencies you have in your application is important. Modern applications typically import dozens—often hundreds—of libraries, increasingly from the open source community, and the possibility that one or more of these contains vulnerabilities increases with the number of dependencies. Since 2017, the canonical example in the industry has been Equifax, a company that was using Apache Struts 2 as part of its infrastructure. As Equifax failed to upgrade or patch its deployment, it suffered a major attack on a known vulnerability.[5] The fact that the company was using a component from an open source project with robust vulnerability reporting meant there were ample opportunities for patching or upgrading the software, which Equifax failed to take, making them our poster child for ensuring knowledge of your dependencies. We will return to the questions surrounding trust in open source software in Chapter 8. Our point here is that without mechanisms to derive trust in the various components that make up the supply chain, all components must be treated as trust anchors. This means due diligence must be considered for *every* component that enters the supply chain (whether open source or proprietary) in order to evaluate the trust relationships within the system.

Types of Trust Anchors

The types of trust anchors that are typically considered explicitly are the ones that are more obviously security-related. These might include cryptography libraries, TPMs, and certificates. As with every other component, there should be a time context to any trust relationship to these specific trust anchors, and the examples illustrate how different these time contexts may look. All components that are acting as trust anchors are almost by definition essential to applications and systems, and the impact of a failure in a trust relationship to anyone may be catastrophic.

Cryptographic Libraries   Cryptographic libraries typically have long lifetimes and, once mature, are rarely revised. Therefore, once a trust relationship has been established with one (which may or may not be as an anchor), it is likely to be acceptable for a long time. However, when cryptographic libraries are revised, it is often due to discoveries of vulnerabilities, and it is important to patch or upgrade them as soon as possible. This means having the ability to monitor appropriate information channels to spot when a revision may be required. For some applications and software lifecycles, this may be simply a matter of an automatically triggered (or regular) new build; but for others, noticing that a new version should be applied is more difficult.

TPMs   TPMs, being hardware, are difficult to revise; but there are lifecycle events associated with them, such as provisioning, which need to be considered in the design, implementation, and operation of a system. They will behave differently based on the state in which they exist at any particular time. In addition, TPMs are also not immune to vulnerabilities and attacks—see, for example, the *TPM-FAIL* vulnerability[6]. When such a

---

[5]Chirgwin, 2017.
[6]Moghimi et al., 2020.

vulnerability is exposed, appropriate experts need to be available to establish whether attacks associated with it might impact the trust relationship and correspondingly impact security. The TPM-FAIL attack, for instance, is only relevant to specific types of operations that TPMs may be performing, and if these are not relevant to the trust relationship, there should be no cause for concern. If, however, the expected actions to be performed by the TPM as a trustee are not defined, it is likely to be difficult to ascertain whether or not a vulnerability is a cause for concern.

Certificates   Certificates have—or should have—lifetimes associated with them, and these should be checked. Any certificate with a longer-than-expected validity or that is lacking an expiration date should ring alarm bells with any party considering a trust relationship to it. Once a certificate's lifetime is completed, it should no longer be trusted for the purpose for which it was used. Equally, if a certificate is proposed for use for two or more purposes, which require different lifetime properties (the signing of an ephemeral software build vs. the establishment of the identity of someone associated with a bank account, for instance), then separate certificates should be used, though they may share the same root certificate. Though certificates are typically less long-lived than cryptographic libraries or TPMs, revocation is sometimes important for them, and mechanisms to allow systems to manage revocation events should be considered when creating trust relationships to them.

All types of trustee systems or components, then, will have a time-based context, but the specific assurances—and mitigations—associated with a particular trust relationship are likely to be unique to that component and to that trust relationship. Sometimes it will be appropriate to specify time as a stand-alone context, but in others, it will be sufficient to consider time as part of a different context, which is the approach we have taken when filling out the tables describing trust relationships earlier in the book. Either way, it is important that an expert in the context *for which the trust relationship is being established* should be involved in considering and describing its properties.

Monitoring and Time

One of the interesting points about monitoring—a process which, by definition, occurs over time—is that although the recording of an action may take place in real time, the analysing of the data rarely does. We examined in Chapter 2 the complexities associated with monitoring information, but if analysis of the data gleaned is not going to be performed immediately, we need to add another layer of complexity: that of storing it. If we are to be able to "trust, but verify", we need to be sure not only that the data to be analysed is correct but also that it is available when we need it. What this means is that we need at least three trust relationships:

- One to the monitoring party, to ensure that the information sent to be stored is correct

- One to the recording party, to ensure that the information actually stored and presented to us is correct (this might be considered two separate trust relationships)

- One to the recording party, to ensure that the information is provided to us on demand

These are requirements that are well-known in the context of logging of data. Logging, which seems at first blush to be a simple operation, actually turns out to be quite complex. By using words such as *correct*, we have skirted over some tricky questions, including how to ensure that ordering of data is correct, that false data cannot be substituted for real, that real data cannot be "replayed" and used again, and that writing to logs is highly available (we have already noted the need for availability of *reading* data). There are also questions to be answered about how frequently updates are made, whether data is confidential (we have concentrated on integrity), and the availability and confidentiality of any backups made. Although this book is not the place for an in-depth discussion of logging, it is worth examining some of the options that may be made when choosing how to log data and some of the benefits and trade-offs they may entail.

Single Database of Record or Distributed   The simplest way to ensure that a data source is consistent is to have only one copy: this becomes the *database of record* and is considered the "source of truth" where all transactions are recorded. Unluckily, this also becomes a single point of failure, whether via malicious attack or misadventure. An alternative is to share data between various locations, whether all locations have all the data or whether different sources receive different subsets of it (typically with some overlap). This allows for reconciling disputed or damaged datasets and better availability properties but is more complex to manage and provides a larger attack surface for malicious actors.

Transactional Logging vs. Lazy Synchronisation   *Transactional logging* is arguably the gold standard for logging services, allowing databases to provide the properties of *atomicity, consistency, isolation*, and *durability* (typically referred to as *ACID*). This practice gives much higher confidence in the correctness of the data but is complex to manage and typically comes with a performance penalty, including the possibility of blocking normal system operation if the parties are unable to complete the transaction. An alternative at the other end of the spectrum is *lazy synchronisation*, which privileges performance and non-blocking operation over immediate ACID (though some or all of these properties may be achieved over time) by choosing when to log events—rather than choosing to log them immediately when they occur. This does raises the possibility that some events may not be recorded in the situation of a failure or denial of services.

Peer-Based Logging   Peer-based logging is an approach where rather than using centralised or authorised entities for log storage and management, peer entities agree to store each other's data, either in a standard distributed or sharded model or by implementing a mechanism such as blockchain. The principle is that if there are enough peers in the system, there should be little temptation to interfere with the data. However, ensuring that this is the case is a more tricky problem than might be expected, particularly when trying to protect against well-resourced attackers, as we saw in Chapter 2 when discussing the *51% attack* in relation to crypto-currencies. On top of this possible problem, the implementation of a blockchain, sharding, or another distribution mechanism may be considered too costly in many situations.

Remote vs. Local   One final consideration is whether data should be stored locally to the system or component that is generating it or stored remotely. Local storage is generally faster, less likely to block or be blocked by external parties, and an easier proposition when establishing a trust relationship. On the other hand, an attack on the local system may well be able to affect the database of log events as well as the system, and errors such as disk filling are more prone to affect the operation of the core system.

Attestation

One of the ways that we can establish a trust relationship to another system is by knowing what it is running. Rather than having to trust a CSP to boot a machine with what we *hope* is on it, if we can be assured that a system contains what we expect, then we have a much better chance of being assured of its likely behaviour and actions. In order to feel so assured, we want as much as possible of the system—hardware and software—to be included in any measurement. We discussed mechanisms for doing this—and some of the pitfalls—in Chapter 5 and also briefly mentioned attestation. Unless the entity reporting the results of a measured or trusted boot process can itself be trusted, we noted, we cannot hold these results as very valuable.

Attestation describes how the results of trust measurements can be provided to other entities; and remote attestation, in particular, describes how these results can be presented to entities that are not on the same physical hardware as the measurement itself. The presenting party is an *attestation service*, and it is important to note that while the potential trustor may need to trust this service to present results, it does not automatically trust the results themselves. In other words, the attestation is the *presentation* of results rather than the proof of their correctness. The trustor still needs to make an evaluation as to whether to create a trust relationship to the measured system—the (potential) trustee. An attestation service can, therefore, act as a trust pivot, with a process and protocol. However, the trustor may wish to consider further information as part of the process: typically a cryptographic signature over the measurement, created by a hardware root of trust with a root certificate that the trustor can verify directly. While we have noted how little thought is generally put into trust relationships in computing, this is where the opposite is true: the Trusted Computing Group, which we have already mentioned, has done a great deal of work on descriptions, processes, and protocols that can be implemented and built on to allow trust measurements and decisions to be made.

As an example, let us consider the operation of Keylime,[7] a remote attestation service that is entirely open source. Keylime describes itself as

> *a TPM-based, highly scaleable remote boot attestation and runtime integrity measurement solution. Keylime enables users to monitor remote nodes using a hardware based cryptographic root of trust.*

We will return to the phrase "runtime integrity measurement" later, but central to Keylime's functionality is remote boot attestation. In fact, it performs exactly the job we described at the beginning of this section, collecting TPM-signed boot measurements from various hosts, transferring them to a central server, and then making them available to other entities that may wish to consume them. Its website notes that it "adheres to the Trusted Computing Group TPM 2.0 specification".

The Problem of Measurement

Another consideration we should have about attestation is that attestation services can only, of course, present information about the measurements of which they are aware, and those measurements only include components that are defined as part of the measurement process. We noted at the beginning of this section that we want as much as possible of the system—hardware and software—to be included in any measurement; but it turns out that in many systems, there are components that are *not* included in such a measurement. In 2016, the broader IT security community took notice of issues that had been raised by some for several years before: that a closed source and opaque hardware component from Intel called the *Intel Management Engine* (IME) operated separately from the main CPU and was not amenable to easy checking from the outside.[8] This is certainly concerning, but there is a broader question of the sheer size and number

---

[7]Keylime.dev, 2020.
[8]See Benchoff, 2016 for a fairly representative article on this issue.

of components being measured. In Chapter 5, we looked at trust relationships between different layers of abstraction. Although we have also discussed the problems that can exist when we need access to further information (which is currently rarely exposed) from other layers and across abstraction boundaries, in the case of a measurement like this, the trust decision is simply binary across the entire measurement set. You have the choice either to trust all or none of it.

It is easy to forget how much code this may entail. A boot measurement might include firmware for multiple devices, a kernel, various boot layers, operating system utilities, and hundreds of user-space libraries. Measuring what this actually means is complex, but let us use one simple metric as an example: the number of lines of code in a standard Linux kernel. At the time of writing, the most recent stable kernel is version 5.13.3[9]—downloading it and then uncompressing and untarring it provides all of the source files. Deleting the documentation and licence files and then performing a line count on the remaining files[10] gives a coarse measure of the amount of code. Version 5.8 reports its total as 61,922,065—over 61 million lines of code (MLOC)! As noted previously, this is a very coarse measurement because real-use kernels are always compiled with options that will remove a great number of these lines of code, including those that are irrelevant for the silicon architecture being targetted (a kernel for an Arm CPU will not include Intel-specific features, for instance) and many that a particular Linux distribution deems unimportant (few desktop distributions will include real-time features). Even given full information about the compilation options and the expertise to work out *which* lines are included and which excluded, the task of going through these and choosing to trust a kernel that the measurement represents is mammoth—and that is before we consider any of the other layers in the stack. Neither are questions that take into account compiler and build options simple: the choices made at build time can have a significant impact not only on the size of the executable(s) created from the kernel sources but also on any number of other properties, including security. At least, in the open source world, we have the opportunity to do *any* of this and to trust the wider community to be performing due diligence and flagging issues. If we decide to use proprietary software, we cannot even start on this task and just have to trust the vendor and any certification bodies that they have chosen to look at their code.

What has this measurement and trust process to do with the context of time, which is the focus of this chapter? We have already looked at one answer, which is that patches and updates may change the code that we are trusting, although the process needs to take this into account, providing "trusted" measurements that include patched or upgraded software. More concerning is

---

[9]For the most recent, see https://kernel.org.
[10]For example, use the command find . -type f -exec wc -l {} \; | awk '{total += $1} END{print total}'.

that the measurement that we have presumably just decided to trust represents the state of the system at *one particular point in time*: when the measurement was performed. Assuming that the point of performing the attestation and verification is to deploy a workload on the measured system (as in the case of a private or public cloud host), the situation around the system changes in three distinct ways as soon as the measurement has been completed once the system is booted and running:

- It may be subject to malicious attacks.
- It is subject to the types of issues we examined in the section "Decay of Trust and Lifecycle" earlier in this chapter.
- It will, as soon as we have loaded our workload onto it, have a larger attack surface (and more software that is also subject to the types of issues noted in the previous point).

This is because we have now moved from *boot time* (at which the system was measured) to *run time*, where the system is in operation; we may also wish to add *load time*, where our workload was loaded onto the system (the period of time when the system was originally set up can be referred to as *provision time*). The fact that these four different stages—boot, provision, load, and run—require different and discrete processes around their security adds further complexity. These processes are likely to be invisible to most tenants of cloud services, despite the fact that they may well be performing similar processes for the layers that they control. These layers of complexity make the establishment of trust more difficult.

The Problem of Run Time

A boot measurement attestation basically puts us in a position where we can decide to trust (or not) the platform (the host system) on which we are going to run our workloads, whether the platform is owned or operated by us or another party (such as a CSP). The problem with run time is that once arbitrary workloads are accepted onto it, it is computationally impossible to be certain that none of them is malicious by analysing them before they run. This is due to the *Church-Turing*[11] *thesis* since it would involve solving the halting problem, which is known not to be solvable by classical computing machines. Even for a smaller (non-arbitrary) set of possible workloads or workload capabilities, providing computational assurance that a malicious workload cannot perform operations that it should not is computationally very expensive. For this reason,

---

[11]Explicitly defined in Kleene, 1952, the relevant outcome of this thesis is that it is possible to create functions for which it is computationally impossible to ascertain whether or not they will ever complete (or "halt").

two alternative approaches have emerged to try to minimise run-time uncertainty and allow trust relationships to carry on beyond boot time into the actual operation of the system. We can think of one of these approaches as proactive and one as reactive.

Access Control Management   Access control management systems restrict the access that processes have to specific operations. This could range from read access to a socket to execute access for a file, to the ability to create new processes or to write to a particular hardware component. There are various approaches and implementations, of which two well-known Linux examples are SELinux[12] and AppArmor.[13] The main drawback with this approach is that in order to constrain workloads, you need to create policies that are tailored closely to the minimum set of operations to which they should be allowed. This means either careful crafting on a per-workload (or workload type) basis or a more "permissive" policy that may not stop all attempts at malicious behaviour.

Integrity Management   Integrity management takes a different approach, starting from the assumption that as long as the initial state of the system (as measured) is trusted, the only concerning operations are those that make changes to those files that have been measured or those that mutate or take advantage of the running state of the system. One approach in Linux, *Integrity Measurement Architecture*[14] (IMA), states as its goals

to detect if files have been accidentally or maliciously altered, both remotely and locally; appraise a file's measurement against a 'good' value stored as an extended attribute, and enforce local file integrity.

(Keylime uses IMA to provide its "runtime integrity measurement solution".) The integrity management approach, though both powerful and complementary to access control management, suffers from the same problems that occur with managing patches and upgrades and can also impose a significant performance penalty on a system, the hit rising with the numbers of files being monitored.

Trusted Computing Base

When we look at the collection of components to which we hold a trust relationship, the term most frequently used is *trusted computing base*[15] (TCB). The Orange Book was central to the adoption of the phrase and defined a TCB as

---

[12]Wikipedia, "Security-Enhanced Linux", 2020.
[13]Wikipedia, "AppArmor", 2020.
[14]Integrity Measurement Architecture, 2020.
[15]Sometimes *Trusted Compute Base*.

contain[ing] all of the elements of the system responsible for supporting the security policy and supporting the isolation of objects (code and data) on which the protection is based. . . . In the interest of understandable and maintainable protection, a TCB should be as simple as possible consistent with the functions it has to perform.[16]

Though the Orange Book became the subject of some criticism, as we saw in Chapter 5, and the concept of a TCB has stood the test of time and is an important one within the IT security space, the danger remains that this description falls foul to Dorothy Denning's concerns about considering trust a property of the system. To avoid this danger, we will consider TCB as encapsulating the concept that we build layers on top of the base and that a TCB represents a set of components that can be

1. Known and defined
2. Evaluated and verified by a trusting party or its agents
3. Expected to continue in the same state
4. Used as the foundation for other services or systems

Property 1 is central to the concept of a TCB. Property 2 allows us to move beyond Denning's concerns about trust as an objective property and consider the TCB as a set of components that can be attested. Property 3 is important since if a TCB changes over time, it is almost impossible for a trustor to maintain a trust relationship to it. Property 4 sets out a TCB's possible use as a trustee.

One of the key parts of the Orange Book's definition of TCB is that it "should be as simple as possible to be consistent with the functions it has to perform"— and this is a core tenet of how TCBs are considered now, with a single alteration, or maybe addition: that the TCB should be as *small* as possible, as well. It is widely understood that the larger the TCB, the larger the attack surface and the larger the number of bugs that it is likely to harbour. On the other hand, a smaller TCB not only turns these two properties on their head but also adds the additional characteristics that a smaller TCB is both easier to audit and conceptually simpler to describe and evaluate architecturally.

Component Choice and Trust

It is for these reasons that choosing the constituent components of a TCB is very important. We mentioned the Intel Management Engine in the previous section. Among the concerns raised by the security community as the role of the IME was made clearer were that although it was, by at least one definition, part of the TCB, booting as it did before the CPU, it was also unauditable (as Intel did not release its specifications) and could not be guaranteed to stay unaltered, as

---

[16]Department of Defense, 1985, p. 66.

executable code could be loaded into it. It thus broke properties 1, 2, and 3 of our list and should not therefore be considered suitable to be a trustee. If any single component or set of components of a TCB comes under such scrutiny, the entire TCB needs to be considered suspect, as it cannot be considered to be a single trustable unit. In our definition, it is not part of the same trust domain, so the TCB cannot be a single unit from the point of view of a trust relationship. The property that a TCB—or any potential trustee component/system—must not be decomposable into different units from the point of view of a single trust domain is central to understanding how trust relationships can—and cannot—be formed.

What, then, constitutes a sensible size for a TCB? That is an almost impossible question to answer (we have already seen how difficult it is to define *size* in a useful way). Maybe a more useful approach is to consider what components might form a TCB and how we can minimise both their size and their number. The size of components is less important as an absolute measure of the number of bytes that executables, libraries, configuration files, etc., take up than as a relative measure of complexity. We have already noted how difficult it is to extrapolate from a set of source files to the eventual size of the executable(s) compiled from it, but a simple count of the number of lines in a file is not necessarily a good measure of relative complexity either. A simple linear flow through a long but well-constructed program with good documentation is likely to be easier to audit than a complex multi-threaded, multi-branch flow in a poorly constructed, ill-documented, but shorter program. Even the language used can make a significant difference: Rust,[17] for example, is a completely open source language designed to be memory-safe, removing[18] many opportunities for developers to create unwitting vulnerabilities in their code.

What about the number of components in the TCB—why should this be important? The first reason is that interfaces between components increase the attack surface of the TCB if they are exposed—intentionally or unintentionally—to components outside the TCB, and a large part of the reason for having a small TCB is to reduce the attack surface available. Attacks may be active (probing interfaces), passive (interception attacks), or replay (taking previous communications across the interface and replaying them, sometimes with alterations, with malicious intent).

The second reason for having a small number of components is that interfaces create possibilities for errors in implementation or for version drift (whether at the API or ABI level).

---

[17]Rust, 2020.

[18]To be more accurate, it does not entirely remove such opportunities, but it makes it much harder for developers to do the wrong thing. In many cases, developers need to make a conscious choice to write code that is likely to expose certain security problems, and blocks of code may even need to be marked with the `unsafe` keyword to pass compiler checks.

The third reason for reducing the number of components in the TCB is not always relevant, but when it is relevant, it is important. In many cases, different components come from different parties (vendors, organisations, or projects). Remember that we wish to have a single trust relationship to the TCB: this may be possible at the level of system operation, but we need, as the trustor, to evaluate and verify the TCB or have an entity acting as our agent do so. This need goes beyond just the source code for the components, but it must include dependencies, compilers, compilation, and build options, maybe even the programming languages employed—and this is before we even start on the question of any firmware or hardware components that also form the TCB. We need to establish trust relationships with each of these components or at least with the entities that produce them, which is generally a more plausible proposition than our doing all the work ourselves.[19]

Given the obvious benefits for security and trust in using open source code, the complexities involved with each consumer of software from an open source project evaluating the code and build options for every project they employ are one of the reasons for the growth in companies providing supported, productised versions of open source projects. Not all companies can or want to build their own versions (of software projects that are typically constantly moving), verify dependencies, perform security checks on all components, find appropriate build options, and then manage operational support. Instead, establishing a trust relationship to a vendor with the appropriate expertise by purchasing a support contract means that the trustor not only gains the benefits from the contract and the expertise of the vendor but is also leveraging the expertise of the broader open source community.

In order to form a trust relationship to the TCB, then, we are going to need either to evaluate *all* of the components within the TCB (or create trust relationships to their providers) and then verify that the measurement that is attested to us is what we expect, or just check the measurement and trust the system on which the TCB resides. It might seem that there is some middle ground where we can check just some of the components, but there is not. The point of the TCB is that it should act as a single, trusted entity—a trustee to which we can establish an operational trust relationship—but if we cannot evaluate whether we can trust each component, then we cannot trust the whole, because a problem with one component means that the entire system is suspect. Operationally, the TCB is acting as a system, which means that from an operational abstraction, it is undecomposable. In short, we either have to evaluate the entire TCB, or we have to trust the system that provides it.

---

[19]However, this approach may be appropriate for certain types of critical or highly sensitive applications.

Reputation Systems and Trust

We discussed reputation in some detail in Chapter 3, where our focus was on human-human or human-organisation reputation considerations. Now that we have transitioned firmly to the realm of trust for computing systems, it is worth looking at reputation in this context. This discussion is appropriate for this chapter because reputation is strongly time-based, and any changes in reputation should be considered if it is one of the measures being used to evaluate assurances when establishing a trust relationship.

Reputation is an area with a lot of overlap between human systems and (particularly) large-scale computing systems such as online marketplaces, but it is not restricted to commercial enterprises. There has been a lot of academic and community work on reputation both within and outside the sphere of security. Although online communities predated the World Wide Web (a classic study being Howard Rheingold's *The Virtual Community*[20]), when the Web started to become populated, multiple communities started to grow, and one of the issues that arose was how to rate information that was posted. Started by Ralph Levien, Advogato[21] was an early social network devoted to free software development, which employed a trust metric to rate and highlight contributions from its members, publishing the design[22] and software implementation.

Another well-known example that is particularly germane to our discussions is *PGP*, key management software named after the initials of what it intended to provide: "Pretty Good Privacy". Leaving aside the legal issues that its inventor, Phil Zimmerman, encountered (he was investigated for three years by the US Customs Service for possibly breaching arms exports controls around cryptography) PGP, and its successor implementations such as *GnomePG* (GPG), implemented a trust model known as a *web of trust*, eschewing centralised authority model, and instead relying on personal trust relationships, where people were physically known to each other—signing each others' keys using public-key cryptography and creating a key chain. Others would act as *introducers*, whereby they would vouch for the trustworthiness—or at least the identity—of other users, who could then be added to a chain held by a particular user. Every user's chain(s) of keys would be different, reflecting the people they knew or to whom they had been introduced.

The problem with this mechanism is one that we have encountered before: what exactly is signified by a signing or an introduction? Are you saying that you believe that an individual is who they assert to be when you sign their key, or that they can be trusted to perform particular actions. If you mean the

---

[20]Rheingold, 2000.
[21]Wikipedia "Advogato", 2020.
[22]Advogato, 2012.

latter, is one of those actions that they are a "trustworthy" introducer? This is a problem of context; but beyond that, the model used by PGP is fairly flat, so there is also no obvious mechanism to track the expected decay in trust along the key chain. In an attempt to reduce some of the problems associated with introducers vouching for people they hardly knew, a culture of *key signing parties*[23] developed, where people (attending a conference, for instance) would meet, provide appropriate identification, and then sign each others' keys. This might seem to provide value by increasing the number of participants in the web of trust and bringing into play the network effect, but it could easily turn out that the peer pressure associated with attending such a party could lead to individuals signing keys for people they hardly knew. The potential for this issue weakened the strength of the Web, which was already overloaded with contexts beyond the simple one of positive identification of an individual. None of this is to suggest that the PGP model was not—and is not—without its merits: there are many people still using it today, and many of them have a deep understanding of both its benefits but also its drawbacks. The broader web of trust that it promised, however, has not materialised, partly due to the issues we have identified but also due to usability problems associated with using PGP keys with other applications.

Many other online reputation mechanisms suffer from not even attempting to make strong assurances about identity and from the ease with which new "identities" can be procured on the Internet, simply in the guise of a unique email address—a problem that has been apparent for some time.[24] Many commerce and travel sites (e.g., Amazon, eBay, and Travelocity) rely on user feedback to build up reputations, but their systems are notoriously brittle, vulnerable both to false improvements to scorings and to malicious attacks on sellers, buyers, or locations.[25]

While these specific issues are not particularly associated with time, there is another: playing the long game, where individuals or organisations spend time acting "properly" in order to build up a positive reputation that will allow them to perform one or more actions that abuse this reputation by breaching the assurances of expected behaviour that have been established over time. This is an issue that is in no sense restricted to computer systems: on 29 November 2019, Usman Khan, a man who had previously been jailed for terrorism offences, killed two people and injured three others in London.[26] He had been participating in a rehabilitation programme for offenders, and it seems that he had been building a reputation and earning trust with those around him in order to allow him to carry out an attack: he had no intention of reforming or being rehabilitated.

---

[23]Brennen, 2008.
[24]Friedman and Resnick, 1999.
[25]See, for instance, Proserpio, Hollenbeck, and He, 2020.
[26]BBC News, 2019.

Similarly, the grooming of children by paedophiles both online and offline often relies on building a reputation over time before abusing the chosen victims. Examples of attackers playing the long game with reputation are less common for online attacks, probably because few computer-computer trust systems rely on reputation but also because a reputation system is rarely the weakest link in the security chain. It is generally easier for attackers to find other weak points that they can attack more quickly rather than waiting for a long-term reputation to be established.

CHAPTER 8

Systems and Trust

We have spent a fair amount of time talking about components and how we need to consider composites of components as systems, looking in detail at systems in Chapter 5. In this chapter, we will concentrate on systems and their position in trust relationships in terms of both the benefits they bring and also the dangers or complications they can introduce. First, however, we will consider briefly what a system might consist of: what are its constituent parts?

System Components

The main focus of this chapter is fairly small systems, though it will become clear pretty quickly that lack of size does not necessarily equate to lack of complexity. Before we move on to such considerations, however, we need to spend a little time thinking about larger systems and what their parts and components might be consist of. In Chapter 3, we defined a system as

> *a set of components—for example, hardware, software, firmware, data, human users—that can be considered a single entity for the purposes of one or more specific architectural views or abstractions.*

Given our focus—which is on the realm of computer-to-computer trust relationships—we have generally been concentrating on hardware and software (with firmware sometimes being considered separately) in automated configurations; but the definition of a system is wider than that, and we should also examine systems driven by user input. In doing so, we can note that the definition specifically includes humans (sometimes referred to, particularly in the earlier days of computing, as *wetware* or *meatware*[1]). Components might also be proactive or reactive, automated or timed. The precise composition of a system should not matter from the point of view of the system-level abstraction, but let us consider why we might consider human interactions in our system. We can start with a large system, such as a mortgage approval system run by a bank. Let us say that I, as a customer of the bank, wish to apply for a mortgage, so I go online and start interacting with the system that manages the process. From my point of view, the system abstraction is fairly clear, and it is to the bank, as well: there is a set of hardware and software systems, with computing resources and access to storage and databases, which, when customers interact with them in expected ways that provide the relevant inputs and outputs, will make a decision as to whether a mortgage should be granted. Part of the process may include calling out to other systems—maintained internally by the bank or by external systems—such as credit or criminal record checks; and at the end, instructions may be passed to various accounts to move money between them. Most of the time, for a modern system, we might expect that the decision of whether or not to approve a mortgage will be entirely automatic—that is, it is performed solely by the software and hardware components—but, from time to time, a human may need to be consulted to make a determination in a case that is in doubt. For the time that this human—presumably an expert with responsibilities specifically associated with this task—is engaging with the software and hardware, they are quite clearly part of the mortgage system, both from my point of view as a prospective customer (though I am likely not even aware of their existence or involvement) and from the point of view of the bank. What is more, the trust relationship that I hold to the system and the trust relationship the bank holds to the system both include this human actor.

It is clear, then, that humans may be part of a system in this context. In the example we have just examined, we have seen how the mortgage approver is involved in the system for part of the time, but we are also aware that they may participate in other activities. Some of these activities will be associated with the work of the bank—maybe the mortgage approver is also a deputy branch manager or has a role as a tax advisor—and some will not—being the chair of the organising committee of the local swimming gala is unlikely to be part of their job description, for instance. There may even be other activities that take place in the context of the mortgage approver's employment at the bank that are

---

[1]Raymond, 2001.

associated with working at the bank and may even be part of their job description but are not explicitly relevant to the bank's day-to-day business, such as being a first aid responder or organising the branch's charitable activities. What is important here is context, of which two examples apply:

- **Bank-related activities**—Those the mortgage approver performs that are related to their position as an employee of the bank

- **Bank business activities**—Those the mortgage approver performs that are directly related to the business of the bank, such as mortgage approvals and tax advice

The reason it is important to understand these contexts is so that we can think about the place of the mortgage approver within the mortgage approval system. When they are undertaking activities with their mortgage approver hat on—that is to say, as a component of the mortgage approval system—they are acting in the same *context* as the other components of the system. Specifically, the mortgage approver and the other components of the system are acting with the agency of the bank. We tend to think of this from the human point of view: our mortgage approver is, legally, likely to be an agent of the bank. But if this is true, then it must be true of the rest of the system, too: the mortgage approval system is an agent of the bank in the context of approving customers (or potential customers) for mortgages. If I am rejected for a mortgage and have occasion to sue an entity over, for instance, evidence that my application was declined due to gender discrimination, then it is the bank to which I (or my lawyers) will present the case, as "the mortgage approval system" is not a legal entity but is acting with the bank's agency. This reflects the discussion we had on agency earlier in the book, but it also leads to an important question: can different parts of the same system perform actions for—that is, have agency for—different entities?

To give a concrete example, let us look at the mortgage approver: when they are acting as part of the system, can they act as the agent for—in the interests of—an entity different from the other parts of the system? The answer to this has to be "no", because otherwise it makes no sense to consider them part of the system. If, for instance, the bank were to discover that the mortgage approver was also employed by a house builder to influence the approver's decisions on approvals in ways that would benefit the builder or damage their competitors, the bank would surely suspend the approver and their involvement in the mortgage approval system. To situate this firmly within the boundaries of our discussions of trust, we can state the point in a different way: trust relationships to a trustee within a specific context always apply explicitly to that trustee. The *system* here, according to our definition, is "considered a single entity for the purposes of one or more specific architectural views or abstractions"—the abstraction in this case being an entity to which a trust relationship can be formed.

When described like this, it seems clear that systems can exercise agency for only one entity within the context of a particular trust relationship, but it is easy to forget that this must be one of the core tests we apply when establishing relationships. Humans are arguably quite bad at considering this—when I go to buy a new car, the salesperson may well attempt to get on friendly terms with me, changing the context of the trust relationship from simply being an agent of the car dealership to one where I am relating to them as a friend whose advice is to be trusted because it is personal and whose feelings I should feel wary of hurting. When they do this, they are attempting to manipulate me and my trust relationship to them by adding another context, without clear flags that I should be forming a new trust relationship (since a new context is being added). Likewise, if we are modelling trust relationships to a system and it appears that the system may be representing more than one entity, it is time to step back and consider whether what we are considering a single system needs to be decomposed into multiple systems, and different trust relationships established with each. This can be extremely complex and even impossible if the components of the system have not been designed with such trust relationships in mind. The principle of *separation of concerns*—where different components of a system (typically a single program or application) encapsulate and manipulate different functions on distinct sets of data—needs to be applied at the macro level as well as the micro level and exposed to potential trustors as part of the design and description of the system.

As we have already noted, one of the key characteristics of systems is that they allow for clear abstractions; but while abstractions provide many benefits, they can also conceal relationships and implementation details that, while not relevant to most users of the system, may have significant implications from a trust point of view. We considered these points in some detail in the previous chapter when we talked about the *trusted computing base* (TCB) the problem for those looking to interact with a system is that, almost by definition, the inner workings of that system are hidden from view and examination. This problem does not end with the TCB, nor can we relegate it to a single point in time: system concepts can—and do—relate to the entire stack and the entire lifecycle of any set of components that we might consider.

Explicit Behaviour

In no way are we trying to suggest that abstractions are a bad idea—without them, modern computing is impossible—but instead, we need to allow a more explicit description of the trust relationships concealed within systems. We actually saw a good example of this in Chapter 3, where we looked at how customers might have chosen to establish a relationship with cloud service provider (CSP) A to provide services because they do not trust CSP B's ability to provide uninterrupted service without being aware that some of CSP A's subsidiary services (e.g., support or bug-reporting services) run on CSP B's cloud, leading to an implicit trust relationship from the customer to CSP B of which the customer is unaware. In some contexts, such dependencies are becoming more of a concern: the rise of legislation such as the European Union's GDPR and the State of California's CCPA, which we have already referenced, means that organisations have to be very careful about where they store and process data, and the use of services based in certain countries or jurisdictions may be disallowed.

The problem with such dependencies and implicit trust relationships in computer-computer trust relationships is how to automate them. This also applies to the consumption of software or hardware directly, rather than as services; but it is compounded in the latter case as humans are more likely to be involved in decisions as to what software or hardware to use unless there is an automated component to the selection, in which case we can describe the availability of this selection as itself a service—our discussion will focus on services but includes consumption in any case where automation is involved. Automation must be a key component to any computer-based system that is to scale beyond simple use cases, and we have said that providers of trustee systems need to deliver sufficient explicit information about encapsulated relationships and the characteristics of a system that flow from these; but how can these providers know what information that they need to expose? There may obviously be issues around commercial confidentiality to consider, but a provider cannot even begin to address these issues if they do not know what potential consumers of their services may wish to know. On the other hand, even if there are no commercial concerns, just listing all the possible relationships and dependencies at every level of abstraction would lead to far too much information to be processed without some sort of framework in which to understand it. The problem is no less complex for the potential consumers, however: how can they know what information to ask for if the abstractions offered by service providers hide encapsulated relationships and dependencies that may be of concern to them?

We can offer an answer to how to start fixing this circular problem: trust contexts. As we have been advocating through this book, an understanding of the contexts in which a trustor interacts with a trustee allows decisions to be made and automated. It provides more than that, however, because it also allows the possibility for a framework with the *intention* of making decisions and *within* which such decisions can be made.

Defining Explicit Trust

The tool that we have been using for describing trust relationships—the trust table—is one we can extend to allow both service providers and consumers of services to make, on the one hand, offers of information, and on the other, requests for information, both within specific contexts. We can start with an existing example that we have already mentioned: the question of the jurisdiction in which data will be stored. First, we can imagine an offer from a service provider (see Table 8.1).

Table 8.1: Trust offer from a service provider

FROM (TRUSTOR)	UNDEFINED	TO (TRUSTEE)	CLOUD SERVICE PROVIDER
Context(s)		Storage of sensitive data related to EU citizens	
Time-specific		Duration of contract	
Action(s)		Data moved to persistent storage	
Expectation(s)		Data marked "EU-sensitive" will only be stored on systems physically residing in EU countries or countries with a relevant treaty; such systems will be wiped before transfer to any country outside such physical locations.	
Assurance(s)		Certifications from relevant country bodies; physical location information provided within TPM, available to be checked by consumer of service.	
Mitigation(s)		Legal recourse; wiping of data by consumer	

We can imagine a similar requirement set from a potential consumer of services (shown in Table 8.2).

Table 8.2: Trust requirements from a service consumer

FROM (TRUSTOR)	CUSTOMER	TO (TRUSTEE)	UNDEFINED
Context(s)		Storage of sensitive data related to EU citizens	
Time-specific		Six months	
Action(s)		Data moved to persistent storage	
Expectation(s)		Data marked "EU-sensitive" will only be stored on systems physically residing in EU countries or countries with a relevant treaty.	
Assurance(s)		Certifications from relevant country bodies	
Mitigation(s)		Legal recourse	

In the case of this service offer and this consumer's requirements, the properties offered by the provider exceed the requirements of the consumer, who should therefore be happy to form a trust relationship to the CSP, assuming that sufficient requirements in other contexts are met. It may be the case, for instance, that there is another context where the ability of the consumer to wipe data is stated as a requirement. This is met in the offer context just described, but if the ability is only provided within the context of this trust context (EU data) and not in the general case, then the consumer should reject the offer unless the only type of data that they might wish to store is EU data.

The example we have just given is now common, given the regulatory contexts in which many organisations operate and the wish to run applications and process and store data in the Cloud; but the assurances provided by CSPs are typically provided at the contractual level rather than the API level. This not only requires information to be extracted from the technical realm into the non-technical, sales/contract-negotiation realm but also means that automating negotiations over such capabilities is well-nigh impossible, and automated or programmatic enforcement of such contractual clauses is often non-existent. Other types of capabilities, on the other hand, may be "baked in" to APIs, rather than explicitly offered, meaning that a human would need to look over the interface descriptions to ascertain, for instance, whether data could be deleted in order to understand whether requirements were met. In the worst case, there might be a need to check API information, other technical documentation, *and* contractual descriptions to work out whether needs are met: it is not uncommon for complex requirements like this to slip through the cracks when purchasing services. And, of course, such a state of affairs is more likely to occur around more complex requirements, which is precisely what we are likely to see when we start considering trust contexts and relationships and as more jurisdictions adopt privacy and data management controls.

These sorts of offers provide added benefits for both parties beyond the obvious ones we have already listed. Two of the most obvious are:

Reducing Service Misuse   When a service is not well-described, it is possible that it will be used for purposes other than those for which it was intended. Though this might seem both unlikely and unimportant, the chances of it are significant if the description of a service does not include contexts important to the consumer or where assumptions are made by either party about the existing *or future* functionality, capabilities, or properties of a service. This can quickly increase the negative impact of such a misuse when assumed (that is, implicit) behaviours in a trustee within a trust relationship do not meet expectations.

Allowing Service Changes   We talked briefly about *version drift*, when the behaviour of the system changes as new versions are produced, when we looked at TCBs. The standard expectation around software is that behavioural changes—whether at the API or ABI level—should be restricted to *major version* changes, which are often identified by a numbering system[2]; other changes to characteristics or behaviours of a system that are not *explicitly* documented may be made within minor changes and may not even be mentioned in change logs. Given the scarcity of statements about trust relationships and the lack of ability to state requirements or offer behaviour around trust, there is no existing mechanism to inform a service consumer of changes in behaviour, and any move to provide such a framework must come as an improvement.

Dangers of Automated Trust Relationships

Providing such a framework to inform customers of changes, then, allows trust relationships and dependencies, which are often currently implicit by necessity, to be made explicit and part of automated service offering and consumption. A note of caution is worth injecting at this point, which is that the ability to automate a system fully is not always the most sensible from a risk point of view. We can see why with a couple of examples where real-life *edge cases* suggest that there is sometimes a place to allow humans to override the trust relationships that might be designed into computer-based systems.

A Hospital Operating Theatre Booking System   Our first example is a hypothetical system to automate and control the booking of the operating theatres in a hospital. Rules are instituted to ensure that only someone logging in as a surgeon or anaesthetist may book an operating theatre and that they must hold the post of at least consultant or equivalent. This might be to avoid the booking of operating theatres by non-qualified staff to "block" periods of time, which might cause scheduling problems based on the availability of staff. We may assume that careful design, implementation, and testing have led to a system that works well and has not run into any problems, and that the trust relationships are locked into the implementation after several months of successful use, but that a feature was added to allow for two or more surgeons or anaesthetists to add a more junior doctor to the permissions list for a 24-hour period in case of holiday clashes or a rise in cases.

This works very well until there is a major terrorist incident close to the hospital. All existing bookings need to be cleared, but the only person "on the ground" with access to the system is a senior nurse. They manage to contact one of the consultant surgeons who is out of the operating theatre, preparing for more incoming casualties but the other surgeon who was about to come on duty was on the way to hospital at the time

---

[2]An increasingly standard example is *semantic versioning* (SemVer); see Preston-Werner, 2020.

of the attack and ended up helping on the scene. The only anaesthetists available are working back-to-back cases in the operating theatres and are unable to come out to deal with the system. In previous emergencies, the relevant authorised persons would have phoned the nurse in charge and asked them to make bookings; but with the new system, there is no way to authorise the senior nurse as an authorised party, so the hospital has to fall back on manual bookings, slowing down a number of processes and putting patients at risk.

The Man Who Stopped WWIII   While our previous example may have seemed serious, our second shows how the ability to override the information provided by automated systems may well have prevented a nuclear war. In 1983, Soviet early warning systems erroneously reported a US missile launch, quickly followed by five more. A lieutenant colonel in the Soviet Air Defence Forces, Stanislav Yevgrafovich Petrov,[3] judged the warning to be a false alarm and failed to follow protocol, which dictated that he should report missile launches to his superiors—who might well have launched a counter-strike, likely leading to a retaliatory launch by the United States.

The fact that trust resided in a human, rather than an automated computer system, allowed a decision to be made that did not naively trust the correctness of the early warning system.

While we might hope that those designing and testing such systems would consider such use cases, it is demonstrably the case that this does not always happen. Neither humans nor computers can reliably predict all possible edge cases that might result in failures with catastrophic impact on the functioning of the system or the environment in which they function—this despite claims around AI/ML systems' ability to make decisions that fundamentally resolve complex mathematical searches and bias amplification. This is one of the reasons risk management should be part of the design phase of any system lifecycle. Considering the very worst cases that a failure might bring about, deciding what their impact would be, and then finding ways to mitigate them is a better approach than designers guessing the likelihood of all the cases they can think of and then working out how (hopefully) to avoid them. This is also a strong argument for diversity within the various phases of a system's lifecycle: the more different ways of thinking are available to the team, the more points of view can be expressed, and the broader the range of possible scenarios considered, avoiding some of the dangers of groupthink that can afflict very homogeneous teams.

---

[3]Wikipedia contributors, "Stanislav Petrov", 2020.

Time and Systems

The question of the importance of time as a context is something that we have already addressed, but what are we doing with this context, and what assurances can we have about it? Decay of trust is the use of time that should be at the forefront of our mind, given the context of this book. It is, however, difficult to define, since exactly how decisions are made will be contingent on the specific context, as discussed in Chapter 7.

To discuss time, we need to consider three possible requirements:

- Knowledge of *wall time*—This is often referred to as *wall-clock time*, or just *real time*,[4] capturing the idea that there is an objective external time on which different parties can agree and that they use as a reference.

- Agreement on *relative time*—Two or more parties may not need an external reference but can agree on the amount of time elapsed after a particular point.

- Explicit *monotonic time*—What is important is not how much time has elapsed but just that time *has* elapsed, so that replay attacks can be avoided, for instance.

In order to get a better feel for some of the inputs that might be used to make decay decisions, let us consider some of the standard uses of time:

Operation Execution   One of the most obvious uses of time is to allow operations to be carried out at a particular time or after a particular amount of time has elapsed. Such an operation could be deleting a file, turning on a light, buying some stock, or one of myriad other operations.

Logging and Correlation   Often, when we are recording events, typically in a log, we record the point at which they happen. There is generally nothing inherently interesting about recording the time; it is usually used for one of two reasons:

   Correlation   When considering various sets of events, particularly on different systems or in different logs, it is often important to be able to correlate them and establish whether they were triggered by the same action.

   Ordering   Ordering is slightly different to correlation in that it generally allows the comparison of different events to establish either whether one might have caused the other or whether, in contrast, there is no possibility of correlation (if, for instance, a file was saved *before* a key-press was entered).

---

[4]Though *real time* can be confusing, as real-time systems have different sets of requirements.

Time-Out   Time is important when considering if an operation should be concluded or cancelled, typically because there was no further interaction. Closing a network connection or blanking a screen because there have been no operations to indicate activity requires the ability to note the passage of time and respond to it.

Authorisation   Certain policies applied to services may only allow them to be authorised between particular times, requiring the service (or, more accurately, the component that authorises access to it) to have access to the time in order to enforce the policy.

Expiration of Tokens   One particular type of authorisation is authorisation via tokens, which may be granted to one entity by another to allow it access to an entity or service. Knowledge of when these expire is important to both the authorised entity (the party holding the token, which needs to know when their authorisation will run and/or when to apply for a new token) and any authorising entities, which will need to make the decision on whether to allow access to services.

Re-keying   Many connection protocols[5] that rely on cryptography require, or at least recommend and allow, re-keying: that is, agreement on a new session key by the parties communicating. This not only reduces the amount of data available to an attacker if the key is compromised (since only a portion of the data communicated will be available under any particular key) but also reduces the amount of cipher text (encrypted data) available for analysis under any particular key, thereby making it more difficult to compromise any key. Re-keying is less typical for data at rest—data that is stored on disk, for instance—but is also available. Techniques for protecting data in use may also make use of re-keying.

Replay Prevention   Some attacks on cryptographic protocols or authorisation protocols rely on reusing previous messages or sets of messages: these are called *replay attacks*. Although one defence against this is to use a *challenge* or *nonce*, which allows a particular set of messages to be identified uniquely, another is to ensure that the passage of time is recorded and that previous messages are not allowed to be replayed.

Transactions   Transactions are sets of actions that are always bundled together, in that they must all complete or all fail. These could be monetary transactions, database commits, or filesystem writes, but in each case, there must be a concept of time to allow the transition between the pre-transaction state and the post-transaction state.

---

[5]See, for instance, the IPsec protocol described in RFC 4301: Kent and Seo, 2005.

While all of these use cases require time, their requirements are different in terms of which of the three types of time they need, as defined at the beginning of the section (wall time, relative time, and monotonic time).

There are a variety of ways in which these different requirements can be met, with the key differences between them from our point of view being whether a third-party source is relied upon (Figure 8.1) or whether one of the parties involved in the existing trust relationship provides the time source (Figure 8.2), in which case there is a new trust relationship context toward this entity. The third option—where each party provides their own source—is not valid, as there can be no agreement on time unless some decision is made as to which source or combination of sources is trusted, which leads us back to the second case of a trust relationship being made to a particular existing party or parties. The difference between the two main cases is important because the trust relationships are significantly different.

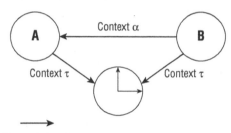

Figure 8.1: External time source.

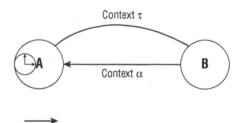

Figure 8.2: Time as a new trust context.

In all cases, in order to act as the basis for a context, time must be considered a primitive. When the time source is provided by one of the parties in the existing sets of trust relationships, there simply needs to be a decision by the other party or parties to set up a trust relationship to this party. An example is shown in Table 8.3, where a server is sending log entries to a logging service. In such a case, there may be multiple servers whose entries may need to be correlated, and it makes sense to choose the entity that will be recording all of the entries to be the time source: in fact, it may be that the server(s) do not include timing information in the entries sent, relying on the logging service to add this as it accepts and records them (though issues such as delays in sending and receiving messages are themselves issues to be considered).

Table 8.3: Trust from server to logging service regarding time stamps

FROM (TRUSTOR)	SERVER	TO (TRUSTEE)	LOGGING SERVICE
Context(s)		Time source	
Time-specific		n/a	
Action(s)		Add time stamps to log entries	
Expectation(s)		Time internally consistent to logging service; millisecond granularity	
Assurance(s)		Very few	
Mitigation(s)		Very few	

Given that we are treating time as a primitive, the assurances available to the trustor are very few. The same goes for mitigations, as the only alternative to using the logging service would be for the trustee to set up a trust relationship with another party or use its own time—both of which remove much of the utility of using the logging service in the first place, since now there can be no consistency of time for logging, and correlation of entries—the reason we gave for this trust relationship—is no longer possible. This will turn out to be an important point when we look at trust domains in Chapter 12. Another interesting point is that the type of time—wall time, relative time, or monotonic time—is irrelevant in this use case, at least from the point of view of the trustee. It may be that the party wishing to perform log correlation needs to be able to check the log entry service's time against wall time, but even this may not be necessary, and the server sending the log entries—the trustee—has no such requirement.

External time sources present more complexities from a trust point of view and need to be considered trust anchors provided by endorsing authorities. This may seem to go against our definition of trust anchors as "static", given that they provide dynamic information; but if we think of time as a deterministic, monotonic progression based on a known (static) starting point,[6] then the definition seems appropriate. Time sources are important for many use cases, as we noted earlier, and a good deal of work has gone into providing time sources that are intended to be trusted. Global navigation satellite systems (GNSS),

---

[6]A definition that does not operate particularly well with scientific understanding of space-time and relativistic effects but is appropriate for most use cases we will be considering.

of which the best known is the Global Positioning System (GPS), can provide accurate time, but there are instances of spoofing that are worrying and mean such options are not appropriate for all systems. There are also a number of public time servers on the Internet that follow the Network Time Protocol (NTP) standard; anyone needing to make decisions about trust relationships to NTP or equivalent time sources should consider the analysis performed by Mizrahi in RFC 7384,[7] which provides an in-depth examination of various attacks, how difficult they are to perform, and what mitigations may be available.[8]

Defining System Boundaries

Boundaries are important for systems because without defining them, we cannot know which components are part of a particular system and which belong to another system. Equally, boundaries are important because they allow change. A well-defined boundary, typically expressed in the software world, at least, is an *API* or an *ABI*, both of which define a semantic boundary: supported (and sometimes excluded) messages and communications via the API or ABI are listed and the expected behaviours and error conditions described. As we saw when we discussed TCBs, this allows for changes to behaviour to be restricted and published, but it also allows for changes on either side of the boundary—by the trustor and trustee in our context—that do *not* need to be described as long as they have no impact on the behaviour defined on the interface. Take a RESTful API,[9] for instance, describing the operations available to update a wiki entry. As long as a system providing such a service adheres to the API description, it does not matter to any clients calling the service over the API whether the system is implemented in Rust, Perl, Erlang, or any other programming language. Again, as long as the system adheres to the service, any part—or all—of the system can be rewritten with no impact on any client services. From the other direction, the system providing the API has no interest in how the client is written—whether it is multi-threaded or single-threaded, for instance—and any changes have no impact on it as long as the API is followed correctly. Note, however, the word *correctly*: this lack of impact is true only if the API fully captures all the behaviours that may impact the service provider (*server*) and client. One example of the impact of threading is the sudden and very negative impact of new multi-threaded web browsers on early implementations of HTTP servers, some of which were single-threaded and suffered from significant performance degradation until they were rewritten to handle multiple threads from the same browser.

---

[7]Mizrahi, 2014.
[8]NTPsec (see NTPsec, 2021) is a framework designed to address some of the known issues.
[9]Erl et al., 2012.

Trust and a Complex System

Let us consider a fairly complex system: the Linux virtualisation stack that we spent some time looking at in Chapter 5. Figure 8.3 is the diagram that we used before.

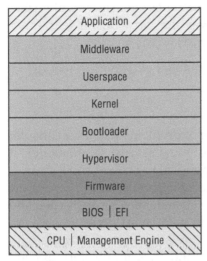

Figure 8.3: Linux virtualisation stack.

It turns out that our diagram is somewhat simplified, as the basic picture focuses on the stack from the point of view of the virtual machine and ignores, for instance, the kernel, which sits at the base of the operating system of the host machine itself. A more complete version might look more like Figure 8.4,[10] though even this depiction ignores a variety of different components that may be present.

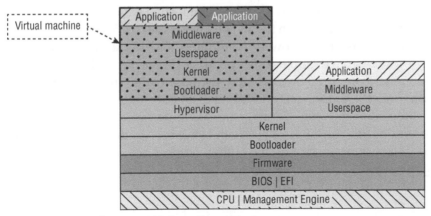

Figure 8.4: Virtualisation stack (complex version).

---

[10]Note that there are multiple approaches to virtualisation, even within Linux, and this picture shows a simplified version of only one.

The first and most obvious question to ask is what we should describe as a system. On one level, the picture represents an entire system, as it is all executing on a single unit of hardware: a host system.[11] Looking from a different point of view, however, we might say that the level we want to consider might be applications—but there are three of these shown in this diagram. For our purposes, we will break things down into two different systems. We will further assume that we can distinguish the two in a way that provides us with interesting issues to consider. We can define these two systems as:

- The virtual machine: all of the components that exist within the virtual machine

- The host: All of the other components

This characterisation may present us with some problems when we consider exactly what is executing, but from the point of view of trust relationships, it makes a lot of sense. If the host machine—the physical hardware and the lower levels of the host—is owned and operated by a CSP (if it is, in fact, part of the Cloud), then all of the components that form the virtual machine are owned and provisioned by a tenant. The picture of a system with layers gives us a way to consider the different components and the trust relationships that come with them. The layers are marked visually, with greys and lines, for the various components. Each pattern represents a different originator of the component(s): let us refer to them as vendors for simplicity. While it is quite possible that each component comes originally from a different entity, we have assumed that some sets are provided by the same vendor, as in the case of the following host components: bootloader, kernel, hypervisor, userspace, and middleware. The expectation here is that this vendor will provide support and patching for all of these components and is therefore an appropriate trustee to whom the trustor—in this case, the host system's owner, the CSP—can form a trust relationship.

We expect that the CSP will wish to run applications of their own—one such is shown at right in the diagram, shown with different shading since it is provided by a different source from the operating system pieces we have already considered. Equally, there are three layers below the bootloader shown in different colours: firmware, BIOS/EFI, and CPU/Management Engine. While the firmware associated with the CPU/Management Engine layer may be provided by a single vendor or vendors for that layer, almost all modern stacks include other physical components provided by other vendors, such as network cards and storage devices.

---

[11]Even this is a simplification: *hyperconverged infrastructure* (HCI) allows for multiple host systems to be combined into a single managed unit, and even cheap personal computers now have multiple CPU cores that may be segmented and operate different instructions.

Having taken a brief tour of the various components in the host stack, let us look at the virtual machine in Figure 8.4, starting from the top down. We show two applications within the virtual machine, each from a different vendor. There is a possibility, of course, that one of these two applications is actually the same application from the same vendor as the one being run on the host machine by the CSP; but since the components within the virtual machine are owned by the tenant, there is necessarily a separate trust relationship: although the trustee may be the same, the trustors—the CSP and the tenant—are different. This also explains why the other key layers—Bootloader, Kernel, Userspace, and Middleware[12]—have different trust relationships associated with them to the ones outside the virtual machine. These components, from the point of view of the applications in the virtual machine, form the trusted computing base that make up the virtual machine. Access to sufficient information to allow each application in the virtual machine to decide whether to establish a trust relationship with the virtual machine TCB should be available to it because the applications and the TCB components are provisioned by the tenant. The trust relationships will, of course, be subject to all of the points we considered in the section on TCBs in Chapter 7; but issues like the management of upgrades should be managed by the same party—the tenant—allowing lifecycle management to be performed as expected and by the relevant party.

It is at this point, however, that we need to muddy the water significantly, because the TCB of the virtual machine also needs to establish a trust relationship to the layers below it: the host machine's components act as a TCB for the virtual machine. This might not seem too large a problem: at least we have an API layer (the hypervisor). However, given the service model espoused by most CSPs, it is extremely unlikely that any tenant can delve deeply enough into the layers below to be fully assured that a trust relationship—even if established at virtual machine provisioning—can be safely and knowledgeably maintained.

In fact, the situation is even worse than we might have hoped, as we have not been totally honest about the interface between the virtual machine and the host: although it looks, from our initial diagram, to be supplied entirely by the hypervisor, the real story is more complex. In order for virtual machines to use hardware devices, access needs to be provided from the host machine. There are a number of ways of doing this, with varying opportunities for the virtual machine to evaluate the extent to which each approach should be trusted, not to mention the varying levels of security associated with each. Equally, although our virtual machine stack shows a bootloader at the bottom, it is normal for a BIOS or UEFI layer to exist below that, and for it to be provided not by the tenant, but by the owner of the host—the CSP in this case—as this allows for easier setup of access to the hardware devices we have just mentioned.

---

[12]Although it is possible to "nest" hypervisors in some contexts, running virtual machines within virtual machines, we will ignore this case: the same arguments and issues apply but can be considered more complex.

We have already discussed in detail the problems associated with system abstractions when establishing trust—and that is when we are operating with well-defined systems. How, then, is the virtual machine—the set of components provided by the tenant—supposed to form a trust relationship to the host system—the set of components supplied by the CSP? The short answer is that, under current models of trust, it is impossible. In order to discover why, we need to consider isolation.

Isolation and Virtualisation

When we examined isolation in Chapter 7, we noted part of the Orange Book's definition of the TCB as

> *all of the elements of the system responsible for supporting the security policy and supporting the isolation of objects (code and data) on which the protection is based.*

This definition might suggest that isolation is absolute and bidirectional, but, like trust, it is not. Let us step back to a simpler representation of a CSP-provided host and consider three entities, as in Figure 8.5.

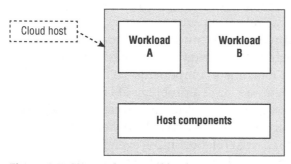

Figure 8.5: Host and two workloads.

· Remember that a virtual machine is simply one or more virtual CPUs and a set of memory pages, all associated with a particular workload. There are three types of isolation that might be of concern to the parties running these components (the CSP and the tenant):

Isolation Type 1—Workload from Workload   The first type of isolation is stopping one workload executing on the host from interfering with another workload (shown in Figure 8.6), whether by affecting its access to resources (a *noisy neighbour* attack), breaking its confidentiality by reading data in its memory pages, or breaking its integrity by altering data in its memory pages. It does not matter whether the workload is malicious by design or has been compromised: the requirement is to protect the other workload from its interference.

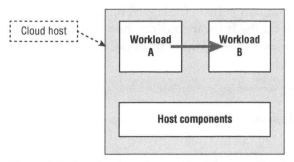

Figure 8.6: Isolation type 1—workload from workload.

Isolation Type 2—Host from Workload   Isolation type 2 (Figure 8.7) is about protecting the host components from a malicious or compromised workload. An attack where this succeeds is sometimes known as a *break-out attack,* as the workload is considered to have "broken out" of the controls imposed on it by the host components (in the case of a virtual machine, these are supplied mainly by the hypervisor and CPU, which has specific instructions available to create and run virtual machines). Stopping attacks of this kind is also important when considering isolation type 1, as the controls used to stop workload-from-workload attacks are provided by the same host components that are likely to be compromised in the event of a successful break-out.

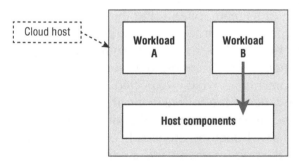

Figure 8.7: Isolation type 2—host from workload.

Isolation Type 3—Workload from Host   The third type of isolation (Figure 8.8) is protecting the workload from the host and is going to be an issue that reappears throughout the rest of the book. There are two key problems faced when trying to isolate workloads from interference from the host: memory and scheduling. The way in which virtual machines are implemented in most architectures is that the hypervisor controls—and is able both to read from and write to—the memory pages allocated to every virtual machine. This means that a key component of the host—under the CSP's control—is able to look into and change the code and data associated with the tenant's workload. Equally, the kernel is in charge of providing CPU cycles to all processes on the host, including the virtual machine, and this means it is able to restrict—in whole or in part—all ability for the virtual machine to execute.

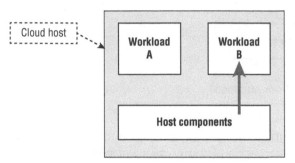

Figure 8.8: Isolation type 3—workload from host.

This final type of isolation deserves deeper consideration. Let us consider how the tenant may try to protect itself—that is, the memory pages associated with it—from the host. The most obvious way to do this is by encrypting them, which, if it can be successfully performed, provides isolation by protecting the confidentiality of the data the pages contain (and may also protect the integrity of the data). However, if the tenant tries to protect itself by encrypting some of this data, it also needs to be able to decrypt it when required, with a cryptographic key that will be in another section of its memory and that the hypervisor—or any appropriately privileged host process—can see. The same goes for the code that will be doing the processing: the hypervisor or other privileged host process can not only see but also change it, so it is impossible even to be sure that the software running in a virtual machine is what is expected.

We have already discussed one technique for ensuring that the software running in a stack is what we expect: measured or trusted boot, which, though not perfect, might at least provide us with some assurances. In order to use these techniques, we need a TPM to do the measurements. We could do this by creating a virtual TPM and making it part of the stack within the virtual machine. However, placing a completely virtual TPM within the virtual machine does not help, as the host can look into that; and even using a virtual TPM with a root of trust in the actual hardware TPM only helps with assurances that the workload was correct at provisioning load-time—when we have already established the host can always alter any of the data in any of the memory pages in the virtual machine. Attempts to attest to the workload owner—the tenant—that the host TCB is trustworthy and will not attack the workload are complex, as we have already seen when considering attestation.

Equally, in order to process data, that data needs to make it into the virtual machine: to be entered into its memory pages. This typically means that it is transferred over a network connection or via storage: both mechanisms are under the control of the host,[13] which means, of course, that they are subject to interference by the host.

With standard virtualisation techniques, there is literally no way to protect a workload from a malicious or compromised host. The host—that is, any party with sufficient privilege to be able to read from or write to memory pages associated with a virtual machine—has control over the virtual machine's memory and its ability to access any resources, including input/output devices like its network, storage, keyboard, graphics cards, and even CPU cycles themselves. In Chapter 10, we will look in more detail at some of the consequences that all of this has on how and when tenants can and should deploy workloads to the Cloud.

The Stack and Time

Setting aside for now the question of isolation, let us consider the stack and how it looks over time. Let us look at the world from the point of view of the application, which is the core part of the stack (or stacks, if we prefer) in which the tenant is interested. Underneath the application are several layers that are controlled by the tenant; but underneath those, there are several layers that are controlled by the host. As we can see from the figure, however, there are several different parties responsible for providing them. For every layer underneath the application, and for which there must be a trust relationship, whether explicit or implicit, there is the question of what happens when updates need to be applied. There is no plausible way that the application or the virtual machine in which it resides can have a trust relationship with the providers of every layer in the stack below it: indeed, one of the major reasons for the virtualisation interface is to provide an abstraction to avoid the need for knowledge of the layers below. This means the tenant must establish a trust relationship with the CSP (which controls the host), which is very clear about the responsibility of the CSP to maintain appropriate relationships with these different providers. We will look at these relationships in more detail when we examine the Cloud and the Edge in Chapter 10.

Beyond Virtual Machines

Our discussion in this section has dived fairly deeply into the world of virtual machines and hypervisors, but almost exactly the same arguments and issues apply to most other types of isolation. Beyond virtual machines, where much

---

[13]Some technologies, like *single root I/O virtualization* (SR-IOV) can allow virtual machines direct access to device memory. SR-IOV is a proprietary standard maintained by the PCI-SIG: see `Pcisig.com`, 2020.

of the isolation is provided by virtualisation instructions provided by the CPU, any situation where a host is executing a workload or workloads for another party raises the question of how all types of isolation are provided, with the most tricky always being type 3 (Figure 8.8). Mainframes have long provided a number of ways of partitioning workloads from each other and the host, but the large majority of workloads today are deployed on hosts employing what is typically now referred to as *x86 architecture* or simply *PC architecture*. This type of hardware virtualisation was introduced around 2005 by both Intel and AMD and was the standard mechanism for isolation until the popularisation of *Linux containers*[14] (or just *containers*) by the company Docker around 2013. Linux containers take a different approach from virtual machines, using various mechanisms in the Linux kernel such as namespaces and control groups (usually shortened to *cgroups*) to provide isolation for aspects of execution such as networking, process IDs, and file system access. The number of cgroups, and hence the number of types of isolation, grew as new controls were added, to encourage the adoption of containers. The immediate and fast-growing popularity of containers was due to a number of factors, including the ease with which they could be deployed and the packaging format, which made the creation and maintenance of new container images relatively simple, at least compared to virtual machines.

The host kernel manages all isolation—through cgroups—and has control over all memory used by the containers (the workloads, in this case) and their execution. Unlike virtual machines, all of the isolation provided by Linux containers is entirely in software, which means that the assurances of isolation provided by type 1 and type 2 are generally considered less strong than for hardware virtualisation. For this reason, various approaches have been proposed to combine the ease of deployment and packaging offered by containers with the stronger run-time isolation provided by hardware virtualisation, of which the best known and most mature is probably Kata Containers.[15] Containers provide no additional type 3 isolation over hardware virtualisation and virtual machines, however, which means that although combined technologies like Kata Containers may improve type 1 and type 2 isolation, there is no improvement in *workload-from-host isolation* (type 3).

Whether containers provide, in general, an improvement in trust options over virtual machine approaches is debatable. Containers rely on the underlying operating system to provide much of the execution environment and so do not provide, for instance, their own kernel or many of the common libraries found on a Linux host. Instead, the application and any further dependencies are

---

[14]Originally known broadly as *Docker containers*, this term has generally been deprecated as the industry has produced non-proprietary standards around containers.
[15]Katacontainers.io, 2020.

bundled into the image, which is then executed by a container runtime such as Docker[16] or CRI-O.[17] This means the nature of the trust relationships from the workload to the host is more explicit and also that there are potentially fewer dependencies from the application to the tenant-controlled layers within the workload—the container image, which is then executed as a running container. In practice, however, the process of creating a container image typically leads to the importing of many—sometimes thousands—different dependent libraries and executables into the workload, often almost invisibly to the tenant. This is exacerbated by the fact that one of the most popular aspects of containers is the ability to take existing container images from public (or private) repositories and either run them as provided or build on top of them to create a new image, which may then be shared back into one or more repositories for use by other parties. While this makes the creation and deployment of containers very easy and has resulted in the creation of a huge public library of available images in a way that never happened for virtual machines, the trust implications are dire. This has created a situation where it is often impossible, as a consumer of a container image that was created through a process of many parties building on top of each parties' prior work, to establish a trust relationship regarding that image because there is no identifiable party or parties to which to form trust relationships.

There have been numerous examples both of compromised libraries being imported into containers[18] and of malicious actors intentionally creating and publicly publishing malicious container images for their own ends—a particular favourite being the mining of crypto-currency[19]—and some of these have even led to compromises in *workload-from-workload* or *host-from-workload* (type 1 and type 2) isolation. In these sorts of circumstances, where it is extremely simple to deploy containers but extremely difficult to enumerate trust relationships, we must consider that containers present real challenges for any environment where trust management is valued, as users can be expected to take advantage of the library's ease of use whilst ignoring the complex issues associated with the trust relationships associated with that use.

Hardware-Based Type 3 Isolation

The lack of type 3 (*workload-from-host*) isolation has been an issue in the industry for some time, and a number of attempts have been made to address it. We will list the main types of hardware isolation here, all of which provide much greater isolation support to workloads than either virtual machines or containers, and will examine them in more detail in Chapter 11.

---

[16]Docker.com, 2020.
[17]CRI-O.io, 2020.
[18]See, for example, Heinz, 2020.
[19]See, for example, Field, 2020.

Hardware Security Modules (HSMs)   HSMs were originally designed for military and defence applications where sensitive material and operations—particularly those associated with cryptographic keys—required strong confidentiality and integrity protections. They were later adopted by financial organisations and certificate authorities. Hardware security modules, as suggested by their name, protect computing and data in hardware, with various levels of protection and tamper-evidence being available (with appropriate certifications). They may be attached directly to the motherboard of a host system (e.g., via a PCI[20] or PCI-X bus), connected to the host via other interconnect mechanisms, or made available over the network—for instance, over a local Ethernet connection. These modules are expensive, do not scale particularly well, and are not typically suited to general computing tasks. Although some are programmable, the obstacles to creating and deploying specific applications to them whilst maintaining appropriate levels of security are high. We discussed HSMs in some detail in Chapter 5.

Field Programmable Gate Arrays (FPGAs)   *FPGAs* are chips that can be shipped on a motherboard but reprogrammed after manufacture. This allows the owner of a host to repurpose them depending on requirements. Their original usage was mainly for networking and telecommunications, but they have other uses, such as neural networks and machine learning. Given that they are physically isolated from the rest of the system, they can provide type 3 isolation; but they are difficult to program for generalised computing, and managing deployment and trust management of new applications is significantly more complex than standard workloads such as virtual machines and containers.

Trusted Execution Environments (TEEs)   *TEEs* differ from HSMs and FPGAs in that they are typically part of the CPU[21] rather than separate components on the motherboard or otherwise accessed by the host. They provide a relatively new approach to type 3 isolation and are being deployed on (typically high-end) server machines as part of standard CPUs. Existing implementations are available from Intel—which pioneered the approach with *Software Guard Extensions (SGX)*[22]—and AMD—which took a different architectural route with their *Secure Encrypted Virtualisation (SEV)*,[23] and further examples have been announced from manufacturers including Arm and IBM. Both of these implementations provide confidentiality protection and integrity protection for workloads' memory pages by encrypting

---

[20]Peripheral Component Interconnect.
[21]Alternative sitings for TEEs include on GPUs or networking components, but no products incorporating such architectures have been announced at the time of writing.
[22]Intel, 2020.
[23]AMD, 2020.

them and only decrypting them while they are being executed within the CPU, thus preventing all other processes, including the kernel and any hypervisor, from being able to view or change the memory associated with the workload. Both also offer attestation to provide the tenant with assurances of the validity of the environment being provided and into which the workload is loaded. One key protection that they do *not* provide is availability, since while the host kernel cannot impact the memory pages associated with the workload, it can starve the workload of compute resources by controlling CPU cycle scheduling. TEEs are relatively cheap in terms of both hardware and deployment costs, and their growing popularity in the public Cloud means that they are becoming easily accessible to tenant organisations.

There is one more type of type 3 isolation mechanism that we could list: *trusted platform modules* (TPMs), which we also encountered in Chapter 5. But because TPMs are not designed for generalised computing such as application workloads, they are not particularly relevant in this discussion.

Open Source and Trust

We have discussed open source in passing at several points in the book already, but we have yet to conduct a thorough examination of the relevance open source has to trust in general. In this chapter, we will look at what trust relationships underpin open source and what impact those relationships have on how open source can be viewed and incorporated into systems. Before continuing, however, it is worth noting that by *open source*, we are referring not necessarily solely to open source software but also to other creations to which open source principles can be applied. We will look at how such principles *are* applied when we consider licences later in this chapter, but suffice it to say that hardware,[1] documentation, and other artefacts may be considered *open source* and are included in our definition and description unless specifically noted.

Distributed Trust

We briefly looked at distributed trust in Chapter 3, where we defined it as "multiple trust relationships spread across different entities, some or all of which may consist of chains of trust". But as we move to consider open source and trust, we need to look at distributed trust in some detail. While we have been

---

[1]One of the leading proponents of open hardware is the OSHWA; see Open Source Hardware Association, 2020.

concentrating on computer-to-computer trust, in order to consider distributed trust, we will go back to looking at human-to-human trust.

The concept of distributing trust across a community is an application of the theory of the *wisdom of the crowd*, posited by Aristotle,[2] where the assumption is that the opinions of many typically show more wisdom than the opinion of one or a few. While demonstrably false in its simplest form in some situations—the most obvious being examples of popular support for totalitarian regimes—this principle can provide a very effective mechanism for establishing certain information. There is a great deal of research on human-to-human relationships based on *social graphs*, which allow the mapping of different interactions between people in different contexts. Rachel Botsman, in her book *Who Can You Trust?*,[3] discusses the website and app UrbanSitter,[4] which is used to find childcare providers online and identifies what we would label as three different contexts for trust: competence, reliability, and honesty. She notes that:

> *In the past, we had to make a lot of decisions based on blind faith or personal experience, but today we can base them on collective experience.*

This collective experience—in this case, that of those who have employed various babysitters and childcare providers—can be harnessed by recording reputational scores within the app, which is acting as an authority (though not necessarily an endorsing authority). Botsman notes that there are some dangers here, and these marry fairly closely with those we have already addressed when discussing reputation.

This distillation of experience allows what we refer to as *distributed trust* and is collected through numerous mechanisms on the Internet. Some apps and websites, like TripAdvisor and Glassdoor, record information about organisations or the services they provide, while others, such as UrbanSitter and LinkedIn, allow users to add information about specific people (see, for instance, LinkedIn's "Recommendations" and the "Skills & Endorsements" sections in individuals' profiles). The benefits that can accrue from these sites are significantly increased by the network effect—the value users gain when more people become involved—since the number of possible connections between members increases exponentially as the number of members increases.

Other examples of distributed trust include platforms like Twitter, where the number of followers that an account receives can be seen as a measure of their reputation and even of their trustworthiness, a calculation we should view with a strong degree of scepticism. Indeed, the company Twitter felt that it had to address the social power of accounts with large numbers of followers and instituted a "verified accounts" mechanism to let people know "that an account of public interest is authentic".[5] Interestingly, the company had to suspend the

---

[2] Aristotle, trans Sinclair, 2000.
[3] Botsman, 2017.
[4] UrbanSitter, 2020.
[5] Twitter, 2020.

service after problems related to users' expectations of exactly what "verified" meant or implied,[6] a classic case of differing understandings of context between different entities.

Distributed trust does not necessarily need to be associated with reputation or mediated by authorities, whether centralised or decentralised, as in the case of many blockchains. One example of a system—or set of systems—which revolves around distributed trust is that of peer-reviewed scientific papers. The concept of peer review is that scientific theories and discoveries are published to the wider scientific community only after they have been reviewed by other experts in the same scientific field, and sometimes by experts in other fields relevant to the paper: for instance, if a paper on quantum mechanics were to make use of mathematical methods not generally associated with the field. Scientific papers that are published without peer review are viewed with considerable scepticism and typically not accepted by the scientific community without at least one round of review.

Although an industry of journals has arisen over time to provide mechanisms for the publishing of peer-reviewed journals, the concept itself does not require their existence. The journals may maintain a board of experts who are available to review submitted papers, or the reputation of the journal itself may be sufficient to convince experts to review submissions, but peer review can be performed by any expert in the field. Another advantage of journals or other institutions that provide facilities for peer review is that they may have processes in place to allow for some anonymisation of the paper's author(s), reviewers, or both. This can reduce the chance of negative or positive reviews by reviewers acquainted with the authors or their reputation, and also of influence on or recrimination by authors toward reviewers before, during, or after the review process.

Peer review—and the industry behind it—is not unproblematic, and criticisms have been aimed at it over many years,[7] not least the danger that discoveries that might lead to paradigm shifts in understanding are disadvantaged compared to papers that uphold the *status quo*.[8] The question of peer review of pharmaceutical trial data has turned out to be particularly contentious. One set of stakeholders—consumers and their advocates—has demanded that new treatments, medicines, and drugs should not be licensed for use without the release of trial data (allowing global peer review), whereas another set—pharmaceutical companies—points to the economic dangers of commercial misuse and theft of their discoveries if information is released, and assert that internal review of results by their own experts should be considered sufficient. Consumers and advocacy groups typically respond with arguments around questions of who benefits most from existing practice—questions that are redolent of those discussed in Chapter 2 related to *security economics*.

---

[6]Cakebread, 2017.
[7]See Smith, 2006, for a good review of some of the criticisms.
[8]Kuhn, 1962.

Whatever the arguments for and against peer review, when combined with the publication of papers, peer review allows for a body of expertise from multiple people to be applied to the results of the paper and for someone who is using the results to have some trust in it that does not necessarily require *them* to hold equivalent expertise. The hope is that papers or theories considered sufficiently important to the wider scientific community—or the public at large—will be subjected to further expert analysis as their importance grows or is suspected: a process that can occur only if they are published widely in the first place.

Distributed trust is not without problems, not least that it leans bodies of expertise away from paradigm shifts (to note the work of Thomas Kuhn again); also, where the information being presented for consideration requires significant technical understanding or expertise, the pool of qualified reviewers may be low, or their review may simply not be available. We will revisit this issue when we look in more detail at open source and security later in this chapter.

How Open Source Relates to Trust

What are we doing when we say "I trust open source software" or even, more broadly, "I trust open source"? The first thing we are *not* doing is making an explicit statement about trust relationships that fits with the methodology we set up in Chapter 1; and it is clear that this is not the sort of statement that allows us to establish computer-to-computer trust relationships. We are firmly back in the human realm, but open source is so firmly established in computing and how organisations run their businesses—particularly in the cloud—that such statements deserve further consideration. We will focus on software, but bear in mind that most of the points we are making can be equally applied to other areas such as hardware and documentation.

Let us suggest what such a statement might typically mean, and then consider what the implications of that meaning might be. We are making a determination that enough of the people who have written and tested the open source software have requirements similar to mine and that their expertise, combined, is such that my risk in using the software is acceptable. There are actually a great number of assumptions about trust being presented here, some of which are very interesting:

- We are trusting architects and designers to design software to meet our use cases and requirements.
- We are trusting developers to implement code well, to those designs.
- We are trusting developers to review each other's code.
- We are trusting technical writers—or anyone associated with documentation tasks—to document the software and its intended operation clearly and correctly.

- We are trusting testers to write, run, and check tests that are appropriate to our use cases.
- We are trusting those who deploy the code to run it in ways that are similar to our use cases.
- We are trusting those who deploy the code to report bugs.
- We are trusting those who come across bugs to report them.
- We are trusting those who receive bug reports to fix them as expected.

There are more, of course, but this list provides us with sufficient starting points to begin our investigation of trust and open source. Of course, when we choose to use proprietary software, the same expectations exist; but in the proprietary case, the trust relationship is much clearer and tighter. It is to a specific vendor, and if any of the expectations just listed are not met, I have the options of choosing another vendor or of working with the original vendor to find ways for those expectations to be met (or changed). In the case of open source software, everything is more nebulous: I may be able to identify at least some of the entities involved (designers, software engineers, and testers, for example), but the amount of power that I, as a consumer of the software, have over their work is likely to be low. There is a strange almost-paradox here, though: we could argue that for proprietary software vendors, the power of the individual consumer or organisational customers over the direction of the software is greater (the vendor faces the stark choice of being paid or not being paid), but the consumer or organisation's direct visibility into what actually goes on, and the concomitant ability to ensure that they get what they want, is reduced when compared to the open source case.

We will spend the rest of this chapter looking at open source in various contexts and teasing out some of the trust assumptions and relationships that exist in our continuing quest to make trust as explicit as possible.

Community and Projects

In the open source software community, the standard unit of engagement is the *open source project* rather than an application or product. An open source project (or just *project*) may become an application, become several, become a software library, be merged into one or more other projects, end up in a commercially supported product, or, after a while, wither and disappear from view if nobody uses it or participation drops below the threshold required to keep people interested. Participants in a project are generally known as *contributors*, a term that is sometimes used to denote a particular role in a project based on measures such as frequency of participation, amount of code submitted over time, and the authority to suggest or approve changes but that we will use more broadly to describe anyone who takes part in the project in a constructive way.

Projects generally have one or more *maintainers*, who are usually in charge of the direction of the project and have the ability to accept or reject changes and publish specific feature sets as a *release*. The number of maintainers for a project is generally low, but a single project may have a single contributor or tens of thousands[9]; and contributors may write code, test code, document code, write use cases, provide graphics or sound resources, provide design or architectural artefacts (or review them), manage marketing, manage and develop build infrastructure, grow and manage the community, and more. The project's *community* is generally considered to include all contributors but also users of the project and/or products derived from it. Growing and maintaining a vibrant community and ecosystem around an open source project is generally considered important to the project's success, and larger projects—or those wishing to grow—often appoint a *community manager*.

As we noted in the earlier section on distributed trust, social graphs have been used extensively to study the relationships between people in different communities, though such analysis is not without its complications.[10] The open source software community has received a great deal of attention due to its large size and the availability of huge amounts of data about different participants and their place in various projects. One interesting study related to trust looked at approaches to estimate trust between open source software developers:

> *Trust is a critical factor for enabling effective online collaboration in open source software (OSS) project teams. OSS team members are more likely to collaborate, share knowledge and accept others' contributions when they trust each other. Trustworthiness also accelerates new member recruitment, and, consequently, brings innovative ideas and work procedures to a project.[11]*

There are at least two assumptions implicit in these statements that are of interest to us. First, that contributors are not likely to be co-located—and hence that their interactions are likely to be online—and, alongside that, that they are not necessarily working for a single organisation, as otherwise, at least some level of trust might be expected by default. Another assumption—borne out by explicit statements later in the paper—is that it is developers who are making the contributions in this study. While we will take *contributors* to mean a much wider set of participants, as outlined earlier, the other two assumptions bear consideration and are typically related.

If one of the aims of a project is to grow a community—and to "embrace innovative ideas and work procedures"—then having a single organisation as the controlling body is not to be encouraged. Indeed, many open source projects have failed to thrive after an organisation ignored the need for a community

---

[9]The largest open source project in existence is widely agreed to be the Linux kernel, founded and still shepherded by Linus Torvalds: see Linux Kernel, The (2020).

[10]See Nia et al., 2010; and Howison, Crowston, and Wiggins, 2020.

[11]Sapkota, Murukannaiah, and Wang, 2019.

and instead decided to declare a project "open source", attach a relevant licence (more on this later), and "throw it over the wall", putting it in the public domain for use by a notional community that fails to materialise. This is generally a recipe for disaster for open source projects, which need to attract diverse contributors, whomever they work for, and wherever they are physically located: hence the need to accept and encourage online communications. It is actually rare for successful open source projects to have a majority of their contributors in physical proximity—other than for specific events like hackathons[12]—and, indeed, it is not uncommon for many contributors never to have physically met their co-contributors on the project.

The paper explores methodologies for measuring trust within the development community of one or more open source projects, and its main aim is not to provide any metrics with regard to the project itself but rather to help those on a project make decisions about whether to accept contributions based on automated measurements of "trustworthiness" for potential or existing developers. The authors do provide a useful review of other work in the area of trust and team cohesion, for instance, but the literature on open source project communities tends to focus on how to measure their vitality or health: for example, the work performed under the auspices of Community Health Analytics Open Source Software" (CHAOSS),[13] a project under the Linux Foundation.

Trust in projects and their communities is, then, difficult to measure, but one of the attractions of open source software can be the lack of any centralised authority that controls the direction, quality, features, and properties of an open source project. Where this lack of centralised control is most evident is in vibrant communities with contributors from diverse backgrounds. Another of the benefits of open source is that in the case of a disagreement arising as to the direction of the project—or when trust is broken among members of the community, or perhaps between some vendor and the community—the software can be *forked*, creating a new project that existing members of the community are free to embrace or not as they see fit.

Projects and the Personal

We have not specifically addressed the issue of distributed trust within the context of open source projects and communities, but the community aspect of open source is actually a driver toward building distributed trust. This is because once you become a part of the community around an open source project, you assume one or more of the roles we identified as being trusted: architect, designer, developer, reviewer, technical writer, tester, deployer, bug reporter, or bug fixer.

---

[12] A *hackathon* is a gathering of developers—and sometimes other project contributors—to work together in a concentrated effort on one more projects or aspects of a single project. See Wikipedia, "Hackathon", 2020.
[13] CHAOSS, 2020.

The more involvement you have in a project, the more you become part of the community, which can, in time, become a *community of practice*. Jean Lave and Etienne Wenger introduced the concept of communities of practice in their book *Situated Learning: Legitimate Peripheral Participation*,[14] where groups evolve into communities as their members share a passion and participate in shared activities, leading to their improving their skills and knowledge together. The core concept here is that as participants learn *around* a community of practice, they become members of it at the same time:

> *Legitimate peripheral participation refers both to the development of knowledgeably skilled identities in practice and to the reproduction and transformation of communities of practice.*[15]

Wenger further explored the concept of communities of practice, how they form, requirements for their health, and how they encourage learning in *Communities of Practice: Learning, Meaning and Identity*.[16] He identified *negotiability of meaning* ("why are we working together, what are we trying to achieve?") as core to a community of practice and noted that without *engagement, imagination*, and *alignment* by individuals, communities of practice will not be robust.

We can align this perspective with our views on how distributed trust is established and built: when you realise that your impact on open source can be equal to that of others who are already contributing to a project, the distributed trust relationships that you hold to members of a community become less transitive. You understand that the impact that you can have on the creation, maintenance, requirements, and quality of the software you are running can be the same as all of those other, previously anonymous (to you) contributors with whom you are now forming a community of practice, or whose existing community of practice you are joining. Then you yourself become part of a network of trust relationships distributed as recognition, and your feeling of inclusion is more personal and at less of a remove than you experience when buying and operating proprietary software.

The process does not stop there, however: a common property of open source projects is cross-pollination, where developers from one project also work on others. This grows as the network effect of multiple open source projects allows reuse and dependencies on other projects to increase and leads to greater take-up across the entire set of projects. It is easy to see why many open source contributors become open source enthusiasts or evangelists not just for a single project but for open source as a whole. In fact, work by Mark Granovetter suggests that too many strong ties within communities can lead to cliques and stagnation, but weak ties provide for the movement of ideas and trends around communities.[17] In other words, if a set of contributors in a community become

---

[14]Lave and Wenger, 1991.
[15]Lave and Wenger, 1991, p. 55.
[16]Wenger, 1998.
[17]Granovetter, 2002.

too inward-looking and rely only on each other for recognition, guidance, and future planning, then that community can cease to flourish. An awareness, instead, of other projects and the communities that exist around them, and the flexibility of ideas across projects, leads to distributed trust extending (albeit with weaker assurances) beyond the direct or short-chain indirect relationships that contributors experience within projects of which they have immediate experience and out toward other projects where external observation or peripheral involvement shows that similar relationships exist between contributors. Put simply, the act of being involved in an open source project and building trust relationships through participation leads to stronger distributed trust toward similar open source projects and, to a lesser degree, simply to other projects that are similarly open source.

Open Source Process

Consuming proprietary software is generally fairly simple: on buying the software (or, more typically, a licence to use it), you download the package (or receive it on physical media—a vanishing delivery mechanism), install it on the appropriate platform, and run it. The software vendor has hopefully provided you with a binary and any required libraries, configuration files, data files, and documentation required, and the software executable runs. In terms of the software, there is a single trust relationship in play in most use cases: that which you (or your organisation) holds to the software vendor. Though this really encompasses multiple contexts and so should actually be considered as multiple relationships, these contexts are typically covered under a single licence grant and commercial agreement. We can model it as in Table 9.1.

Table 9.1: Trust from software consumer to software vendor

FROM (TRUSTOR)	SOFTWARE CONSUMER	TO (TRUSTEE)	SOFTWARE VENDOR
Context(s)		Fitness for use, including ability to run on advertised platform, security, resilience, performance properties, etc.	
Time-specific		Length of licence	
Action(s)		Software runs on platform	
Expectation(s)		No functional bugs, no security bugs or backdoors, performance acceptable, etc.	
Assurance(s)		Legal agreement; reputational damage to vendor if problems occur	
Mitigation(s)		Legal recourse, change vendor, unfavourable reports to press, others in the sector, etc.	

The commercial agreement is likely to include other elements such as support, security patching, and possibly upgrades to new versions as they become available. In the case of open source, things are rather different. There are two main approaches to consuming open source projects: we will deal with the first here and the alternative—using a vendor—in the section "Supply Chain and Products".

Trusting the Project

We have already looked at the question of what it means to say "I trust open source", but what happens when we actually look at trust at the project level, as a consumer of software? We would love to be able to create a single trust relationship table, such as the one for proprietary vendors in Table 9.1, and apply it to open source software, but this is immediately problematic: who should the trustee be? Once we delve a little deeper, it becomes clear that this is far from our biggest problem. Let us start at the project level and think about what metrics we might need to collect in order to decide whether to trust the software that the specific open source project provides. As an example, we will consider the case where we are looking to use a library that provides some cryptographic protocol implementation. What do you need to know, and what are your choices? Assuming that the decision has been made to use an open source implementation, what criteria might be used to select an appropriate project?

Here is a list of some of the more obvious—and more easily available—measures that you might choose to examine in order to allow you to make a determination about trusting an open source project[18]:

Documentation   Availability of documentation is easy to check, and a lack of documentation, gaps in specific areas, or existing but out-of-date documentation are all issues that should raise immediate concerns. Documentation should include not just a description of how to use the software but also the requirements (in terms of features, usability, and other properties) it is designed to meet.

Test Coverage   Assuming that there is sufficient documentation, what is the status of tests for the code? Untested code is untrustworthy code because even if you know what an implementation is *supposed* to do (as described by documentation), there is no way to know whether it actually meets the requirements.

Number of Contributors   A high number of contributors is not necessarily the sign of a healthy or well-designed and implemented project, but projects with small numbers of contributors may not survive if one or more key members leave for whatever reason.

---

[18]CHAOSS has a working group related to this area (see CHAOSS, 2020a), though the level of activity at the time of writing is fairly low.

Details of Core Contributors   For some consumers of software, the provenance of the software may be important. A high number of contributors from a single organisation may signal that the project is open source in name only and really a vanity project by that organisation, meaning that the ability of consumers to get involved with the project or shape the future feature and functionality roadmap may be impaired. Equally, for an organisation based in country A with poor diplomatic or business relationships with country B, a strong preponderance of contributors from country B may be a cause for concern, particularly if the organisation is involved in government or sensitive market sectors. Another metric may be the percentage of contributors in academia: is the project more of a research project than an implementation aimed at commercial use? Given the interest in anonymity among many open source proponents, pseudonymity is fairly common for some projects, meaning that it is not always easy to track the organisational, national, or institutional affiliation of all contributors.

Attribution   A growing area of interest around supply chain management is not just the identity and affiliation of core contributors but also that specific code can be tracked to them. A common way to do this is to require contributors to tie contributions to their identities (typically via capabilities provided by the repositories that host the project artefacts). Mechanisms such as attaching a developer certificate of origin[19] (DCO) further allow contributors to make assertions about their right to contribute the code under the relevant licence (to avoid unintentional copying of proprietary code, for instance).

Code Contribution Activity   Neither the number of contributors nor their affiliation provides sufficient insight into the health of the code itself. If there are very few contributions, this may signal either that the community is lacking momentum or that it has reached a level of maturity where contributions tend to be grouped around new features rather than spread across the code base.

Bug and Feature Management   Most software comes with bugs, and most software can be improved or extended to other use cases with the addition of new features and functionality. If you are intending to use the cryptographic library that this project provides within a production environment, then being able to report bugs (and have them fixed!) and request features is an important factor to consider. Reviewing how bug reporting and feature requests are managed and how the criteria applied to them ("most interesting" vs. "most pressing for users") suit your requirements will help.

---

[19]Wikipedia, "Developer Certificate of Origin", 2020.

Of course, given that the project is open source, there is nothing to stop developers in your organisation from getting involved—in which case it is important to understand the prioritisation and appetite for acceptance of bug fixes by the maintainer(s) and how welcoming the community is to new contributors.

Community Activity (Vendors, Chat, Issues, etc.)   General activity in a project is a good measure of health (see the work of CHAOSS previously cited), and if there is involvement from contributors outside the core developer group, welcoming chat rooms, etc., this may be a good sign that the project is healthy. Another positive measure is the existence of vendor-backed, productised implementations of the project (a subject to which we will return), as this suggests good market acceptance of and appetite for the project.

Vulnerability Reporting and Management   Vulnerability reporting and management processes, though not the most interesting parts of a project to many contributors, are very important for security-related projects. Without them, consumers who are employing software in production environments are at risk of being exposed to vulnerabilities that are not fixed quickly in open source projects.

This list is not exhaustive but does highlight a number of the issues that might need to be considered. We should note that, with the exception of code contribution activity, we have not considered the impact of time as a context, and questions of managing decay of trust (discussed in Chapter 7) should also be included.

Trusting the Software

Earlier, we talked about "the software that the specific open source project provides" but concentrated on evaluating the project and its community. These are not, of course, what we are directly consuming: our actual interest is in the software, whether libraries or binaries—we will refer to them both as the *package*—which are both artefacts of the project. Code does not just come into being out of thin air and then become a binary executable or library: there are steps involved and a process to be followed. In the case of proprietary software, all of this is hidden from the consumer, for good or ill; but in the case of open source software, the various parts are visible, and all of them are vital to examine when deciding whether to trust an open source software package.

We will continue with our example, where the package in which we are interested is an implementation of a cryptographic library. In order to keep the example simple, we will assume that the development team comprises a single maintainer of the package and multiple contributors (we can ignore other project-level measurements at this level). The contributors provide code (and tests, documentation, etc.) to the project, and the maintainer provides builds—compiled binary/library packages—for you to consume, rather than your taking the source code and compiling it yourself. This is a library to provide cryptographic capabilities, so it is fairly safe to assume that we care about its security: we will assume that the maintainer is sufficiently careful to ensure that there is good (and up-to-date) test coverage and that the integrity of the code that is submitted is protected (through controls applied by the repository in which it resides, for instance). We will present five core categories that need to be considered as part of our decision as to whether to "trust the package". As always, this list is not exhaustive but aims to identify some of the key issues:

Build   Although the process of compiling source code into binaries may seem like the least complex or vulnerable part of the process, it is the cornerstone: without good *build hygiene*, you may not only end up with compromised packages but, even worse, not be able to tell whether a package is compromised. We know from the wisdom of Ken Thompson that without trust in all components of the entire build stack, there is a danger that compromised packages may be created. What we need, in fact, is to consider the entirety of the build system as a trusted computing base (TCB) and manage our trust in that. The maintainer, who performs the task of building the software, needs to establish trust in the build system: a "clean" host and stack, with the minimum set of appropriate, up-to-date and validated compilers and libraries required for the build process. One oft-followed practice for builds of sensitive packages is to maintain a separate virtual machine image containing an operating system and build tooling image and to instantiate it into a clean virtual machine for each build instance; it is, of course, important to consider the other elements in the host stack when this is done.

If the package is created with untrusted tools, then how can we trust it at all? We need to establish—and preferably audit—the measures that the maintainer takes to ensure the hygiene of the build environment. An additional data point is the provision of appropriate documentation and tools to allow the package to be created as a *repeatable build*. This allows other people—such as those consuming the package—to follow the same steps as the maintainer and check that the package they create is the same as that created by the maintainer. Any differences in the output between the maintainer's build and a repeated build are signals of one of the following: the build documentation is incorrect; the maintainer has incorrectly followed the documentation; the re-builder has incorrectly followed the documentation; the maintainer's build system is compromised; the builder's build system is compromised; or the integrity of the package inputs has been compromised.

Integrity   When we talk about *package inputs*, we are referring generally to the code, any configuration files, compilation flags, and other dependencies that are required to make the package, many of which may sit outside the build system. Code and configuration files directly related to the project are likely to come from the project repository, but dependencies may well be gathered at build, compile, or link time and used as inputs into the build process (this allows the build system to pick up the most recent version of libraries and binaries on which the build relies without having to store them in the repository and rely on the other processes to update them). If, somehow, a compromise is injected into the build process, which could come from code, compiler flags, system libraries, or other sources, then we obviously should not trust the package. Equally, we want to know exactly which version of the source code is being used as the basis for the package we are consuming so that we can track features—and bugs. The same should apply to the version of the compiler used (if it is a compiled language). As mentioned previously, having a repeatable build is a great bonus here, though if the build process itself is compromised, then the integrity of the inputs a re-builder takes may be affected in the same way as those of the maintainer, meaning that there is no sign of any difference.

Responsiveness   What we mean by *responsiveness* is related to two measures we considered when looking at the trust at the project level: *bug and feature management* and *vulnerability reporting and management*. Here though, we are specifically interested in how responsive the maintainer is to changes. Generally, for a package that we are deploying in a production environment, we want stable features tied to known versions; but this requirement is somewhat turned on its head for bug and (in particular) security patches, where we are looking for quick acceptance of changes into the package. If the maintainer does not accept patches in a timely manner, then there is cause for concern about the overall security of the package and our trust in it over time.

Provenance   We discussed details of core contributors and attribution at the project level, but the maintainer should have a slightly different concern. All code is not created equal, and one of the things which a maintainer should be tracking is the provenance of contributors. If a large amount of code in a part of the package that provides particularly sensitive features is suddenly submitted by an unknown contributor with a pseudonymous email address and no history of contributions of security functionality, this should raise alarm bells. On the other hand, if a group of contributors employed by a company with a history of open source contributions and well-reviewed code submit a large patch, this is probably less troublesome. This is a difficult issue to manage, and there are typically no definite "OK" or "no-go" signs, but the maintainer's awareness and management of contributors and their contributions is an important point to consider. It is worth noting that a web-of-trust approach to reputation, often tracked through identity tokens such as PGP keys, is a standard approach to address the question of provenance without relying on identity disclosure or an intermediated verification process. While this is not without its flaws (as we noted when we discussed reputation systems in Chapter 7), alternatives such as requiring the use of identities backed by government-issued documentation raise real concerns for minorities, those in oppressive regimes, and those worried by future shifts in such a direction.

Expertise   An evaluation of expertise is arguably the most difficult and complex of the package trust issues to address. The project may be fortunate enough to have a maintainer who is excellent at managing all of the previous points but is just not an expert in certain aspects of the functionality of the contributed code. As a consumer of the package, however, we need to be sure that it is fit for purpose, and that may include, in the case of the security-related package we are considering, being assured that the correct cryptographic primitives are used, bounds-checking is enforced on byte streams, proper key lengths are used, or constant-time implementations are provided for particular primitives, to give three separate examples. There is also a need to understand and evaluate the impact of any dependent packages the project is consuming (see the next section for more on this point). All of these tasks are extremely difficult and require significant subject matter expertise in a number of disparate fields, so the job of maintainer can easily become a full-time one if they are acting as the expert for a large and/or complex project—an option that may not be available to them or the project. Indeed, best practice in such cases is to have a team of trusted, experienced experts who work either as co-maintainers or as a senior advisory group for the project. Alternatively, having external people or organisations (such as industry bodies) perform audits of the project at critical junctures—when a major release is due or when an important vulnerability is patched, for instance—allows the maintainer to share this responsibility.

It is important to note that the project does not magically become "secure" just because it is open source, but that the community, when it comes together, *can* significantly improve the trust that consumers of a project can have in the packages it produces.

Once we consider these areas, we then need to work out how we measure and track each of them. Equally important, how can we be sure that the views and priorities of the maintainer are aligned with ours, the consumer of the software? Who is in a position to judge the extent to which any particular maintainer is fulfilling each of the areas?

It is clear that trust in the package can only be as strong as our trust in the maintainer. There are many, many open source projects, and fewer of them than we might like—even those that are security-related—are lucky enough to have maintainers who are sufficiently skilled in the various fields of expertise we have identified to provide a fully "trustable" package. We need to trust maintainers in multiple contexts. Luckily, we can fall back on distributed trust to some extent here, but that assumes there are sufficient experts in the community who are engaging with the projects in which we are interested[20] and aligned with the values and priorities about which we care the most.

This may all seem a little daunting, but at least in the case of open source projects, you *can* look into all of these issues, as opposed to the proprietary case, where you need to trust the vendor of the software about most if not all of them. There also exists another mechanism by which you can consume open source software, which we will address now.

Supply Chain and Products

We have looked at a use case where a single library is being packaged and consumed, but the real world is generally more complex than that. Not only is it quite likely that any production application will be consuming multiple packages, but we also need to be aware that each of those packages is likely to be consuming other packages. Each of these may well be consuming packages, and some of these dependencies may be common between the various components that are being consumed.

While we can spend a great deal of time evaluating the project and the processes that produce the cryptographic library we are consuming, and while we can leverage our distributed trust in the open source community, the amount of assurance we can have about the trustworthiness of every package and dependency can only decrease as their numbers increase. If even one package is compromised, as in Figure 9.1, the security of the application we are deploying may be significantly reduced.

There is growing interest in mapping and managing these issues; this falls under the more general field of *supply chain management*, which includes other issues such as licence management and is equally applicable to open source and proprietary software packages. This interest stems mainly from concerns that organisations could be liable if customers were affected by an issue arising from software on which they have not performed the same sort of due diligence on their software supply chain as is standard for non-software-based industries. The open source community, keen to encourage wider adoption of open source,

---

[20]The Open Source Security Coalition (OSSC), a project under the Linux Foundation, exists to try to identify key open source security projects and to help improve various aspects of their processes.

has embraced this trend: dependency-checkers for licensing, known vulnerabilities, and common bugs are now common, with integration into continuous integration/continuous deployment (CI/CD) systems allowing for automation. In an attempt to allow more complicated tracking, open source projects like Rekor[21] are beginning to track the more complicated dependencies and attribution questions that we have already examined in this chapter.

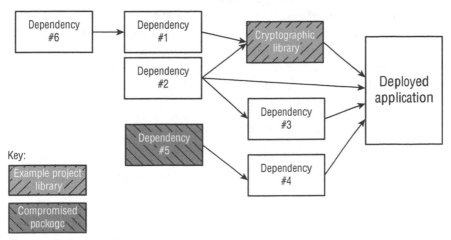

Figure 9.1: Package dependencies.

All of these tools still require the consumer of packages to manage the due diligence process and find appropriate expertise inside their organisations to evaluate the risks associated with the software supply chain, which is likely to be a complex and lengthy undertaking. Whatever the organisation's interest in open source and its belief in distributed trust as a basis for risk assessment, the model of being able to form a commercial agreement with a single vendor, with associated trust relationship(s), as we modelled at the beginning of this chapter, allows for much simpler risk management. All the added complications of having to manage patching, upgrading, and lifecycle management, which we examined in previous chapters, add to the benefits associated with a vendor-centric model.

In the early 2000s, Red Hat, Inc. became the first commercial vendor of open source software to target enterprises,[22] rather than personal users, as its business model. Rather than licensing the software itself, it sold subscriptions to businesses and other institutions, including support, updates, and security fixes as part of the model. Other businesses followed, providing enterprises

---

[21]Rekor, 2020.
[22]Red Hat, 2020.

with the opportunity to tap into the benefits of the open source development model, community, and commonwealth while mitigating many of the risks. So successful was this approach that the market for open source software is now worth many billions of dollars, and Red Hat was acquired by IBM for $34 billion in 2019. Nor was Red Hat the first: many other companies have created successful businesses around open source, such as MySQL, the first open source software company acquired for over $1 billion.

Such commercial vendors of open source address the issues we have discussed around dependency checking, build management, and project trust assessment themselves by employing experts, performing testing and builds, and actually becoming active in open source projects through providing staffing and other resources. As a result, they can provide a number of benefits to the organisations that consume their products, including

- A single entity for commercial agreements
- Support, upgrade, and security update services
- Guarantees of indemnity from possible licence infringement
- Dependency checking
- Build management
- Version management
- Patent-infringement protection

Many vendors also provide packaged (and supported) versions of multiple open source projects as products, managing integration and coordinating versioning between them.

Some feel that companies that charge for, or productise, open source software go against the ethos of the movement and see the "free" aspect of open source[23] as inseparable from the movement.[24] The foundation of the Open Source Initiative was partly to allow the community to differentiate between various approaches to distribution of open source (of which there are several), and partly to provide guidance regarding licences and make clear what is considered "within" the open source movement and what is not.

This move to a single vendor from a community model does, of course, change the trust model when consuming packages. However, one of the benefits of choosing this approach is that if a vendor ceases trading or drops a product line, a dependent project is forked, or the consuming organisation becomes unsatisfied with the approach, the consumer can still go back to community project consumption model. Vendors of commercial open source software also

---

[23]To disambiguate the uses of the word *free* in English, the phrase "free as in beer, not just free as in speech" is sometimes used. Some communities have adopted the term *libre* to further clarify the reference to the right to freedoms, rather than that software is free of cost.
[24]Stallman, 2016.

point out that consumers of their products benefit from the wider community and the distributed trust they leverage whilst adding further value in the areas noted in our list. But the core benefit to organisations is a much-increased ability to evaluate, manage, and mitigate risk. All in all, the vendor model addresses most of the complexity we have addressed in the previous sections and allows trust relationships and commercial agreements to be implemented in exactly the same way as for proprietary software whilst enjoying the benefits offered by open source—one of which, security, we will cover in the following section.

Open Source and Security

One recurring question around open source software is whether proprietary software is somehow "safer"—by which people usually mean "more secure"—than open source. Some answer "no" and assert that proprietary code is more secure precisely because its source code cannot be read and inspected for vulnerabilities by would-be bad actors, a view sometimes referred to by its detractors as *security through obscurity*. The opposing view—that open source is, in fact, more secure than proprietary software—is frequently supported by the *many-eyes hypothesis*. This is derived from a proposition sometimes known as Linus's Law: "Given enough eyeballs, all bugs are shallow". The idea is that all bugs will be found and fixed in open source software, as long as there are enough people looking to find them. We need to delve more deeply into both of the arguments presented.

The first point we should restate is one we have made before: that writing software is hard and writing security code, or even "secure" code, is much harder. We have looked at many of the issues of design, implementation, and formal proofs and can expect that pretty much all software—open source or proprietary—will include bugs. This is as true for security software as it is for any other software project (if not more so). For this reason, *code review*—the practice of another developer poring over the initial developer's code—and *functional testing*—the practice of writing and performing tests to show that software functions as expected—are considered basic tenets of software development. The point of the many-eyes hypothesis is that the pool of available code reviewers for open source software is almost immeasurably larger (tens or hundreds of thousands of people) than the pool for proprietary software (a few people within a team at a software vendor, and maybe some auditors), so the chances of finding (and fixing) bugs is concomitantly significantly increased. This, however, leads us to the two main problems with the many-eyes hypothesis in the context, in particular, of security software:

> **The "If You Build It, They Will Come" Fallacy**   Around 1994, there was a list online of all the websites in the world, and if you added your website to that list, people would visit. In the same way, it may once have been

the case that the number of open source security projects was so small that there was a good chance that, as a new one was added, people would find it and review the code. Those days (if they ever existed) are long gone, and although there are some mechanisms emerging for core open source security projects to receive regular review (such as the work of the Open Source Security Coalition), we cannot assume that such review is automatic simply by dint of the existence of an open source project with a security capability or impact.

Availability of Qualified Eyes   The second problem is related to the complexity of security software and the wide breadth of skills and expertise required to write software that exhibits strong security properties—a point to which we alluded in the section "Trusting the Software" earlier in this chapter. The availability of people with such skills is limited, as few software developers specialise in security, which means that the number of "eyes"—people with the time and skills—available to provide appropriate code review (and architectural, design, test, and documentation review) is significantly fewer than the wider pool of developers on which the many-eyes hypothesis is based.

This does not mean, however, that we should accept the opposing view: that proprietary software is somehow more secure because it is *not* open source. The frequency with which serious vulnerabilities are discovered in proprietary software, either by non-invasive attacks such as fuzzing or by reverse engineering and compilation of binary packages, is high, and attackers seem to have few problems finding them. And not only are there fewer eyes—expert or not—available to review proprietary software, but the designs and architectures are also hidden from view, with dangers of organisational groupthink and hierarchical pressure much more likely to expose themselves in a closed source environment.

One response to the suggestion that companies open up their code is that "it needs to be closed in order to protect our intellectual property". This is particularly weak when we consider the requirement for expert review for security primitives, protocols, and algorithms, and should raise immediate questions from anyone considering using software from organisations that peddle this defence.[25]

Let us return to our two problems with the many-eyes hypothesis: how can these be addressed? Our answers must work on several fronts:

- Train developers to know when they are creating security-critical code, and ensure that architecture, design, and code review is performed by sufficiently expert eyes.

---

[25]These are all issues clearly related to those we identified when we discussed the release of pharmaceutical trial data in the section "Distributed Trust" earlier in this chapter.

- Train developers to know when to reuse libraries and applications from existing projects rather than creating their own (which just creates more work and risks re-implementation of existing capabilities with lower levels of security).

- Train more people into security, thereby increasing the number of experts available for review.

- Encourage—and fund—community initiatives to identify widely used security projects and direct expert review toward them.

- Ensure that enterprise vendors of products based on open source projects perform due diligence on them and their dependencies, and provide resources to help remediate issues where found.

We noted earlier in this chapter that direct individual involvement in open source projects is not the only way to participate in the community, and improving the quality and security of projects. Consumption of open source software via commercial vendors also benefits the broader community—as long as those vendors themselves enthusiastically participate in open source projects and encourage the communities around them.

Whether open source software truly provides inherent benefits to security, its ubiquity within the enterprise and government computing ecosystem, from mobile phones to public cloud, from automobiles to spacecraft, is such that it is important that we are able to consider the impact it has on trust. As we have described in this chapter, the difference in *how* open source software is created is only one aspect of the trust relationships that need to be considered for any system that includes it.

Trust, the Cloud, and the Edge

In Chapter 5, we noted a common joke in cloud computing:

There is no cloud: it's just somebody else's computer.

In this chapter, we will delve deeper into the impact of this statement on trust and also consider another important computing environment: what has become known as "the *Edge*". Let us attempt a definition of *Edge computing* to allow us to disambiguate it from *cloud computing*. While there is some overlap, there are some differing characteristics that will be of interest to us as we look at trust in each context. Edge computing addresses use cases where consolidating compute resources in a centralised location (the typical cloud computing case) is not necessarily appropriate. This pushes some or all of the computing power out to the edges of the network, where it can process data that is generated at the fringes rather than having to transfer all the data over what may be low-bandwidth networks for processing. There is no generally accepted single industry definition of Edge computing, but examples might include:

- Placing video processing systems in or near a sports stadium for pre-processing to reduce the amount of raw footage that needs to be transmitted to a centralised data centre or studio
- Providing analysis and safety control systems on an ocean-based oil rig to reduce reliance and contention on an unreliable and potentially low-bandwidth network connection

- Creating an Internet of Things (IoT) gateway to process and analyse data from environmental sensor units (IoT devices)

- Mobile Edge computing, or multi-access Edge computing[1] (both abbreviated MEC), where telecommunications services such as location and augmented reality (AR) applications are run on cellular base stations rather than in the telecommunication provider's centralised network location

In cloud computing, the hosting model views computing resources as being consumed by tenants. In the Edge case, the consumer of computing resources is often the owner of the systems providing them (though this is not always the case). Another difference between these two environments is the size of the host providing the computing resources, which may range from very large to very small (in the case of an IoT gateway, for example). While not always the case, Edge environments typically have smaller hosts than cloud environments. One important factor about most modern Edge computing environments is that they employ the same virtualisation and orchestration techniques as the cloud, allowing more flexibility in deployment and lifecycle management over bare-metal deployments.

Table 10.1 compares the various properties typically associated with cloud and Edge computing and points out a number of differences.

Table 10.1: A comparison of cloud and Edge computing

	PUBLIC CLOUD COMPUTING	PRIVATE CLOUD COMPUTING	EDGE COMPUTING
Location	Centralised	Centralised	Distributed
Hosting model	Tenants	Owner	Owner or tenant(s)
Application type	Generalised	Generalised	May be specialised
Host system size	Large	Large	Large to very small
Network bandwidth	High	High	Medium to low
Network availability	High	High	High to low
Host physical security	High	High	Low

Table 10.1 notes two different types of cloud computing: *public* and *private*. The latter is sometimes characterised as *on-premises* or *on-prem* computing, but

---

[1]ETSI, 2020.

the point here is that rather than deploying applications to dedicated hosts, workloads are deployed using the same virtualisation and orchestration techniques employed in the public cloud. The only difference is that the hosts and software are owned and managed by the owner of the applications. Sometimes these services are actually managed by an external party, but in the case of a private cloud there is a close commercial (and concomitant trust) relationship to this *managed services provider*. Equally important, single tenancy in a private cloud is assured (assuming that security is maintained), as only applications from the owner of the service are hosted.[2] Many organisations will mix and match workloads to different cloud deployments, employing both public and private clouds (a deployment model known as a *hybrid cloud*) and/or different public clouds (a deployment model known as *multi-cloud*). All these models—public computing, private computing, and Edge computing—share an approach in common: in most cases, workloads are deployed not to bare-metal servers but to virtualisation platforms.

Deployment Model Differences

From a trust point of view, what are the requirements that we are looking to meet, and what is special about each of the models and their offerings? We are looking to establish trust relationships to the host system with assurances about security and have identified *confidentiality*, *integrity*, and *availability* as key metrics. Given that all of the approaches are based on one or more virtualisation technologies (we identified hardware-enabled virtual machines and Linux containers as the main incumbent technologies in Chapter 5), and given the difficulty of providing assurances around availability at the virtualisation layer, we must assume such assurances will need to be made by a contract component or system and monitored by the orchestration or application systems. Luckily, availability (the ability to continuing processing) is generally fairly easy to monitor, unlike the integrity and (to an even greater extent) confidentiality of workloads.

Another characteristic that the three approaches share is scale. They all assume that machines will host multiple workloads—though the number of hosts and the actual size of the host systems is likely to be highest in the public cloud case and lowest in the Edge case. This high *workload density* makes public cloud computing in particular economically viable and is one of the reasons that it makes sense for organisations to deploy at least some of their workloads to public clouds. Cloud service providers (CSPs) can employ economies of scale that allow them to schedule workloads onto their servers from multiple

---

[2]This is a somewhat simplistic view that we will examine in more detail in Chapter 12.

tenants, balancing load and bringing sets of servers in and out of commission infrequently (these activities are costly in terms of both computation and time). Owners and operators of private clouds, in contrast, need to ensure that they have sufficient resources available for the maximum possible load at all times and do not have the opportunity to balance loads from other tenants unless they open their on-premises deployment to other organisations, which would mean transforming themselves into CSPs and putting themselves into direct competition with existing CSPs. It is this push for high workload density that is one of the reasons strong workload-from-workload (type 1) isolation is needed; refer back to Chapter 8, Figure 8.6.

In order to be able to maintain high density, cloud owners need to mix workloads from multiple tenants on the same host. Tenants are mutually untrusting; in fact, they are likely to be completely unaware of each other. If the host is doing its job well, its tenants will be unaware of the presence of other workloads on the same host they occupy. More important than this property, however, is a strong assurance that their workloads will not be negatively impacted by workloads from other tenants. Although negative impact can occur in other contexts to computation—such as storage contention or network congestion—the focus is mainly on the isolation that hosts can provide.

The likelihood of malicious workloads increases with the number of tenants but reduces significantly when the tenant is the same as the host owner—which is the case for private cloud deployments and some Edge deployments. Thus, the need for host-from-workload isolation (type 2; refer back to Chapter 8, Figure 8.7) is higher for the public cloud—though the possibility of poorly written or compromised workloads means that it should not be neglected for the other types of deployment.

One final difference between the models is that for both public and private cloud deployments, the physical vulnerability of hosts is generally considered to be low,[3] whereas the opportunities for unauthorised physical access to Edge computing hosts are considered to be much higher. When we considered trusted computing bases (TCBs) in Chapter 7, we discussed the importance of considering hardware components as part of the TCB but did not talk in detail about what it might mean to compromise a hardware component. Chapter 11 is devoted to hardware, and we will discuss this issue in much more detail. It is a fundamental principle of computer security that if an attacker has physical access to a system, the system must be considered compromised, as it is, in almost all cases,[4] possible to compromise the confidentiality, integrity, and availability of workloads executing on the system.

---

[3]Though this idea assumes that people with authorised access to physical machines are not malicious, a proposition that cannot be guaranteed but for which monitoring can at least be put in place.
[4]The cases where this principle does not always hold are an important aspect of the discussion on hardware and trust.

What Host Systems Offer

Table 10.2 shows the characteristics of workload density and vulnerability to physical compromise as they apply to the three types of deployment we are considering.

Table 10.2: Host system criteria for cloud and Edge computing environments

	PUBLIC CLOUD COMPUTING	PRIVATE CLOUD COMPUTING	EDGE COMPUTING
Workload density	High	Medium	Low
Vulnerability to physical compromise	Low	Low	High
Type 1 isolation (workload from workload)	High importance	Low importance	Depends on tenancy model
Type 2 isolation (host from workload)	Important	Low importance	Medium importance

We could compare this approach with the "legacy" approach to deployments, with one workload per host. Although the problems of isolation are generally removed in the legacy approach, workload density is reduced to a minimum. Vulnerability to physical compromise depends, of course, on the deployment scenarios.

What Tenants Need

Having considered the interests of the owners and operators of the hosts, we need to return to our main concern: the interests of the workload owners—the tenants. What are they concerned about? First, we need to remind ourselves that what we are exploring in this book is computer-to-computer trust relationships and the extent to which they are possible. In order to support this ambition and allow the sorts of automation that it allows, the tenants need access to computational assurances around the following issues, which we have addressed in earlier chapters. Note that our use of language will be a little loose—a point we will remedy after our initial list.

Isolation   Without isolation, there can be no assurances around security: specifically, confidentiality and integrity (we have already noted that assurances around availability are almost impossible to offer at the virtualisation layer).

Type 1—Workload from Workload   Workload-from-workload isolation is extremely important to tenants in multi-tenancy deployments as they have no trust relationship with other tenants and must therefore assume them to be malicious. This type of isolation is less relevant in single-tenancy deployments but should not be ignored, given the possibilities of compromised workloads on the same host.

Type 2—Host from Workload   Host-from-workload isolation generally is not directly important to tenants, as it aims to protect the host. However, in the situation where a workload on a host (or on a host in the same trust domain—a point to which we will return in Chapter 12) is malicious and manages to break type 2 isolation, all other workloads are at risk and should be considered compromised, even if the host itself was previously trusted.

Type 3—Workload from Host   Workload-from-host isolation is important to tenants in all deployments where the host is not trusted or the chance of an initially trusted host being compromised is significant (where, for instance, the chance of compromise due to physical vulnerability is high).

Hardware Root of Trust   A hardware root of trust may be useful to anchor the trust the workload holds in the host's TCB.

Attestation   Attestation is a mechanism that can be used to present measurements to the workload or tenant to allow them to evaluate assurances. But unless the attestation is itself performed by hardware components, rather than within software, the expectation should be that any attestations provided after provisioning time may be invalid, as the software providing them may have been compromised.

Trust in TCBs   As we noted in Chapter 7, without a TCB, a workload can have few assurances that it will run as expected. The problem, as we noted in Chapter 8, is that in the virtualisation scenario, there are at least two different TCBs that the tenant must trust:

Own TCB   It should normally be expected that the workload's own TCB is trusted at deployment time. But without type 1 isolation, there can be few assurances that the workload will not be compromised by another workload. And without type 3 isolation, we have few assurances that the workload will not be compromised by the host.

Host TCB   It may be possible to offer assurances to the workload and/or tenant about the trustworthiness of the host TCB at deployment (at least of the host, if not the workload), but longer-term assurances are more difficult, and trust in the host's TCB should be expected to decay over time.

Now that we have stated the main principles of the tenant's requirements from a host, we need to clear up the loose language. On a number of occasions, we talked about the host being "trusted". We know by now that any such use of language is dangerous: what is the trust relationship—or relationships—that underpin such a statement, and can they be backed up computationally?

The final set of requirements around TCBs turns out to be central to understanding and addressing our concerns. Let us return to the discussion on virtual machines that we had in Chapter 8. We were considering the use case of a workload in a virtual machine in a host owned and operated by a CSP. We established that the workload (which is executing in a virtual machine) has to have multiple trust relationships to the host machine in multiple contexts, which is challenging when the host machine is difficult to define as a single system. At the very least, however, the workload needs to be considered a separate system from the rest of the host machine because (as we noted in Chapter 4), systems can only exercise agency for one entity within the context of a particular trust relationship. Without type 3 isolation, where the workload is protected from actions performed by the host, this is impossible.

This problem is not alleviated with the use of other common types of virtualisation: *Linux containers* and *serverless computing*. Serverless computing (despite its name) actually does require servers; but the tenant uses computing resources on CSP-owned hosts to execute short-lived workloads, which can be conceptualised as single-function instances—hence another name of serverless computing: *function as a service*. In neither of these cases is type 3 isolation provided—in fact, both type 1 and type 2 isolation are software-based rather than hardware-based, arguably providing weaker protections in both these contexts.

This inability to isolate the workload from actions performed by the host is a core point. Unless we can separate the workload and its associated agency (from the tenant) from the host (with associated agency from the CSP), there can be no well-defined trust relationships. The CSP can overrule or subvert the agency of the tenant by causing the workload to act in ways that are unexpected and unplanned. This has a major impact on a subject that we have so far only touched on briefly, but to which we will devote an entire chapter, Chapter 12. Trust domains, as defined in Chapter 3, are:

Sets of entities of components that can be considered to comprise a single unit from the point of view of a trust relationship.

By this definition, a virtual machine running in a host cannot sit within the tenant's trust domain because, without type 3 isolation, its operation is under the control of the host. If the tenant requires assurances about the functioning of the virtual machine, there needs to be one or more trust relationships from the tenant to the host or the entity that owns/runs the host, typically the CSP. If a tenant has a sensitive workload—that is, a workload whose data, algorithm, or execution requires protection in terms of at least confidentiality, integrity, and availability—then the tenant cannot have any assurances beyond those offered by the trust relationship to the host.

Mutually Adversarial Computing

There has been little dedicated study of the trust relationships that exist within and around cloud computing, and a 2016 study by Jens Lansing and Ali Sunyaev noted that:

> *trust has received little attention in the context of cloud computing, resulting in a lack of understanding of the dimensions of trust in cloud services and trust-building antecedents.*[5]

Later in the paper, they state that, to the best of their knowledge, "no study investigates the IT artifact, neither as a trust antecedent nor as a trustee".[6] We would generally use terms such as *component* and *system* to allow us to be more specific about what they refer to as "IT artifacts". Nonetheless, a useful point that they make is that "users will consider cloud service to be predictable if they are confident that resources will be provisioned as requested." Another paper on "trust in online environments", published in 2008, gives us a clue as to how trust in particular contexts of cloud computing (such as the ability to offer type 1 isolation) may have led to tenants assuming that trust could be assumed in other contexts:

> *We suggest that the target of trust is usually an object (such as trust in the ability and integrity of a recommendation agent that is a component of a Web site), the availability of which leads to a behavioural belief (that using the Web site would lead to an efficient product search), which in turn influences the adoption of that Web site.*[7]

What this tells us is that tenants—at least those who are not aware of the relevant risks or who are not under regulatory regimes where the risks are made explicit—are likely to have made risk assumptions based on behavioural beliefs that are *not only computationally impossible to verify but also unlikely to be covered by commercial agreements*. This leads to significant business risk, which is (as noted in the extract from the paper we have just seen) often implicit, based on behavioural belief rather than rational modelling.

---

[5]Lansing and Sunyaev, 2016, p. 58. The authors' focus in the paper is on areas such as functionality, reliability, and predictability, none of which are fully aligned with our main interest in security, but the study is well worth reading.
[6]Lansing and Suyaev, 2016, p. 66.
[7]Gefen, Benbasat, and Pavlou, 2008, p. 281.

Many organisations operate in legal or regulatory contexts such as the United States' *Health Insurance Portability and Accountability Act* (HIPAA), the *European Union's General Data Protection Regulation* (GDPR), national telecommunications provision regulations, or the financial industry's *Payment Card Industry Data Security Standard* (PCI-DSS). This means that where they are tenants, any workloads that they deploy are likely to be subject to a regulatory framework, whether they deploy them in a private cloud, the public cloud, or on the Edge. When they wish to deploy a workload in the public cloud, on a CSP's host, they need to ensure that they are employing a service that provides sufficient safeguards to meet the relevant provisions—though there is a risk, as we have noted, that organisations may not realise that the capabilities they require are not provided by default. If the services *are* to provide the appropriate capabilities, this may amount to a large burden and needs to be made explicit. Even if a CSP *can* meet such requirements—we might say "require such assurances"—it may be that the CSP must insist that any workloads requiring such assurances are labelled to this effect and may be charged at a higher rate. This type of deployment also requires that the tenant:

- Be aware of regulations that are relevant to the workload

- Know that there is a requirement for them to gain assurance that the CSP is able to meet any relevant provisions

- Be able to control where their workloads execute (where they are *scheduled*, in the language of cloud orchestration)

- Log where and when all of their workloads are executed, to allow for appropriate auditing.

These requirements are complex and may be costly, and it is no surprise that many organisations that are subject to these types of legal or regulatory requirements choose not to deploy sensitive workloads to the cloud, even when the legal or regulatory environments allow it—and many do not—and even to hosts owned by CSPs that are able to meet some or more of these requirements. The only way to fix the issue of having to hold a trust relationship to the CSP in such a way—or, to take a different view, to allow the virtual machine to sit in a separate trust domain to the rest of the host—is to provide a mechanism to allow type 3 isolation.

The final statement seems extreme, and it is intended to be. And it must also lead us to some extreme reappraisals of how we think about using the public cloud or any other set of computing resources that we do not control, such as a private cloud or Edge computing.[8] The problem is that underlying all of the previous discussions about the relationships between hosts and workloads is a fundamental asymmetry in standard virtualisation techniques, which has

---

[8]And, of course, beyond: how many of the components of your mobile phone are you able to evaluate and verify?

major impacts on how organisations should consider their approaches to cloud computing in particular:

> *A CSP can have computational assurances that a tenant's workloads cannot affect its hosts' normal operation, but no such computational assurances are available to a tenant that a CSP's hosts will not affect their workloads' normal operation.*

In other words, the tenant has to rely on commercial relationships for trust establishment, whereas the CSP can rely on both commercial relationships and computational techniques. Worse yet, the tenant has no way to monitor the actions of the CSP and its host machines to establish whether the confidentiality of its workloads has been compromised (though integrity compromise may be detectable in some situations): so even the "trust, but verify" approach is not available to them. In a world where all organisations are trustworthy, or where no workloads contain sensitive data or workloads, this might be acceptable; but this is not the business or commercial environment we outlined where regulatory, legal, or just business concerns do not allow such a lack of controls.

In order to think about public cloud computing (where the host acts with the agency of the CSP, not the tenant) and Edge computing (where even in the single-tenant model, the host is considered more vulnerable to physical compromise. Therefore, it cannot be assumed to be operating with the agency of the owner) in a way that allows us to model workloads as computationally separate from hosts. We therefore need to be able to show that they can run as *separate systems*, as otherwise there is no way for them to establish trust relationships to each other. In fact, rather than considering the host a friendly helper, we need to move to considering it a potential adversary—in the same way hosts have to assume that workloads are potential adversaries through outright malicious intent or compromise. This is what we mean by *mutually adversarial computing*.

This does not mean automatically assuming that every CSP is malicious or that no workloads should be deployed onto CSPs' hosts. Most CSPs will be benevolent—at least within the range expected in a commercial relationship—but they may be subject to different legal and regulatory regimes from their tenants. They are also vulnerable to compromise by internal actors (employees and contractors) and external threats. Though those vulnerabilities may also exist for their tenants, the profile of likely attackers may well be different, which means that any threat and attacker modelling needs to consider both the CSP and the tenant's situation.

What this *does* mean is that we need to realise that the risks associated with running workloads in different deployment contexts vary by situation and that we need to consider the risk profile we are willing to accept for different types of workloads processing different types of data at different times. A large part of this realisation must centre around the fact that we cannot assume a clearly definable trust boundary between the infrastructure owner and the workload. If such a trust boundary is required in order to allow us to calculate, manage, and mitigate risk for particular workloads, then the lesson has to be that those workloads are not appropriate for deployment on that particular host environment. We have concentrated on the case of the CSPs—public cloud service providers—in this chapter, but all of these points apply to private cloud deployments and the Edge, with different emphases on the various choices and risks.

Mitigations and Their Efficacy

Virtualisation and its various commercial applications—public cloud, private cloud, and Edge—are here to stay; and while this chapter aims to raise the visibility of some particular problems associated with their use, it is not this book's intention to try to dissuade organisations from employing all or any of them. Rather, we wish to encourage more explicit modelling of trust relationships, permitting calculations around risk to take place and allowing informed decisions about appropriate mitigations. In this section, we discuss some examples of mitigations that may be appropriate and consider their efficacy and applicability for particular types of use cases.

Commercial Mitigations

The first type of mitigation to consider is within the commercial sphere. A great deal of this book is concerned with technical considerations around trust in the computing sphere, but we must not lose sight of the fact that the technical serves the commercial. We only write applications and deploy them in order to serve the commercial or business activities of the organisations with which we are associated, including activities that are not profit-related or that are associated with non-profit-generating organisations such as charities or government.[9] Given this reality, we should always consider that the most appropriate mitigation may be associated with actions within this realm. Such mitigations may include (but are certainly not limited to):

- Deciding to assess the risk based on its likelihood and expected impact on the organisation

- Negotiating contractual agreements with the trustee (such as the CSP) to reduce the organisation's exposure to risk

- Taking out insurance to cover possible impacts on the organisation

Sometimes, creating complex technical solutions to complex problems that exist partly outside the technical sphere—as is the case with trust relationships—is

---

[9]Even this may not be entirely accurate, of course—there are certainly deployments of leisure-related applications that may be associated with individuals, for instance—but we will assume that individuals should also be making risk assessments associated with such activities.

not the most efficient or appropriate way to manage risk. In these cases, the simplest—and cheapest—approach is coordination with business-related parts of the organisation to find alternatives to technical solutions.

Architectural Mitigations

Architectural mitigations involve considering the workload and its context and identifying whether there are ways to manage the risks associated with it in ways that do not require technical measures to be applied to change specific trust characteristics of the different components.

The first consideration is what components of an application require the types of protection provided by isolation—these are typically, as we have seen, confidentiality, integrity, and availability. As we have already discussed, providing protection of availability is almost impossible in a standard virtualisation context. If this type of protection is required for a component, then we already have a clear requirement. This component needs to be deployed in a bare-metal environment or in a virtualisation context where we can form a trust relationship to the host system in which we can establish sufficient assurances that this expectation will be met. The appropriate mitigation in this case, might involve making the architectural decision to ensure that all instances of this component are deployed on our private cloud instance rather than on the public cloud.

This leads us to a second consideration, which is how best to "componentise" our application. One of the advantages of virtualisation and distributed computing in general is the opportunity to separate an application or system into multiple components and deploy them into different execution contexts. Rather than thinking of an application as a single, monolithic program that has a single set of trust and security requirements, it may be that we can identify the logging and auditing functions as requiring higher levels of protection and associated isolation properties than other parts of the application. If this is the case, we may decide to separate these functions out and run them in a different execution context separately. This model, where applications are considered multiple components that run with clear execution boundaries, and where some components may even provide services to multiple applications,[10] is known as a *microservices architecture*. Setting up rules where microservices are deployed to different hosting environments based on their requirements allows those parts of an application that have lower trust requirements to be deployed on the public cloud. For instance, it might be while those with higher requirements can be deployed in the private cloud or instances of the public cloud with more stringent controls in place. For example, if a CSP offers services that provide higher

---

[10]An authentication microservice might be used by several applications or different layers of the same application, for instance.

levels of isolation assurance than standard offerings, these might be employed for microservices whose requirements they meet.

We should note that there is a danger associated with such componentisation strategies. While such strategies allow for easier decisions to be made about deployment options, they may also lead to a fracturing of applications into forms that do not allow system abstractions to be consistently applied. They also increase the difficulty of trust domain management. We will address some of these concerns in Chapter 12.

Decisions around architecture may also be applied at other architectural boundaries, such as different layers of the application stack. For an application with a presentation layer, web layer, application layer, and database layer, for instance, opportunities arise to consider the risk, trust, and security policies that are applicable for each and to manage deployment options based on the requirements that arise from such considerations.

While much of our focus on applications in this context has been on their execution and the protection of their computational resources—code and data—we should not ignore opportunities for protection of other aspects such as storage and networking. While confidentiality and integrity concerns can often be addressed with encryption in both networking and storage contexts, encryption is not always applicable. This may be because computational isolation contexts do not allow for key management to support it or because multiple components need to access the data. In these cases, there are various opportunities to isolate network traffic or stored data using techniques such as VPNs, VXLANs (forms of network segregation), or just ensuring that data only ever exits a trust domain in encrypted form—meaning all components that need to access it in unencrypted format must be deployed *within* that trust domain. The use of cryptographic hashes may also provide some of the protections around integrity that may be required in certain use cases.

Another mitigation that bears consideration is monitoring. It may not always be possible—or price-appropriate—to employ the other techniques we have outlined, whereas monitoring of specific components may be cheaper and may provide sufficient risk mitigation to allow their deployment in "less secure" environments. Indeed, in some cases, this monitoring may extend well beyond the components themselves and be part of a wider risk-reduction strategy. Some organisations monitor communications over their organisational boundaries such as email or chat communications, looking for possible leakage of information that should be subject to confidentiality protections.

Finally, it is worth noting that there are certain mitigations that may apply to Edge deployments that are not available or relevant in the public cloud context. This is particularly true if rather than considering the set of Edge hosts as homogeneous, we think of their potentially having different characteristics. Assuming that we have some control over the estate of deployed Edge hosts to which we may deploy workloads, we may be able to configure them to operate with different properties. It may be the case, for instance, that while most of the Edge hosts we manage will support multiple tenants, we can configure and manage a different set so that they will be associated with a single tenant or sets of tenants that have well-defined trust relationships between them or between their workloads. This may reduce the requirements for strong type 1 and type 2 isolation workloads deployed on this set of hosts. Equally, while it may be too expensive to provide strong physical protections for the entire set of Edge hosts, the risk profile associated with a subset—and their workloads—may make it appropriate (and cost-effective) to apply stronger physical protections to these.

Technical Mitigations

Technical mitigations may be software or hardware related. Chapter 11 is devoted specifically to hardware mitigations, so we will instead briefly list some software-related mitigations here. We must remember, though, that none of these provide the level of type 3 isolation (workload from host) that allows for the deployment of more sensitive workloads. Decisions around the appropriateness of mitigations should always be considered through the lens of business and commercial risk rather than as solely technical choices. Some of the technical mitigations that may be considered include:

- Access control management (e.g., SELinux and AppArmor)
- Integrity management (e.g., IMA)
- Boot measurement technologies

For more information on any of these, please refer to earlier chapters, including Chapter 7.

CHAPTER 11

Hardware, Trust, and Confidential Computing

This chapter finally gets to the bottom—pretty much literally—of many of our discussions about trust, in that without a root of trust in hardware, our search for trust in computing is likely to be fruitless, as we have seen. For more details of the mechanisms that provide the underlying components, Ross Anderson's *Security Engineering: A Guide to Building Dependable Distributed Systems*[1] is the canonical work in the field, and it is strongly recommended that readers turn to it for further reference. Rather than attempt a survey of many different types of hardware and how they relate to trust, we look at the two key sets of properties that hardware may enforce or strengthen and then at what happens if hardware components are compromised. Our final section explores how hardware can help systems to impose and enforce boundaries, as we apply our understanding of hardware and isolation to trust and trusted computing bases (TCBs) explicitly and consider the opportunities that present themselves for explicit trust relationships around *trusted execution environments* (TEEs).

---

[1] Anderson, 2021.

Properties of Hardware and Trust

There are two properties of hardware components that we have identified as important to our quest for understanding trust: *isolation* and *root of trust*. We have considered both to some degree earlier in the book; here, we will look at how hardware components provide them.

Isolation

Much of the interest we have shown in isolation has been in the realm of execution, and we have considered three types in detail: *workload-from-workload* (type 1), *host-from-workload* (type 2), and *workload-from-host* (type 3). It is worth noting that these are not industry-standard appellations but labels that we have adopted to try to make clear exactly the properties for which we may be looking. Up to now, we have spent little time understanding how they are provided by hardware. In order to understand hardware isolation, we need to look at the context in which it arose: virtualisation. Virtualisation as a concept is older than might be expected, dating from the 1960s, and refers to the ability of a hardware system to create a simulated computing environment in which software can be run as if it had its own dedicated hardware: the software runs in a virtual machine (VM), and there may be multiple VMs per physical host (one of the reasons for virtualisation is the economic driver to make more efficient use of hardware resources).

Hardware-assisted virtualisation, where the hardware provides isolation, was introduced in the IBM System/370 in 1972 and came to the x86 computing world in 2005 when Intel provided CPU-based support, followed by AMD in 2006. There are various types of virtualisation, some mixing hardware and software techniques, but it is the capabilities offered by hardware-assisted virtualisation that are of most interest to us. The key point about hardware-assisted virtualisation with regard to isolation is that it allows the *guest operating system* to operate as if it were the only operating system using the hardware, protecting the *host operating system* from interference by processes running in the guest system.[2]

The most common approach to running *guests* on a host is to have a full operating system (such as GNU/Linux or Microsoft Windows) running virtualised. However, alternatives exist such as *library operating systems*, which provide cut-down *unikernels* or *microkernels*, implementing a reduced set of operations to support specific use cases such as quick boot-time requirements, high-performance networking, and execution of applications written in particular programming languages. In all

---

[2]The specifics of this form of isolation, and approaches such as *para-virtualisation*, which mix hardware-assisted and software virtualisation, vary by implementation (in both software and hardware) but generally are not germane to our discussion.

cases, the standard approach to loading and running guests is for a *hypervisor* to manage the operation of the guest, including (importantly, from our point of view) mapping and managing memory pages. Memory pages on the host are mapped to VMs so that guests can operate, and sometimes the memory pages are shared between multiple VMs to allow for higher *workload density* (where the data is the same and either read-only or currently untouched by any of the guests). Two of the key tasks of the hypervisor are to ensure that no memory pages associated with the host operating system are mapped to guests[3] and that memory pages are only accessible by the guests to which they are assigned.

Hardware-assisted virtualisation aims to deny guests access to the underlying host operating system and the hypervisor (type 2 isolation) and to isolate guests from each other (type 1 isolation). However, the fact that the hypervisor—which sits outside the virtualisation boundary imposed by the hardware—has both read and write access to the memory pages that are allocated to the guest explains why type 3 isolation is incompatible with standard virtualisation techniques.

Hardware-assisted virtualisation is not the only technique to provide isolation: physical boundaries such as *hardware security modules* (*HSMs*), co-processors, and physical separation of hardware in different chassis all provide ways to separate systems, all with different trade-offs around security, management, and ease of operation. Nor is isolation restricted to execution: techniques exist to provide for the separation of both network traffic and stored data. *Air-gap networks* are arguably the safest way to provide isolation of data flow between systems[4] and are historically the mechanism used to maintain separation between high-security networks such as those maintained by government and military agencies. Looking at virtualisation techniques, *single root I/O virtualization* (SR-IOV) can allow guest VMs to communicate directly with network or storage cards, bypassing host memory—though the lack of type 3 isolation means the host can still access the traffic as it passes through or resides in guest memory pages.

Roots of Trust

Another important service provided by hardware components is their use as roots of trust for a system, though we should not lose sight of the fact that trusted platform modules (TPMs)—the most common hardware roots of trust in modern computing systems—themselves include a certificate from an endorsing authority (such as the manufacturer) to allow entities to decide whether to accept the trust pivot they can provide. HSMs can perform a similar service, though

---

[3]This is something of a simplification, particularly in the case of para-virtualisation, as there may be some sharing: it is more accurate to say that the hypervisor restricts unauthorised access to memory pages associated with the host operating system.

[4]Or were, until the advent of cheap and portable storage, given the near ubiquity of USB ports in modern hardware and cheap mobile cellphones.

they may require more provisioning in order to allow a system to form a trust relationship to them—which may be seen as a positive in some situations where explicit trust pivots are beneficial.

What is particularly interesting about TPMs in the context of virtualisation and the cloud is for *what* specifically they are providing a root of trust.[5] The standard use for a root of trust is the *trusted computing base* (TCB) of the host system, and this is the main context for which TPMs were originally employed (ignoring their use for *digital rights management* [DRM], an example of security economics that we have already considered). We represent this use case in the diagram shown in Figure 11.1.

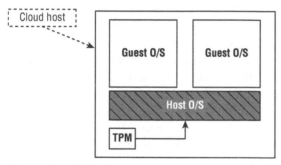

Figure 11.1: TPM—host usage.

Here, the host operating system—or at least the parts of it that make up the TCB—can be measured, and the TCB can act as a root of trust, providing some assurances to the owner of the host system about the integrity of the system. An alternative use case might be to pass control of the TPM to a virtualisation guest (for instance, a hardware-assisted VM or a Linux container) to allow measurements—such as of the supplied firmware and the kernel image—that we might hope would provide the owner of the guest to have some assurances about its integrity. This is represented in Figure 11.2.

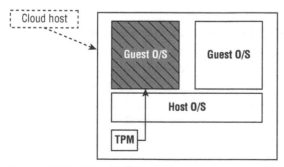

Figure 11.2: TPM—guest usage.

---

[5]For a detailed technical description of some of the various options and an attack based on some weaknesses in standard models of TPMs used in virtualisation contexts, see Lauer and Rudolph, 2019.

It turns out that two immediate problems arise with this, however. The first, as we noted earlier, is that the owner of the guest needs to trust not only the guest TCB but also the host TCB. In the arrangement shown, there is no measurement of the host system, so the guest can have no trust in the host TCB. The second problem is the mechanism by which the TPM is mapped to the guest: if we are not careful, it could be done in such a way that the host operating system could interfere with any measurement being sent to the guest. In fact, this second concern is irrelevant, as the host can always change any measurement data provided to the guest before it can be used or transmitted to the guest owner. One way to try to address these issues might seem to be to measure the host operating system and then measure the guest operating system, passing both measurements to the guest: this practice would provide assurances to the guest that the host operating system was what was expected. Unluckily, as we noted when we examined TCBs, this does not help with our trust issue either. Since the host operating system is owned by another entity—which may be malicious or compromised—then the fact that the TCB was trusted at provisioning time is (again) irrelevant: the host owner can make whatever changes they wish to the host during runtime. Trying to set up the host system to avoid such changes requires a significant rearchitecting of the overall system and basically moves the host into the trust domain of the guest, making the guest the owner of the system and negating much of the point of virtualisation in the first place.

There are two further techniques that are sometimes employed in cloud deployments and deserve our attention: *software TPMs* and *virtual TPMs* (*vTPMs*). Industry definitions are not consistent, so we will provide our own in order to allow us to disambiguate the differences:

Software TPM   This is a TPM that is implemented in software and under the control of the host. In some cases, the host operating system may map measurements to a physical TPM, but (as opposed to a vTPM) all such operations are exposed to (and therefore not isolated from) the host.

vTPM   This extends the functioning of a hardware TPM via capabilities rooted in the hardware of the TPM itself, allowing certain of its functions to be shared by more than one entity, including virtualisation guests. These functions are mapped directly to the various entities (host and guests) from the hardware.

The trust characteristics of these approaches are very different, as is clear from Figure 11.3 and Figure 11.4.

As we can see, in the case of a software TPM, the TPM (and therefore all measurements) is fully under the control of the host operating system, which provides the implementation of the TPMs for each guest operating system. It might seem that there is no point in such an arrangement, since in order for this approach to provide any improved assurances to the guest owner, they

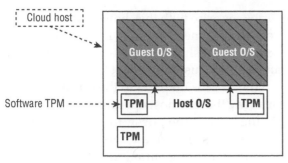

Figure 11.3: TPM—software TPM.

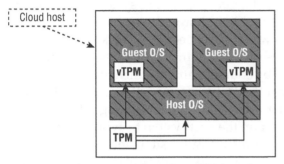

Figure 11.4: TPM—vTPM (based on a TPM).

must trust the host owner. In fact, there are occasions where software TPMs of this type can help guests, as long as there is an appropriate trust relationship to the host owner.

Although much of our focus in this book has been on the more extreme requirements of systems with regard to trust between computer systems, we have noted examples of broader contexts, such as where risk is managed via commercial relationships. In these or similar cases, the trust required by the guest in the hardware operating system may be a secondary consideration, and other benefits may accrue from the use of a TPM. For instance, it may be the case that the guest owner's assurances around the integrity of the guest operating system before it is instantiated are low, or that the guest operating system is provided by the host from local storage rather than by the guest owner itself. In both of these examples, having a measurement of the guest operating system come from an entity trusted to provide such a service may be appropriate. The dangers, of course, are that such trust relationships are rarely explicit and also that the host operating system may itself be compromised: any attacker might attack the software TPM as an obvious vector to attacking the guest operating system.

There are also other possible benefits to a software TPM beyond trust relationships associated with virtualisation: a number of applications at either the operating system or the user level may wish to make use of functionality expected to be provided by a TPM, particularly in the case where the guest may be unaware that it is running in a virtualised context, providing such capabilities will allow for a wider range of deployment options. The hardware TPM associated with a host itself could also provide a measurement of the host operating system, of course (though this is not represented in Figure 11.3), but does not itself provide a particularly strong assurance about either the longer term, time-based context of trust in the host TCB or any measurements of the host TCB that are sent to the guest.

The alternative—using a vTPM (where available in the hardware and offered by the host owner, which needs to enable such functionality for the guests)—addresses some of the concerns we have with the other approaches but still does not deal with the issue of a malicious host or one that is compromised after measurement. Having a vTPM provides benefits to guest applications similar to having a software TPM. Another benefit that overcomes a limitation of standard TPM deployments, which we did not mention when discussing the option of mapping the physical TPM to a guest, is that without extended capabilities, TPMs cannot be shared between multiple entities, meaning that supporting multiple guests is impossible.

While the use of a vTPM does not stop a malicious or compromised host from interfering with a guest's operation or prevent the host from changing the measurement data reported within the host, it does move the attack vector and may require more sophisticated attacks across the host-guest barrier than a direct attack on the software TPM within a host. Another benefit can be found in models of deployment where some functions of virtualisation, such as the hypervisor, are isolated from the host operating system (the model employed by Xen, for instance). The different models of TPM deployment are not the only variations between these virtualisation models, whose broader differences are beyond the scope of this book. But it should be noted that the precise virtualisation implementation offered by cloud service providers (CSPs) is unlikely to be exposed to either the guest operating system (to allow system-to-system trust decisions) or the guest owner (to allow informed risk and trust decisions at the commercial level).

Physical Compromise

There is a general principle in IT security that if an attacker has physical access to a system, that system should be considered compromised, which is why physical access to hardware is considered the highest level of control over information systems.[6] In our terms, "if an attacker has physical access to a system, then any assurances around expected actions should be considered reduced or

---

[6]See Ylonen et al., 2015, p. 2.

void, thereby requiring a re-evaluation of any related trust relationships". We briefly looked at tampering when we first considered hardware roots of trust in Chapter 5, particularly in relation to HSMs. Tampering is the typical concern when considering physical access, but exactly what an attacker will be able to achieve given physical access will depend on a number of factors, not least the skill of the attacker, the resources available to them, and the amount of time they have physical access. Scenarios range from an unskilled person attaching a USB drive to a system through short-duration *evil maid*[7] attacks and long-term access by national intelligence services. We should extend our scope beyond access to provisioned systems—whether running or not—and those that have yet to be provisioned or even necessarily assembled and those that have been decommissioned.

In our discussions of the supply chain, we have concentrated mainly on software, though we also noted in Chapter 2 the concerns that some governments (and organisations with nationally sensitive functions) have around hardware sourced from countries with whom they do not share entirely friendly diplomatic, military, or commercial relations. Even this scope is too narrow: there are many opportunities for other types of attackers to attack systems at various points in their lifecycles. *Dumpster diving*, in the context of IT security, is an old and well-established technique: where attackers look for sensitive paperwork (such as proprietary manuals), old computers, and hardware that have been thrown out by organisations but not sufficiently cleansed of data. At the other end of the scale, an attacker who was able to get a job at a debit or credit card personalisation company and then gain information about the cryptographic keys inserted in the bank card magnetic strips (or, better yet, chips) might be able to commit fraud that was both extensive and very difficult to track down. None of these attacks require damage to systems, but they do require physical access to systems or the manufacturing systems and processes that are part of the systems' supply chain.

An exhaustive list and description of physical attacks on systems is beyond the scope of this book (Anderson's *Security Engineering: A Guide to Building Dependable Distributed Systems*[8] is an excellent resource on this topic), but some examples across the range of threats, such as those shown in Table 11.1, may give an idea of the sort of issues that may be of concern.

The extent to which systems are vulnerable to these attacks varies enormously; it is particularly notable that systems deployed at the Edge, as defined

---

[7] An evil maid attack assumes that an attacker has brief access (on the order of tens of minutes, for example) to a hotel room where computer equipment such as a laptop is stored: whilst there, they have unfettered access but are expected to leave the system looking and behaving in the same way it was before they arrived. This places some bounds on the sorts of attacks available to them, but such attacks are notoriously difficult to defend against.

[8] Anderson, 2021.

in Chapter 10, are particularly vulnerable to a number of them. This is typically either because it is difficult to apply sufficient physical protections to such systems or because attackers may be able to achieve long-term physical access with little likelihood that their attacks will be discovered—or, if they are, with little danger of attribution to the attackers. Another interesting point about the majority of the attacks noted in Table 11.1 is that they do not involve physical damage to the system and are therefore unlikely to show tampering unless specific measures are in place to betray them. Providing as much physical protection as possible against some of the more sophisticated and long-term attacks, alongside visual checks for tampering, is the best defence for techniques that can lead to major, low-level compromise of the TCB.

Table 11.1: Examples of physical system attacks

ATTACK	LEVEL OF SOPHISTICATION	TIME REQUIRED	DEFENCES
USB drive to retrieve data	Low	Seconds	Disable USB ports/ software controls
USB drive to add malware to operating system	Low	Seconds	Disable USB ports/ software controls
USB drive to change boot loader	Medium	Minutes	Change BIOS settings
Attacks on Thunderbolt ports[9]	Medium	Minutes	Firmware updates; turn off machine when unattended
Probes on buses and RAM	High	Hours	Physical protection of machine
Cold boot attack[10]	High	Minutes	Physical protection of machine/TPM integration in boot process
Chip-scraping attacks	High	Days	Physical protection of machine
Electron microscope probes	High	Days	Physical protection of machine

---

[9]See, for example, Ruytenberg, 2020.
[10]A cold boot attack allows an attacker with access to RAM to access data recently held in memory.

In fact, understanding the extent of the TCB, the sensitivity of the system (and its guest workloads, where applicable), and the availability of mitigations are all important considerations when deciding what defences should be applied, what types of trust relationships should be established to the system, and how the context of time should alter those relationships.

Confidential Computing

One of the most important characteristics of systems is their ability to provide abstractions by exposing interfaces rather than their inner workings. These interfaces can be thought of as encapsulating particular functionality as a way to simplify components into more easily understood building blocks or as the boundaries around systems. Once a system can be bounded, opportunities arise to measure it, control it, and, most important in our focus, *isolate its operation*. Within software, the most often used type of runtime boundaries are threads and processes provided by the operating system (and/or languages). Both threads and processes have their own lifecycles, contexts, and rules for operation; and both provide isolation from their peers. As we move to more complex systems and more sensitive environments, boundaries become more visible and heavyweight, but there is a trade-off: almost every system needs to communicate externally to be of any use, which means there needs to be some permeability across boundaries. We can add to this the challenge that humans have managing many complex architectures and designs and the intrinsic redundancy of functionality in many systems (due partly to their use of commodity hardware and software components designed for applicability in multiple contexts). When taken together, it is unsurprising that accidental or malicious crossing of these boundaries is commonplace.

Much of the field of IT or cybersecurity is concerned with addressing these boundary problems, so let us briefly state, in simple terms, what we are looking for in terms of trust relationships from one entity to another in how data is managed and what this may mean in terms of boundaries. We will present three contexts: data in transit (on the network—Table 11.2), data at rest (in storage—Table 11.3), and data in use (executing—Table 11.4). As we are concentrating on boundaries and isolation, we will look at confidentiality and integrity as our core concerns.

We have already discussed various techniques, including software-based (particularly those related to cryptography) and physical (such as SR-IOV or, in a more extreme case, air-gapping), to provide assurances around networking and storage. We have also noted how weak these measures are when corresponding assurances around protection for data in use are not forthcoming. When applied to the execution of guest workloads on the cloud, the last of the trust relationships listed in Table 11.4 translates into what we have been calling *workload-from-host*

Table 11.2: Trust and data in transit

FROM (TRUSTOR) ENTITY A	TO (TRUSTEE) ENTITY B
Context(s)	Network data confidentiality and integrity
Time-specific	Dependent on relationship
Action(s)	Transmission and reception of data
Expectation(s)	Confidentiality cannot be breached by a third party. Integrity cannot be breached by a third party.
Assurance(s)	Mathematical or physical

Table 11.3: Trust and data at rest

FROM (TRUSTOR) ENTITY A	TO (TRUSTEE) ENTITY B
Context(s)	Storage data confidentiality and integrity
Time-specific	Dependent on relationship
Action(s)	Storage and retrieval of data
Expectation(s)	Confidentiality cannot be breached by a third party. Integrity cannot be breached by a third party.
Assurance(s)	Mathematical or physical
Mitigation(s)	TBD

Table 11.4: Trust and data in use

FROM (TRUSTOR) ENTITY A	TO (TRUSTEE) ENTITY B
Context(s)	Execution of workload (data and code)
Time-specific	Dependent on relationship
Action(s)	Execution of data by code
Expectation(s)	Confidentiality cannot be breached by a third party. Integrity cannot be breached by a third party.
Assurance(s)	Mathematical or physical

(type 3) isolation; the rest of this chapter examines the implications of supporting the establishment (and maintenance) of this type of trust relationship.

This use case has become known as *confidential computing* and is understandably of significant interest to organisations that wish to take advantage of the benefits of cloud and Edge computing but whose regulatory regimes or risk appetite do not allow them to deploy workloads using standard virtualisation techniques on hardware and systems that they do not and cannot control. The Confidential Computing Consortium, created as a Linux Foundation project in 2019, exists as a body to "accelerate the adoption of trusted execution environment (TEE) technologies and standards"[11] and has as its members all of the main silicon vendors and a number of the leading global CSPs. Though the exact scope of the use cases covered by confidential computing has yet to be fully agreed upon within the industry, the Confidential Computing Consortium aims to help define the core requirements and also to act as a space within which open source projects related to TEE usage can flourish and interact. We will devote the rest of this section to looking at various technologies that can be used to address and enable confidential computing, considering the impact of the boundaries that each provides and also the types of assurance provided by each. It is important to note that not all of these techniques are hardware-based; in a white paper,[12] the Confidential Computing Consortium provides a helpful diagram to show some of the technologies that can be applied (shown in Figure 11.5).

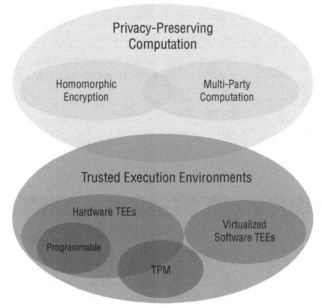

Figure 11.5: Venn diagram of various technologies used to protect data in use. (Disclaimer: Some terms have multiple competing definitions, so boundaries are often fuzzy.)

Source: Confidential Computing Consortium, 2020a.

We have already touched on TEEs in the section on hardware-based type 3 isolation in Chapter 7 and spent considerable time discussing TPMs, but we have not touched on homomorphic encryption. *Homomorphic encryption* refers

---

[11]Confidential Computing Consortium, 2020a.
[12]Confidential Computing Consortium, 2020, p. 8.

to a set of mathematical techniques in which certain programmatic operations are to be performed on encrypted data without having to decrypt the data first. This means that if such a set of operations can be provided as a workload, it can execute on a host with which it does not require a trust relationship with regard to confidentiality or integrity protection (though it still requires availability protection, of course). While this provides exciting opportunities for a small set of workloads, the chances of homomorphic encryption techniques being applicable to most general computing tasks are low, at least in the near to medium term. The Confidential Computing Consortium white paper also notes the existence of *software TEEs*, differentiating them from *hardware TEEs*. The paper defines *hardware TEEs* thus:

> *A hardware-based TEE uses hardware-backed techniques to provide increased security guarantees for the execution of code and protection of data within that environment. This assurance is often missing in approaches that do not use a hardware-based TEE.*

We accept the concerns expressed regarding software-based TEEs in this definition and do not consider software TEEs as providing sufficient protections to be worth considering for the types of trust relationships with which we are concerned, so we will refer to hardware TEEs solely as *TEEs* for the rest of the book.

The Confidential Computing Consortium white paper also provides a table[13] comparing three of these techniques: hardware-based trusted execution environments (HW TEEs), homomorphic encryption, and secure elements (e.g., TPM), three technologies that are usually the easiest to implement using standard systems and that can provide strong isolation boundaries for runtime execution protection. We have reproduced an adapted version in Table 11.5 and added HSMs.

Table 11.5: Comparison of data protection techniques

	HARDWARE TEE	HOMOMORPHIC ENCRYPTION	SECURE ELEMENT (E.G., TPM)	HSM
Data integrity	Y	Y (subject to code integrity)	Keys only	Y
Data confidentiality	Y	Y	Keys only	Y
Code integrity	Y	No	Y	Y
Code confidentiality	Y (may require work)	No	No	Y
Programmability	Y	Partial	No	Depends
Attestability	Y	No	Y	Depends

---

[13]Confidential Computing Consortium, 2020, p. 8.

All of these techniques provide boundaries that can be enforced to create systems to which trust relationships can be built: that is, they can all provide assurances in the context we have labelled *execution of workload (data and code)*. The methods they use to allow such assurances to be provided differ:

Hardware TEE   Chip-level instructions for encrypting memory pages and decrypting them only in the appropriate execution context.

Homomorphic Encryption   Mathematical techniques to protect the data being processed.

TPM   Physical boundary—whether as a separate chip on a motherboard or as separate IP blocks[14] on a CPU, with protections.

HSM   Physical boundary, enhanced by tamper-evidence and tamper-protection mechanisms.

Which of these approaches are the most appropriate for our needs? From our point of view, our key interests are confidentiality and integrity protection. Table 11.5 separates the protection of a workload's code from the data it is processing—a distinction we have not examined up to now. There are certainly use cases where keeping a workload's code confidential is not required: for example, if it is open source or implements well-known cryptographic protocols. But even when there is nothing confidential about the code, the mere fact of the code's existence as part of the workload may be sensitive information. If, for instance, a workload includes logging code that is widely used in the industry, there might be no need to keep the code's existence confidential for a host that is well-behaved. But if the host becomes compromised or is malicious, the very knowledge of what the workload *is* may be enough for the host to attempt to disrupt the workload's operation—for example, by restricting its access to computation resources. For our purposes, then, both data and code confidentiality protection are required (alongside integrity protection for both); this is reflected in the context label *execution of workload (data and code)*. We note that only hardware TEEs and HSMs can provide this protection, though Table 11.5 notes that this "may require work" for code confidentiality for some hardware TEEs. We can require that support for this property will be one of the assurances offered by a potential trustee system.

Another key attribute that we require is *programmability*—our main interest is in general computing workloads, and neither homomorphic encryption nor TPMs offer this capability. Some HSMs are able to accept applications, but implementing HSM-ready applications is difficult; provisioning them is complex, and when we look at the *scalability* attribute, we note that this is low for HSMs, ruling them out for many of our workloads in the cloud and Edge.

---

[14]An *IP block* is a set of functionality that can be created on an area of silicon, combined with other blocks on a chip.

In terms of providing type 3 isolation for general computing workloads, then, TEEs (hardware-based TEEs, specifically) offer us opportunities that go beyond standard virtualisation mechanisms and are not available from the other technologies we have examined—at least, not to the same level or with the same availability. In the next two sections, we will look at the TCB models provided by TEEs and then what trust models are available in deployments that employ TEEs.

TEE TCBs in detail

There are two main technologies currently available to provide trusted execution environments: *process-based* and *VM-based*. At the time of writing, the only technology using process-based TEEs is Intel's SGX, and the only technology on the market using VM-based TEEs is AMD's SEV, though IBM have announced a technology they call *Protected Execution Framework*[15] (*PEF*), and Intel have announced *Trust Domain Extensions*[16] (*TDX*). The TCBs associated with the two approaches vary quite significantly, so it is worth describing them in order to allow us to compare the options for TCBs[17]:

Process-Based TEEs   In the process-based model, processes that are accessing the TEE are split into two parts: those that are trusted and those that are untrusted (where these terms relate to the confidentiality and integrity protection provided). All data within the trusted part of a process is encrypted, as it resides within encrypted memory pages. The untrusted part of the process sits in unencrypted memory and is responsible for all communications with the rest of the host.

VM-Based TEEs   In the VM-based model, the standard virtualisation boundary is enhanced: by encrypting all memory pages associated with the VM are encrypted by the TEE and so are not directly readable or/and writable by the hypervisor or other host-based software processes. All processes within the VM are considered trusted. The basic implementation of a VM-based TEE is one or more vCPUs, to which (encrypted) memory pages can be added.

One of the differences between process-based TEEs and VM-based TEEs is that though process-based TEEs provide type 3 isolation, they do not provide type 2 isolation, meaning that the rest of the host does not have protection from malicious processes (or parts of processes) running within the TEE instance. Another is that VM-based TEEs require a mechanism to interact with the vCPU and memory, in the form of a kernel of some

---

[15]Hunt and Pai, 2019.
[16]Intel, 2020a.
[17]A more detailed comparison is available in Simon and Sturmann, 2019.

kind to provide process management, memory addressing, and other tasks. This does not need to be a full operating system kernel but could be a microkernel or unikernel. In the process-based TEE case, however, the host operating system provides the kernel; and though the processes that are accessing the TEE need to be managed and made aware of their execution environment, the amount of software infrastructure that needs to be provided in order to run an application may be lower.

The phrase *amount of software infrastructure* leads us inexorably to the question of the *trusted computing base (TCB)*. Let us start with the assumption that the type 3 isolation provided by the TEE provides sufficient assurances that we are happy to form a trust relationship to the TEE instance (an assurance for which we will provide an example a little later). Where this is the case, it is immediately clear that the TCB we need to consider is significantly changed from our previous case. Let us look at Figure 11.6, the diagram of the virtualisation stack that we introduced in Chapter 7.

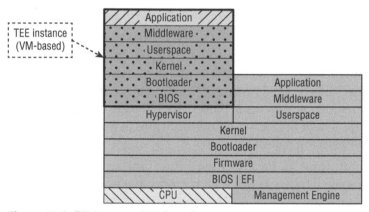

Figure 11.6: TEE instance (VM-based).

We have made some changes to the diagram:

- We show an additional layer in the VM, which we excluded for simplicity in our previous discussion: the BIOS.

- We have assumed that only one application will be running within the TEE instance.

- We thickened the line around the workload to emphasise the extent of the TEE protection.

- We have given all layers on the host (with the exception of the CPU) the same shading.

The reason for the last point is why TEEs bring such enormous possible benefits to trust relationships: it is possible to set up a TEE instance in such a way that the *only* trust relationship it needs to have with a component of the host system is with the CPU (and any associated firmware). This is an enormous change and, in the public cloud deployment scenario, raises the possibility of removing any need to trust the CSP at all in the contexts of confidentiality and integrity protection. This can be achieved through attestation but is complex and therefore easy to implement in ways that have significant negative impacts on the intended trust model.

We discussed attestation mainly in the context of measured and trusted boot mechanisms, but it is a vital part of the process of establishing trust. In order to consider both of our TEE types—process-based and VM-based—let us modify our diagram in a way that allows us to separate the two key components of interest to us at this point: the application and the TEE runtime (shown in Figure 11.7).

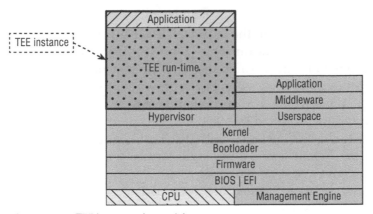

Figure 11.7: TEE instance (generic).

Although TEEs can be used in a variety of contexts, we will continue to describe the party wishing to use one as the *tenant* and what they wish to run as the *workload*. In order to have the assurance that its workload is going to execute correctly, a tenant needs to be able to establish:

- That the TEE runtime is what is expected and has not been altered in the process of being loaded
- That the application is what is expected and has not been altered in the process of being loaded

In both cases, this is a question of establishing the integrity of the component. This can be performed by attestation. We can also safely assume that the tenant wishes to ensure that the TEE runtime—which forms the TCB for the application—is unlikely to be compromised, a point to which we will return shortly.

The exact mechanisms for performing attestation vary between implementations by the silicon vendors but can be roughly categorised as falling into one of two approaches: *pre-load attestation* and *post-load attestation*. Both approaches rely on the CPU to perform a measurement of the TEE memory pages and provide a cryptographically signed measurement to the requesting party (the tenant, in our case). The CPU is a trust anchor in this context and is able to sign the measurement with a cryptographic key for which the CPU vendor is the endorsing authority. The CPU vendor then sends all of the information to the tenant, with some additional information that is dependent on the silicon vendor's implementation. The tenant should then check the following information provided as part of the measurement:

- Cryptographic validity

- Root of trust from the endorsing authority

- Expected value against known previous valid measurements, which are created before provisioning and made available to the tenant's attesting service

The last point varies depending on the approach taken—pre-load or post-load attestation—but in both cases, the outcome of the attestation (if it has been successful) is that the tenant is now assured that the TEE instance is valid and the tenant now has an established session key with which to communicate with the TEE instance, allowing any further material (code or data) to have its confidentiality and integrity protected by standard encryption protocols. This session key is unique to the TEE instance, with different keys produced even when there are multiple TEE instances on a single host, and is not reused if a TEE instance is deleted and a new one created.

The specific differences between pre-load and post-load attestation are important to understand, and we list them here.

Pre-Load Attestation   For pre-load attestation, the TEE is measured in its "empty" state before anything has been loaded into it (see Figure 11.8). The actual loading of components can take place separately, but the precise order is irrelevant to the attestation process, which has already completed. Validation of the measurement is simple, as creating a measurement of the known empty state is easily performed in advance.

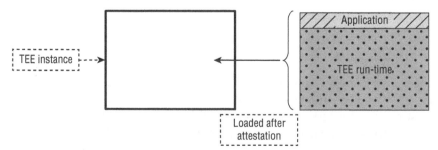

Figure 11.8: Pre-load attestation.

Post-Load Attestation   For post-load attestation, at least some components are loaded into the TEE instance before measuring takes place. The following diagrams show three examples: full workload loading (Figure 11.9), loading of the TEE runtime (which subsequently loads the application) (Figure 11.10), and loading of a runtime loader (which then loads the TEE runtime, which subsequently loads the application) (Figure 11.11). Creating measurements for the post-load attestation cases presents different challenges depending on the option chosen.

Full Workload Measurements   Where the full workload is loaded before attestation, the tenant must have a measurement of the entire workload image ready, meaning that any change to the application or the TEE runtime necessitates a re-measurement—which then needs a secondary attestation process as well. This may be appropriate when the workload image is created by the tenant (which may be more likely for process-based TEEs, where any runtime may be created with the image at application compilation time) or provided by a vendor, such as an *appliance image* to be run as a single VM. In other cases, however, where the tenant does not provide both the application and the runtime or where either may be updated or upgraded independently of the other, this option can be more difficult to manage, and providing patches in such a situation may require frequent measuring.

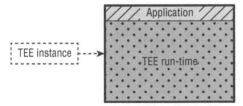

Figure 11.9: Post-load attestation—full workload.

TEE Runtime Measurements   In this use case, the application and TEE runtime are decoupled, with only the TEE runtime being measured. As long as the tenant is happy with the measurement provided, it can provide the application to be loaded by the runtime using the session key, which is established as part of the attestation. This approach has the benefit that the tenant does not need to perform a measurement of the application as part of the process, and the TEE runtime measurement can be created either by the tenant or by another party, such as the vendor providing the TEE runtime. This means the application and the TEE runtime can be revised separately, and this makes managing workloads much simpler, particularly in cases such as DevOps or Agile development, where the application is frequently updated but the execution environment (the TEE runtime) is fairly stable.

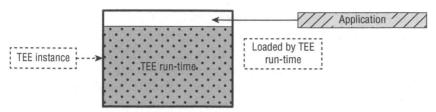

Figure 11.10: Post-load attestation—TEE runtime.

Runtime Loader Measurements   This use case requires the least measurement of the options presented, as only the loader of the TEE runtime is measured. It is likely that this can be fairly stable, with few changes, meaning that the management of both the application and the TEE runtime can be decoupled and the application and TEE runtime can be upgraded or updated independently. The runtime loader does not even necessarily need to know ahead of time what the TEE runtime will be, since as long as it is loaded with the session key established during attestation (and conforms to whatever execution expectations the loader expects), the tenant is free to provide whatever combination of application and TEE runtime it wishes for every TEE instance.

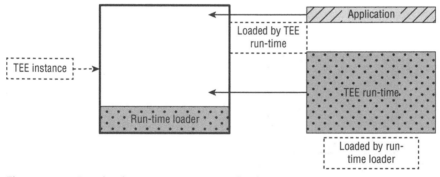

Figure 11.11: Post-load attestation—runtime loader.

Trust Relationships and TEEs

What are the trust relationships that we need to consider in the context of TEEs? The good news is that there are far fewer than the alternative virtualisation approaches we have considered. We do need to consider two different use cases, however, and the one chosen for a particular deployment may have a significant impact on both the development and deployment of the application:

SDK-Centric   In SDK-centric deployments, applications are designed and compiled with the aid of a *software development kit* (*SDK*) provided by a third-party vendor or open source project. The application is therefore created with the "knowledge" that it will be executing in a TEE context.

This approach is particularly suited to process-based TEEs, where (unless a runtime is provided, as described in the following approach) the application needs to be able to interact with the external, untrusted parts of the host. In some cases of SDK-centric deployments, a TEE runtime may also be provided; but in either case, the application will compile against libraries that are specific to the TEE environment(s) the SDK supports. Examples of SDKs for TEEs include Asylo,[18] the Enclave Development Platform,[19] and the Open Enclave SDK[20] (an open source project within the Confidential Computing Consortium).

Runtime-Centric   Runtime-centric deployments provide a runtime environment in which the application can execute. While the application may need changes to operate within any constraints that the TEE and the runtime environment impose, these are generally minor. The advantage of this approach is that when the runtime can provide a familiar application binary interface (ABI), it may allow applications to run in TEE instances with few or no changes. Examples might include library operating system approaches that could include support for languages such as Python, system interfaces such as WebAssembly's[21] *WebAssembly System Interface* (*WASI*[22]), VMs such as those supporting Java, or implementations of broad system interfaces such as POSIX[23] (e.g., ELF support via a Linux operating system) or OCI[24] (e.g., CRI-O).

The trade-offs that need to be made when choosing between these options are important, and there may often be a compromise between ease of use and security. It may be possible to take a standard operating system—a Linux distribution or Windows, for instance—and run it as the TEE runtime, but this can present significant problems. The first is memory usage: while VM-based TEEs generally have larger memory footprints than process-based TEEs,[25] one of the disadvantages of TEE use is the lower workload density available on host systems on which they are deployed. As memory pages allocated to TEE instances are encrypted on a per-instance basis, the opportunities for sharing them across workloads is removed, so equivalent workloads occupy more space when deployed in TEEs than using standard virtualisation. The second trade-off is the

---

[18]Asylo, 2020.
[19]Fortanix, 2020.
[20]Open Enclave SDK, 2020.
[21]WebAssembly, 2020.
[22]Konka et al., 2020.
[23]The Open Group, 2020.
[24]Open Containers, 2020.
[25]Note that restrictions on the size and numbers of TEE instances are relaxing as newer generations of supporting hardware become available, but this does not improve the issues with workload density.

size of the TCB: a smaller TCB is always preferred over a larger TCB, as there is less opportunity for bugs and backdoors and hence a reduced attack surface.

Another important issue to address is the behaviour of the TEE runtime in its interactions with the host system. The two key protections we expect when deploying an application to a TEE instance are confidentiality and integrity, and while the application's execution and interactions are entirely contained within the TEE, these are assured (to the extent of our trust relationship to the implementation). As soon as there is any interaction with the host system or any entity outside the TEE isolation boundary, there is a danger that confidentiality, in particular, may be compromised.

The most obvious example of this danger occurs in data storage. If an application within a TEE wishes to store some persistent data, this requires interactions with external components (such as a hard disk local to the host machine). If the data is to have confidentiality protection applied to it, then either the application must know to encrypt the data (requiring changes to the application logic) or the runtime must provide transparent encryption services.

In fact, there exists a variety of ways in which a standard operating system within a TEE instance may leak information to the host system, and the situation is even more complex when virtualisation-aware runtimes are considered. Other components, such as peripheral devices connected to the CPU across a PCI bus, perform tasks such as off-loading computation for performance (e.g., GPUs and network accelerator cards) and present a significant risk to the confidentiality and integrity guarantees of confidential computing. While the addition of TEEs to such components may allow these guarantees to be reintroduced, the complexities involved in setting up and maintaining trust relationships to them are also significant.

The most common example of such a leaky system at the time of writing is Linux containers, which we have already discussed. The container packaging format might seem to be an excellent fit for TEE deployments, but it falls down in two important areas. The first area is the size of the TCB, which is typically very dynamic as (generally opaque) dependencies are fulfilled at packaging time, and the second area is the interactions that container runtimes (such as CRI-O, referenced earlier) expect to have with the host system. In order to manage their operation, containers need to communicate information about the workload they are executing with the *pod* (a set of containers running on a single host machine) in which they are situated. This means that either the container runtime needs to be adapted to run in a TEE as a stand-alone runtime for a pod run by the host operating system—which would necessitate a design that would leak information to the host—or the entire pod would need to be run within a TEE instance. While the latter is certainly possible, any benefits that would have been gained from reducing the size of the TCB are immediately reversed since an entire operating system *and* pod management application need to be run within the TEE instance.

There are benefits, then, to designing and implementing a TEE-aware runtime that protects the application from having to be aware of the context in which it is running. A variety of projects and products are available, making different choices around the trade-offs that we have just discussed, including Enarx,[26] Graphene,[27] and SCONE.[28]

How to establish a trust relationship to the TCB is the key question about trust in the code from which the TCB is built. We explored the issues of trust and open source in some depth in Chapter 8. The TEE runtime is a perfect example of a component where open source can provide excellent opportunities for the wider security community to audit design and implementation. Providing repeatable builds from open source software allows vendors to check measurements of the TEE runtime for themselves, allowing them to establish their own trust relationships (via distributed trust in the community) rather than having to seek assurances from vendors that their proprietary design and code is free from bugs and backdoors. Tenants can also check for themselves whether vulnerabilities found in any open source components are fixed, a task that is typically much more difficult in proprietary software.

How Execution Can Go Wrong—and Mitigations

Having described what we are hoping for—a workload executing in a TEE instance with confidentiality and integrity protection, with no trust relationship to the owner of the host or any component of the host system beyond the CPU and CPU firmware—let us consider what problems may arise with this scenario, and some mitigations. This will allow us to propose an architecture that hopefully meets our requirements and also allows for the minimum number of trustees and trust relationships. The Confidential Computing Consortium white paper provides a helpful list of threats[29] that may be considered in scope and out of scope, and we will start by accepting their set of out-of-scope threats:

- Sophisticated physical attacks that require long-term and/or invasive hardware

- Upstream hardware supply-chain attacks such as attacks at chip manufacturing time or key injection/generation time

It should come as no surprise that these are among the more sophisticated of the physical attacks we described earlier in this chapter in the section "Physical Compromise". Designers of TEEs have attempted to provide protections for many of the less sophisticated attacks, but even with TEEs, there are some

---

[26]Enarx, 2020.
[27]OscarLab, 2020.
[28]SCONE, 2020.
[29]Confidential Computing Consortium, 2020, pp. 10–11.

areas against which it is extremely difficult to defend. Let us look at some other attacks and issues that may affect our ability to accept assurances for workloads executing in TEE instances. We take a somewhat different approach to the Confidential Computing Consortium white paper on these points, looking not just at attacks but also at possible weaknesses in the design and implementation of systems utilising TEEs. For the sake of simplicity, we will talk about TEEs being associated with CPUs, though they could similarly be implemented in other components such as GPUs:

Incorrect TEE Design or Implementation   There is little that users of TEEs can do directly to protect against weaknesses or vulnerabilities in the design or implementation of TEEs and the supporting protocols by silicon vendors. Tenants can, and should, consider the risks associated with their use and mitigations based on their risk profile, and should also be ready to react to the discovery of new vulnerabilities by the research or security community. In many cases, particularly where no patch or fix is made available by the silicon vendor (to the associated firmware, for example), the best mitigation may be to cease use of the particular implementation with which the vulnerability is associated, though this may be difficult if the workload implementation is closely tied to a particular TEE design (which is particularly likely for SDK-based deployment approaches).

It should be noted that not all vulnerabilities will necessarily be "fatal" to a particular TEE implementation's security: it may be possible to mitigate or fix some in the firmware shipped with the CPU without having to make changes to the CPU parts themselves (which typically are long-lived and require a new generation of chips for fixes to be made available). Vulnerabilities that can be fixed in firmware may also require changes to the attestation protocol associated with the TEE implementation and corresponding changes to the tenant's processes for attestation validation, including, at minimum, a change in policy to enforce that known-vulnerable versions of firmware are excluded from use.

No Direct Trust Relationship to the CPU Vendor   At the time of writing, the majority model of silicon manufacture is the design and implementation of hardware by one organisation (often with actual fabrication being performed by a third party with whom the vendor has strong commercial trust relationships): this is standard for vendors such as AMD, IBM, and Intel. In these cases, the vendor of the chip is the party to which the tenant needs to establish a trust relationship. Another model exists, however, such as the Arm silicon ecosystem and some growing open source hardware models, where one vendor designs the hardware (or its components) and a licensee implements the silicon (with some possible changes) and then fabricates it (or has a third party do so, again with strong commercial trust relationships in place). In such a situation, the question arises as to the appropriate party to which the tenant should establish a trust relationship. The obvious answer is that it should be to the licensee, which should provide cryptographic signatures to prove their relationship to the CPU, but licensees may be reluctant to be held as the endorsing authority for a design they did not originate. Another option would be for a foundation to be set up that all licensees join and that acts as an endorsing authority. Such an organisation would need to be managed carefully to ensure that appropriately strong commercial trust relationships to the foundation could be set up. Such relationships are essential so that if, for instance, an error were found with a licensee's TEE implementation, the trustor (the tenant) would have appropriate levels of recourse and the trusted party (the foundation, in this example) would have sufficient involvement and authority to be capable of addressing the error: for example, by issuing a revocation certificate. Issues of reputation—individual and foundation-level—are also relevant in this context.

Side Channels   We separate vulnerabilities associated with side channels from *incorrect TEE design or implementation* for two reasons: first, silicon vendors may consider at least some side-channel attacks out of scope for their implementations[30], and second, it may be possible to mitigate some of them using techniques within the TEE instance.[31] This latter expectation— that mitigations will be applied within the TEE instance—is generally related to side attacks associated with cryptographic key generation and usage and raises difficult issues for users of TEEs.

Where workloads are SDK-based, or where the TEE runtime is specifically designed for TEE deployment, there are opportunities for the SDK to provide appropriate mitigations (such as providing constant-time cryptographic implementations); but where standard operating systems are used as the TEE runtime, or the TEE runtime is otherwise not TEE-aware, the onus is on the application developer to provide mitigations. This is clearly not an option for applications that are not themselves aware that they are running in a TEE; and for those that are TEE-aware, the expertise required to provide and test such mitigations is rare in today's workforce, and individuals specialised in this field may be able to command uniquely high pay. It is clearly simpler to scale such efforts by providing TEE-aware mitigations in the TEE runtime than to expect application developers to manage such efforts.

---

[30]See, for example, Claburn, 2019.
[31]See, for example, Sharwood, 2018.

Randomness and Entropy Management   Many cryptographic operations require a dependable source of randomness or *entropy*. Provision of sufficient entropy to components that need it has been a complex issue throughout the history of modern computing, but most systems now provide entropy from a variety of sources (mainly hardware-related) and combine them to provide an easily consumed source. Given that TEEs are designed for sensitive workloads that are likely to require entropy, the availability of a dependable source in each TEE instance should be a requirement of any TEE design, and, critically, it should have its confidentiality and integrity protected from the host system. Even when these requirements are met, however, it is easy for workloads to misuse entropy when implementing sensitive functions—or to use it inadequately. This is another area, like constant-time cryptography, where a TEE runtime, if it is TEE-aware, can help mitigate errors or poor design within the application by ensuring that the entropy sources it provides are appropriate for use by applications.

BIOS Provision   Earlier in this chapter, we talked about Figure 11.6, an altered diagram in which we included an extra layer within the TEE: a BIOS. The reason we introduced the BIOS layer in this diagram is that in order to allow standard operating systems to execute with minimum alteration in cloud deployments, it is normal practice for the CSP to provide a BIOS layer to simplify communications with the host. While this practice may be acceptable in a standard virtualisation deployment, CSPs have started to supply VM-based TEEs to tenants using the same practice. We reproduce this diagram in Figure 11.12 with an important change: the shading of the BIOS layer.

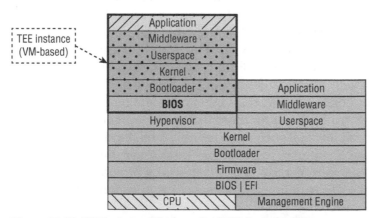

Figure 11.12: TEE instance (VM-based)—BIOS from the CSP.

It should be clear that accepting any component from the CSP immediately changes the trust relationships associated with the workload, as any such component—including the BIOS, which has access to low-level operations—adds the CSP back into the set of trustees: a move we explicitly excluded when we specified that we wished to have *no trust relationship to the owner of the host or to any component of the host system*. This dependency on the BIOS, an easily overlooked aspect of a CSP-provided TEE, inserts CSPs into trust chains from which many tenants may believe they (the CSPs) are excluded. This should be a major area of concern for tenants, regulators, and auditors of these services.

Application Compiled by an Untrusted Party   A different issue arises when applications are prepared by an untrusted party for deployment into TEE instances. Some CSPs currently provide services where they simplify the deployment of applications by removing the complexity of compilation and preparation for their deployment by creating a TEE-ready workload image from the application code or image (typically by recompiling the workload image using a toolkit for an SDK-centric framework). While it is possible that a tenant might be able to take the compiled version and try to reconstruct it in order to check its behaviour, this is unlikely to be plausible and would defeat much of the point of the service, which is intended to simplify the process of application deployment for tenants. An alternative way to simplify the process is to integrate the SDK (or any changes required for a runtime-centric deployment) into an *integrated development environment* (IDE), though if this is run in an untrusted context (that is, outside the tenant's trust domain), then the problem has been transferred to a different component, as another trustee has again been added to the process.

Attestation Validation by an Untrusted Party   We have not yet looked in detail at the entities and components involved in the attestation process from the tenant's point of view. It is clear that the entity performing the attestation validation is central to the establishment of the trust relationship to the TEE and the trust pivot of the TEE instance to the tenant's trust domain. The attestation client, then, must be explicitly trusted by the tenant, as its confidentiality and integrity must be protected. Integrity is important to ensure that measurement checks cannot be falsified; and confidentiality is important as the attestation client holds the session keys for communication with the TEE instance, the compromise of which would allow a party such as the host to see or change any part of the workload.

Any deployment that does not allow the tenant attestation client to execute as a trusted agent is therefore completely flawed from the point of view of the requirements we have specified. This means that in order to meet these requirements, the tenant attestation agent *must not* be hosted by the CSP—or by any other party to which the tenant does not have an explicit and current trust relationship in this (extremely important) context. The only exception to this requirement would be if the tenant attestation agent were itself executing within a TEE instance, in which case there must be a bootstrapping mechanism in order to allow *this* TEE to be set up in the first place. This is not impossible to arrange, but many of the existing offerings of TEE instances by CSPs (at the time of writing) provide attestation services for their tenants, thereby inserting themselves directly into a trust relationship from which they should be explicitly excluded if tenants are to be provided with the levels of confidentiality and integrity that TEEs *can* provide, and which auditors and regulators should rightfully be expecting. Attestation services are complex—and likely outside the expertise of many tenants—but trusting CSPs to provide them leads to circular dependencies that are incompatible with the trust relationships being described.

Compromise of Attestation Pre-Measurement Integrity   In order to have sufficient assurance that the TEE instance is correctly set up and the chosen workload should be executed within it, it is clearly vital that the attestation measurement should be trusted. If the integrity of the measurement from the CPU is somehow compromised, which may be detected through the attestation process, then the tenant should simply stop the provisioning process and refuse to send the workload to the TEE instance. However, the tenant attestation client needs to compare the attestation measurements with stored pre-measurements of the TEE instance (whether in the pre-load or post-load attestation model). If these pre-measurement vectors have been compromised, there is no way for the tenant to discriminate between a valid measurement and an invalid measurement of its workload. The pre-measurements are therefore vital and should be signed by a trusted party so that the tenant attestation agent can check their validity, though integrity protection of the public certificates associated with such signatures is equally important. Special care should be taken with the chain of trust here, as any party trusted to sign the pre-measurements should be considered within the trust boundary.

Runtime TCB Is Not or Cannot Be Audited   As we have discussed before, *trustworthiness* is not an intrinsic property, and trust relationships are based on assurances in particular contexts. If a tenant is to have appropriate assurances associated with the contexts of confidentiality and integrity protection toward the runtime TCB, it is important that the runtime TCB can be audited for appropriateness for the use cases to which it will be put. In order for this to be the case, auditing must be performed—either by a trusted party, aware of the specific assurances required by the tenant, or through the efforts of the wider community if the runtime TCB is open source. It should be noted (as covered in Chapter 8) that though providing the runtime TCB as open source allows many more opportunities for auditing, this is no guarantee that the TCB will be audited by those with appropriate expertise, or, if it is, that it will be audited with a focus on the appropriateness for any specific use case. Tenants should consider this question when deciding whether to deploy a particular workload or workload type.

Runtime TCB Has Errors   Whilst related to auditability, there is always the possibility that a runtime TCB may contain design or implementation errors or other faults introduced during compilation. Constant-time cryptography, for instance, may require very specific compile-time options to be applied, which, if missed, may reduce protections against side-channel attacks. Supporting repeatable builds from open source projects allows tenants—and the wider community—to validate all aspects of the lifecycle of the runtime TCB, from the design through the implementation, choice of build toolchain, and build process itself—and then to suggest and implement improvements. Repeatable builds are, however, themselves a complex issue and the subject of a variety of projects.

Runtime TCB Is Too Large   We have already noted the dangers associated with large TCBs, and this is especially applicable to the TEE runtime. The likelihood of compromise is, of course, increased as the attack surface is increased, which is an almost inevitable result of an increased runtime TCB. Compromise may be particularly difficult to spot in a TEE instance as some standard techniques for protection and monitoring—including memory inspection—are reduced, and there is typically no trusted party to perform them anyway.

There are some interesting design decisions that can be applied to TEE runtimes around how to reduce the runtime TCB: an example is the inclusion or exclusion of a networking stack. It is to be expected that most applications will require access to networking (though some might only require access to storage IO, for instance), and it might be expected that the network stack would be best placed within the TEE runtime. If a broad systems interface approach to the TEE runtime is adopted, such as a full operating system kernel or Java runtime, a network stack is likely to be included by default. However, networking stacks (e.g., TCP/IP) are typically large and notorious for containing vulnerabilities. We know that even critical bugs can take years to be identified and fixed,[32] and bringing them into the TEE runtime is likely to add further delay as the provider must create and test a new version before distributing it. An alternative is to use the network stack provided by the host but ensure that all data is already encrypted before transmission out of the TEE instance. Similar questions can be applied to other subsystems such as storage, with the benefits of simplicity needing to be balanced against the possibility of a significantly smaller runtime TCB.

Runtime TCB Is Not TEE-Aware   In addition to questions such as reduction of TCB size and management of sensitive cryptographic operations, there

---

[32]A study of the Linux kernel in 2016 found that the average age of even those bugs labelled *Critical* was 3.3 years—see Cook, 2016.

are other issues that TEE runtimes cannot address if they are not designed to be running in a TEE context. In particular, these include assumptions about isolation (both its availability and its requirement), which are likely to lead to the sorts of vulnerabilities around leakage of information to the host system that we have already addressed when looking, for instance, at Linux container runtimes. It is difficult to identify all the other possible weaknesses as they will depend both on the TEE runtime and the TEE implementation.

Minimum Numbers of Trustees

One of the core lessons from this book is the importance of establishing and maintaining as few trust relationships as possible, but the number of trust relationships is arguably less important than the number of trustees. Once mechanisms have been established to derive assurances from a particular trustee in a specific context, it is likely to be simpler to derive assurances in other contexts from the same trustee than it is to establish mechanisms to derive assurances from a new trustee. However, we must beware of the halo effect of establishing trust relationships in different contexts with the same trustee just because we have one in an existing context.

Part of the mission of this chapter has been to show how TEEs can provide significant improvements to security (through confidentiality and integrity protection) if the host system and owner can be removed as a trustee. In this section, we will briefly show how this works in the best case and identify a few possible complications.

Figure 11.13 shows our ideal situation, where the only organisational trust relationships (in the contexts of confidentiality and integrity protection for the tenant's workload) are to the CPU vendor and the TEE runtime vendor—where the latter may be supplemented or replaced by a distributed trust relationship to the open source community.

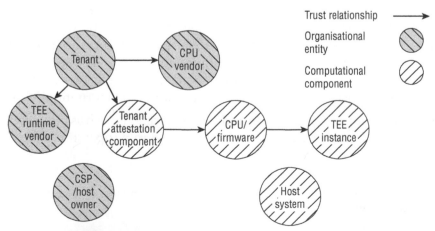

Figure 11.13: TEE trust relationships (ideal).

The tenant needs to have a trust relationship to the tenant attestation component. But as long as all the other requirements we have stated are met, the tenant can establish a trust relationship to the CPU/firmware, and that relationship can then extend to the TEE instance, providing a transitive trust relationship (not explicitly shown) from the tenant to the TEE instance, which is assumed in this diagram to include both the TEE runtime and the tenant's application.

Problems begin when any of the issues identified in the section "How Execution Can Go Wrong—and Mitigations" arise (and are not sufficiently mitigated). As we can see in Figure 11.14, if any of the implicit trust relationships represented by dotted lines are established, a trust relationship is formed from the tenant to the CSP/host owner.

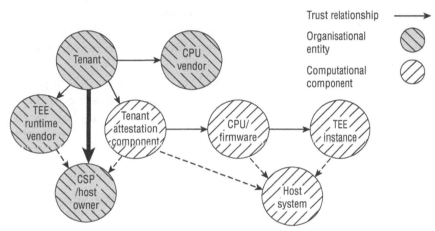

Figure 11.14: TEE trust relationships (implicit).

What is most concerning about implicit trust is both the number of different ways in which this can happen and how easily they can occur with little knowledge of the tenant. Combine this inclusion of implicit trust with offerings from CSPs, which *explicitly* allow these situations, and it is easy to see that the options for deploying applications with strong type 3 isolation to the public cloud (and, correspondingly, to the Edge) are limited. While we should not ignore the fact that some organisations will be happy to deploy into such scenarios based on their risk profile and mitigation strategies, the danger, as always with trust, is that there are many opportunities for implicit trust relationships that undermine the explicit risk appetites and policies of such organisations, and also few existing approaches that provide strong type 3 isolation and explicit, visible trust relationships.

Explicit Trust Models for TEE Deployments

Our focus on TEEs to this point has been on a fairly simple trust model where there is a single tenant with an application it owns running in a TEE instance with a TEE runtime provided by a vendor to which the tenant can establish a direct trust relationship. The real world—where organisations have multiple direct and transitive trust relationships with multiple third parties—is not so simple. As we have just noted, even getting to a situation where tenants can deploy workloads with explicit trust models such as the simple one we have just propounded is complex, given the existing offerings for cloud or Edge. There is growing interest in the industry in the ability to model and deploy more complex trust relationships such as those needed for *multi-party computation* (MPC), backed by the types of assurances offered by TEEs. An example of this is an open source enterprise blockchain called Corda,[33] which uses TEE instances to support specific trust model relationships required for certain sets of financial transactions.

We can expect to see more examples of complex trust models emerging, and there is a need for both theoretical and implementation work to support them. An oft-cited example is that of pharmaceutical research, where a pharmaceutical company may wish to access data sets from multiple independent health providers with requirements that

- The integrity of the data sets must be maintained.
- The health providers' data is kept entirely confidential from other health providers.
- The pharmaceutical company, while able to perform analysis and run computations over the data set, does not have direct access to the data but only to the results.
- The computations can take place in the public cloud.
- All parties are able to confirm that all of these requirements are met.

While these requirements are fairly complex, we can create trust models that reflect them: a simple example is provided in Figure 11.15, though even this does not provide a clear overview of the various parties and relationships. More work needs to be undertaken to provide trust modelling tools that are accessible to the industry and can be applied to the sorts of models that are beginning to emerge.

One of the reasons it is difficult to show a diagrammatic representation of such a trust model is that the trust relationships change over time as different

---

[33]R3, 2020.

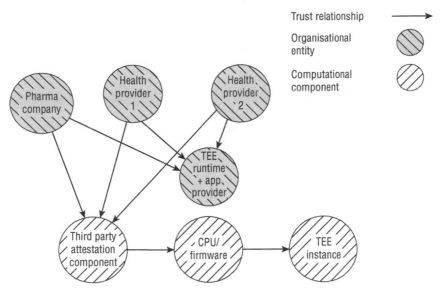

Figure 11.15: A complex trust model.

parts of the system are brought up, attestation takes place, computational components and data are loaded, further attestations are performed for different parties, computation takes place, and the system is then brought down. Time is a key context in trust, as we know, and this becomes particularly clear as we start to examine more complex trust models.

Trust Domains

Although starting a conversation with an IT security or cybersecurity practitioner by talking about *trust domains* is likely to gain a nod of recognition, the concept is not common in the field. Despite that, the book has been converging on the domain as a core concept, one that offers major benefits when considering trust models, architectural frameworks, and approaches to implementation. In Chapter 3, we defined trust domains thus:

> *Trust domains are sets of entities or components that can be considered to form a single unit from the point of view of a trust relationship. All entities share and are subject to the same set of policies. Such a trust relationship must—as with all trust relationships—be bounded by context(s).*

There are times when a *system*—one of the other concepts central to this book—does not provide a unit of abstraction that is large enough for complex trust and security architectures. Before we discuss exactly what we have in mind, let us compare two other similarly named constructs: trusted system domains and trust frameworks.

Trusted system domains   The Trusted Computing Group defines a *trusted systems domain* as follows:

A logical grouping containing infrastructure assets, service providers (operators), users, applications and information where a trusted context has been established and governed by a consistent set of operational and security policies.[1]

This definition shares our concept that all entities or components are governed by the same set of policies; and although it specifies a particular set of entities, it seems fairly similar to our definition of trust domains. It certainly is in general accord with our approach. Delving a little deeper into what a trusted context means, however, it seems that the concept of a trusted systems domain is related to specific devices, since a trusted context, as we will later see from the same source, requires "understanding of the identity and compliance levels of the device and operational parties involved".[2] This is unsurprising, given the scope of the document and working group that created it (the Multi-Tenant Infrastructure working group). So, while this definition is a useful validation of the approach we are taking, it does not represent the same concept.

Trust Frameworks   Another concept is presented in the NIST document "Developing Trust Frameworks to Support Identity Federations", though here the context is federated identity management:

[U]sers are enabled to federate their identity through common, shared authentication processes and access multiple online organizations and services. Federated identity management is inherently based on trust. Organizations must trust the federated identity management processes of the other federation participants in order to allow access to users that were authenticated by another entity. The rules for federated identity management are known as trust frameworks and the organizations that agree to follow such rules and participate are known as identity federations.[3]

Again, the very specific context of federated identity management does not accord directly with ours—though identity is an important primitive to which we will return later in this chapter.

A third approach to comparing similarly named concepts is to examine one that might seem to be in direct opposition to what we are proposing: *zero trust*. We spent some time examining and critiquing zero trust—or how the concept is often applied—in Chapter 5. There are, however, as we noted in that section, some positive aspects to zero trust as a concept. Not the least of which is that it raises the issue of trust in the first place, though the contexts of the trust relationships implied by the term are rarely made sufficiently explicit for our needs. Let us concentrate in this current section on the positive aspects of the zero-trust concept and how they relate to *trust domains*.

One of the most defining aspects of the concept of zero trust—and one of the reasons for its existence—is the rejection of the idea that boundaries, and

---

[1]Trusted Computing Group, 2013, p. 10.
[2]Trusted Computing Group, 2013, p. 11.
[3]Temoshok and Abruzzi, 2018, p. 1.

in particular network boundaries, can be usefully established and managed in a modern, distributed computing deployment. Zero trust started, at least in part, as a reaction to the complexity of firewall and routing rules and the impossibility of managing them in a real-time, adversarial enterprise setting. One of the dangers of using the word *domain* in the context of *trust domain* is that we might be seen as trying to take the (retrograde) step of insisting on static collections of locally networked machines, whose contact with other trust domains is managed and mediated solely by firewalls and routers. This is not what we intend with the phrase "[a]ll entities share and are subject to the same set of policies." Let us compare a definition of zero trust from NIST's *Zero Trust Architecture* publication:

> *Zero trust (ZT) is the term for an evolving set of cybersecurity paradigms that move defenses from static, network-based perimeters to focus on users, assets, and resources. . . . Zero trust assumes there is no implicit trust granted to assets or user accounts based solely on their physical or network location (i.e., local area networks versus the Internet) or based on asset ownership (enterprise or personally owned).[4]*

One key point that should strike a positive note is the declaration that "there is no implicit trust granted" on physical or network location or asset ownership. We would simplify this statement to reflect that no trust should be granted implicitly and also to add that there is a need for context in trust relationships.

There is one area in which zero trust aligns well with our views on trust: the importance of time. The NIST publication states the following as the fourth tenet of zero-trust architectures:

> **4. Access to individual enterprise resources is granted on a per-session basis.** *Trust in the requester is evaluated before the access is granted. Access should also be granted with the least privileges needed to complete the task. This could mean only "sometime recently" for this particular transaction and may not occur directly before initiating a session or performing a transaction with a resource. However, authentication and authorization to one resource will not automatically grant access to a different resource.[5]*

The use of session as a unit of time here reflects the transactional, web-based focus of zero trust, whose nascence from a Web 2.0, enterprise approach to architecture covers only some of the layers and types of components in which we are interested. While the appropriate time context for some trust relationships may be the length of a session—as we saw with the whisky purchase transaction example—there are other situations—such as for a trust relationship from a tenant workload to a host system—where a different type of measure is appropriate. In this case, the requirements for time will need to be defined as part of the trust relationship, and the different options available should make

---

[4]Rose et al., 2020, p. ii.
[5]Rose et al., 2020, p. 6.

up part of the trust actions description associated with a potential trustee. The lack of definition in the phrase "sometime recently" also grates, compared to the levels of specificity that we intend to enshrine in trust relationships.

Zero-trust architectures, when applied appropriately, actually attempt to address many of the same issues with which we are concerned. But our interest in various granularities of systems and refusal to consider the host system or appliance as the standard unit of trust means that there is divergence in the two approaches.

The Composition of Trust Domains

What might trust domains look like, given the starting points that we have established and the ways we think about systems? First, let us consider some of the possible uses of trust domains. We will start with the example of a bank (Figure 12.1) and then look at an organisation that deploys workloads to a variety of locations, including private and public clouds, in a distributed architecture.

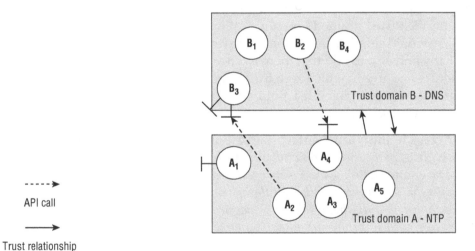

Figure 12.1: Trust domains in a bank.

Trust Domains in a Bank

Trust Domain A—NTP Trust domain A provides NTP (network time protocol) services to systems in the bank and comprises five entities, two of which (A_1 and A_4) expose APIs: interfaces that can be used by systems in other trust domains in the bank. These are the only interfaces through which components that are part of other trust domains can communicate with trust domain A, and monitoring may be put in place to ensure that other information flows are noticed (and trigger remedial action).

Trust Domain B—DNS   Trust domain B provides DNS (Domain Name Service) services to systems in the bank and itself comprises four entities, one of which (B_3) exposes APIs—interfaces that can be used by systems in other trust domains in the bank. These are the only interfaces through which components that are part of other trust domains can communicate with trust domain B, and monitoring may be put in place to ensure that other information flows are noticed (and trigger remedial action).

Relationships between A and B   There is a trust relationship from trust domain A to trust domain B in the context of DNS by which trust domain A is assured that DNS lookups provided by the official interfaces exposed by trust domain B will be valid.

Component A_2 connects to one of the interfaces exposed by trust domain B in order to get DNS lookup information that it can share with other components in trust domain A.

There is a trust relationship from trust domain B to trust domain A in the context of NTP by which trust domain B is assured that NTP lookups provided by the official interfaces exposed by trust domain A will be accurate within a tolerance acceptable to domain B.

Component B_2 connects to the interface exposed by trust domain A in order to get NTP lookup information that it can share with other components in trust domain B.

Providing these descriptions allows us to see that the two domains need very little information about each other. They only need to know about

- Any trust relationships that exist from one to the other, whether as trustor (to ensure that only operations that are appropriate are carried out) or trustee (so that the assurances expected by the other party can be met).

- The details of any interfaces that are relevant to the operation of the trustor

There is no need for one trust domain to have any knowledge of the internal workings or composition of the other. We might be tempted to think of each of these as a system, rather than a trust domain, if it were not for the fact that from the point of view of each, the number of entities and how they are put together probably exceeds what we might expect from a system.

Another reason for thinking of these as trust domains, rather than systems, presents itself when we add another trust domain. Following from our earlier example in Chapter 8 of a mortgage approval system, we now include trust domain C (Figure 12.2). Trust domain C comprises not just our mortgage approval system but also other functions of the bank, including all personal lending services. It may be that there are multiple differentiated systems within trust domain C. But from the point of view of how these systems are managed and, maybe, within a risk and liability context, they are considered part of the same trust domain. With reference to our definition of a trust domain, *all entities within the trust domain share and are subject to the same set of policies.*

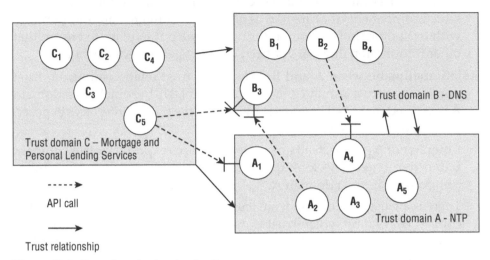

Figure 12.2: Trust domains in a bank—2.

Trust Domain C—Mortgage and Personal Lending Services   Trust domain C provides mortgage and personal lending services to customers of the bank and to systems in the bank and comprises five entities, none of which exposes APIs in any contexts in which we are currently interested.

There is a trust relationship from trust domain C to trust domain A in the context of NTP by which trust domain C is assured that NTP lookups provided by the official interfaces exposed by trust domain A will be accurate within a tolerance acceptable to domain C.

There is a trust relationship from trust domain C to trust domain B in the context of DNS by which trust domain C is assured that DNS lookups provided by the official interfaces exposed by trust domain B will be valid.

Component C_5 connects to the interface exposed by trust domain A in order to get NTP lookup information that it can share with other components in trust domain C.

Component C_5 also connects to the interface exposed by trust domain B in order to get DNS lookup information that it can share with other components in trust domain C.

Any trust relationships between trust domains A and B, and any communications that exist between them, are irrelevant to trust domain C.

It is easy to see that these types of diagrams may become complex very quickly, but one of their benefits is that they can be used to provide different views that are relevant to different contexts. We can simplify the diagram to present a view of the world that is relevant to those who manage trust domain C, for instance (Figure 12.3).

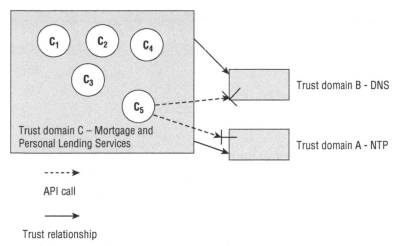

Figure 12.3: Trust domains in a bank—C's view.

Another view would be appropriate for those interested in auditing the various trust relationships and dependencies between different trust domains in the bank (Figure 12.4).

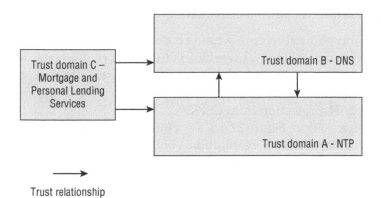

Figure 12.4: Trust domains in a bank—trust domain view.

A final example would be for someone wishing to understand that trust domains depended on a particular trust context and how interfaces were being called—in this case, NTP (Figure 12.5).

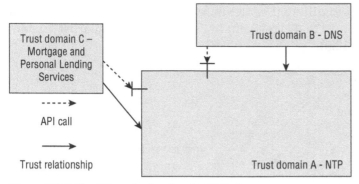

Figure 12.5: Trust domains in a bank—NTP view.

All of these diagrams expose different views on trust-related contexts with different types of abstraction. Diagrams exposing different systems and their interactions with each other are not new when considering enterprise architectures—in fact, entity-relationship diagrams are a commonly used tool. But the addition of trust considerations as per our examples allows for an important new perspective. Most importantly, this new idea introduces simplified abstractions that enable viewers of these diagrams whose role is unrelated to the operation, management, or composition of the IT infrastructure (by which we also include those humans involved in its work) but who *are* concerned with risk management to have a concise and comprehensive view.

Trust Domains in a Distributed Architecture

Let us consider a distributed architecture where an organisation has an on-premises (*private*) cloud and also deploys workloads to an external system: a *public cloud* system managed by a *cloud service provider* (CSP). Crucially, one of the workloads the organisation wishes to deploy has sensitive data that requires confidentiality and integrity protection from CSPs.

Our first diagram in this section, Figure 12.6, shows four trust domains: three within the organisation and a CSP. The organisational boundary is denoted by a dashed line, which does not necessarily indicate a physical or logical boundary from the point of view of network traffic, for instance. The *Web services division* trust domain has trust relationships to the *On-premises private cloud* trust domain and to the *CSP* trust domain, which allow the web services division workloads (which are considered *non-sensitive* and do not require strong confidentiality and integrity protections) to be deployed on host systems in either of those trust domains. The workloads that the *Financial audit group* trust domain wishes to deploy, on the other hand, *are* considered sensitive; a risk assessment has led to a trust relationship to the *On-premises private cloud* trust domain, allowing workloads to be deployed on host systems in that trust domain, but there is no corresponding trust relationship to the *CSP* trust domain.

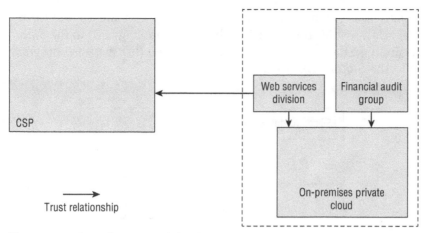

Figure 12.6: Trust domains and the cloud—1.

The second diagram about trust domains, Figure 12.7, shows workloads deployed from the *Web services division* trust domain into the *CSP* trust domain and from the *Financial audit group* trust domain into the *On-premises private cloud* trust domain. The *Financial audit group* trust domain is blocked by policy and architectural controls from deploying a workload to the *CSP* trust domain.

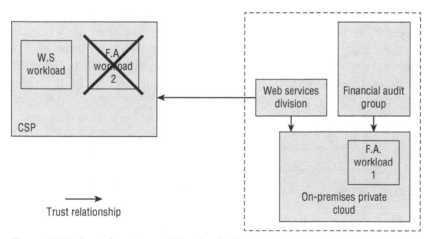

Figure 12.7: Trust domains and the cloud—2.

Figure 12.8 shows two more trust domains and associated trust relationships. The first additional trust domain is that of the *Silicon vendor,* whose CPUs are incorporated into at least some of the hosts of the *CSP* trust domain. The second additional trust domain is the *Risk management group* trust domain, which is part of the organisation. It has established a trust relationship to the *Silicon vendor* trust domain in the context of trusted execution environment (TEE) validation. The *Financial audit group* trust domain has formed a trust relationship to the *Risk management group* trust domain in a context that allows it to form a transitive trust relationship (not explicitly shown in the diagram) to the *Silicon vendor* trust domain in the same context as that from the *Risk management group* trust domain to the *Silicon vendor* trust domain.

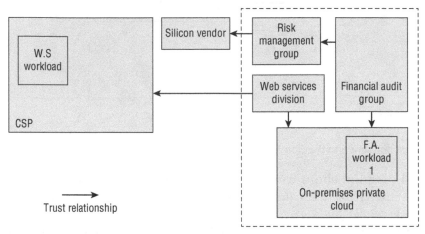

Figure 12.8: Trust domains and the cloud—3.

Figure 12.9 shows a new component in the *On-premises private cloud* trust domain: an attestation client. A second trust relationship from the *Financial audit group* trust domain is also shown, in the context of providing validation of TEE instances associated with the *Silicon vendor* trust domain's TEEs. Additionally, the *Financial audit group* trust domain has instigated the creation of a TEE instance.

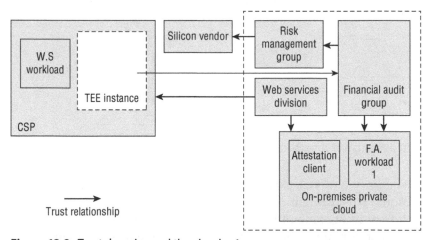

Figure 12.9: Trust domains and the cloud—4.

In our final diagram (Figure 12.10), the attestation of the TEE instance and workload in the *CSP* trust domain has been successful, and the workload has started executing on a host in the *CSP* trust domain. However, as shown by the workload's appearance in the *Financial audit group* trust domain, a trust pivot has been performed, and the workload actually exists within the *Financial audit group* trust domain and not the *CSP* trust domain. This workload can now be set up as an entity within the *Financial audit group* trust domain, subject to the same policies as the rest of the domain.

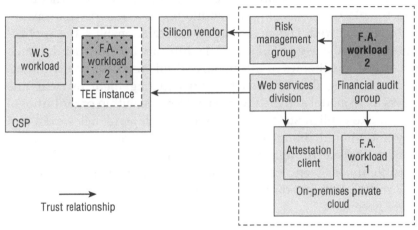

Figure 12.10: Trust domains and the cloud—5.

An important lesson that presents itself (as we note the appearance of the second workload from the *Financial audit group* trust domain in the *Financial audit group* trust domain itself) is that trust domains do not need to be associated with computer systems or components. There is no need for any computing capability within the *Financial audit group*, as long as appropriate communications can be made to the various other trust domains in line with the trust relationships that have already been established (and should be checked in line with their time contexts).

Another point to note is that none of the trust domains spans the organisational boundary. It is possible to consider trust domains that might do this, but one of the defining characteristics of a trust boundary is that all entities within it share the same set of policies. It is difficult to imagine how this might be possible across organisational boundaries unless the context of the trust domain *itself* crosses these boundaries. This might be the case where two organisations that share a trust domain are governed by a third—in other words, they are subsidiary organisations—but it is difficult to conceive of other examples.

In fact, where trust domains exist across organisational boundaries, such as when auditing firms or subcontractors do work for another organisation, it is common practice to impose an additional intra-organisational boundary: this is generally referred to as an *ethics wall* or *firewall*, which

> *as it is used in the business world, describes a virtual barrier intended to block the exchange of information between departments if it might result in business activities that are ethically or legally questionable.*[6]

This use case allows us to realise an additional use for trust domain diagrams and modelling: the placement of components and use of a trust pivot to ensure that risk policies are followed. The modelling of trust relationships, the application of the trust pivots, the use of TEEs, and the introduction of trust domains have emerged as the core themes of this book, and this use case finally allows us to consider them all together. The benefits to risk management are clear: this technique allows us to model and architect trust domains within organisational contexts and to make explicit statements about what dependencies exist and how they may and should change over time. The application of these trust domains can be modelled through the drafting of the policies shared within each, and possible inconsistencies noted. Flows between trust domains can be monitored, and unauthorised or unexpected communications noted and remedied where necessary.

Trust Domain Primitives and Boundaries

Given the importance of policies to the definition of trust domains, it should come as no surprise that they are important to our understanding. This section considers policies and other primitives we may need in order to define, establish, and manage trust domains. We then move on to questions around boundaries between trust domains, how they can be managed, and some of the issues that management brings.

Trust Domain Primitives

There are a number of different *primitives* (or fundamental elements) associated with trust domains, but the most obvious, and the one to which all the others can be related, is policy. In this section, we spend some time looking at policy in relation to trust domains; then we look at other primitives.

---

[6]Kenton, 2000. It should be noted that the use of the word *virtual* in this context does not refer to virtualisation within computing, but to the fact that the barrier is not physical—though physical elements and virtualisation techniques may be employed.

Trust Domains and Policy

Policies can be applied to many aspects of computing, and their use is central to many areas of IT security. Policies have a lifecycle, which may look like this:

1. *Creation* to satisfy governance and risk requirements
2. *Validation* to ensure the policies' applicability and accuracy
3. *Application* against the entities for which the policies are relevant
4. *Monitoring* to ensure the continued application of the policies
5. *Enforcement* to respond to any issues as internal or external events or stimuli are exerted
6. *Revision* as the environment, risk model, or governance requirements change
7. *End of life* as the policy is no longer required

When we note that entities within a trust domain share the same set of policies, this does not mean that all policies are equally applicable to all entities. A policy that all customer data at rest should be encrypted is irrelevant to a network switch, for instance. Its applicability to data stored on paper may depend on context—there may be examples of requirements to store ciphertext on paper in some contexts—but is more likely that equivalent policies (such as storing customer data in locked cabinets when not in use and keeping careful control of the keys and their management) need to be created that are consonant with those for the IT systems. This issue is why policies should be created within the context of risk and governance, so that appropriate policies (and monitoring, etc.) can be established and maintained across the trust domain.

Table 12.1 lays out examples of policies that a particular trust domain might include.

Table 12.1: Examples of policies in trust domains

TRUST DOMAIN	FINANCIAL AUDIT GROUP	ENTITY/SYSTEM TYPE	STORAGE— HARD DRIVE, SSD, USB DRIVE
Context(s)		Customer data	
Time-specific		Key rotation (yearly); key rotation (on discovery of vulnerability or exposure)	
Action(s)		Data encrypted	

Continues

Table 12.1: (*continued*)

TRUST DOMAIN	FINANCIAL AUDIT GROUP	ENTITY/SYSTEM TYPE	STORAGE—HARD DRIVE, SSD, USB DRIVE
Expectation(s)		Data encrypted using AES-128 or higher; appropriate cipher suite	
Monitoring		Daily automated scans for unencrypted data	

TRUST DOMAIN	FINANCIAL AUDIT GROUP	ENTITY/SYSTEM TYPE	HUMAN
Context(s)		Customer data	
Time-specific		Quarterly review; on promotion; on role change; on retirement; on move to another department; on leaving company	
Action(s)		Data confidentiality maintained	
Expectation(s)		Information must not be disclosed to anybody outside the financial audit group	
Monitoring		Quarterly reminders; questionnaires to department heads; reporting of infractions; email scanning	

TRUST DOMAIN	FINANCIAL AUDIT GROUP	ENTITY/SYSTEM TYPE	DEPARTMENT HEAD (HUMAN)
Context(s)		Customer data	
Time-specific		Quarterly review; on promotion; on role change; on retirement; on move to another department; on leaving company	
Action(s)		Data confidentiality maintained	
Expectation(s)		Information must not be disclosed to anybody outside the financial audit group except customer or government-appointed auditor	
Monitoring		Quarterly reminders; questionnaires to department heads; reporting of infractions	

Readers will note a strong similarity between these policy descriptions and our trust relationship descriptions, but with *assurance(s)* changed to *monitoring* and without any *mitigations* listed: we will return to the question of mitigation in the "Centralisation of Control and Policies" section later in this chapter. The reason for these similarities is that a trust domain is a set of entities that present a consistent trust profile to other trust domains or external entities and systems. In order to present a consistent trust profile, the other domains, entities, or systems must have behaviours that are assured to fit expectations—as with trust relationships—and are shared. In other words, each entity within a trust domain has a trust relationship to every other component, but one that is transitive through the owner(s) and enforcer(s) of the policy set and is also shared between all members of the trust domain. This assumes the existence of some authority or authorities within a trust domain, which we address, along with mitigations, later in this chapter. The mechanism of a trust domain, then, provides several advantages over an amorphous set of components with inter-dependent trust relationships. The key advantages are as follows:

Consistency   Rather than having to poll each member of the trust domain and check for consistency, policies can be applied across all members.

Reduction in Complexity   A network of trust relationships would require either a complex set of transitive relationships or a number of trust relationships growing exponentially with the addition of entities. A trust domain, however, allows a single set of policies to be maintained across the trust domain.

No Knowledge of Peer Entities   In a trust domain, if an entity wishes to communicate with another entity in the same trust domain, neither needs to have details of the other in order to establish trust relationships. As long as the identity of the other entity, and its current inclusion in the trust domain, can be established, then each entity can be assured of the expected behaviour of the other.

Monitoring   One of the onerous requirements of trust relationship maintenance is the difficulty in monitoring or receiving other assurances of expected behaviour. Within a trust domain, monitoring and enforcement of behaviour are managed at the trust domain level rather than at the individual relationship level.

External Interfaces   External interfaces to a trust domain are well-defined, which benefits not only external entities, which know where these interfaces are to be found, but also internal entities, which know (through policy) whether or not they may communicate with other entities, and if so, which ones.

It should be noted that not all policies are of the type that we might expect within the scope of computing or even formal organisational structures. We have already noted that trust domains may in fact not include any computing systems or components—the policies in this case may be formal rules or even the norms and expectations associated with a professional body or a community of practice. Relying on such informal or unwritten rules rather than codifying them may make risk management more complex, but there are some contexts where acknowledging the existence of such rules may be sufficient.

Other Trust Domain Primitives

In this section, we look briefly at some of the other primitives that may be required to establish and operate a trust domain.

Identity   The ability to establish identity is required in order for all entities within a trust domain to identify each other when required and for other entities to ascertain and verify that entities are part of a particular trust domain. Trust domains may operate *local certificate authorities* (CAs) for their own identity management, or they may defer to external CAs (which may still be "local" in that their scope is, for instance, only organisation-wide) to whom they have appropriate trust relationships. The use of such an external CA allows trust domains to have an identity associated with them so that authentication, encryption, and other operations may be performed over the interfaces exposed to other trust domains.

Authentication and Authorisation   Though separate operations, authentication and authorisation are both tied to identity and will exist as part of the policy for the trust domain in which entities are operating, whether that is in terms of intra-domain or inter-domain communication.

Cryptography   Though it may be possible to operate a trust domain without cryptographic primitives, many operations (including identity and authentication) may rely on it. An easily overlooked requirement for a trust domain is a consistent policy with regard to cryptographic usage, including acceptable cipher suites, key lengths, key lifetimes, and revocation processes.

Trust Pivots   While trust pivots are not required for trust domain management, the ability to move entities in and out of trust domains provides great opportunities for trust management—trust pivots are one of the key methods available for managing trust. We have seen a number of mechanisms for this, the most relevant in the context of computing and the cloud being TEEs, which allow the movement of execution environments (workloads) containing data in use between trust domains.

Time   Another important primitive to be considered for trust domains is a set of shared policies with regard to time. This is important for logging and monitoring, but also for the establishment of the timeliness of policies (the equivalent of the time contexts for trust relationships). A shared *source of truth* for time, policies regarding the frequency of adjustment, policies related to appropriate behaviour should timeouts occur, and tolerance for drift should all be considered for a trust domain, though in the simplest of cases (where there are only co-located human resources to be considered), a simple wall clock, visible to all, may suffice.

Logging   Though individual entities are not expected to manage monitoring services (unless that is their role within the trust domain), logging of events is important to allow the appropriate trust domain authorities to validate continued adherence to policies.

Boundaries

Earlier, we noted some of the similarities and differences between trust domains and the concepts associated with zero trust. One of the differences was the realisation that boundaries are something that we *do* need to consider (whilst accepting the wisdom in doubting the impermeability of network boundaries enforced by firewalling and routing). One of the advantages of adopting the concept of trust domains is their applicability at various levels of granularity; and while we have concentrated on their use at the level where workloads, host systems, and humans are standard entities, they can be applied at other levels as well: for instance when considering components in a single computer system, an IoT subsystem, or a vehicle, whether a motorcycle or a warship. It is worth listing some of the types of boundaries that might be considered when thinking about isolation either between entities within a trust domain or between trust domains themselves:

- Air-gaps between networks
- Network subnets
- Virtual networks (e.g., VXLAN[7])
- Computing hardware components (e.g., CPU, GPU, TPM, HSM)
- Virtualisation constructs (e.g., Linux containers, VMs)
- Threads and processes
- TEEs

The reason boundaries are important to us is that this is where we can find two important aspects of trust: isolation and interfaces. We know that isolation is extremely difficult to ensure in many contexts (even when systems and components are designed with isolation in mind, as we have seen when considering side channels). Where a boundary exists, there is the possibility of checking for leakage of information, as well as policing the data that is passed over approved interfaces. Side effects—and emergent properties of systems—can complicate the management of isolation[8]; but without explicit requirements on interfaces and

---

[7]Mahalingham et al., 2014.

[8]A canonical example from outside the context of computing is an enemy agent noting the delivery of cold weather gear ahead of troop movements and being able to derive information about likely deployments from this information, even in the absence of direct intelligence as to the location of planned activities.

defined expectations with regard to behaviour, it is impossible to know what the *correct* functioning of a system should look like, let alone what mitigations should be put in place in case of problems.

Centralisation of Control and Policies

Policy management and enforcement are complex, particularly when applied across multiple contexts in a distributed deployment. At the time of writing, policy management is still an emerging field; and while frameworks such as the open source Open Policy Agent[9] are gaining some interest, it is unclear whether all the complexities around providing federated, distributed, high-availability solutions for enterprise use at scale have yet been addressed.

In the context of trust domains, we advocate for a combination of *minimum viable governance* and *management by exception. Minimum viable governance* is a concept normally applied to project or organisational management, but it is also applicable to our context and involves implementing only those policies that are required for smooth functioning of a system: in our case, the risk and/ or governance requirements on the trust domain. It can be combined with *management by exception*, where monitoring is concentrated not on checking for normal operation but on detecting anomalous behaviour (that is, exceptions from the norm) and remediating them. Clear definition of *nominal behaviour*— that is, behaviour that is within limits of acceptable operation, rather than setting a (possibly unattainable) standard for *perfect behaviour*—further allows for exceptions from expected behaviour to be monitored without over-reacting to events that may not turn out to expose the trust domain to unacceptable risk.

We have been wary of suggesting particular models for managing policy, particularly as models and architectures are still emerging. There is a need to balance, for instance, the lessons from zero-trust architectures that may become the norm in some organisations. Centralisation of control and policy management for organisations needs to be balanced against the differing requirements of the organisations' various trust domains, and we can expect to see hierarchical and/ or federated models being adopted. It is important to note that all of the various policy lifecycle steps need to be managed. While, for instance, monitoring may be performed by a separate entity or component from enforcement, there is a clear need for communication and well-defined responsibilities between them. The good news is that while the field of policy management is still in its infancy, many of its component parts, such as monitoring and configuration management, along with models for delegation of control to decentralised authorities such as groups and departments, are already available and well-understood within the enterprise software space.

---

[9]Open Policy Agent, 2020.

The fact that some components are available and well-understood, however, should not negate the fact that there are still lessons to be applied from our discussions around trust, including how monitoring agents from different trust domains, for instance, might execute within a specific trust domain, and the importance of time in trust relationship management. There also needs to be careful thought about the correlation of monitoring events from disparate trust domains. We addressed this issue previously when we discussed abstractions—that vulnerabilities and attacks that span abstractions are difficult to correlate if cross-abstraction collections are unavailable, yet the confidentiality that results from having separate trust domains may be compromised for systems or trust domains when they are made available to other trust domains. Without a *super-domain* populated by experienced security professionals, in which information from all domains is collected and from which remediating actions can be initiated, this situation becomes an intractable problem. In the real world, where certain business functions, such as legal and executive, may need to maintain confidentiality protection for some of their data from all other functions, including IT and security, the creation of a super-domain is not always possible: the trust arrangements are too complex. A classic example is where database administrators need access to database tables that contain information such as the salaries and remuneration packages of senior executives. This, again, is an area where sensible thinking about risk management needs to take precedence over purely technical solutions.

One final point that needs to be taken into account is that any mechanism that revolves around mutual trust between multiple entities, and where external trust relationships are made to the collective whole, has a major Achilles' heel. If one component is compromised, the immediate assumption must be that *all* components are compromised. This presents a difficult problem when mitigating risk within complex trust domains. In a completely automated world of trust management, there is a danger that when a system fails, it must always fail *closed*. This is a typical approach often taught to security professionals: if a system is known or suspected to have been compromised, then it should be shut down ("closed") and no longer available to other components or systems that may be using it.

This, security professionals are taught, minimises risk. As we have noted, however, risk is not one-dimensional; and although shutting down a backup storage server that may have been compromised reduces the risk of further loss of data, for instance, it may do so at the expense of business continuity. The CEO or CISO of a large organisation (and its auditors) may prefer to be exposed to the risk of some data loss if that means the organisation's order management and fulfilment systems can continue to function for the last three days of the financial quarter.

For this reason, *failsafe* or *fail closed* may not always be the preferred option for systems. It turns out that one of the benefits of well-defined trust relationships is that trustors may have enough scope to make their own decisions about whether to continue to accept actions associated with trustees in certain situations. In this manner, a level of *service degradation* may be designed into a system so that even if a trustee's operation falls outside the *nominal* range, operations can continue. Vitally, this decision needs to be made by the trustor, rather than the trustee. Also, there needs to be some way to communicate changes in the state of the trustee service to the trustor—whether directly from the trustee by another party (to whom the trustor has an appropriate trust relationship in this context) or via the trustee itself, where possible. We should also remember that, although our main focus in this book has been around security, there are other types of operational degradation (such as performance or resilience) in which trust relationships may exist.[10]

Earlier, we noted the need for processes around revocation of compromised cryptographic keys within a trust domain, but, depending on the makeup of the domain, there may be a requirement to clean or re-form the entire trust domain. The fragility of the trust domain to compromised keys within a domain is one of the problems that zero trust attempts to solve, and it is a known weakness of mutually trusting systems. This is another situation where technical solutions on their own are unlikely to be sufficient. The fact that well-formed trust domains explicitly accommodate heterogeneous entity types (including humans, virtualised and non-virtualised computing, paper management, etc.) provides increased possibilities for resilience when considered from the perspective of risk management. "Technology-only" solutions will always have vulnerabilities, as they cannot fully reflect the real world; we must avoid taking such a one-dimensional approach, ignoring the interactions between various components and entities and allowing humans to have their place where appropriate.

---

[10]See Ford, Parsons & Kua, 2017, for some interesting insights into designing systems to prioritise particular behaviour and fitness for particular requirements.

A World of Explicit Trust

At the beginning of this book, we explored what it means to say that we *trust*, and we stated that our interest was more in computer-to-computer trust than in trust involving humans. As we have gone further into what *trust* may mean to us, we have come full circle when we looked at trust domains, which can mix humans and trust but which use the same building blocks to be explicit about what we are trusting to do what, how, with what assurances, and when. While our focus has been on trust as related to security, we have tried to avoid talking about trust as a mechanism solely in that context but instead have considered it as a tool that can be used to address other characteristics or properties of systems, such as resilience. Most important, we have presented trust as a tool to help manage risk, but one that, when applied to the realm of computer-to-computer interactions, can provide more quantifiable information around risk than is typically available using current techniques. This last chapter allows us to consider what looks different in a world where risk is explicit within the context of computer-to-computer interactions.

Tools for Trust

None of the tools we have presented in this book are revolutionary, but all provide new ways of modelling systems that allow various parties to consider the impact of trust relationships. We present some of the key concepts and tools here as a summary:

Trustor/Trustee Separation   One of the core aspects of the definition of a trust relationship is the realisation that trust relationships are asymmetric and that, for any context, there is no necessary expectation of a reciprocal relationship from a trustee to a trustor. Being able to separate entities and consider explicitly the relationships they have to one another allows us to understand better what assurances can actually be made about the interactions between them.

Trust Relationship Description   One important tool to allow architects and designers of systems to describe trust between trustor and trustee in different contexts is a table describing the properties of a specific trust relationship, a template for which is shown in Table 13.1. We strongly advise separate instances for each context (though time should always be considered for each context modelled).

Table 13.1: Example of a trust table

FROM (TRUSTOR)	TO (TRUSTEE)
Context(s)	
Time-specific	
Action(s)	
Expectation(s)	
Assurance(s)	

Endorsing Authorities and Trust Anchors   We have extended the concepts of endorsing authorities and trust anchors beyond the context of certificate authorities and shown how endorsing authorities can allow trust relationships established *outside* the scope of computer-to-computer interactions into this realm, using trust anchors as a mechanism to provide the *root of trust* or *bottom turtle* that is vital for establishing chains of trust.

Distributed Trust and Open Source   We have looked at various ways that trust can be established and shown that distributed trust in a community can provide an alternative to a centralised endorsing authority. In particular, we have provided an explanation of how and why open source communities may provide benefits in many contexts—including security—where supply chain risk management is required and how we can evaluate such a community's ability to provide those benefits.

Trust Pivots   The introduction of trust pivots provides a way to describe how components and systems can establish different trust relationships and move between trust domains, in combination with endorsing authorities (whether distributed or centralised) and trust anchors. We have also shown how trust pivots are a key mechanism for managing trust in the cloud and on the Edge.

Virtualisation and Trust   Virtualisation (via various mechanisms) is one of the core technical mechanisms by which the cloud and the Edge function, but the trust relationships it brings are complex, ill-understood, and exist in multiple contexts. The risks associated with the typically implicit trust relationships held between tenants (and their workloads) and cloud service providers (and their hosts) has been an important theme in this book. The impact of having to consider multiple trusted computing bases (TCBs) and the question of whose control they sit under has also led to major questions around where trust can reside and where risks must be mitigated.

Isolation and Boundaries   Defining trust relationships requires a clear understanding of where one component or system ends and another begins. From there, dependencies between entities can be examined and risks considered. We have concentrated on isolation of execution, particularly on the opportunities offered by trusted execution environments (TEEs) for the emerging field of confidential computing.

Trust Domains   Equipped with descriptions of all the preceding concepts, we introduced trust domains as a way to combine these concepts in ways that can be used at the organisational level, modelling relationships between different groups of entities, including human and non-human actors and both within and between organisations. The intention, as always, is to provide ways to expose, understand, and mitigate risk.

The Role of the Architect

Throughout the book, we have discussed *architecting* as one of the key steps in the creation of components and systems. Although the architect role is typically associated with software, we include hardware architecture in this context, particularly given the attention we have paid to the importance of hardware components within the realm of trust. The role of architect[1] is a complex one and requires a good technical background combined with an understanding of business context and processes. To this, we would add that architects should have a clear eye on trust as one of their key concerns if they are going to apply considerations about risk to the systems they design. In this section, we consider two major concerns that we believe an architect should manage as part of the process of creating a system: the system and the trustee.

---

[1]See Monson-Haefel (ed.), 2009, and Spinellis and Gousios, 2009, for two good surveys of the field.

Architecting the System

An architect should be able to engage with technical details where necessary, but another of their responsibilities is to rise above implementation details and look at the system as a whole, mapping out the individual components of a system and teasing out the interactions between them. Added to that is a need to look at the interactions the system will have with other parties, both planned and unplanned. Sometimes—as in a standard host system architecture—the units of consideration will be modelled as layers, while on other occasions, the communications are between distributed components executing on different platforms owned and operated by different parties (trust domain modelling lies strongly in the latter camp).

Where there is information flow—between layers and domains and over boundaries—there is risk. Much of this book has centred on protecting the confidentiality and integrity of data and information, both in intended and unintended communication flows. Risk can accrue in other ways, however, with availability and resilience both featuring as concerns, as we discussed when considering service degradation in the last chapter. The architect's role is *not*, however, always to reduce risk; it is to identify and *expose* risk at appropriate layers. By this, we do not, of course, mean that architects should find ways to increase risk; but just that there are times when risk can best be managed either by going outside the domain of the architect (by considering issues such as business risk, for instance) or by using tools and mechanisms that may be unavailable to them, such as insurance or human guards and physical security measures. Being able to expose and quantify these risks is a skill that takes time to gain and, where security in particular is concerned, requires a mindset that can turn a system on its head and allow the architect to look for the weakest parts of their thinking and consider how an attacker would exploit them.

Interfaces and boundaries are always the most likely points of failure—whether malicious or unintended—and they are also where trust relationships are established and maintained: this should now come as no surprise to us, given how the two topics are so intertwined. As the architect exposes risk, they have the opportunity to model the trust relationships that are associated with an interface and be explicit about what requirements are being put on other components in a way that is complementary to purely functional specifications but allows risks to be mitigated and managed. The architect can separate different contexts, consider the impact of time on any relationships, and actually allow the system they are designing as a trustor to make risk-informed decisions about trust relationships: which to build, which to avoid, which to drop, and which to monitor.

The Architect and the Trustee

The flip side of thinking about the trust relationships that one system will form to other systems is for the architect to consider the place of the system as a trustee: the recipient or target of those trust relationships. Once this is understood, it needs to be defined and advertised, whether as a passive artefact for design-time binding or as a more active artifact for provisioning or runtime binding. This is the function of the *trust action description*, an entity within the architectural domain whose importance we have noted but that we have spent little time defining. This section will briefly define what a trust action description might look like and the information it may include, but note that this is a new construct requiring more research and development within the community.

Whether or not a formal trust action description is provided for a system or its interfaces, there are some aspects that an architect must consider, most of which are very familiar to us from our description of trust relationships from the trustor to the trustee. A key point here is that the architect of the trustee system should aim to have a good understanding of not only the functional uses to which the system may be put but also the trust contexts and risk concerns of potential trustors. Without this information, there is a real danger that the architect will either create a system not fit for purpose or be unable to provide a trust action description that is sufficient or expressive enough for potential trustors—who are, after all, the system's expected users:

Included Contexts   If a trust action description is to be useful, it must include any contexts in which the system is designed to act as trustee. These should be as specific as possible and allow potential trustors to evaluate the use of the trustee system in terms of the risks associated with the context. Available mitigations in a context may not be known to the architect (as they may fall outside the architect's domain) but should be listed where possible and applicable.

Excluded Contexts   As important as contexts that are included are contexts that are explicitly *excluded*. Examples might include a system that is *not* designed to support real-time processing or one that is considered resilient against attacks by actors with certain sets of resources but not against nation-state actors.

Behaviours and Assurances   Within any context, there are expected behaviours and assurances that can be associated with it. This is an area where abstraction may be important: rarely is there a strong requirement to expose the implementation details of behaviours to potential trustors, and doing so may restrict future updates and upgrades to a system.

Dependencies   The exception to exposing information about behaviour is when the service being offered has dependencies that may impact the decision of the trustor as to whether to establish a trust relationship to the system. This is an area where a good knowledge of the system's potential trustors is required in order to allow appropriate information to be provided.

Known Side Channels and Unspecified Behaviours   Somewhat related to the issue of excluded contexts is the question of side channels and unspecified behaviours associated with the system. Where possible, the architect should specify any side channels against which protections are not available within the system itself. It is not always economically or logistically appropriate to provide all possible protections, such as enterprise-level tamper evidence for a system expected to be used for home gaming, and noting that behaviour of the system is unspecified should the system be tampered with goes some way to help ensure its appropriate use, alongside the list of included and excluded contexts.

Protections   While protections against some attacks or failure modes may not be provided by the system itself, it may be that trustors can implement some protections themselves, as we saw when discussing constant time cryptographic implementations as protection against certain side-channel attacks.

System and Service Degradation Options   Where systems and the services they provide are able to offer different degradation options, listing and defining these within the trust action description allows trustors to establish trust relationships that can react over time to changes in the service provided. The options provided should be very carefully tied to contexts and the assurances offered, as degradation may well vary across different contexts—it may be possible to maintain integrity protection across an interface while not being able to guarantee confidentiality under high load, for instance.

API Hooks   Most interfaces, at least in the software world, are represented by APIs. While APIs rarely (if ever) include information about trust, there are opportunities for adding it. If a trustor wishes to make use of a particular behaviour and requires assurances related to it, registering this interest at the API level allows the trustee system to bear this in mind when considering service degradation during future runtime operations. Or, the system may be able to reduce the number of trustors to which particular assurances are made (by altering the available trust action description) if there is a danger that too much load will be put on the system, for instance.

Coda

I believe that more explicit consideration of trust is an obvious next step within the field of computer systems and that the existing discussions of the field have lacked the theoretical underpinnings and descriptive frameworks that allow software engineers, architects, and other practitioners in the field to build and operate systems. I believe passionately that risk should be part of the language understood and spoken not just by security experts but by all those involved in the lifecycle of computer systems. Furthermore, such discussions of risk must not exist solely within the context of hardware and software but be expressed in the language of business and organisations: the context in which our systems operate. The enormous popularity of the cloud has led to more conversation about risk and trust, but not enough. Without the languages and frameworks to discuss trust, cloud and edge deployments expose organisations to more risk, just as they extend their reach and their ability to operate more quickly and efficiently in global markets.

Trust and risk lurk in all areas of the field of computing, from the smallest IoT device to the largest supercomputer, from wind turbines to online gaming, and from financial markets to educational institutions. It is time to talk about risk, expose it, and apply techniques and tools to it that exist in a shared community of practice within which architects take a central but non-exclusive place. I hope that this book forms part of the foundations of that ongoing community of practice and the discussions it occasions.

References

Abate, A. (2017). Formal verification of complex systems: model-based and data-driven methods. *MEMOCODE '17: Proceedings of the 15th ACM-IEEE International Conference on Formal Methods and Models for System Design September 2017*, 91–93.

Abdul-Rahman, A. and Hailes, S. (1997). A distributed trust model, https://www.nspw.org/2009/proceedings/1997/nspw1997-rahman.pdf (accessed 20 December 2019).

Advogato. (2012). Advogato's Trust Metric. https://web.archive.org/web/20120930213545/http://advogato.org/trust-metric.html (accessed 25 August 2020).

AMD. (2020). AMD Secure Encrypted Virtualization (SEV). https://developer.amd.com/sev (accessed 18 October 2020).

Anderson, R. (2021). *Security Engineering: A Guide to Building Dependable Distributed Systems, 3e.* Hoboken, NJ: Wiley.

Anderson, R. and Moore, T. (2006). The economics of information security. *Science, New Series* 314 (5799): 610–613.

Anderson, R. and Moore, T. (2009). Information science: where computer science, economics and psychology meet. In: *Philosophical Transactions: Mathematical, Physical and Engineering Sciences 367 (1898, Crossing Boundaries: Computational Science, e-Science and Global e-Infrastructure II. Selected Papers from the UK e-Science All Hands Meeting 2008*, 2717–2727.

Anderson, R., Moore, T., Nagaraja, S., and Ozment, A. (2007). Incentives and information security. In: *Algorithmic Game Theory* (ed. N. Nisan, T. Roughgarden, E. Tardos, and V.V. Vazirani), 633–650.9. Cambridge University Press.

Arends, R. et al. (2006). RFC 4033: DNS security introduction and requirements. Tools.ietf.org. https://tools.ietf.org/html/rfc4033 (accessed 23 July 2020).

Arends, R. et al. (2006a). RFC 4034: Resource records for the DNS security extensions. Tools.ietf.org. https://tools.ietf.org/html/rfc4034 (accessed 23 July 2020).

Arends, R. et al. (2006b). RFC 4035: Protocol modifications for the DNS security extensions. Tools.ietf.org. `https://tools.ietf.org/html/rfc4035` (accessed 23 July 2020).

Aristotle (?4C BCE; 2000). *The Politics (Classics) Revised Edition* (trans. T.A. Sinclair). London: Penguin Group.

Asylo. (2020). Asylo: An open and flexible framework for enclave applications. `https://asylo.dev` (accessed 12 December 2020).

Axelrod, R. (1990). *The Evolution of Co-operation*. London: Penguin Group.

Baier, A. (1986). Trust and antitrust. *Ethics* 96 (2): 231–260.

Barker, E., Smid, M., and Branstad, D. (2015). NIST special publication 800–152: A profile for U.S. federal cryptographic key management systems. NIST. `https://nvlpubs.nist.gov/nistpubs/SpecialPublications/NIST.SP.800-152.pdf` (accessed 22 March 2020).

Bateson, P. (1988). Biological evolution of cooperation and trust. In: *Trust: Making and Breaking Cooperative Relations* (ed. D. Gambetta), 14–30. Oxford: Basil Blackwell.

BBC News. (2019). London bridge attacker had terror conviction. `https://www.bbc.co.uk/news/uk-50610215` (accessed 25 August 2020).

Benchoff, B. (2016). The trouble with Intel's management engine. Hackaday. `https://hackaday.com/2016/01/22/the-trouble-with-intels-management-engine/` (accessed 24 August 2020).

Berman, A. (2018). Retail giant Carrefour launches blockchain food tracking platform for poultry in Spain. *CoinTelegraph*. `https://cointelegraph.com/news/retail-giant-carrefour-launches-blockchain-food-tracking-platform-for-poultry-in-spain` (accessed 21 June 2020).

Bogard, W. (1996). *The Simulation of Surveillance: Hypercontrol in Telematic Societies*. Cambridge University Press.

Botsman, R. (2017). *Who Can You Trust? How Technology Brought Us Together—And Why It Could Drive Us Apart*. London: Penguin Random House.

Boyens, J., Paulsen, C., Moorthy, R., and Bartol, N. (2015). NIST special publication 800–161: supply chain risk management practices for federal information systems and organizations. `http://dx.doi.org/10.6028/NIST.SP.800-161` (accessed 22 March 2020).

Brennen, V.A. (2008). The keysigning party HOWTO. Cryptnet.net. `https://www.cryptnet.net/fdp/crypto/keysigning_party/en/keysigning_party.html` (accessed 25 August 2020).

Buchan, N.R. (2009). The complexity of trust: cultural environments, trust, and trust development. In: *Cambridge Handbook of Culture, Organizations, and Work* (ed. R.S. Bhagat and R.M. Steers), 373–417. Cambridge University Press.

Cakebread, C. (2020). Twitter stops its verification program after giving its 'verified' badge to the organizer of the Charlottesville 'Unite The Right' rally. *Business Insider*. `https://www.businessinsider.com/twitter-suspends-account-verifications-after-backlash-2017-11` (accessed 15 November 2020).

Carroll, L. (1889). *Sylvie and Bruno Concluded*. London: MacMillan and Co.

CHAOSS. (2020). https://chaoss.community (accessed 16 November 2020).

CHAOSS. (2020a). Wg-Risk. https://github.com/chaoss/wg-risk (accessed 17 November 2020).

Cheshire, C. (2011). Online trust, trustworthiness, or assurance? MIT Press Journals http://people.ischool.berkeley.edu/~coye/Pubs/Articles/Cheshire_DAED_Trust.pdf (accessed 23 August 2020).

Chirgwin, K. (2017). Equifax couldn't find or patch vulnerable Struts implementations. *The Register* https://www.theregister.com/2017/10/02/equifax_ceo_richard_smith_congressional_testimony (accessed 23 August 2020).

Chomsky, N. (2015). *Masters of Mankind: Essays and Lectures 1969-2013*. London: Penguin Random House.

Claburn, T. (2019). If there's somethin' stored in a secure enclave, who ya gonna call? Membuster! *The Register*. https://www.theregister.com/2019/12/05/membuster_secure_enclave/ (accessed 13 December 2020).

Clark, D. (2014). The role of trust in cyberspace. In: *Trust, Computing, and Society* (ed. R.H.R. Harper). Cambridge University Press., 17-37.

Coleman, J.S. (1986). *Individual Interests and Collective Action: Selected Essays*. Cambridge University Press.

Commoncriteriaportal.org. (2020). *Common Criteria*. www.commoncriteriaportal.org (accessed 24 May 2020).

Confidential Computing Consortium. (2020). Confidential computing deep dive white paper v1.0. https://confidentialcomputing.io/wp-content/uploads/sites/85/2020/10/Confidential-Computing-Deep-Dive-white-paper.pdf (accessed 28 November 2020).

Confidential Computing Consortium (2020a). What is the Confidential Computing Consortium? https://confidentialcomputing.io/ (accessed 17 December 2020).

Cook, K. (2016). Security bug lifetime. https://outflux.net/blog/archives/2016/10/18/security-bug-lifetime/ (accessed 16 December 2020).

Cramer, R., Damgard, I.V., and Nielsen, J.B (2015). *Secure Multiparty Computation and Secret Sharing*. Cambridge University Press.

CRI-O.io. (2020). https://cri-o.io (accessed 18 October 2020).

Dasgupta, P. (1988). Trust as a commodity. In: *Trust: Making and Breaking Cooperative Relations* (ed. D. Gambetta), 49–72.

De Cremer, D. (2015). Understanding trust, in China and the West. *Harvard Business Review*. https://hbr.org/2015/02/understanding-trust-in-china-and-the-west (accessed 6 June 2021).

Denning, D.E. (1993). A new paradigm for trusted systems. https://www.researchgate.net/publication/234793347_A_New_Paradigm_for_Trusted_Systems (accessed 3 April 2020).

Department of Defense. (1985). Trusted computer system evaluation criteria. https://csrc.nist.gov/csrc/media/publications/conference-paper/1998/10/08/proceedings-of-the-21st-nissc-1998/documents/early-cs-papers/dod85.pdf (accessed 24 May 2020).

Deutsch, M. and Krauss, R.M. (1960). The effect of threat on interpersonal bargaining. *Journal of Conflict Resolution* 6: 52–76.

Docker.com. (2020). Container runtime. https://www.docker.com/products/container-runtime (accessed 18 October 2020).

e-Residency. (2019). What is e-Residency? | How to start an EU company online. https://e-resident.gov.ee/ (accessed 28 December 2019).

Enarx. (2020). What is Enarx? https://github.com/enarx/enarx/wiki (accessed 12 December 2020).

Engquist, M. and Leimar, O. (1993). The evolution of cooperation in mobile organisms. *Animal Behaviour* 45: 747–57.

Erl, T., Carlyle, B., Pautasso, C., and Balasubramanian, R. (2012). *SOA with REST: Principles, Patterns and Constraints for Building Enterprise Solutions with REST*. Upper Saddle River, NJ: Prentice Hall.

Ethereum. (2021). What is Ethereum? https://ethereum.org/en/what-is-ethereum/ (accessed 2021-07-04).

ETSI. (2020). Multi-access edge computing (MEC). http://www.etsi.org/technologies/multi-access-edge-computing (accessed 19 November 2020).

Farrell, H. (2009). Informal institutions without trust: relations among mafiosi in Sicily. In: *The Political Economy of Trust*. Cambridge University Press, 171–200.

Ferguson, N. and Schneier, B. (2003). *Practical Cryptography*. Hoboken, NJ: Wiley.

Feiner, L. (2019). IBM closes its $34 acquisition of Red Hat. CNBC. https://www.cnbc.com/2019/07/09/ibm-closes-its-34-billion-acquisition-of-red-hat.html (accessed 18 November 2020).

Field, R. (2020). Attackers found building malicious container images directly on host. InfoQ. https://www.infoq.com/news/2020/09/Malicious-Container-Images/ (accessed 18 October 2020).

Fortanix. (2020). Enclave development platform. https://fortanix.com/products/runtime-encryption/edp/ (accessed 12 December 2020).

Friedman, E.J. and Resnick, P. (1999). The social cost of cheap pseudonyms. http://citeseerx.ist.psu.edu/viewdoc/summary?doi=10.1.1.39.6921 (accessed 25 August 2020).

Fukuyama, F. (1995). *Trust: The Social Virtues and the Creation of Prosperity*. London: Hamish Hamilton.

Gambetta, D. (1988). Can we trust trust? In: *Trust: Making and Breaking Cooperative Relations* (ed. D. Gambetta), 213–238.

Gambetta, D. (1988a). Mafia: the price of mistrust. In: *Trust: Making and Breaking Cooperative Relations* (ed. D. Gambetta), 158–175.

Gefen, D., Benbasat, I, and Pavlou, P.A. (2008). A research agenda for trust in online environments. *Journal of Management Information Systems* 24 (4): 275–286.

Gibson, W. (1993). *Virtual Light*. New York: Viking Press.

Goodin, D. (2008). Linux guru Hans Reiser convicted of first-degree murder. https://www.theregister.com/2008/04/29/hans_reiser_found_guilty/ (accessed 17 November 2020).

Granovetter, M. (1982). The strength of weak ties: a network theory revisited. In: *Social Structure and Network Analysis* (ed. P.V. Marsden and N. Lin), 105–130. Beverly Hills: Sage Publications.

Grimshaw, M. (2009). The audio uncanny valley: sound, fear and the horror game. *Games Computing and Creative Technologies: Conference Papers (Peer Reviewed)*. Paper 9.

Hardin, R. (2001). Conceptions and explanations of trust. In: *Trust in Society* (ed. K.S. Cooke). New York: Russell Sage Foundation, 3-39.

Hardin, R. (2002). *Trust and Trustworthiness*. New York: Russell Sage Foundation.

Harper, R.H.R. (ed.) (2014). *Trust, Computing and Society*. Cambridge University Press.

Heap, S.P.H. and Varoufakis, Y. (1995). *Game Theory: A Critical Introduction*. London: Routledge.

Heinz, M. (2020). Analyzing Docker image security. Towards Data Science. https://towardsdatascience.com/analyzing-docker-image-security-ed5cf7e93751 (accessed 18 October 2020).

Hern, A. (2017). Google will stop scanning content of personal emails. *The Guardian*. https://www.theguardian.com/technology/2017/jun/26/google-will-stop-scanning-content-of-personal-emails (accessed 28 May 2021).

Hobbes, T. (ed. R. Tuck) (1692; 1996). *Leviathan*. Cambridge University Press.

Hoffman, P. and McManus, P. (2018). RFC 8484: DNS queries over HTTPS, DoH. Tools.ietf.org. https://tools.ietf.org/html/rfc8484 (accessed 21 July 2020).

Horrible Histories. (2017). Invention of the English mile. https://youtu.be/5FPTxAEC6DY (accessed 9 February 2020).

Housley, R. (ed.) (2009). RFC 5484: Digital signatures on internet-draft documents. Tools.ietf.org. https://tools.ietf.org/html/rfc5485 (accessed 13 June 2020).

Housley, R. (ed.) (2018). RFC 8358 Update to digital signatures on internet-draft documents. Tools.ietf.org. https://tools.ietf.org/html/rfc8358 (accessed 13 June 2020).

Howison, J., Crowston, K., and Wiggins, A. (2020). Validity issues in the use of social network analysis for the study of online communities. Zenodo. http://dx.doi.org/10.5281/zenodo.913303 (accessed 16 November 2020).

Hunt, G. and Pai, R. (2019). Protected execution facility. Platform Security Summit. https://www.platformsecuritysummit.com/2019/speaker/hunt (accessed 7 December 2020).

I, Robot. (2004). (film) Directed by Alex Provas. Hollywood: 20th Century Fox.

Inclusive Naming Initiative. (2021). About the Inclusive Naming Initiative https://inclusivenaming.org/about (accessed 2021-04-07).

Intel. (2020). Intel Software Guard Extensions. `https://software.intel.com/content/www/us/en/develop/topics/software-guard-extensions.html` (accessed 18 October 2020).

Intel. (2020a). Intel Trust Domain Extensions (Intel TDX). `https://software.intel.com/content/www/us/en/develop/articles/intel-trust-domain-extensions.html` (accessed 7 December 2020).

Integrity Measurement Architecture. (2020). Integrity Measurement Architecture (IMA) / Wiki / Home. Sourceforge.net. `https://sourceforge.net/p/linux-ima/wiki/Home/` (accessed 24 August 2020).

International Organization for Standardization. (1994). ISO/IEC 7498-1:1994.

ISO/IEC 7498-1:1994 Information technology — Open Systems Interconnection — Basic Reference Model: The Basic Model (see `https://www.iso.org/standard/20269.html`).

International Telecommunication Union. (2001). Recommendation X.509, information technology – open systems interconnection – the directory: authentication framework, COM 7-250-E Revision 1.

Katacontainers.io (2020). Kata Containers—open source container runtime software. (online) `https://katacontainers.io/` (accessed 18 Oct 2020).

Katz, I. (2020). Have we fallen out of love with experts? BBC News. `https://www.bbc.co.uk/news/uk-39102840` (accessed 9 February 2020).

Kent, S. and Seo, K. (2005). RFC 4301: Security architecture for the internet protocol. Tools.ietf.org. `https://tools.ietf.org/html/rfc4301` (accessed 19 September 2020).

Kenton, W. (2020). Chinese wall. Investopedia. `https://www.investopedia.com/terms/c/chinesewall.asp` (accessed 21 December 2020).

Keylime.dev. (2020). `https://keylime.dev` (accessed 24 August 2020).

Kleene, S.C. (1952). *Introduction to Metamathematics*. North-Holland.

Konka, J. et al. (2020). Welcome to WASI! bytecodealliance. `https://github.com/bytecodealliance/wasmtime/blob/main/docs/WASI-intro.md` (accessed 12 December 2020).

Kuhn, T.S. (1962). *The Structure of Scientific Revolutions*. University of Chicago Press.

Lansing, J. and Sunyaev, A. (2016). Trust in cloud computing: conceptual typology and trust-building antecedents. *ACM SIGMIS* 47 (2), 59–96.

Lauer, H. and Rudolph, C. (2019). Bootstrapping trust in a 'trusted' virtualized platform. CYSARM '19, ACM, London.

Lave, J. and Wenger, E. (1991). *Situated Learning: Legitimate Peripheral Participation*. Cambridge University Press.

League Against Cruel Sports. (n.d.). Hunting on national trust land. `https://www.league.org.uk/nationaltrust` (accessed 4 January 2020).

Linux Kernel. (2020). The Linux Kernel Archives. `https://kernel.org` (accessed 18 November 2020).

Lloyd, R. (1999). Metric mishap caused loss of NASA orbiter. CNN (September 30). http://edition.cnn.com/TECH/space/9909/30/mars.metric.02/ (accessed 9 February 2020).

MacKenzie, D. (2001). *Mechanizing Proof: Computing, Risk, and Trust*. MIT Press.

Mahalingham, M. et al. (2015). RFC 7348: Virtual eXtensible Local Area Network (VXLAN): A framework for overlaying virtualized layer 2 networks over layer 3 networks. Tools. ietf.org https://tools.ietf.org/html/rfc7348 (accessed 21 December 2020).

Mill, J.S. (1863). *Utilitarianism*. London: Parker, Son, and Bourn.

Mills, D. et al. (2010). RFC 5905: Network Time Protocol version 4: protocol and algorithms specification. Tools.ietf.org. https://tools.ietf.org/html/rfc5905 (accessed 21 Jul 2020).

Mizrahi, T. (2014). RFC 7384: Security requirements of time protocols in packet switched networks. Tools.ietf.org (online) https://tools.ietf.org/html/rfc7384 (accessed 26 Sep 2020).

Mockapetris, P. (1983). RFC 882: Domain names – concepts and facilities. Tools.ietf.org. https://tools.ietf.org/html/rfc882 (accessed 21 Jul 2020).

Mockapetris, P. (1983a). RFC 882: Domain names – implementation and specification. Tools. ietf.org https://tools.ietf.org/html/rfc883 (accessed 21 Jul 2020).

Moghimi, D., Sunar, B., Eisenbarth, T., and Heninger, N. (2020). TPM meets timing and lattice attacks. https://tpm.fail/tpmfail.pdf (accessed 23 August 2020).

Monson-Haefel, R. (ed.) (2009). *97 Things Every Software Architect Should Know: Collective Wisdom from the Experts*. Sebastopol, CA: O'Reilly Media.

Nakamoto, S. (2008). Bitcoin: a peer-to-peer electronic cash system. https://bitcoin.org/bitcoin.pdf (accessed 21 June 2020).

National Trust. (n.d.). Our position on trail hunting. https://www.nationaltrust.org.uk/features/our-position-on-trail-hunting (accessed 4 January 2020).

Nia, R., Bird, C., Devanbu, P., and Filkov, V. (2010). Validity of network analyses in open source projects. *Proceedings of the 7th IEEE Working Conference on Mining Software Repositories (MSR 2010)*.

Nock, S. (1993). *The Costs of Privacy: Surveillance and Reputation in America*. New York: A. De Gruyter.

O'Neill, O. (2002). *A Question of Trust: The BBC Reith Lectures 2002*. Cambridge University Press.

Open Containers. (2020). OCI image format specification. https://github.com/opencontainers/image-spec (accessed 12 December 2020).

Open Enclave SDK. (2020). https://openenclave.io/sdk (accessed 12 December 2020).

Open Group. (2020). *IEEE Std* 1003.1 2017. https://pubs.opengroup.org/onlinepubs/9699919799/ (accessed 12 December 2020).

Object Management Group. (2017). Unified Modeling Specification version 2.5.1. https://www.omg.org/spec/UML/2.5.1/PDF (accessed 24 May 2020).

Open Policy Agent. (2020). Policy-based control for cloud native environments: Flexible, fine-grained control for administrators across the stack. `https://www.openpolicyagent.org/` (accessed 21 December 2020).

Open Source Hardware Association (2020). Open Source Hardware Association. (online) `https://www.oshwa.org/` (accessed 14 November 2020).

Open Source Security Coalition. (2020). `https://github.com/Open-Source-Security-Coalition/Open-Source-Security-Coalition` (accessed 17 November 2020).

Opensource.com. (2021). What is open source? `https://opensource.com/resources/what-open-source` (accessed 28 May 2021).

Opensource.org. (2020). The Open Source Definition. `https://opensource.org/osd` (accessed 16 November 2020).

Opensource.org. (2020a). News | Open Source Initiative. `https://opensource.org` (accessed 16 November 2020).

OscarLab. (2020). Graphene Library OS with Intel SGX Support. `https://github.com/oscarlab/graphene` (accessed 12 December 2020).

Paine, T. (1791, 1792; 2000). The rights of man. In: *Common Sense and The Rights of Man*, 57–278. London: Phoenix Press.

Pcisig.com. (2020). Welcome to PCI-SIG. `https://pcisig.com` (accessed 11 October 2020).

Postel, J. (ed.) (1981). RFC 791: Internet Protocol, Darpa internet program protocol specification. Tools.ietf.org. `https://tools.ietf.org/html/rfc791` (accessed 23 May 2020).

Preston-Werner, T. (2020). Semantic versioning 2.0.0. `https://semver.org/spec/v2.0.0.html` (accessed 13 September 2020).

R3. (2020). The Corda platform – open source + enterprise. `https://www.r3.com/corda-platform` (accessed 16 December 2020).

Rathburn, B.C. (2011). *Trust in International Cooperation*. Cambridge University Press.

Raymond, E.S. (ed.) (1996). *The New Hacker's Dictionary*, 3e. MIT Press.

Raymond, E.S. (ed) (2001). The jargon file. `http://www.iwar.org.uk/hackers/resources/faq/jargon.htm` (accessed 22 August 2020).

Red Hat. (2020). Our history. `https://www.redhat.com/en/about/brand/standards/history` (accessed 18 November 2020).

Rekor. (2020). Project Rekor. `https://github.com/projectrekor` (accessed 18 November 2020).

Rescorla, E. (2000). RFC 2818: HTTP over TLS. Tools.ietf.org. `https://tools.ietf.org/html/rfc2818` (accessed 08 March 2020).

Rheingold, H. (2000). *The Virtual Community: Homesteading on the Electronic Frontier*, Revised Edition. MIT Press.

Robinson, A. (2020). Twitter will ban "deceptive" faked media that could cause "serious harm". The Verge. `https://www.theverge.com/2020/2/4/21122661/twitter-deepfake-manipulated-media-policy-rollout-date` (accessed 29 May 2021).

Rose, S., Borchert, S., Mitchell, S., and Connelly, S. (2020). NIST special publication 800–207: zero trust architecture. https://nvlpubs.nist.gov/nistpubs/SpecialPublications/ NIST.SP.800-207.pdf (accessed 17 December 2020).

Ross, R., McEvilley, M., and Oren, J.C. (2016). NIST special report 800-160: systems security engineering (online). https://nvlpubs.nist.gov/nistpubs/SpecialPublications/ NIST.SP.800-160.pdf (accessed 25 March 2020).

Ross, R., McEvilley, M., and Oren, J.C. (2016a). NIST special report 800-160: systems security engineering—volume1.https://nvlpubs.nist.gov/nistpubs/SpecialPublications/ NIST.SP.800-160v1.pdf (accessed 25 March 2020).

Rossi, F. (2019). Building trust in artificial intelligence. *Journal of International Affairs* 72 (1): 127–134.

Rousseau, J.-J. (1762). *The Social Contract*. Amsterdam.

Russell, N.S. (2015). The problem with a trust-but-verify approach. *Psychology Today*.https://www.psychologytoday.com/gb/blog/trust-the-new-workplace- currency/201507/the-problem-trust-verify-approach (accessed 3 January 2020).

Rust. (2020). www.rust-lang.org (accessed 25 August 2020).

Ruytenberg, B. (2020). Thunderspy. https://thunderspy.io (accessed 5 December 2020).

Sabbagh, D. (2011). Radio 4's long wave goodbye. *The Guardian*. https://www .theguardian.com/media/2011/oct/09/bbc-radio4-long-wave-goodbye (accessed 22 August 2020).

Sapkota, H., Murukannaiah, P.K., and Wang, Y. (2019). A network-centric approach for esti- mating trust between open source software developers. *PLOS ONE* 14 (12): e0226281.

Schelling, T. (1960). *The Strategy of Conflict*. Harvard University Press.

Schneier, B. (1997). Essays: why cryptography is harder than it looks. Schneier on Security. https://www.schneier.com/essays/archives/1997/01/why_cryptography_is .html (accessed 21 March 2020).

Schneier, B. (2012). *Liars and Outliers*. Hoboken, NJ: Wiley.

SCONE. (2020). SCONE confidential computing. https://sconedocs.github .io (accessed 12 December 2020).

Sharwood, S. (2018). Intel shrugs off "new" side-channel attacks on branch prediction units and SGX. *The Register*. https://www.theregister.com/2018/03/28/intel_shrugs_off_ new_sidechannel_attacks_on_branch_prediction_units_and_sgx (accessed 13 December 2020).

Shirey, R. (2007). IETF security glossary, version 2. https://tools.ietf.org/html/ rfc4949 (accessed 11 March 2020).

Simon, A. and Sturmann, L. (2019). Current trusted execution environment landscape. Red Hat. https://next.redhat.com/2019/12/02/current-trusted-execution- environment-landscape/ (accessed 7 December 2019).

Singhal, A., Winograd, T., and Scarfone, K. (2007). NIST special publication 800-95: guide to secure web services. https://nvlpubs.nist.gov/nistpubs/Legacy/SP/nistspecial- publication800-95.pdf (accessed 22 March 2020).

Smith, R. (2006). Peer review: a flawed process at the heart of science and journals. *Journal of the Royal Society of Medicine* 99 (4):178–182. https://www.ncbi.nlm.nih.gov/pmc/articles/PMC1420798 (accessed 15 November 2020).

Spinellis, D. and Gousios, G. (2009). *Beautiful Architecture*. Sebastopol, CA: O'Reilly Media.

Stallman, R. (2016). FLOSS and FOSS. GNU.org. https://www.gnu.org/philosophy/floss-and-foss.en.html (accessed 18 November 2020).

Stallman, R. (2019). Linux and the GNU system. Free Software Foundation. https://www.gnu.org/gnu/linux-and-gnu.en.html (accessed 24 May 2020).

StatCounter Global Stats. (2020). Mobile operating system market share worldwide, April 2020. https://gs.statcounter.com/os-market-share/mobile/worldwide (accessed 24 May 2020).

Temoshok, D. and Abruzzi, C. (2018). NISTIR 8149: developing trust frameworks to support identity federations. https://nvlpubs.nist.gov/nistpubs/ir/2018/NIST.IR.8149.pdf (accessed 15 March 2020).

Thompson, K. (1984). Reflections on trusting trust. https://www.cs.cmu.edu/~rdriley/487/papers/Thompson_1984_ReflectionsonTrustingTrust.pdf (accessed 14 September 2021).

Trusted Computing Group. (2013). Trusted multi-tenant infrastructure work group reference framework. https://trustedcomputinggroup.org/trusted-multi-tenant-infrastructure-reference-framework (accessed 11 March 2020).

Trusted Computing Group. (2017). TCG glossary. https://trustedcomputinggroup.org/wp-content/uploads/TCG-Glossary-V1.1-Rev-1.0.pdf (accessed 10 March 2020).

Trusted Computing Group. (2020). Welcome to Trusted Computing Group. https://trustedcomputinggroup.org (accessed 9 May 2020).

Turing, A. (1950). Computing machinery and intelligence. *Mind* LIX (236): 433–460.

Tversky, A. and Kahneman, D. (1982). Judgment under uncertainty: Heuristics and biases. In: *Judgment Under Uncertainty: Heuristics and Biases* (ed. D. Kahneman, P. Slovic, and A. Tversky), 3–20. Cambridge University Press.

Twitter. (2020). About verified accounts. https://help.twitter.com/en/managing-your-account/about-twitter-verified-accounts (accessed 15 November 2020).

UrbanSitter. (2020). Find babysitters—child care and sitter services—Urbansitter. www.urbansitter.com (accessed 15 November 2020).

Waitzman, D. (1990). RFC 1149: A standard for the transmission of IP datagrams on avian carriers. Tools.ietf.org. https://tools.ietf.org/html/rfc1149 (accessed 23 May 2020).

Wang, F. and De Filippi, P. (2020). Self-sovereign identity in a globalized world: credentials-based identity systems as a driver for economic inclusion. Frontiers in Blockchain. https://www.frontiersin.org/articles/10.3389/fbloc.2019.00028/full (accessed 21 June 2020).

WarGames. (1983). (film) Directed by J Badham. Hollywood: United Artists.

WebAssembly. (2020). Specifications. `https://webassembly.org/specs` (accessed 12 December 2020).

Weiss, A. (2006). In our trusty cage. *NetWorker 10 (3, Trusted computing: who will control the PC of the future?)* New York: Association for Computing Machinery.

Wellman, B. (1988). Structural analysis: from method to metaphor to theory and substance. In: *Social Structures: A Network Approach* (ed. B. Wellman and S.D. Berkowitz), 19–61. Cambridge University Press.

Wenger, E. (1998). *Communities of Practice: Learning,* Meaning and Identity. Cambridge University Press.

Werbach, K. (2018). *The Blockchain and the New Architecture of Trust.* MIT Press.

Wikipedia contributors. (2020). Advogato. `https://en.wikipedia.org/w/index.php?title=Advogatoandoldid=963267223` (accessed 25 August 2020).

Wikipedia contributors. (2020). AppArmor `https://en.wikipedia.org/w/index.php?title=AppArmorandoldid=969815810` (accessed 24 August 2020).

Wikipedia contributors. (2021). Boeing 737 MAX groundings. `https://en.wikipedia.org/wiki/Boeing_737_MAX_groundings` (accessed 28 May 2021).

Wikipedia contributors. (2020). Developer certificate of origin. `https://en.wikipedia.org/w/index.php?title=Developer_Certificate_of_Originandoldid=958782843` (accessed 17 November 2020).

Wikipedia contributors. (n.d.) Externality. `https://en.wikipedia.org/w/index.php?title=Externalityandoldid=937436483` (accessed 25 January, 2020).

Wikipedia contributors. (n.d.) Hackathon. `https://en.wikipedia.org/w/index.php?title=Hackathonandoldid=987960708` (accessed 16 November, 2020).

Wikipedia contributors. (n.d.) List of cognitive biases. `https://en.wikipedia.org/w/index.php?title=List_of_cognitive_biasesandoldid=931544009` (accessed 3 January, 2020).

Wikipedia contributors. (2020). Morris worm. `https://en.wikipedia.org/w/index.php?title=Morris_wormandoldid=937243574` (accessed 8 March 2020).

Wikipedia contributors. (2020). Security-enhanced Linux. `https://en.wikipedia.org/w/index.php?title=Security-Enhanced_Linuxandoldid=949954519` (accessed 24 August 2020).

Wikipedia contributors. (2020). Stanislav Petrov. `https://en.wikipedia.org/w/index.php?title=Stanislav_Petrovandoldid=977680016` (accessed 13 September 2020).

Ylonen, T., Turner, P., Scarfone, K., and Souppaya, M. (2015). NIST internal report 7966—Security of interactive and automated access management using Secure Shell (SSH). `https://nvlpubs.nist.gov/nistpubs/ir/2015/NIST.IR.7966.pdf` (accessed 25 March 2020).

Index

A

Abate, Alessandro, 90
Abdul-Rahman, A., 79–80
ABI (application binary interface), 164, 165, 167, 179, 191, 198, 267
abstraction, 75, 188
access control management, 177, 246
accountability, assurance and, 67–78
ACID (atomicity, consistency, isolation, and durability), 172
acquirer bank, 117, 129
Advogato, 181
agency
  defined, 8–10
  and intentionality, 62–65
  trust relationships and agency in worked example, 136–144
Agile, 265
AI (artificial intelligence), 42, 46, 193
air-gap networks, 249
air-gapping, 256
Alibaba, Alibaba Cloud, 97
Amazon, AWS, 97
AMD, 206, 208, 248, 261
Anderson, Ross, 47, 50, 247, 254
animal rights campaigns, 44
animals, trust relationships with, 69
anthropomorphism, 45–47
anti-authority movement, 37
antiscience movement, 35, 36
anti-vaccination (anti-vaxxers) movement, 36
Apache Struts 2, 170
AppArmor, 177

application binary interface (ABI), 164, 165, 167, 179, 191, 198, 267
Application layer
  in Internet Protocol, 95
  in OSI, 95
application programming interface (API)
  API call, 284, 286, 287, 288
  API hooks, 306
  as boundary, 198
  capabilities as "bakedin" to, 191
  controls of, 123
  as defining contract, 17
  definition of as mitigation, 164
  as describing functional behaviour of difference layers, 101
  RESTful API, 198
  similarities of trust action description to, 59
  as standard mechanism for specifying behaviour of component, 146–147
  use of side effects regarding, 50
architects
  of computer systems, 94
  role of, 303–306
  and trustees, 305–306
architecture
  distributed architecture, 288–292
  microservice architecture, 244
  x86 architecture, 206
  Zero Trust Architecture, 283
Aristotle, 212
Arm, 208, 270
artificial intelligence (AI), 42, 46, 193
Asimov, Isaac, 76n21

assurance
  and accountability, 67–78
  defined, 67
  use of term, 24
Asylo, 267
asymmetric cryptography, 35, 88, 114, 157
atomicity, consistency, isolation, and durability
    (ACID), 172
attackers, target of, 164
attacks
  from within, 43–45
  break-out attacks, 203
  Dumpster diving, 254
  evil maid attacks, 254
  examples of physical system attacks, 255
  local attacks, 135
  noisy neighbour problem/attack, 202
  remote attacks, 135
  side-channel attacks, 147–148, 271
  timing attacks, 147
  when execution goes wrong, 269–270
  in worked example, 134–135
attestation
  post-load attestation, 263, 265, 266
  pre-load attestation, 263, 264
  remote attestation, 113
  role of, 173–177, 238
attestation service, 173
attribution, as measure to make determination
    about trusting an open source project, 221
authentication
  as trust domain primitive, 296
  two-factor authentication, 117
  use of concept in computer systems, 11
authorisation
  as standard use of time, 195
  as trust domain primitive, 296
  use of concept in computer systems, 11, 12
authority
  certificate authorities (CA). *See* certificate
      authorities (CA)
  change away from trusting established
      authorities, 36
  endorsing authorities, 33–35, 54, 61, 70, 115,
      118, 152
  etymology of, 33
  extra-territorial authorities, 32
  institutional authority, 34
  non-territorial authorities, 32, 33
  secondary authorities, 33
  trust based on, 33–37
automated trust relationships, dangers of,
    192–193
availability, 11, 71
avalanche effect, 110
Axelrod, Robert, 25–26, 32, 42

B
Baader-Meinhof effect, 38
backup files, 51
Baier, A., 20
behaviours
  explicit behaviour, 188–192
  nominal behaviour, 298
  non-deterministic behaviour, 163
  perfect behaviour, 298
  system behaviour, 17–18, 126, 164
  use of term, 47
being explicit, importance of, 145–150
best practice, 148
best-known practice, 148
bias
  cognitive bias, 38–41, 46
  on evaluation of conjunctive and disjunctive
      events, 40
  normalcy bias, 39, 40
Bible, as example of secondary authority,
    33
BIOS | EFI, 98, 99, 104, 112, 199
Bitcoin, 151, 157
"Bitcoin: A Peer-to-Peer Electronic Cash
    System" (Nakamoto), 151
blockchains, 36, 45, 151–156
Boeing 737 MAX 8 aircraft, 9, 89n27
boot measurement, 174, 175, 176, 246
boot time, 176, 248
Bootloader, 98, 104, 199
bot, 46
Botsman, Rachel, 212
bottom turtle, 302
boundaries
  in systems, 198–209
  as tool for trust, 303
  of trust domains, 297–298
breaking by patching, 164–165
break-out attack, 203
Buchan, Nancy, 68
bug and feature management, as measure to
    make determination about trusting an open
    source project, 221–222
build, as category to consider as part of decision
    on whether to "trust the package," 223
build hygiene, 223
burn-in periods, 166

C
California Consumer Privacy Act (CCPA),
    51
the Campaign for Nuclear Disarmament (CND),
    as non-territorial authority, 32
categorisation, use of concept in computer
    systems, 11

certificate authorities (CA)
  examples of, 35
  how they work, 114–125
  Internet certificate authorities, 115–116, 117,
    120, 129, 133
  local certificate authorities, 115, 116–119, 296
  trust contexts in, 118
  types of, 115
  use of term, 118
certificate chain, 115, 117, 118, 119, 120, 121, 149,
  162, 163
certificates
  developer certificate of origin (DCO), 221
  endorsement key (EK) certificate, 118
  ephemeral certificates, 149
  root certificate. *See* root certificate
  self-signed certificate, 115
  as type of trust anchor, 170, 171
cgroups, 206
chain of trust, 23, 35, 40, 55–56, 60, 64, 114, 115,
  117, 149–150, 162, 163, 274
CHAOSS (Community Health Analytics Open
  Source Software), 217
Cheshire, Coye, 20, 86
children, trust relationships with, 68n15
China, United States' government's view of
  telecommunications from, 49, 50, 108
Church-Turing thesis, 176
CIA (confidentiality, integrity, and availability)
  triad, 71
cipher text, 114
Clark, David, 14–15
climate change, denying validity of scientific
  consensus on, 36
cloud computing
  as compared to Edge computing, 234
  joke about, 97, 233
cloud service provider (CSP)
  as employing economies of scale, 235–236
  examples of, 97
  expressing trust in, 70–75
cloud stacks, 97–99, 103–106
CND (the Campaign for Nuclear Disarmament),
  as non-territorial authority, 32
code contribution activity, as measure to make
  determination about trusting an open source
  project, 221
code review, 229, 230
cognitive bias, 38–41, 46
cognitive dissonance, 38
Coleman, J.S., 32, 65, 70
collective experience, basing decisions on, 212
collision resistance, of hash functions, 111
collisions, hash as having, 110
Common Criteria, 100

Communist International (Comintern or the
  Third International), as non-territorial
  authority, 32
*Communities of Practice: Learning, Meaning and
  Identity* (Wenger), 218
community, use of term in open source projects,
  216
community activity, as measure to make
  determination about trusting an open source
  project, 222
Community Health Analytics Open Source
  Software (CHAOSS), 217
community manager, use of term in open source
  projects, 216
community of practice, use of term in open
  source projects, 218
components, choice of and trust, 178–180
computer system, use of phrase, 125
computer-to-computer trust, lack of discussion
  about, 2
computing systems
  as not fundamentally trustworthy, 12
  as placed into trust relationships with other
    systems and ultimately humans and
    organisations, 12
  trust definitions in, 79–85
confidential computing, 256–279
Confidential Computing Consortium, 258, 259,
  267, 269
confidentiality, 11–12, 71
confidentiality, integrity, and availability (CIA)
  triad, 71
consensus algorithm, 156, 157, 158, 159
consensus mechanisms
  in blockchains, 155–156
  vulnerability of, 45
constant-time implementation, 147
Container Engine, 98
containers
  Linux containers, 122, 206–207, 239, 268,
    297
  virtualisation and, 97–99
contract
  between components, 16–17
  expressing trust in, 70
  legal contracts as alternative to trust, 65–66
  smart contracts, 158–159, 160
contributors
  details of core ones as measure to make
    determination about trusting open source
    project, 221
  number of as measure to make determination
    about trusting open source project, 220
  use of term in open source projects, 215
copyleft movement, 37

correctness, defining of in system behaviour, 17–18
correlation, as standard use of time, 194
CPU/Management Engine, 98, 99, 112
credit card associations, 116, 129, 136, 137
CRI-O, 207, 267, 268
critical national infrastructure, 48–49
cross-pollination, in open source projects, 218
crowd, wisdom of the, 212
cryptocurrency, 36, 152, 156, 157, 158
cryptographic hash functions, 110–112, 157
cryptographic key generation, 147
cryptographic primitives, 12, 88, 110, 225
cryptographic protocol, 12
cryptographic root certificate, 35
cryptography
  asymmetric cryptography, 114, 157
  mathematics and, 87–89
  public-key cryptography, 35, 114, 181
  as trust domain primitive, 296
crytographic libraries, as type of trust anchor, 170
CSP (cloud service provider)
  as employing economies of scale, 235–236
  examples of, 97
  expressing trust in, 70–75
cultural power, as type of endorsing power, 35
cyber-security, 10

D
Dasgupta, P., 20
data at rest, trust and, 256, 257
data in transit, trust and, 256, 257
data in use
  trust and, 256, 257
  Venn diagram of various technologies used to protect, 258
Data link layer, 95
data protection techniques, 259
database of record, 172
de facto standards, as type of endorsing power, 34
debit card associations, 117
deconstructionism, 36
deep fakes, 46
Denning, Dorothy, 99, 100
deployment
  explicit trust models for TEE deployments, 278–279
  fire and forget approach to, 166
  model differences between cloud computing and Edge computing, 235–240
  runtime-centric, 267
  SDK-centric, 266–267
Derrida, Jacques, 36

Deutsch, Morton, 42
developer certificate of origin (DCO), 221
"Developing Trust Frameworks to Support Identity Federations" (NIST), 282
DevOps approach (to software), 168, 265
DigiNotar, 116, 135, 149
digital rights management (DRM), 47–48, 250
digital signatures, 157
distributed architecture, trust domains in, 288–292
distributed trust
  community aspect of open source as driver toward building of, 217, 218
  defined, 56–57
  details of, 211–214
  importance of reputation to relationships of, 60, 62
  as tool for trust, 302
DNS lookup, 132, 133, 135
DNS over HTTPs protocol (DoH), 132
Docker, 206, 207
documentation, as measure to make determination about trusting an open source project, 220
domain name system (DNS) server, 133
Domain Name System Security Extensions (DNSSEC), 135
DRM (digital rights movement), 47–48, 250
Dumpster diving, 254

E
East India Company, as endorsing authority, 34
edge cases, examples of, 192–193
Edge computing ("the Edge"), 233–234
ELF support, 267
ELIZA, 46
emergent properties, 148
Enarx, 269
Enclave Development Platform, 267
encryption, 11–12, 114, 258–259
endorsement key (EK) certificate, 118
endorsing authorities
  as backing up contracts, 70
  blockchains and, 152
  certificate authorities (CA) as, 115, 118
  credibility and authority of, 115
  defined, 54
  establishment of, 33–35
  gathering information from multiple ones, 61
  reputation as alternative to, 61
  as tool for trust, 302
enforcement, as alternative to trust, 66
Enquist, Magnus, 59
ephemeral certificates, 149
Equifax, 170

Ethereum, 158
European Union, General Data Protection Regulation (GDPR), 51, 241
evil maid attack, 254
exclude list, 145
execution, how it can go wrong, 269–277
execution mode, 146
execution of workload (data and code), 260
expert reappraisal, 166
expertise, as category to consider as part of decision on whether to "trust the package," 225
expiration of tokens, as standard use of time, 195
explicit actors, 149
explicit behaviour, 188–193
explicit trust, 54, 189–192, 278, 301–306
external time source, 196, 197
externalities, defined, 50
Extinction Rebellion, 32, 65
extra-territorial authorities, 32

F

fail closed, 300
failsafe, 300
fallacy of sunk costs, 39
Farrell, Henry, 31
Ferguson, Neils, 87
fiat currency, 156
fibre-seeking backhoes, 166
field programmable gate arrays (FPGAs), 208
51% attack, 45, 173
fire and forget approach (to deployment), 166
Firmware, 98, 99, 104, 112, 199
fiscal power, as type of endorsing power, 34
formal verification, mathematics and, 89–91
FPGAs (field programmable gate arrays), 208
framing effect, 38
frequency illusion, 38
Fukuyama, Francis, 30, 65, 70
full workload measurements, 265
function as a service, 239
functional testing, 229

G

Galen, 33
Gambetta, Diego, 5, 20–21, 23, 31, 66, 67, 79, 80, 116
game theory
  defined, 24
  importance of in IT and computing, 47
  Prisoner's Dilemma, 24–27, 31, 42, 59
  reputation and generalised trust, 27–28
  role of, 87

General Data Protection Regulation (GDPR) (EU), 51, 241
generalised trust, 27–28
Gibson, William, 37
Glassdoor, 212
global navigation satellite systems (GNSS), 197–198
Global Positioning System (GPS), 198
Global Thermonuclear War, 42
GnomePG (GPG), 181
Google, Gmail, 8–9
gossiping, 60
Gove, Michael, 36
Granovetter, Mark, 218
Graphene, 269
guest operating system, 248
guests, running of, 248

H

hackathon, 217
Hailes, S., 79–80
Hardin, R., 20
hardware, properties of hardware and trust, 248–253
hardware root of trust, 84, 106–125, 152, 174, 238
hardware security modules (HSMs), 108, 109–110, 112, 115, 208, 249–250, 260, 297
hardware TEEs, 258, 259, 260
hardware-assisted virtualisation, 248, 249
Harper, Richard, 19, 20, 48
hash functions, use of, 110
Health Insurance Portability and Accountability Act (HIPAA) (US), 240
Heap, S., 25
Hobbes, Thomas, 29–30, 32, 34
Holocaust deniers, 36
homomorphic encryption, 258–259, 260
host operating system, 248
host systems, what they offer, 237–240
HSMs (hardware security modules), 108, 109–110, 112, 115, 208, 249–250, 260, 297
HTTPS, 135
Huawei, 49, 50, 108, 169
humans, and trust, 19–52
human-to-human trust, defined, 20
HW TEEs (hardware-based trust execution environments), 258, 259, 260
hybrid cloud, 234
hyper-correction, 119
Hypervisor, 98, 103, 104, 105, 106, 112, 199

I

I, Robot (film), 76n21
IANA (Internet Assigned Numbers Authority), 133

IBM, 208, 228, 248, 261

IDE (integrated development environment), 273

identification, use of concept in computer systems, 11

identity, as trust domain primitive, 296

IETF Security Glossary, on trust definitions, 84–85

"If You Build It, They Will Come" fallacy, 229–230

illusion of validity, 38

imbalance of proof, 67

IME (Intel Management Engine), 174

Imitation Game (a.k.a. Turing Test), 45

implicit trust, 54, 61, 62, 63, 132, 189, 277, 303

in the cloud, running of applications, 97

incorrect TEE design or implementation, 270

individuals, trust of, 37–45

institutional authority, 34

institutional trust, 28–32

integrated development environment (IDE), 273

integrity
  as category to consider as part of decision on whether to "trust the package," 224
  as part of CIA triad, 71
  use of concept in computer systems, 11, 12

integrity management, 177, 246

Integrity Measurement Architecture (IMA), 177

Intel, 206, 261

Intel Management Engine (IME), 174

intentionality, 58–59, 62–65

Internet Assigned Numbers Authority (IANA), 133

Internet certificate authorities, 115–116, 117, 120, 129, 133

Internet layer, in trust relationship from Link layer, 101–102

Internet Protocol, 94, 95, 101–102

introducers, 181, 182

IP block, 260

Irigaray, Luce, 36

irrational escalation, 39

isolation
  as characteristic in definition of system, 125–127
  isolation type 1—workload from workload. *See* isolation type 1—workload from workload
  isolation type 2—host from workload. *See* isolation type 2—host from workload
  isolation type 3—workload from host. *See* isolation type 3—workload from host
  as need of tenants, 237
  as property of hardware components, 248–249
  as tool for trust, 303
  and virtualisation, 202–205

isolation type 1—workload from workload, 97, 202–203, 206, 207, 236, 238, 248, 249

isolation type 2—host from workload, 97, 203, 206, 207, 236, 238, 248, 249

isolation type 3—workload from host, 97, 203–204, 206, 207–209, 238, 248, 249, 256–257, 262

issuer bank, 117, 129

IT security, 10

K

Kahnemann, Daniel, 39–40

Kata Containers, 206

Kernel, 96, 98, 104, 105, 106, 199

kernel space, 96

key ceremonies, 115

key pair, 114

Keylime, 174, 177

Khan, Usman, 182

Krauss, Robert M., 42

Kristeva, Julia, 36

Kubernetes, 72n20

Kuhn, Thomas, 34

L

Lansing, Jens, 240

Lave, Jean, 218

layers. *See also specific layers*
  in computer systems, 94
  trust in Linux layers, 102–103

lazy synchronisation, 172

League Against Cruel Sports, 44

legal contracts, as alternative to trust, 65–66

Leimar, Olof, 59

Leviathan: Or the Matter, Form and Power of a Commonwealth, Ecclesiastical and Civil (Hobbes), 29

Levien, Ralph, 181

Liars & Outliers: Enabling the Trust That Society Needs to Thrive (Schneier), 28

library operating systems, 248

Lightman, David (fictional character in *WarGames*), 8

Link layer, in trust relationship from Internet layer, 101–102

LinkedIn, 212

Linus's Law, 229

Linux
  container stack, 98
  containers, 122, 206–207, 239, 268, 297
  ELF support via, 267
  kernel, 216n9
  layers in, 96–97

trust in Linux layers, 102–103
virtualisation stack, 98, 199
Linux Foundation, 217, 258
load time, 176, 204
local attacks, 135
local certificate authorities, 115, 116–119, 296
logging, 48, 50–51, 109, 128, 145, 146, 172, 173, 194, 196–197, 244, 266, 296, 297
logical positivism, 35
Lysenko, Trofim, 33

M

machine learning (ML), 46
machine-to-machine trust, lack of discussion about, 2
"Mafia: the Price of Mistrust" (Gambetta), 31
maintainers, use of term in open source projects, 216
malfunction, unintentional, understanding possibilities available for, 17
malicious compromise, understanding possibilities available for, 17
managed services provider, 234
management by exception, 298
many-eyes hypothesis, 229–231
mathematics
   and cryptography, 87–89
   and formal verification, 89–91
   and trust, 87–89
MD5, 110
mean time to failure (MTTF), 165
mean time to repair (MTTR), 165
measured boot, 108, 112–114, 173, 204, 263
measurement
   boot measurement, 174, 175, 176, 246
   full workload measurements, 265
   problem of in attestation, 174–176
   runtime integrity measurement, 174, 177
   runtime loader measurements, 266
meatware, 186
MEC (mobile edge computing), 234
MEC (multi-access edge computing), 234
metaphors, use of, 16
microkernels, 248
microservice architecture, 244
Microsoft
   Azure, 97
   "Patch Tuesday," 165n2
Middleware, 97, 98, 104, 199
minimum trustable entity, 126
minimum viable governance, 298
misconceptions of regression, 40
misplaced trust, 75–78, 127
mistrust, defined, 19
mitigations

architectural mitigations, 244–246
to availability of support, 166
to avoid exposure to vulnerabilities, 163–164
to breaking by patching, 165
commercial mitigations, 243–244
efficacy of, 243–246
to MTTF and MTTR failures, 165
to target of attackers, 164
technical mitigations, 246
to upgrades and changes, 164
to user error, 166
when execution goes wrong, 269–277
Mizrahi, 198
ML (machine learning), 46
mobile edge computing (MEC), 234
monitoring, 21–24, 171–173, 245
monotonic time, 194, 196, 197
Moore, Tyler, 47, 50
moral systems, impact of on cooperation between humans, 42
MTTF (mean time to failure), 165
MTTR (mean time to repair), 165
multi-access edge computing (MEC), 234
multi-cloud, 234
multi-party computation (MPC), 278
mutual trust, 11, 30, 299
mutually adversarial computing, 240–243
MySQL, 228

N

Nakamoto, Satoshi, 151, 156–157
NASA, as operating authority, 133
National Institute of Standards and Technology (NIST) (US)
   "Developing Trust Frameworks to Support Identity Federations," 282
   Special Report 800-160: Systems Security Engineering—Volume 1, 127
   on trust definitions, 80, 83
   Zero Trust Architecture, 283
National Trust, on trail hunting, 44
negotiability of meaning, 218
Network layer, 95
network stack, 94–96, 97, 101–102, 132, 145, 275
Network Time Protocol (NTP), 198
"A New Paradigm for Trusted Systems" (Denning), 99
Nock, Steven, 36
noisy neighbour problem/attack, 77, 202
nominal behaviour, 298
non-decomposability, 93
non-deterministic behaviour, 163
non-functional requirements, 147–148
non-human or non-adult actors, trust of, 68–69

non-repudiability/non-repudiation, 154, 155, 157
non-territorial authorities, 32
normalcy bias, 39, 40
NTP (Network Time Protocol), 198

O
observer-expectancy effect, 39, 40
OCI, 267
OEM (original equipment manufacturer), 118
O'Neill, Onora, 30–31
on-premises (on-prem) computing, 234
Open Enclave SDK, 267
Open Policy Agent, 298
open source
  how it relates to trust, 214–219
  and security, 229–231
  as tool for trust, 302
  use of term, 211
Open Source Initiative, 228
open source movement, 37
open source process, 219–226
open source projects, 215–219, 220
Open Source Security Coalition (OSCC), 226n20, 230
open source software, 23n9, 158, 227–228
OpenStack, 72n20, 77
operation execution, as standard use of time, 194
oracles, 37, 159
"Orange Book" (United States Department of Defense), 99, 177–178, 202
orchestrator, defined, 72
ordering, as standard use of time, 194
organisation, trust relationships with, 69
original equipment manufacturer (OEM), 118
OSCC (Open Source Security Coalition), 226n20, 230
OSI, 94, 95

P
p2p (peer-to-peer) systems, 124
package dependencies, 227
package inputs, use of term, 224
Paine, Thomas, 34
patches, application of, 164–165
Payment Card Industry Data Security Standard (PCI-DSS), 241
PC architecture, 206
peer review, 213–214
peer-based logging, 173
PEF (Protected Execution Framework), 261
perfect behaviour, 298
permissioned blockchains, 152–156, 157–158, 159

permissionless blockchains, 152, 156, 157, 158, 159
Petrov, Stanislav Yevgrafovich, 193
PGP ("Pretty Good Privacy"), 181, 182
physical compromise, 253–256
Physical layer, 95
PKI (public key infrastructure), 35, 85, 114, 116, 117, 118
platform configuration register (PCR) slots, 112
policy engines, 123
POSIX, 267
post-load attestation, 263, 265, 266
power
  cultural power, 35
  fiscal power, 34
  utility power, 35
power supply units (PSUs), 165
Practical Cryptography (Ferguson and Schneier), 87
pre-image resistance, of hash functions, 111
pre-load attestation, 263, 264
Presentation layer, in OSI, 95
"Pretty Good Privacy" (PGP), 181, 182
"The Price of Mistrust" (Gambetta), 66
primary trustee, 23
primitives, 12, 87, 88, 89, 110, 162, 196, 197, 225, 230, 292–297
Prisoner's Dilemma, 24–27, 31, 42, 59
private blockchains, 152
private clouds, 97, 234, 235, 236, 237, 241, 243, 244, 288, 289, 290, 291
private key, 114
process-based technologies, 261
process-based TEEs, 261, 262, 265, 267
processes
  expressing trust in, 70
  open source process, 219–226
programmability, attribute of, 260
pro-individualist movement, 37
proof of work, 157n5
Protected Execution Framework (PEF), 261
provenance, as category to consider as part of decision on whether to "trust the package," 224–225
provision time, 176
PSUs (power supply units), 165
public blockchains, 152
public clouds, 97, 159, 176, 209, 231, 234, 235, 236, 237, 241, 242, 243, 244, 263, 277, 288
public key infrastructure (PKI), 35, 85, 114, 116, 117, 118
public time servers, 198
public-key cryptography, 35, 114, 181

Q

qualified eyes, availability of, as problem with many-eyes hypothesis, 230

R

ransomware, 62
Rathburn, Brian, 27–28
Reagan, Ronald, 43
Red Hat, Inc., 227, 228
regression, misconceptions of, 40
re-keying, as standard use of time, 195
Rekor, 227
relative time, 194, 196, 197
remote, vs. local, 173
remote attacks, 135
remote attestation, 113
replay prevention, as standard use of time, 195
reporting, role of in creating trust, 21–24
reputation
   collecting information, 60
   defined, 58
   gathering information from multiple
      endorsing authorities, 61
   and generalised trust, 27–28
   importance of to transitive and distributed
      relationships, 60
   reputation systems and trust, 181–183
   as strongly time-based, 181
   use of term, 59
responsiveness, as category to consider as part
   of decision on whether to "trust the
   package," 224
RESTful API, 198
"revolt from within," 44
RFC 5485, 109
RFC 7384, 198
Rheingold, Howard, 181
The Rights of Man (Paine), 34
risk
   as arising in four categories, 13–14
   defined, 13
   importance of in IT and computing, 15–18
   trust as way for humans to manage, 13–15
Roman Catholic Church, as non-territorial
   authority, 32, 33, 34
root certificate, 35, 54, 63, 115, 119–122, 152, 171,
   174
root keys, 115
root of trust, 54, 107, 108, 112, 115, 119, 152, 204,
   248, 249–253, 302. *See also* hardware root of
   trust
root servers, 133
Rossi, F., 46
Rousseau, Jean-Jacques, 29
run time, 176–177

runtime integrity measurement, 174, 177
runtime loader measurements, 266
runtime-centric deployment, 267
Russell, Nan, 43

S

scalability, attribute of, 260
Schneier, Bruce, 28, 42, 67, 87
SCONE, 269
SDK (software development kit), 266, 267
SDK-centric deployment, 266–267
SDN (software-defined networking), 122
second pre-image resistance, of hash functions,
   111
secondary authorities, 33
second-guessing, 42n40
second-order problem, 166
secure boot, 108, 113
secure elements, 259
Secure Encrypted Virtualisation (SEV), 208, 261
security
   cyber-security, 10
   IT security, 10
   open source and, 229–231
   relationship of trust to, 75
   through obscurity, 229
   trust as important to, 12
security economics, 47, 48, 51, 250
*Security Engineering: A Guide to Building
   Dependable Distributed Systems* (Anderson),
   247, 254
self-driving cars, as entity to trust, 9
self-signed certificate, 115
self-sovereign identity (SSI), 36
SELinux, 177
separation of concerns, 188
serverless application, 97
serverless computing, 239
service changes, allowance of, 191–192
service degradation, 300
service misuse, reduction of, 191
service-level agreements (SLAs), 166–167
Session layer, 95
SEV (Secure Encrypted Virtualisation), 208, 261
SGX (Software Guard Extensions), 208
SHA-256, 110
side channels, vulnerabilities associated with,
   271
side effects, 50, 146
side-channel attacks, 147–148, 271
simple cloud virtualisation stack, 104
single database of record or distributed, 172
single root I/O virtualization (SR-IOV), 249, 256
*Situated Learning: Legitimate Peripheral
   Participation* (Lave and Wenger), 218

SLAs (service-level agreements), 166–167
smart contracts, 158–159, 160
The Social Contract (Rousseau), 29
social contract theory, 29
social location, defined, 25
software development kit (SDK), 266, 267
software development lifecycle, 168
Software Guard Extensions (SGX), 208
software lifecycle, 168–171
software supply chain, 169
software TEEs, 259
software TPMs, 251–253
software-defined networking (SDN), 122
SR-IOV (single root I/O virtualization), 249, 256
SSI (self-sovereign identity), 36
stacks
    network stack, 94–96, 97, 101–102, 132, 145,
        275
    simple cloud virtualisation stack, 104
    and time, 205
    trust in cloud stacks, 103–106
    virtualisation stack, 97, 98, 112, 113, 199, 262
standards, importance of, 37
standards bodies, as type of endorsing power,
    34
subjective probability, use of term, 23–24
sunk costs, fallacy of, 39
Sunyaev, Ali, 240
supply chain
    management of, 226
    and products, 226–229
    trust anchors, trust pivots, and, 169–170
support, availability of, 166
suspiciousness, 60
system behaviour
    causes of perturbation of, 164
    defined, 126
    defining of correctness in, 17–18
system boundaries, defining of, 198–209
system calls (syscalls), 104
system design, 93–99
systems
    applying socio-philosophical definitions of
        trust to, 86–91
    architecting of, 304
    complex systems, 199–202
    contexts of, 127–128
    defined, 53–54, 93, 185–186
    defining boundaries of, 198–209
    defining of trust in, 15–17
    importance of, 125–128
    isolation in, 125–127
    time and, 194–198
    and trust, 185–209
    "trusted" systems, 99–106

T
tampering, 108–109, 254
TCB (trusted computing base). *See* trusted
    computing base (TCB)
TCG (Trusted Computing Group), 84, 108, 174
TCSEC (*Trusted Computer System Evaluation
    Criteria*) ("Orange Book") (United States
    Department of Defense), 99–100
TDX (Trust Domain Extensions), 261
TEE instance (generic), 263
TEE instance (VM-based), 262, 272
TEE runtime, 263, 265, 266, 267, 269, 271
TEE trust relationships (ideal), 276
TEE trust relationships (implicit), 277
TEEs (trusted execution environments). *See*
    trusted execution environments (TEEs)
tenants, what they need, 237–240
territoriality, defined, 32
test coverage, as measure to make
    determination about trusting an open source
    project, 220
Thompson, Ken, 90, 91, 102, 158, 169
threats, Confidential Computing Consortium's
    white paper on, 269
"The Three Laws of Robotics" (Asimov), 76n21
time
    boot time, 176, 248
    external time source, 196
    importance of, 161–183
    load time, 176, 204
    monitoring and, 171–173
    monotonic time, 194, 196, 197
    as new trust context, 196
    provision time, 176
    relative time, 194, 196, 197
    run time, 176–177. *See also* TEE runtime
    stacks and, 205
    standard uses of, 194–195
    and systems, 194–198
    TEE runtime, 263, 265, 266, 267, 269, 271
    as trust domain primitive, 296
    wall time, 194, 196, 197
time sources, 197
time-out, as standard use of time, 195
timing attacks, 147
TNC (Trusted Network Connect), 84
TPM-FAIL vulnerability, 170–171
TPMs (trusted platform modules). *See* trusted
    platform modules (TPMs)
transactional logging, vs. lazy synchronisation,
    172–173
transactions
    on blocks within blockchain, 153
    as standard use of time, 195
transitive trust, 55, 60, 61, 113, 114, 123, 163

transitive trust relationship, 61, 66, 113, 155, 277, 278, 290
Transport layer, 95
TripAdvisor, 212
The Trolley Problem, 76n21
trust
    according to Gambetta, 20–21, 23
    as affected by time, 5, 7, 25, 100
    alternatives to, 65–67
    as applied to game theory, 25
    applying socio-philosophical definitions of to systems, 86–91
    as asymmetric, 5, 6, 7, 25, 100
    based on authority, 33–37
    blockchain promoting trust, 154
    chain of, 23, 35, 40, 55–56, 60, 64, 114, 115, 117, 149–150, 162, 163, 274
    in cloud stacks, 103–106
    and complex systems, 199–202
    component choice and, 178–179
    as contextual, 5, 6, 25, 100
    corollaries to definition of, 2, 5–7, 25, 100
    decay of, 161–168, 194
    defined, 1–2, 5–8, 100
    defining of in systems, 15–17
    definitions of in computer systems, 79–85
    distributed trust. See distributed trust
    explicit trust, 54, 189–192
    expressions of, 69–75
    generalised trust, 27–28
    hardware root of, 84, 106–125, 152, 174, 238
    how open source relates to, 214–219
    humans and, 19–52
    from hypervisor to kernel, 105
    implicit trust, 54, 61, 62, 63, 132, 189, 277, 303
    importance of being explicit when describing, 145–150
    as important to security, 12
    of individuals, 37–45
    institutional trust, 28–32
    from kernel to hypervisor, 105
    in Linux layers, 102–103
    mathematics and, 87–89
    misplaced trust, 75–78, 127
    mutual trust, 11, 30, 299
    within network stack, 101–102
    NIST definitions of, 80
    of non-human or non-adult actors, 68–69
    open source and, 211–231
    of others, 41–45
    of ourselves, 37–41
    properties of hardware and trust, 248–253
    range of views around, 3
    relationship of to security, 75
    reputation and generalised trust, 27–28

reputation systems and, 181–183
    role of monitoring and reporting in creation of, 21–24
    root of. See root of trust
    systems and, 185–209
    tools for, 301–306
    transitive trust, 55, 60, 61, 113, 114, 123, 163
    use of as operations, 53–78
    virtualisation and, 303
    as way for humans to manage risk, 13–15
    web of, 181
"trust, but verify," 43, 169
trust action description, 59, 62, 63, 305, 306
trust anchors
    CPU as, 264
    defined, 54
    insertion of, 63–64
    preparation of, 64
    root certificates known as, 35
    and supply chain, 169–170
    as tool for trust, 302
    types of, 170
trust chain, 55–56, 115, 273. See also chain of trust
Trust Domain Extensions (TDX), 261
trust domains
    in bank, 284–288
    boundaries of, 297–298
    centralisation of control and policies of, 298–300
    composition of, 284–292
    defined, 57–58, 239, 281
    in distributed architecture, 288–292
    and policy, 293–295
    primitives of, 292–297
    as tool for trust, 303
    trust domain A–NTP (network time protocol), 284, 286, 287, 288
    trust domain B–DNS (Domain Name Service), 285, 286, 287, 288
    trust domain C–mortgage and personal lending services, 285–286, 287, 288
trust frameworks, 282
trust models
    complex trust model, 279
    explicit trust models for TEE deployments, 278–279
    web of trust, 181
trust operations, and alternatives, 53–78
trust pivots
    defined, 54–55
    preparation of, 64
    and supply chain, 169–170
    as tool for trust, 302–303
    trust certificate as, 119–122
    as trust domain primitive, 296

trust relationships
  as affected by time, 2
  and agency in worked example, 136–144
  with animals, 69
  as asymmetric, 2
  automated trust relationships, dangers of,
      192–193
  with blockchain system, 155
  with children, 68n15
  as contextual, 2
  defining of, 21
  examples of regarding CSPs, 73
  four cases of, 3–5
  in game theory, 27
  from laptop to DNS server, 138
  between Link layer and Internet layer, 101–102
  NIST definitions of, 81
  no direct trust relationship to CPU vendor as
      weakness in design and implementation
      of systems utilising TEEs, 270–271
  with organisations, 69
  with others, 41–45
  with ourselves, 37–41
  shipping company trust relationship with
      blockchain system, 155
  shipping company trust relationship without
      blockchain system, 153
  TEE trust relationships (ideal), 276
  TEE trust relationships (implicit), 277
  and TEEs, 266–269
  as tool for trust, 302
  transitive trust relationship, 61, 66, 113, 155,
      277, 278, 290
  from web browser to laptop system, 137, 139,
      141, 142
  from web browser to web client, 141
  from web browser to web server, 138, 139, 140,
      141, 142
  from web server to acquiring bank, 144
  from web server to host system, 143
  from web server to web browser, 144
  without blockchain system, 153
  writing requirements for, 145
trust tables
  example of, 302
  role of, 189
  shipping company trust relationship with
      blockchain system, 155
  shipping company trust relationship without
      blockchain system, 153
  trust from bash shell to login program, 103
  trust from hypervisor to kernel, 105
  trust from Internet layer to Link layer in IP
      suite, 102
  trust from kernel to hypervisor, 105

trust from server to logging service regarding
    time stamps, 197
trust from software consumer to software
    vendor, 219
trust offer from service provider, 190
trust relationship from laptop to DNS server,
    138
trust relationship from web browser to laptop
    system, 137, 139, 141, 142
trust relationship from web browser to web
    client, 141
trust relationship from web browser to web
    server, 138, 139, 140, 141, 142
trust relationship from web server to
    acquiring bank, 144
trust relationship from web server to host
    system, 143
trust relationship from web server to web
    browser, 144
trust requirements from service consumer,
    190
*Trust: The Social Virtues and the Creation of
    Prosperity* (Fukuyama), 30
trusted boot, 108, 112–114, 149, 173, 204, 263
Trusted Computer System Evaluation Criteria
    (TCSEC) ("Orange Book") (United States
    Department of Defense), 99–100
trusted computing base (TCB)
  compromise of, 255
  considering the entirety of build system as,
      223
  defined, 177–178, 202
  described, 177–183
  final set of requirements around, 239
  guest TCB, 251
  host TCB, 238, 251, 253
  own TCB, 238
  as standard use for root of trust, 250
  TEE TCBs, 261–278
  trust in, 238
  of virtual machines, 201
Trusted Computing Group (TCG), 84, 108, 174
trusted execution environments (TEEs)
  adoption of, 258
  described, 208–209
  hardware TEEs, 258, 259, 260
  process-based TEEs, 261, 262, 265, 267
  software TEEs, 259
  TEE instance (generic), 263
  TEE instance (VM-based), 262, 272
  TEE runtime, 263, 265, 266, 267, 269, 271
  TEE TCBs in detail, 261–279
  TEE trust relationships (ideal), 276
  TEE trust relationships (implicit), 277
  trust relationships and, 266–269

VM-based TEEs, 261–262, 263, 267, 272
weaknesses in design and implementation of
    systems utilising TEEs, 272–276
Trusted Network Connect (TNC), 84
trusted platform, defined, 7
trusted platform modules (TPMs)
    as compared to HSMs, 109–110
    as component example, 108, 126
    in confidential computing, 260
    defined, 84
    as doing measurements, 204
    as generally coming with endorsement key
        (EK) certificate, 118
    guest usage, 250
    as hardware roots of trust, 152, 249
    host usage, 250
    in measured boot and trusted boot,
        112–114
    software TPMs, 251–253
    as standard use for root of trust, 250
    TPM 2.0 specification, 174
    TPM-FAIL vulnerability, 170–171
    as type 3 isolation mechanism, 209
    as type of trust anchor, 170–171
    virtual TPMs (vTPMs), 251–253
trusted systems domain, defined, 281–282
trustee
    architect and, 305–306
    defined, 53
    as entity being trusted, 3
    identifying real trustee, 47–52
    minimum number of, 276
    primary trustee, 23
    trustor/trustee separation, 302
trustor
    defined, 53
    as entity doing trusting, 3
    possible inability of monitoring actions by,
        21
    trustor/trustee separation, 302
trustworthiness, 20, 28, 40, 82, 83, 86, 181, 212,
    216, 217, 226, 238, 274
Turing, Alan, 45
Turing Test, 45
turtles, use of term, 106–107
Tversky, Amos, 39–40
Twitter
    as example of distributed trust, 212–213
    use of, 46–47
two-factor authentication, 117
type 1 isolation mechanism. See isolation type
    1—workload from workload
type 2 isolation mechanism. See isolation type
    2—host from workload
type 3 isolation mechanism. See isolation type
    3—workload from host

U
uncanny valley, 46
un-decomposability, 125
Unified Modeling Language (UML), 99
unikernels, 248
unintentional malfunction, understanding
    possibilities available for, 17
United States
    Civil Rights movement, 65
    government's view of telecommunications
        from China, 49, 50, 108, 169
University of Maryland, as operating authority,
    133
unpermissioned blockchains, 152
upgrades and changes, impact of, 164
UrbanSitter, 212
user error, 165–166
User Mode, in Linux, 96
user space, 96
user-experience design (UXD), 166
userland, 96
Userspace, 97, 98, 104, 199
utility power, as type of endorsing power, 35

V
validity, illusion of, 38
Varoufakis, Y., 25
verification
    as alternative to trust, 67
    mathematics and formal verification, 89–91
Verisign, 133
version drift, 179, 191
Virtual Light (Gibson), 37
virtual machine (VM), 97, 199, 201, 202
virtual TPMs (vTPMs), 251–253
virtualisation
    and containers, 97–99
    hardware-assisted virtualisation, 248, 249
    isolation and, 202
    and trust, 303
virtualisation stack, 97, 98, 112, 113, 199, 262
The Virtual Community (Rheingold), 181
VM (virtual machine), 97, 199, 201, 202
VM-based technologies, 261
VM-based TEEs, 261–262, 263, 267, 272
vTPMs (virtual TPMs), 251–253
vulnerabilities
    discovery of, 163
    Equifax experience of attack on known
        vulnerability, 170
    reporting and management of as measure to
        make determination about trust open
        source project, 222
    TPM-FAIL vulnerability, 170–171
    in worked example, 134–136

W

wall time, 194, 196, 197
WarGames (film), 8, 42
web of trust, 181
WebAssembly System Interface (WASI), 267
Wenger, Etienne, 218
wetware, 186
whisky, purchasing of, as worked example,
   128–144
Who Can You Trust? (Botsman), 212
"Why Cryptography Is Harder Than It Looks"
   (Schneier), 67
wisdom of the crowd, 212
worked example, purchasing whisky, 128–144
workload density, of public cloud computing,
   235

workloads
   defined, 97
   deployment of, 206
   examples of ones more generic, 73
   examples of ones specific to organisations or
      sectors, 72
   key rule for deployment of, 77–78

X

x86 architecture, 206

Z

Zero Trust Architecture (NIST), 283
zero trust (ZT), 124–125, 282–284
zero-trust networks, 122–125